Cambridge Medieval Textbooks

THE WARS OF THE ROSES

Cambridge Medieval Textbooks

This is a series of specially commissioned textbooks for teachers and students, designed to complement the monograph series Cambridge Studies in Medieval Life and Thought by providing introductions to a range of topics in medieval history. This series combines both chronological and thematic approaches, and will deal with British and European topics. All volumes in the series will be published in hard covers and in paperback.

For a list of titles in the series, see end of book.

Hannah Daw

This is a new interpretation of English politics during the extended period of political crisis beginning with the majority of Henry VI in *c.* 1437 and lasting at least up to the accession of Henry VIII in 1509.

The later fifteenth century in England is a somewhat baffling and apparently incoherent period which historians and history students have found consistently difficult to handle. The grand interpretations of the Whig historians and their successors made sense of it by doing violence to everything that was important in the period. The large-scale 'revisionism' inspired by the classic work of K. B. McFarlane led to the first real work on politics, both national and local, but has left the period in a disjointed state: much material has been unearthed, but without any real sense of direction or coherence.

This book places the events of the century within a clearly delineated framework of constitutional structures, practices and expectations, in an attempt to show the meaning of the apparently frenetic and purposeless political events which occurred within that framework – and which sometimes breached it. At the same time it takes cognisance of all the work that has been done on the period, including recent and innovative work on Henry VI.

– political → focus on Warwickshire

THE WARS OF THE ROSES

Politics and the constitution in England,
c.1437–1509

CHRISTINE CARPENTER

CAMBRIDGE
UNIVERSITY PRESS

CAMBRIDGE UNIVERSITY PRESS
Cambridge, New York, Melbourne, Madrid, Cape Town, Singapore, São Paulo

Cambridge University Press
The Edinburgh Building, Cambridge CB2 2RU, UK

Published in the United States of America by Cambridge University Press, New York

www.cambridge.org
Information on this title: www.cambridge.org/9780521268004

First published 1997
Reprinted 1999, 2002

A catalogue record for this publication is available from the British Library

Library of Congress Cataloguing in Publication data
Carpenter, Christine.
The Wars of the Roses: politics and the constitution in England, *c.* 1437-1509/
Christine Carpenter.
p. cm. – (Cambridge medieval textbooks)
Includes bibliographical references and index.
ISBN 0 521 26800 1 (hb). – ISBN 0 521 31874 2 (pb)
1. Great Britain – Politics and government – 1399–1485. 2. Great Britain –
Politics and government – 1485–1509. I. Title.
II. Series.
JN137.C37 1997
942.04–dc21 97–7038 CIP

ISBN-13 978-0-521-26800-4 hardback
ISBN-10 0-521-26800-1 hardback

ISBN-13 978-0-521-31874-7 paperback
ISBN-10 0-521-31874-2 paperback

Transferred to digital printing 2006

For Helen Castor, Richard Partington,
Benjamin Thompson, Julian Turner and
John Watts

CONTENTS

ILLUSTRATIONS

PREFACE

This work owes its existence primarily to all those students who have sat in front of me for a Cambridge 'supervision' (i.e. tutorial) since 1973; it must by now be a very large number. Their agonies have not been in vain, for, even by asking the most banal questions – perhaps above all by asking the most banal questions – they have forced me to examine my most fundamental assumptions about medieval England. Indeed, the principal merit of the broad outline papers of history as still taught at Cambridge, combined with the weekly essay and the weekly hour's tuition on the essay, is that both teacher and taught have to learn to think about historical development in broad conceptual terms. Without the teaching that I began to do at Cambridge in my fourth year of research, I should never have understood where my collection of trees about fifteenth–century Warwickshire fitted within the large wood of English political, constitutional, social and economic change from before the Conquest until well into the early-modern period. It was indeed the formative moment in my development as a historian, even if at times the agony was mine rather than the students', as I struggled to keep one jump ahead of them on a week's reading on each of up to four different topics in a single week.

Others to whom I am deeply indebted are those colleagues, past and present, at Cambridge and elsewhere, who, perhaps even without knowing it, have nurtured my understanding of politics and political society in late–medieval England in the last few years. The medievalists' list must, as always, start with my former research supervisor Dr Gerald Harriss, who has remained constantly encouraging; he has also remained spiritually my supervisor, in that, where our interpretative ways have parted, I have known that this was a sure sign that I must be very careful to be able to justify myself to myself. Among Cambridge medievalists, past and present, I must also thank Dr Edward Powell, Dr Rosemary Horrox (who kindly read chapters 8, 9 and 10 and pointed out mistakes and ambiguities), Dr Rosamond McKitterick, Professor Barrie Dobson and Professor Sir James Holt. But it will be clear from this book how heavily I have leaned on Tudor and Stuart historians for advice and inspiration. I must start with the late Professor Sir Geoffrey Elton, from whom I learned so much in my final year as an undergraduate, but more recently pride of place must go to Dr John Morrill and Professor Wallace MacCaffrey, not forgetting the stimulus I have had from Drs Jenny Wormald, Steven Gunn, Steven Ellis and George Bernard and Mr Patrick Higgins. None of the historians listed above bears any responsibility for any egregious errors or wild theories offered here but all should have my thanks for help, inspiration and at times saving me from worse. I must also thank William Davies of the Cambridge University Press for his customary kindness and patience while waiting for the completion of my efforts (this one was due in on 31 December 1985, but he tells me this is not a record). Almost finally, there is 'The Group': two of its members have already been mentioned by name. One day, its role in making me feel four times a year in recent years that the life of an academic historian in a university might after all be worth living will be directly acknowledged with a dedication. But, for now, the dedication must go to a group whom I supervised as both undergraduates and research students and who have since in every case but one gone on to become academic historians in their own right. John and Helen were kind enough to read the manuscript right through and comment on it, saving me repeatedly from error and not infrequently from incoherence: naturally, any errors and incoherence that remain I claim entirely for my own. Helen was kind enough to let me give a 'trailer' for much of her remarkable work on the Duchy of Lancaster; I hope no-one will give me the undeserved credit for it and I trust my remarks will whet the appetite of all historians of the period for her book. All five have taught me a very large part of the history I know, and I can only say, 'Thank you'.

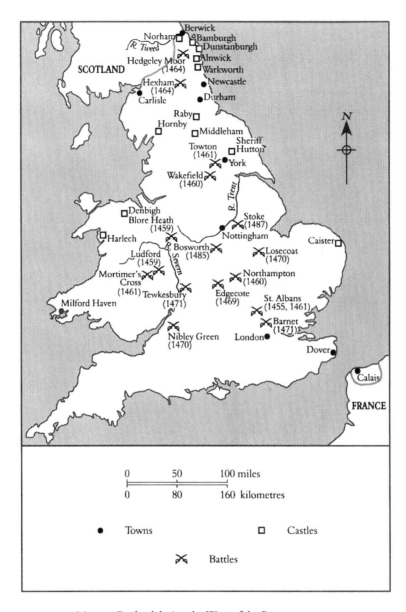

SCOTLAND

Berwick
Norham
Bamburgh
Dunstanburgh
Alnwick
Hedgeley Moor
(1464)
Warkworth
Hexham
(1464)
Newcastle
Carlisle
Durham

Raby
Hornby
Middleham
Sheriff
Towton
(1461)
Hutton
York
Wakefield
(1460)

Denbigh
Blore Heath
(1459)
Stoke
(1487)
Harlech
Nottingham
Caister
Ludford
(1459)
Bosworth
(1485)
Losecoat
(1470)
Mortimer's
Cross
(1461)
Northampton
(1460)
Tewkesbury
(1471)
Edgecote
(1469)
St. Albans
(1455, 1461)
Milford Haven
Nibley Green
(1470)
Barnet
(1471)
London
Dover

Calais

FRANCE

R. Tweed

R. Trent

Severn

N

| 0 | 50 | 100 miles |
| 0 | 80 | 160 kilometres |

● Towns □ Castles

⚔ Battles

Map 1   England during the Wars of the Roses

INTRODUCTION

This is not, strictly speaking, a book about the Wars of the Roses. The theme of the book is much better summed up in the sub-title: 'Politics and the constitution in England *c.* 1437–1509'. You will not find here the story of how the name 'Wars of the Roses' came to be applied to what happened in England between 1455 and 1485. Nor will you find an explicit discussion under the headings normally used in considering the causes of the Wars of the Roses: the dynastic problem, the financial problem, the effects of the French war, and so on. Though that does not mean that these issues will not be seriously addressed. What you will find is a broader account of how governance was supposed to work in fifteenth-century England and of how and why governance and politics went wrong in this century, how they were put right and what the effects were of both the crisis and its rectification. In the course of this account, the political events from the later 1430s will be recounted and explained.

As I shall show in the next chapter, it does not make much sense to look at the Wars in isolation because they have never been discussed without reference to what came before and after. Since the middle of the last century, they have always been used as a touchstone for the health of the late-medieval body politic, or polity (essentially what we would now call the state), and the search for their causes has almost invariably gone back to perceived weaknesses in kingship dating back to the previous century. For that reason alone, it is essential to examine the development of the polity from at least the time of Edward III (1327–77), in whose reign much of the evil is supposed to have originated. Even if the idea of long-term weaknesses is rejected, we shall see that it is not possible to understand the course of politics in England in the fifteenth century without a grasp of the nature of kingship and polity in late-medieval England. Equally, the importance of dynastic rivalries in causing the Wars cannot be evaluated without looking at the consequences of the deposition of Richard II in 1399 and assessing the strength of the monarchy under the first two Lancastrian kings. Henry VI's minority and his majority up to 1450 also require discussion to see if they sowed the seeds of later conflict, as it has often been alleged that they did.

The book is not intended to be used as a work of reference for the entire history of the period; there are plenty already that fulfil this function, and some of these are listed in the bibliography. Its purpose is to show the student how to approach a very difficult period with a difficult and problematic historiography. Other interpretations will be discussed where this is essential, in order to understand the nature of existing analysis before considering an alternative view, but the main purpose of the book is to cut a way for the reader through the thickets of interpretation and events. Throughout, attention will be firmly focused on what good and bad kingship meant; in particular what was expected of the ruler by the nobles and gentry, the people who enabled monarchy to work and who had most to gain or lose from good or bad rule. That means that we need to look at local government and politics, on which a lot of work has been done in recent years, as much as at government and affairs at the centre. Attention will therefore be given to the implications for the localities of developments in national politics and, conversely, of the impact of the shires on national politics. It will be seen that we are still in a state of ignorance in many important areas. This is especially true of our grasp of power structures in the shires and of what really happened in the localities in the fifteenth century and why. But by being explicit about what we do not know, and avoiding answers that can only be fudges when we do not yet have the information to answer them properly, it is often easier to make sense of a historical problem.

For all these reasons, the reader will be taken back to the first principles of medieval governance at every level. Chapters 2 and 3 will run through the government and the political structures of fifteenth-century England and this will entail some discussion of how they came to be as they were. The fourth chapter will offer an assessment of Henry VI's father and grandfather, Henry IV and V, examining the legacy they left him, and of Henry's own minority. All these are in a sense preparatory to the main narrative, which begins in the following chapter with Henry's adult rule. Readers who are put off by the analytical chapters at the start, especially those who are new to the period, may like to begin with chapter 4, but they would be well advised when they have read the whole book to go back to the first three chapters which are essential to a proper understanding of the narrative.

Note that footnotes are used for the following purposes: to attribute direct quotations in the text; for further explanation of points in the text or clarification of technical terms; for internal reference; occasionally to reference specific works mentioned in the text. All other references to, and discussions of, the historical literature will be found in the bibliographical essays, one for each chapter, at the end of the book.

I

SOURCES AND HISTORIOGRAPHY

The Wars of the Roses have been a problem to historians almost from the moment they occurred. Contemporary or near-contemporary narrative accounts are largely devoid of any explanation for what happened. The vigorous monastic historical tradition of earlier centuries was by this time largely defunct. In the fifteenth century its place was taken by a number of town chronicles, mostly from London, which have interesting moments but tend to purvey bitty information, interspersed with lists of urban officers and accounts of urban events, and lack the unity and penetration of many earlier works. There are a small number of accounts of particular episodes and periods in the Wars of the Roses, written, it seems, by people close to the participants and events. These include 'Warkworth's Chronicle' (on the first fourteen years of Edward IV), the 'Arrivall' (dealing with Edward IV's return in 1471), and the 'Chronicle of the Lincolnshire Rebellion'. The best and most penetrating of these is undoubtedly the 'Croyland Continuations', covering the period from 1459 to 1486.

Towards the end of the period, the new 'humanist' history begins to appear, not with entirely beneficial effects. It is much more coherent but prone to moralising and to putting words in the mouths of historical figures. Dominic Mancini's 'Usurpation of Richard III' is, on the face of it, a straightforward account of events by an informed observer and it has in the past been treated as a reliable source. It is now apparent that Mancini was seriously handicapped not only by his ignorance of English and lack of access to high places, but also by a 'humanist' perspective which drove him to moralise and to find a pattern in events which may not have been there. This is especially true of his account of the behaviour of Richard of

Gloucester, which he made to look carefully planned. The most celebrated humanist historians who wrote with any direct knowledge of this period were Polydore Vergil, who was commissioned to write his 'Anglica Historia' by Henry VII, and Sir Thomas More, who wrote the famous 'History of King Richard III'. In neither work is the recounting of historical truth the main purpose and, in both, pieces of useful information, which the authors may have taken direct from participants or eye-witnesses, have to be extracted with care from the surrounding fiction.

To sum up, no coherent account of the politics of the Wars of the Roses could be written from chronicle evidence alone; to a great extent, all that could be produced from them is a purposeless list of events. There is none of the psychological insight and acute analysis of events to be found in earlier histories, especially those from the late twelfth to early fourteenth centuries. That is no doubt why, as we shall see, historians have found it hard to analyse the politics of the period. However, this lack of good contemporary accounts has been indirectly beneficial. First, it is now realised that some medieval histories, especially perhaps the richest and outwardly most rewarding ones, may be using rhetorical devices and may not always be literally truthful accounts of events; this is an alarming thought that need be of little concern to the historian of the fifteenth century, who can make such limited use of this type of source. Secondly, it has proved impossible to say anything much about politics and governance in the fifteenth century without prolonged and detailed research. That meant that for a long time not much was said, but it now means that there is a depth of research on the period, especially into local politics and local disputes, unique in medieval political history.

What the fifteenth century did have is the extraordinary collections of gentry letters: Paston, Stonor and Plumpton. Used with care these give us a dazzling insight into local society and politics. However, these too have added to the difficulties in dealing with the period. First, as K. B. McFarlane, the greatest historian of the period, pointed out, the absence of noble letters has too often fed a prejudice we shall shortly be looking at. This was that, in contrast with the gentry, the nobles were ignorant illiterates, devoid of the ability to write, to think at any profound level or even to behave like human beings.[1] Secondly, as we shall see, the early publication of the fullest set, the 'Paston Letters', which happens also to be the most lurid and the most atypical, only reinforced existing beliefs about the barbarity of the period. This does not mean that all three collections are

[1] K. B. McFarlane, 'The Wars of the Roses', *England in the Fifteenth Century*, ed. G. L. Harriss (London, 1981), p. 231; McFarlane, *The Nobility of Later Medieval England* (Oxford, 1973), p. 229.

not wonderful and inexhaustible sources but, as yet, they have not, with one exception, been used in any very systematic way.[2]

The earliest of the accounts of the Wars of the Roses which are far enough removed to be called history in the modern sense link our discussion of the sources to the historiography. These are the summary chronicles of Stowe, Hall and Holinshed written in the sixteenth century. They use earlier works (not all of them still extant) and to that extent are not entirely useless as original sources, but their moralising purpose is plain. It has, in fact, been the misfortune of the fifteenth century rarely to be studied for its own sake but nearly always as an episode in a longer process, 'an age of transition', as it has not infrequently been called. This tradition goes right back to some of these earliest historians. In a schema brought to fruition by Edward Hall in the mid-sixteenth century and memorably dramatised by Shakespeare, they saw the deposition of Richard II as the cause of the evils of the following century. The divisions of this time were only healed in 1485, when Henry VII became king and, by marrying Edward IV's daughter Elizabeth, united the red rose of Lancaster and the white of York.[3]

When 'professional' history began to be written in the second half of the nineteenth century, it was forced to rely principally on these early narrative sources, however inadequate, and this was doubtless partly why there was so little attempt to understand the motives of the main protagonists. There was simply too little that could be used in these mostly very bald accounts. But that was not the only reason for the draining of all excitement and richness from what was after all a period when political events could hardly be described as boring. It was at this point that there was the first modification of the Tudor interpretation, but it still left the fifteenth century as a staging post on the way to further developments. In this case, however, it could be said to have been joined by all the periods of English history, since what is known as 'the Whig interpretation of history' made a fetish of continuity and progress. Its focal point was a particular view of the English constitution. Most people would now use the word 'constitution' in a neutral sense, to mean the way in which a country or state is constituted. By this we mean the institutional framework, if there is one, and the customs, laws, practices and ideas which determine the way this framework operates, its relationship

[2] The exception is the work of Dr Helen Castor on the Duchy of Lancaster in East Anglia, which makes fruitful combined use of the Paston letters and more formal governmental and private sources. Most of this very important work (see further comments in chapters 3–5) is still not yet in print but references are given in the bibliographies for chapters 4 and 5 to the parts of her work that have already been published.

[3] Readers who wish to explore the history of the whole 'Roses' tradition are referred to S. B. Chrimes, *Lancastrians, Yorkists, and Henry VII* (2nd edn, London, 1966).

to the political classes within the country and their relationship to each other. But, to the Whig historians, 'constitution' meant the English constitution as they perceived it in their day, which was one of limited, parliamentary monarchy. Thus, 'constitutional' was an approving term, meaning proceeding by way of parliamentary (or, before parliament, pseudo-parliamentary) checks on the executive.

It was a view of history that emerged in the middle decades of the nineteenth century. It laid emphasis on the gradualness of constitutional change in England and, in relation to this, on England's privileged uniqueness to have achieved change without revolution. The focus of this achievement was parliament, seen as the forum for the preservation of the subject's liberties against the executive power of the crown. And within parliament particular importance was given to the Commons, the forerunners of the House of Commons, whose gentry and merchant members were perceived as a middle class, the direct ancestors of the triumphant middle class of Victorian England. In the monumental *Constitutional History of England* by William Stubbs, the great Whig synthesis for the middle ages, the fifteenth century played an important part. To him the greatest rulers were those who understood that their monarchy would be at its strongest if they allied themselves with the emerging power of parliament. Thus, the first of his outstanding heroes was Edward I, whom he saw as reigning in partnership with parliament, especially the knights in the Commons. And the second was Henry IV, who was thought to have a parliamentary title to the crown, and to have initiated the 'Lancastrian constitutional experiment', in which the king deliberately shared power with his subjects: 'he reigned as a constitutional king; he governed by the help of his parliament, with the executive aid of a council over which parliament both claimed and exercised control'.[4] Then, in the majority of Henry VI, it became clear that constitutional development 'had outrun the capacity of the nation'[5] and what had been liberty became licence. England disintegrated into a mass of warring factions, the nobles taking the lead in irresponsibility, and it could only be rescued by a form of despotism introduced by Edward IV (who, for reasons that are far from clear, gets an extraordinary moral dressing-down from Stubbs) that was brought to its fruition by the Tudors. These ideas about the late fifteenth century were reflected in the contemporaneous work of J. R. Green, who invented the 'new monarchy', established by Edward IV and developed by his successors, something he saw as alien to England in its despotic ability to function without parliament. Embedded in the whole 'Whig' approach was a reverence for institutions – in this case parliament – and a contempt

[4] W. Stubbs, *The Constitutional History of England*, iii (4th edn, 1890), pp. 73–4.
[5] Stubbs, *Constitutional History*, p.294.

for politicians, unless they were perceived to be built on a statesmanlike
Victorian model, that made it almost impossible to say anything worthwhile about the tangled and sometimes violent politics of fifteenth-
century England.

Stubbs' version of the late middle ages has been extraordinarily durable.
It received further support from Charles Plummer, who in 1885 produced
an edition of Sir John Fortescue's *Governance of England*, a work written
during the reign of Edward IV to explain the collapse of Henry VI's
government and prevent a recurrence. Plummer believed that Fortescue
had put his finger correctly on the causes of monarchical failure in the
fifteenth century: financial weakness, 'overmighty subjects', who were
richer than the king and could therefore outbid him for his subjects'
loyalty, and the presence of armed bands of retainers who could be used
against the monarch. This last phenomenon he christened 'bastard feudalism'. This phrase conveyed the idea that 'true' feudalism, which meant
lordship founded on a grant of land by a lord to his man, in return for the
dependant's military service, had been replaced during the fourteenth
century by a debased dependency resting on money and contract. Using
the earliest modern edition of the Paston letters, Plummer showed the evil
effects of this system in local government, the first of many to draw
prolonged attention to this issue.

As this persuasive picture of the later middle ages developed, so the
reign of Edward III (1327–77) was seen, by both Stubbs and many
subsequent historians, to have a pivotal role in the decline of monarchical
power during the fifteenth century. It was held that Edward's acute need
for money to finance the Hundred Years War against France had led him
into making unwise concessions. In so far as this involved enhancing the
power of parliament, especially of the Commons, by giving it greater
control over taxation, as the price of securing taxes for the war, that was to
be approved. However, in other respects Edward's actions were held to be
deleterious, especially as their purpose, the pursuit of foreign war, was in
itself deemed inappropriate to England's interests, defined as they were in
terms of the growth of constitutional liberty. It was argued above all that
he had allowed far too much power to be devolved into the hands of the
nobility.

The most serious charges were these. First, he had permitted the nobles
to raise men for his army by contract. This was seen to be the cause of the
growth of bastard feudalism: soldiers, recruited for war by contract because
the numbers that could be raised by feudalism were now inadequate for
the king's campaigns, went on to serve their masters in peace. Once back
in England, these men, 'incapacitated by long warfare for the pursuits of
settled and peaceful life, and ready to follow their masters on any turbulent

enterprise',[6] became an endemic cause of instability. Not only were they intrinsically violent, but the fact that they were attached to their lords by money and contract rather than by the more durable tie of land was held to have introduced a market in allegiance. Retainers changed their lords at will, creating an unsettled society, and forcing lords to carry out ever more outrageous illegal acts and perversions of law and government to retain their loyalty. Secondly, Edward III was supposed to have offered freedoms to the nobility with regard to their land, in return for support for his wars, which seriously undermined the power of the crown. He was the first king freely to give the licences that the nobles, as direct tenants of the crown, still needed to grant their lands away. This enabled them to give their lands to trustees, or feoffees as they were called. Consequently, they could avoid the equivalent of the death duty that the heir had to pay on succeeding to the land and prevent crown control over marriages of heiresses and underage heirs. The argument then continued that the king thus lost valuable revenue on the one hand and on the other the ability to prevent the creation by marriage of large magnate agglomerations of land. Great noble rebels, like the duke of Lancaster, who deposed Richard II in 1399, and Warwick the Kingmaker, who made and broke kings, were said to have owed their existence to this development.[7]

Thirdly, Edward was blamed for the way he treated his own family. He had six sons, of whom five survived into adulthood.[8] The families of all his four surviving younger sons became possessed of important noble estates and titles, either through their own marriages, or through those of their children, and it was through the sons of Edward III that all the possible candidates for the throne from 1399 to 1485 could make their claim. It was therefore alleged that Edward was at fault for the deposition of his grandson and immediate successor, Richard II, in 1399, because it was done by the duke of Lancaster, Edward's grandson, Henry. According to this interpretation, Henry had the power to remove the king because Henry's father, John of Gaunt duke of Lancaster, Edward's third son, had been married by his father to the Lancaster heiress. This deposition was then said to have destabilised English politics because Lancaster's claim to

[6] Sir John Fortescue, *The Governance of England*, ed. C. Plummer (Oxford, 1885), p. 15
[7] This accusation against Edward has proved remarkably durable. It is made in M. McKisack, *The Fourteenth Century 1307–1399* (Oxford, 1959), pp. 261–2, where this highly technical subject can be pursued. Her account of Edward is generally favourable to him but sees the policy as a source of later weakness. The issue lingers on in later discussions of the reign: see below, pp. 41–3.
[8] McKisack (*Fourteenth Century*) has two Williams who died in infancy in her genealogy of the House of Plantaganet. That would make seven sons, but the Great Gate of Trinity College, Cambridge, which has the names and shields of Edward's sons, has only one William, William of Hatfield.

the throne could be contested by the descendants of Edward's second son, Lionel of Clarence, who ultimately became the Yorkist claimants.[9] Moreover, the plethora of possible claimants to the throne in the fifteenth century was also laid at Edward's door, as the result of the marriages of his other younger sons. An additional sting to this accusation was the fact that the duke of Lancaster was so particularly powerful in 1399 because his father and grandfather, his immediate predecessors as dukes of Lancaster, had been given enormous 'palatinate' authority within the Duchy of Lancaster[10] by Edward III, another facet of his policy of strengthening the nobility to secure their support in war.

Both Plummer and Stubbs saw the fifteenth century as 'an age of transition' and curiously they were joined in this by the most surprising allies, Karl Marx and some of his subsequent followers. Marx too, for different reasons, thought the old order was breaking down in the later middle ages, and for him too a key element in the process of change was the dissolution of feudalism. Both schools of history, we can see with hindsight, were made acutely aware of historical change by the changes in nineteenth-century society going on around them. Particularly noted was the advent of new non-landed wealth, which is mirrored in the idea of a transition in the late middle ages from the permanence of dependent relationships based on land, to ones that were more commercial and therefore more subject to change. Although the 'new monarchy' has long since been laid to rest, we shall see in looking at Henry VII that the idea of a change from a 'medieval' to a 'modern' world at the end of the fifteenth century has been hard to shake off even in the late twentieth century. In fact, this is a historiographical division that goes all the way back to the 'Enlightenment' of the eighteenth century, when the idea was put forward that Europe only began to become civilised at the end of the middle ages, and that in England this happened in 1485. Once it had grafted on to it the Marxist concept of a change from 'feudalism' into 'capitalism', beginning some time towards the end of the middle ages and coming to fruition in the eighteenth century, then historians were well on the way to a periodisation that we still use and now call 'medieval', 'early-modern' and 'modern'. It is not surprising that historians like Stubbs and Plummer, as near-contemporaries of Marx, living in the same country, should have responded similarly to the changes going on around them.

The first challenges to Stubbs came paradoxically from historians who accepted his parameters but moved the arguments within them. Most of

---

[9] See genealogy, pp. 82–3.
[10] This is discussed and explained below, p. 54.

these were from the so-called Manchester school of medievalists, which developed towards the end of the nineteenth century and in the first two decades of the twentieth. Of these the greatest was T. F. Tout. These were the first medievalists self-consciously to espouse the cause of 'professional history' in England. Unlike his predecessors, who had been conscientious exploiters of the limited number of documents from the vast governmental archive then coming into print, Tout went to the archive itself. He was the first historian to make extensive use of the records of the English government. But he was also part of a generation that was trying to free itself of Stubbs, in writing not only 'professional' but what we would now call value-free history. The reverence for professionalism, the study of mainly administrative documents, the belief in the objective truth they offered, and the reaction against the Whig picture of English history as one big parliamentary debate, together produced a vogue for administrative history. The great heroes were now the administrators and the kings who recognised their worth. However, in Tout there was a twist, for he still accepted the notion of 'conflict for the constitution' but shifted it into a struggle for control of the king's central government. He believed that the household was the hub of potentially despotic monarchical authority and that the barons were trying to control the king by forcing him to rule through the more institutionalised parts of government, which he called 'the departments of state'. In practice this meant that for Tout medieval history ended in 1399 with the deposition of Richard II, the king responsible for 'the last avowed attempt at autocracy' through the household.[11] He accepted the idea of Lancastrian constitutionalism and therefore supposed that the struggle was over until the arrival of Tudor despotism.

However, an American follower of the school, J. F. Baldwin, an assiduous searcher among the growing corpus of printed documents of the central government, did take the story into the fifteenth century by placing the centre of conflict in the council. He was of the opinion that there was a feudal or baronial view of the king's council, which was that it should be a body representative of the nation, through which the monarch could be subject to control, and a royal view, that, at its most extreme, valued the council as a purely professional body entirely under the domination of the king. As in previous interpretations of the period, Richard II is seen to be the most 'royalist' of the medieval kings and, after baronial dominance of the council under Henry VI, the royal victory is sealed under Edward IV and Henry VII. But the novelty in Baldwin's work was that, in place of assumptions about the despotism of the earlier Tudors, a balanced council

---

[11] T. F. Tout, *Chapters in the Administrative History of Medieval England* (6 vols., Manchester, 1920–33), i, p. 229.

of representative and professional elements is held to emerge under Henry VIII.

Here we have another aspect of the reaction to Stubbs, the re-evaluation of the Tudors, which was to have important implications for the fifteenth century, but especially for the reign of Henry VII. The Tudor monarchy had in fact already been celebrated in the work of J. A. Froude, a contemporary of Stubbs. Already in violent reaction against the whole Whig school, he extolled the Tudors, despotism and all, taking from the Whigs only the delight in the Reformation, which others of Froude's political leaning had tended to see as a wrong turning. He found in the sixteenth century the origins of empire and, in an odd twist to Whig insularity, the beginnings of England's special imperial position. He extolled nationalism against internationalism. For him the great hero was Henry VIII. It has been rightly pointed out that it is from Froude that we get the picture of 'merrie England' located in the sixteenth century.

But it was with the reaction against Stubbs that the Tudors really came into their own. Related to the other factors that produced the new school – a school that was professional in both the way it did history and its reverence for administrators – was the movement in England in the last three decades of the century for greater governmental efficiency. For obvious reasons, this was another incitement to look with a new eye at periods that had appeared despotic to the Whigs but could be taken to be marked by efficiency rather than tyranny. The kings to emerge with the greatest credit from this were the first two Tudors. Henry VIII was the hero of A. F. Pollard, one of the most eminent of the 'efficiency' school, while Henry VII, who had remained rather grey in comparison with his son, appeared suddenly to be great by virtue of his very greyness, the ultimate self-effacing bureaucrat. The most significant novelty of this interpretation, and another which was clearly influenced by contemporary concerns, was its emphasis on the importance of the monarchy's financial health. This theme had been there since Sir Francis Bacon's portrait of Henry VII, written in the early seventeenth century, with its focus on Henry's wealth and how he garnered it. Indeed, it was potentially present even earlier in Fortescue's diagnosis of the ills of fifteenth-century monarchy and his list of remedies. However, the royal finances in the fifteenth century had been curiously absent from analysis of the king's weakness in that period; for example, Stubbs, who refers to the king's poverty when expounding Fortescue, does not develop the point in the main substance of his discussion of the Lancastrian kings. Fortescue's principal role for the Whigs had been to figure as an early theorist of English parliamentary liberty. Only Plummer, writing his introduction to Fortescue's *Governance* nearly a decade later, when the efficiency movement was well under way, drew attention to the wealth of Edward IV and Henry VII as a major basis of their rule. Gradually Henry was elevated to his present position as the man whose 'unmedieval' qualities of hard work, respect for money and disrespect for barons made the world safe for Tudor monarchy. Consciousness of the importance of money can already be seen in the work of J. H. Ramsay, starting from the 1890s, which makes serious, if naive, efforts to assess the state of the finances of the medieval kings.

Although some of this post-Stubbs work did take the fifteenth century before the rise of the Tudors seriously, none of it added significantly to historians' understanding of the century. We have seen that the focus remained on institutions, even if less on parliament, and there was little of interest to say about institutions for most of the fifteenth century. It was only the study of political history which could bring any life back to the period. Indeed, the new history was, if anything, more hostile to the nobles and noble politics than its predecessor, obsessed as it was with the virtues of faceless administrators functioning throughout the middle ages, regardless of the incompetence and indiscipline of the nobility, and in the fifteenth century these appeared especially incompetent and lacking in discipline. The new approval of the Tudors still left most of the fifteenth century and the whole late-medieval period under a cloud. The difference was that it was now seen no longer as the cause of the decline of liberty in the sixteenth century, but as a time that had to be got through before things improved. The administrative historians made the period look worse because some of them began to examine the records of the local administration, including the Justices of the Peace. These seemed to give added authority to the verdict on the period that Plummer had taken from the Paston letters and appeared especially to emphasise the inadequacies of Edward III. It was Edward who had allegedly allowed the administration of justice to slip out of the king's hands into those of local societies, represented by the JPs, where it became the plaything of local 'bastard feudal' politics.

There is one last group in the professional movement that concerns us, and that is the legal historians. The greatest of these was F. W. Maitland, arguably one of the greatest historians of all time. Most of his work was done on much earlier periods, but he brought a genuine breath of fresh air to the whole debate by suggesting two things. First, that the English common law, the other gift of history that was supposed to have made England great and unique, was irrational and unscientific and secondly that it had been studied in a completely anachronistic and irrational manner. For almost the first time there was introduced the heretical notion that England's past was not just a pale reflection of its present but that the past just might, to use a famous quotation, be 'another country'. Maitland's work has been and remains hugely influential, although sadly, as we shall see, more in the earlier than the later middle ages.

In introducing professionally studied legal history, Maitland brought to the forefront of research the one part of formal government that was indubitably important to all medieval landowners, the king's law. The institutional history that had prevailed all the way through in this period, and had focused on parliament, administration and council, at last fixed on an institution whose importance could be recognised without anachronism. It was also an institution whose ideas permeated much of the thinking of the political society of crown, government and landowners.[12] There was a further benefit, which was that historians' attention was directed to the Year-Books, the digests of legal arguments and opinions produced for the training of lawyers, which began to appear in the later thirteenth century. Here at last, mixed in with a mass of discussions of other issues, were to be found informally expressed views on what the powers of the crown and its relation to governmental institutions really were. Attention was also drawn to some of the main legal texts of the fifteenth and early sixteenth centuries, such as Lyttleton, St Germain and Starkey. We shall see in the next two chapters how enormously important the law is to any understanding of England in the late middle ages.

A predictable quantity of debunking of the Whig interpretation ensued from this legal wing of the 'professional revolution', as it was discovered that there was no sense of a 'constitution' in the modern sense in the fifteenth century; that fifteenth-century kings had no parliamentary title; that parliament was very much the king's own institution; that there was no suddenly established supremacy of statute under the Lancastrians; that the only constraint on medieval kings was their subordination to the law but that force alone could compel them to keep it. Thus all the major planks of Stubbs disappeared. The leading figures here are T. F. T. Plucknett, a legal historian whose main work was on Edward I, and a more conventionally trained historian, S. B. Chrimes, who wrote in 1936 what should have been a seminal work on the fifteenth-century constitution from the perspective of legal records. He also used the work of fifteenth-century legal writers like Fortescue, whose work was now pressed into a different service.

But what should have been a straight path to the exit from what had become a Whig prison proved not to be so. It is not altogether easy to explain why. Partly it was a simple matter of Chrimes' book's appearance so close to the war years, so that there was no time for its influence to spread; by 1945, as we shall shortly see, it had been supplanted as a point of

---

[12] For more on law in ideas and in governance, see below, pp. 22–9, 47–54, 59–63.

departure for a new interpretation of the period. More important was its overemphasis on legal history as constitutional history. Chrimes produced an excellent non-Whig definition of the constitution: 'that body of governmental rights and duties which exist in a state at any time in virtue of their recognition by law, custom, convention, practice or opinion. By this definition, even the most extreme despotism is a constitution.'[13] However, his insistence that there was a law of the constitution and that constitutional history was essentially legal history was clearly too limiting, especially in its failure to engage with the practices of government. This led Chrimes to pass by the magisterial and unavoidable work of Tout and his school.[14]

Perhaps most damaging of all was Chrimes' failure to force himself beyond the Stubbsian parameters. Every question examined in his book makes sense only to those familiar with the Whig agenda. And this inability to break out of the framework is common to all the other post-Stubbs historians up to this time. Of those we have not looked at, Petit-Dutaillis and Lefebvre, two French historians who produced studies and notes on Stubbs between 1908 and 1929, went in for an extreme form of debunking, by no means unique to them, which denied all motives beyond pure self-interest to either kings or barons at any time in the middle ages. The historical pedigree of this approach can be seen from the fact that the translation of their work was published by Manchester University Press and that they refer approvingly to Tout. Though whether the latter would have endorsed all of this is another matter. Nevertheless, it was a view of medieval English history that was to have a lot of mileage in it where the fourteenth and fifteenth centuries were concerned.[15]

C. L. Kingsford, in a series of lectures published in 1925, tellingly called *Prejudice and Promise in Fifteenth-Century England*, went further than all previous historians in finding some worth in the century but he too was ultimately unable to get beyond Stubbs. He took the Froude view of the sixteenth century and tried to show that the fifteenth was not a sink of iniquity but the prelude to England's greatness a hundred years later. He puts before the reader Lollardy as the origin of the Reformation (an idea with a long history behind it), the growth of the English vernacular as the harbinger of the great Elizabethan literary age, west country pirates as the forerunners of the Elizabethan buccaneers, Froude's own prelude to empire. He even uses the Paston letters in conjunction with the Stonor

---

[13] S. B. Chrimes, *English Constitutional Ideas in the Fifteenth Century* (Cambridge, 1936), p. xix.
[14] He did in fact later produce what was essentially a 'digest' of Tout's work in *An Introduction to the Administrative History of Mediaeval England* (Oxford, 1966) but he never married his work on the law to administrative history.   [15] See below, pp. 21–2.

letters, published recently by Kingsford himself, and unpublished legal records (then almost entirely unexplored territory) to show that the violence depicted in the Paston letters was unusual. He exploits the conclusions of Thorold Rogers, a distinguished late-nineteenth-century historian of wages and prices, to show that underneath all the conflict the English yeoman prospered as never before, and he celebrates the prosperity of fifteenth-century London. He is indeed the first historian of the century to note that there was by no means unadulterated and all-consuming conflict throughout the crisis of 1450–85. And he tries to produce a responsible statesman to set beside the heroes of sixteenth-century England, in the duke of Suffolk, impeached and murdered in 1450. In the context this seems ludicrous, but we shall see later that, if for the wrong reasons, he may well have been on to something. He too, however, accepted unquestioningly the notion of a 'Lancastrian constitutional experiment' and parliamentary title, and, although trying to minimise the 'lack of governance', assumed that it existed, and was concerned about indentured retainers.

To borrow the language of historians of science, a new paradigm was needed, and it was provided by K. B. McFarlane, the one indisputably great historian to have worked primarily on the fifteenth century, and almost the first to study it for its own sake, neither as the degrading of something good nor as the prelude to something better. Before the war there were already signs that he had rejected the Stubbs perspective, but his real influence came after, starting in 1945 with, to all intents and purposes, the first attempt to explore the workings and effects of bastard feudalism. Instead of sweeping generalisations there was carefully studied fact; instead of assumptions there was perceptive thought. Perhaps the most important contribution of McFarlane's work to the subject of bastard feudalism was to do away with the prevalent idea that retainers were normally hired thugs or men originally engaged for war and brutalised by their experience, and to direct attention to the normality of the relationship, whether in peace or war. In showing that retainers were in most cases either members of the gentry or rising professional men, he put an end to the Whig view that these men represented the dross of fifteenth-century society, while the parliamentary Commons stood for all that remained good; in McFarlane's work we can see that they were to a large extent the same people. He also pointed out, tellingly, that there were plenty of retainers about in Tudor England, when the Tudors were supposed to have brought peace to England by doing away with the evils of bastard feudalism. Moreover, in his work on the late-medieval nobility, he made it clear that the gentry were not part of a parliamentary middle class but incorporated with the nobles into the landed classes.

He was also to make a significant contribution to a new understanding of both feudalism and bastard feudalism which has really only gained headway among historians of all periods of medieval English history in recent years. Typically, English historians had treated both primarily as different ways of raising troops for war. In his 1945 paper McFarlane accepted the generally held premise that, by the end of the thirteenth century, weakening of feudal lordship had made feudal tenure an inadequate means of doing this, and that the rise of the indentured retainer was mainly due to the need for an alternative means of raising troops. In common with previous writers, he thought that the emergence of bastard feudalism indicated the appearance of the 'cash nexus' at the expense of older forms of loyalty based on land tenure. However, he later came to the conclusion that the change from feudalism to bastard feudalism was more to do with the lord's peacetime needs and that feudalism was not so very different from bastard feudalism. The primary purpose of both was not to provide troops for war but to create bonds between nobles and lesser landowners. The money payment was not the essence of the relationship, which remained one of personal allegiance and mutual benefit. In general, he thought that the differences between a supposedly stable and peaceful feudal early middle ages and an unstable and violent bastard feudal later middle ages owed more to the relative lack of legal records up to *c.* 1300 and their rapid growth thereafter than to any real distinction.

Historians of feudal society have recently been moving in the same direction, increasingly discussing the feudal tie as a social phenomenon and less as a method for raising soldiers; and their work is revealing that allegiances could be as complex and changing as anything found in the fourteenth and fifteenth centuries. At the same time, studies of late-medieval local societies and noble followings, or 'affinities' as they are known, have revealed a far more stable world than was supposed. Chopping and changing of allegiances was rare and a lesser landowner would normally attach himself, often by family tradition, to a leading noble in his locality and stay with him. This was in much the same way that, because of the tenurial relationship, the feudal followers of a baron would live in the vicinity of his estates. So, thanks to McFarlane and those who followed in his footsteps, we now know that there was nothing intrinsically 'wrong' with the social system of late-medieval England, and that in itself it was not remarkably different from what came before. Thanks also to both McFarlane and historians of the earlier middle ages, we have realised that the words 'feudalism' and 'bastard feudalism' do not describe particular institutions which really existed but are convenient short-hand for certain types of social relations at particular periods of history. That is why, if used, they tend to be put, as here, in inverted commas, and that is how they will be used henceforward in this work.[16]

In his article of 1945 McFarlane also put forward what was to prove one of the principal foundations for his radical revision of the century; this was the rejection of the idea running through much of the nineteenth-century historiography that there was a fundamental weakness in fifteenth-century government and, instead, his attribution of the periods of failure to inadequate kingship. This in itself, combined with the re-evaluation of 'bastard feudalism', was a huge step forward, for the two insights shifted attention away from alleged long-term causes, hitherto discussed with a remarkable lack of precision, and towards the precise nature of late-medieval kingship and detailed study of the actions of the kings. In keeping with this change of focus was McFarlane's insight, revolutionary and massively influential across the whole of late-medieval English political history, that the history of this period should not be primarily of institutions but of people; that 'the real politics' of the period consisted of the king's 'daily personal relations with his magnates'.[17] Almost at a stroke arid institutional history, once it was shown to be an anachronism, could be abandoned and the politicians – kings and nobles, the ones who made things happen – could take centre-stage.

Three things followed from this. First, it became necessary to study the nobles; for almost the first time, the stock 'wicked baron' was being replaced by a series of skilful portraits of individual figures, based on meticulous research and emphasising the uniqueness of each. Secondly, in pursuing these studies, McFarlane had to break out of the almost complete reliance on royal records which had been the norm since the emergence of the Tout school and make use of the private archives of the nobles. This meant that the political world was no longer being seen exclusively through the eyes of kings and bureaucrats but that the perspective of what might be called consumers of government was for the first time being introduced. From this vantage, what had approvingly been referred to as strong government might look unnecessarily interfering, and nation-wide disorder might come to be seen less as the product of noble ambition and indiscipline and more as the unwelcome result of feeble kingship. This led McFarlane thirdly to the conclusion that it was not conflict between kings and nobles that was the norm in the later middle ages, but co-operation.

It is hard to exaggerate the impact of McFarlane's work, especially at Oxford, where he taught. A whole generation of students there was inspired to work on what had been a very neglected century; nearly all the political historians of fourteenth- and fifteenth-century England today,

---

[16] This is all discussed further below, pp. 49–52.   [17] McFarlane, *Nobility*, p. 120.

including the present writer, are, academically speaking, 'children' or 'grandchildren', even 'great grandchildren', of McFarlane. His inspiration led to systematic study first of numbers of individual nobles and then of local gentry societies, the second leading on naturally from McFarlane's interest in the relations of 'bastard feudalism'. Vast amounts of unpublished documents have been read, and classes of document scarcely explored before have been investigated, especially the limited surviving archives of the gentry and the difficult and voluminous records of the royal law courts, with rich results. From the work of McFarlane and his successors, as they have looked at first the nobles and then the gentry, we have come to realise how able, well-educated and, above all, rational most of these people were. Perhaps the most obvious benefit of this deeper knowledge has been the vindication of Kingsford; the recognition that there was plenty of life in England going on outside the periodic crises. This is seen most notably now in the general agreement that the Wars of the Roses ended not in 1485 but in 1471, to be restarted almost by accident in 1483.

The effect of McFarlane's work was by no means confined to the period of the Wars of the Roses. Since he was rightly minimising the importance of long-term causes to the travails of the fifteenth-century monarchy, all the other reigns embraced by an interpretation that placed the fifteenth century at the end of a period of long-term monarchical and governmental decline had to be re-examined. Above all, as the key reign in the synthesis that was finally being discarded under the inspiration of McFarlane, Edward III's was due a reassessment. It must be said that Edward's reign as a whole still causes historians problems which, as we shall see, have a strong bearing on their handling of the origins of the Wars of the Roses.[18] However, McFarlane's work has been applied directly and indirectly to restore Edward's reputation in most of the areas where he had been most severely taken to task. Partly this came naturally from the realisation that Edward's military needs did not create 'bastard feudalism', but that this new pattern of social relations among the landed aristocracy was growing naturally out of changes in society. Like all social changes, it occurred over a long time and could hardly have been accomplished by the whim of a single man, however powerful. But also fundamental to rethinking Edward's reign was McFarlane's point about king and nobles being normally on the same side rather than opposed.

Once it was grasped that both this idea of natural opposition and historians' hostility to foreign war were nineteenth-century anachronisms, it could be seen that Edward was an effective leader who shared with his nobility an enthusiasm for war and had nothing to fear from their power.

---

[18] See below, pp. 32–3, 41–2.

The dukes of Lancaster, for example, were given such great powers in the north because, if the king was fighting the French, he needed to delegate the defence of the northern borders against the Scots. In any case, unusually powerful nobles were nothing new in the later middle ages – they are found all the way back to the Norman Conquest and beyond – and were not directly caused by the king's failure to maintain his rights over noble lands. The Lancaster lands, the greatest of the late-medieval agglomerations, were in fact created for a member of the royal family, Edward I's younger brother, and, from 1399, returned to the crown permanently. The financial profits to the king from his control over noble lands were also seen to be insignificant. They had been in decline ever since Magna Carta had severely curtailed them in 1215 and by Edward's reign were more a source of aggravation than a serious means of funding the crown. The new taxation itself, it has been shown, did not involve the surrender of any significant monarchical powers, but rather made the king who had access to all this money for war hugely powerful.[19] And to blame the Wars of the Roses on Edward for having large numbers of sons and marrying some of them into noble families, just because the events of a hundred years later made these relationships important, is to study history backwards with a vengeance. In fact, like his grandfather, the acclaimed Edward I, all he was doing was endowing his children at no cost to the crown. The monarchy in 1377, at Edward III's death, was in fundamentally good order and Richard II was deposed because he ruled inadequately.[20]

Consequently, it was understood that the deposition itself and the arrival of the Lancastrian kings was not a source of long-term weakness. Once Henry IV had shown himself able to survive his first few shaky years, and the exploits of his son, Henry V, had set an almost irremovable gloss on the dynasty, the Lancastrians had no need to prove their worth in order to remain kings. The unchallenged accession of a nine-month-old baby, Henry VI, in 1422, at a moment in the French war when the last thing that England needed was a baby on the throne and a long minority, proves the point. McFarlane-inspired work on Henry V has shown the health of the monarchy under an able king, and the lengths to which the king could push his authority to maintain the peace at home and fight an ambitious and expensive war abroad. Work on Henry IV has shown how even a usurper, facing a mass of internal and external threats, whose health broke down as soon as his position had become reasonably secure, could rule with moderate effectiveness.[21]

The realisation that England was not full of undisciplined armed 'thugs' and that the monarchy was inherently stable, even strong, has led to the

[19] See below, pp. 29–32.   [20] This is discussed further below, pp. 41–3, 65.
[21] For more on these kings, see below, chapter 4.

minimising of the extent of violence during the Wars of the Roses. It is understood that armies were mostly not large and campaigns were short and that the potential for large-scale destruction between 1455 and 1485 was much less than has been supposed. We shall see that there is still some discussion of how much devastation there was, resulting both from the wars and from the failures of government, but no-one is now pressing for a return to the picture of wholesale destruction over a thirty-year period.[22]

However, the McFarlane legacy has proved problematic. He was a perfectionist who was reluctant to publish his research and he died prematurely and suddenly in 1966, leaving his work incomplete; much of it was published after his death and nowhere is there the extended treatment of the nobility on which he spent much of his working life. It is consequently not entirely clear what the McFarlane legacy is, since, like the Bible or the works of Karl Marx, it can be interpreted in different ways. One of these has become the predominant orthodoxy since McFarlane's death. It starts from McFarlane's stress on personal politics and brings in another aspect of his work. McFarlane, being very much alive to what was going on in other periods, was much taken by the pioneering work of Lewis Namier on patronage politics and the creation of political followings by the distribution of rewards in eighteenth-century England. This drew his interest to 'prosopography', an important part of the Namierite method, meaning the writing of history by means of card-index biographies of numbers of minor political figures, in this case to show their connections with more important politicians. It was of course an ideal method for the study of the 'bastard feudal' followings of the late-medieval nobles. But in his admiration for Namier and his concern to remove institutions from late-medieval politics, McFarlane at times placed what is perhaps undue weight on patronage and reward, particularly what the king had to offer, as the all-purpose lubricant of politics at this time.

In a great deal of subsequent writing on the period this idea is absolutely central, even to the point where it is suggested that the king functioned best as the centre of his own 'bastard feudal' network based on the crown lands, and it has deeply contradictory implications. For a start, the conviction that effective kingship to a large extent stood or fell by how well the king managed his patronage is profoundly inimical to McFarlane's central belief in the normal coincidence of royal and noble interests, for it implies that the nobles had to be bought over. It can therefore lead to a contempt for magnate aspirations – words like 'greedy', 'self-seeking', 'grasping', even 'thugs', are in common use – and an enthusiasm for what is still approvingly called 'strong kingship' which is highly reminiscent of

[22] See below, pp. 258–60.

everything that came before McFarlane and is wholly out of place in interpretations which claim to take their starting-point from him. There is an almost universal agreement that politics were entirely about individual ambition and conflict over the spoils of monarchy, and that political actions were motivated almost exclusively by intense personal feeling. This is a curious and intellectually self-limiting return to the period when the only escape historians could see from the Whig tradition was to deny any dignity at all to any period of medieval politics. With the assumption that rampant individualism was the norm, it becomes extremely difficult to discuss collective political action, such as deposition of a king, among the landed classes. Historians have been reduced to two alternatives. Either they have to fall back on crude divisions between 'ins' and 'outs', which leaves no room for those, often the majority, who do not fit conveniently into either group, so that they then have to create an ever-growing band of 'moderates'. Or they feel obliged to find a personal cause for every participant in collective acts of resistance. Related to this dim view of landowners' political sophistication is the belief, often implicit but some-times explicit, that, if nobles were not fighting the French abroad, they would be fighting each other or the king at home.[23] In this view, contrary to almost everything that has been discovered about them since the 'McFarlane revolution', they were nothing but ignorant and violent soldiers.

Another return to the past has been the stress on the royal finances, reminiscent of the 'efficiency school', since the king's ability to distribute patronage successfully to the competing multitudes must be underpinned by solvency. This has tended to carry with it a continuing reverence for good monarchical housekeeping in the name of avoiding a generally undiagnosed reliance on parliament. Not only is all this alien to almost everything McFarlane had to say on the period, but the stress on strong kingship, noble baseness, royal wealth and patronage is in effect the adoption of the Fortescue recipe, and *The Governance of England*, the work by Fortescue outlining this policy, was dismissed by McFarlane in these words: 'Fortescue's overrated and misleading pamphlet'.[24] These are not the only items from past interpretations still lying around; there is still quite a lot of Tout in the treatment of Richard II's household, some subliminal Baldwin hovering over the treatment of the council throughout the middle ages, a fair amount of Plummer in the discussion of 'bastard feudalism' and disorder. As all this implies, historians are still clinging to 'long-term causes' in their interpretation of the 'Wars of the Roses', rather than following McFarlane's advice by examining what went wrong in one

---

[23] This is part of the 'war state' interpretation, for which see below, pp. 41–3.
[24] McFarlane, '"Bastard Feudalism"', *England in the Fifteenth Century*, p. 23.

particular period. It is therefore perhaps symptomatic of this lingering permeation by earlier work that Edward III's pivotal reign still awaits the full-scale study that has been urgently required ever since McFarlane's work nullified the accepted account of this king. A book on the Wars of the Roses published as recently as 1988 could still refer to 'the more fundamental structural weaknesses of monarchy inherited from Edward III'.[25] There is also one other long-term cause that has emerged since the war, the product of a period when economics were thought by many to lie at the base of all history, and that is the argument that the Wars occurred not because the nobles were too rich and overmighty but because they were too poor. This contention, which, while coming from a very different direction, has a lot in common with the all-pervasive 'patronage' interpretation, will be examined in the next chapter.

There is, of course, nothing intrinsically wrong in rejecting McFarlane's ideas in favour of a return to earlier frames of reference. The trouble is that doing it in the name of McFarlane produces confusing history. Each of the older interpretations was, like McFarlane's revision, intellectually complete on its own terms; it is therefore impossible to try to keep an amalgam of them, at least without going back to first principles to explain why certain elements might be retained. This jumbling together of different hypotheses is symptomatic of the larger reason why late-medievalists have tended not to make the best use of McFarlane's profound insights, which is their unwillingness to think about concepts. Although the explosion of research on the fifteenth century since the McFarlane revolution has produced much interesting work, it has tended to enlarge factual knowledge rather than to increase our understanding, because historians have been reluctant to think about the framework of government and power within which these events were occurring. That has meant that they have no analytical framework of their own in which to place all this fact. The combined effect of emphasis on patronage and individual interest and fear of returning to the discredited Stubbsian paradigm has been to turn historians away from the central questions that still need to be asked: where power lay and how it was created and used, the mechanisms of government, the interrelationship of national and local government, of high and low politics, what effective kingship was thought to be.

The result has been a failure to make the best use of what has been discovered during this period of intensive research. We now know a lot about the events and personalities of national politics; we also have a lot of information about events in the localities; we know very little about how these political arenas were connected and operated on each other. One

[25] A. J. Pollard, *The Wars of the Roses* (London, 1988), p.66.

historian has attempted to argue, contrary to one of McFarlane's key insights, that the Wars of the Roses welled up from the localities to the centre, by 'an escalation of private feuds',[26] rather than that the feuds and the Wars were caused by failure at the centre. But this interesting hypothesis could not be sustained because the work failed to elucidate the mutual impact of centre and localities. Equally, because we lack a context for national politics, it is extremely difficult to understand these either, despite the fact that some of the most interesting work has been done on some of the great politicians of both fourteenth and fifteenth centuries. Part of the problem is that the institutions of government, once studied to the exclusion of all else, are usually ignored or, if examined at all, are considered in a curiously nineteenth-century manner, as if there was no other way of accommodating them and they were completely divorced from the business of kingship and politics. Yet these institutions, especially the means of enforcement linking centre to localities, are indispensable to political history. They must now be examined not in isolation but as one element in the complex business of government. The lack of a conceptual framework is undoubtedly why long-term causes and older interpretations have remained attractive options amid the sometimes remorselessly close analysis of national politics. Once the analysis has been carried out in the absence of such a framework, the historian, left with nothing but a body of fact, has sometimes reached for an older synthesis. However antithetical it may be to the approach which gave rise to the study of politics, it is simply the only one available.

In fact what all these unasked questions about power and governance amount to is what we used to know, under a rather different guise, as 'constitutional history', and, curiously, despite the apparent readiness to carry around much of the baggage of past interpretations, the one historian late-medievalists are terrified of being identified with is Stubbs, the author of the *Constitutional History*. And yet, it is evident that McFarlane, in rejecting Stubbs as anachronistic, wanted not to deny the existence of a late-medieval constitution, but rather to replace Stubbs' constitution with something that grew out of an understanding of what the leading late-medieval politicians as a group thought they were up to. It was important to McFarlane to study the nobility as a whole. He later grew more critical of prosopography, finding its emphasis on material rewards to the exclusion of any other kind of motivation too self-limiting, but he did value it as a way of making some contact, albeit 'dimly', with 'thinking, living individuals ... not romanticised and above all not to be patronised'.[27] All the same, he realised that the nobles had 'corporate traditions as well as a

---

[26] R. L. Storey, *The End of the House of Lancaster* (London, 1966), p. 27.
[27] McFarlane, *Nobility*, p. xxxvi.

sense of their own interests'[28] and he was anxious to go beyond the evidence for actions, which is almost all we have, to the exploration of motives. In this he was unconsciously working towards what has become known as 'the new social history' long before it affected historical studies in Britain. This is a history, originating in France and heavily influenced by the social sciences, which studies how societies and the social groups within them operate, along with their attitudes or 'mentalities'. This kind of social history, like McFarlane's work on the nobility, can absorb the study of politics as an essential aspect of the activities of a particular group. In fact, it is very much the kind of political history that is lacking for this period: one where nobles can be studied not just individually and in isolation. All this is a far cry from assumptions about individualism and ambition that leave no space for further discussion of motives. If one essential prerequisite for understanding the late-medieval constitution is to examine the great landowners as a body, and indeed lesser ones as well, then another is self-evidently to look at the nature of kingship. However, this also is forced into a dead-end if the debate has been summarily cut off with strong kings and patronage politics.

It could therefore be suggested that we have reached the end of the useful pursuit of one part of McFarlane's legacy and should now stand back and begin to think about the others. It is also becoming apparent that the weakest part of McFarlane's work was his propensity to treat the king as if he was no more than 'the good lord of all good lords',[29] and therefore to neglect the public dimension of kingship which made the king and his government different from any of his subjects. So we need to amalgamate McFarlane's revolutionary concern with the aspirations of the nobles, from which we have learned also to study the gentry, with a renewal of interest, albeit on different terms, in the public face of governance. What this entails specifically is looking at the constitution of the body politic and at how it functioned, and at the ideas of the landowners, the political classes of this constitution, both individually and collectively. We must try to explain why they did what they did and how they justified it to themselves and to each other. Self-evidently, since a lot of what they did was conditioned by the constitutional framework, and the framework itself was affected by ideas on what it should be, the two problems are closely related. There is plenty of groundwork, both within and outside the subject area, to help us in changing the nature of the debate. We have first the vast amount of knowledge garnered on the period, much of it from unpublished sources. Then, despite the cautions given earlier, we can still learn a lot from our more constitutionally minded predecessors. For

[28] *Ibid.*, p. xxxii.   [29] *Ibid.*, p. 119.

example, their large-scale conceptual thought could be usefully allied to
the detailed and more sophisticated understanding we now have as the
result of our more miniaturist specialised work; if we are more rigorous in
relation to evidence, their thinking was more rigorous than ours.

In one sphere particularly we can and are learning a lot, and that is
through the inheritance of Maitland in legal history. This has now fused
with the new social history, to generate the study of law in society through
most periods of English history. In late-medieval England, where the law
was so important to landowners,[30] this approach can tell us an enormous
amount about the preoccupations of local landed societies, about how they
regarded the government whose law they consumed and about how the
linkages between government and provinces operated. It is also an obvious
approach to the old questions about 'bastard feudalism': the degree to
which England in this period was disordered and the origins of disorder.
Sadly, the Maitland inheritance in this new guise has struck a deeper chord
with early medievalists than with later ones but it has nevertheless had some
impact here. There is also work done on earlier and later periods which can
show us how to examine political actions for evidence of political motives
and how to evaluate the true meanings, within their contexts, of the words
used in what is sometimes called political discourse. This is another area
which has proved problematical to historians since McFarlane. The tendency, especially in dealing with the statements made by the Yorkists in the
1450s, has been to assume that all political statements are cloaks for
self-interest. This is a circular argument, which then justifies the assumption that all politicians in this period were out for what they could get and,
in doing so, defeats any attempts at deeper analysis of motivation. At the
same time, it is used in a very arbitrary manner, so that Suffolk's protesta-
tion before he went to negotiate peace on Henry VI's behalf is taken at face
value,[31] while York's comments on Henry VI's government are denied any
sincerity. Again, we need to rethink our way of dealing with politics in this
period. One way out of this impasse is the suggestion that whether a
political statement or programme was meant seriously or not is beside the
point; what mattered is that it was made in a certain way using a certain
language, and these things tell us what the norms of political discourse
were. To sum up everything that has been said here about a new approach
to the history of the period, we are no longer looking for long-term *causes*
but that does not mean we should not be looking at long-term *circumstances*,
the inescapable parameters of constitution and society within which politics occurred. The following two chapters will examine those parameters.

---

[30] See below, pp. 27–8, 47–8.   [31] See below, p. 100.

2

THE GOVERNANCE OF ENGLAND IN THE
FIFTEENTH CENTURY I: KINGS, KINGSHIP
AND POLITICAL SOCIETY

·

THE KING AND HIS POWERS: INWARD AND
OUTWARD DEFENCE

In late-medieval England no-one had any doubt that governance was really about kingship. By the fifteenth century the king of England sat at the head of an all-encompassing legal and fiscal system. He had a sophisticated central governmental machine, that had been developing almost continuously since the Conquest, with a chancery to make grants and send out his instructions in the form of writs, a treasury to collect and store his money, an exchequer to audit his accounts and chase up debts, and a large army of professional bureaucrats to staff his government. The growth of central government, much of it in response to the needs occasioned by the Hundred Years War, was given concrete expression in the growth of Westminster as the place where the expanding bureaucracy was located. It was the king whose abilities and ambitions determined whether there would be rule or anarchy. How had he come to acquire such power? The answer lies in the twin duties assigned to him as the defender of the realm: to preserve peace internally and to protect the realm against its external enemies. The most significant element of the first obligation was the defence of the landed property of his landed subjects. This was partly because land was almost uniquely the basis of wealth but more important was the fact that it was the basis of power – something we shall look at later on in this chapter.[1] Indeed it could be argued that landowners had first accepted any kind of ruling authority in order to provide themselves with a defender and guarantor of their land against each other. To help them fulfil

---

[1] See below, pp. 35–6.

this obligation, the kings of England, since the time of Henry II (1154–89), had had at their disposal an increasingly complex and sophisticated system of law. The main function of this was to defend the landed property of all free men, by which was meant all those who were allowed to bring their pleas before the king's law. To a large extent that meant the landed aristocracy, barons and knights, later nobles and gentry, since it was held that most peasants should be regarded as unfree, or unable to use the king's courts.[2]

At first, since they had themselves given the law to their subjects, to regulate the subjects' dealings with one another, kings saw no reason themselves to feel constrained by their law; they would, for example, continue to take the lands of barons who were in debt to them long after it had ceased to be lawful for any subject, however powerful, to take the land of another free man without due process of law. However, Magna Carta in 1215 had established the principle that the king must obey his own law and, despite the efforts of successive kings to ignore it, by the fifteenth century this was a long-accepted premise of rule. Thus, kings were by this time theoretically subordinated to their own law, which meant that they were not supposed to make arbitrary attacks on the landed property of their free subjects. A king who ruled entirely in his own interests and took free men's property and its fruits without observing proper process was held to be a tyrant, the antithesis of a king. Increasingly during the thirteenth and fourteenth centuries there developed the idea that the realm of England was a community, possessed of certain rights, of which Magna Carta was the first and most definitive statement. However, paradoxically, kings were set above all other forms of authority, answerable only to God; even if they broke or disregarded the law there was no legitimate way of bringing them to account. There was good reason for this: a king who could be constrained by a subject was in no position to act with equal impartiality towards all his subjects. This, an important enough attribute of kingship before the law existed, became inescapable once the ruler had command of a legal system that could make or break landowners. If he himself had to be discouraged from attacking his subjects' property, it was if anything still more important that he had the power to prevent his landed subjects attacking each other.

Late-medieval English kings were consequently not only exceedingly powerful in being at the head of this system but even more powerful in being unchallengeably at its head. But their authority was yet greater. If we return to the other side of defence of the realm, defence against outward enemies, it too had brought enormous powers to the monarchy. Foreign

---

[2] However, by the fifteenth century, most of the peasants had to all intents and purposes become free and were using the king's law increasingly.

warfare required large sums to fund it, ever greater sums as the cost of equipment and size of armies grew throughout the middle ages. For the rulers of what was almost an island, England's kings had carried a surprising weight of military responsibility. Not only were there the other countries of the British Isles to be fought against and, they hoped, eventually subjugated, but since the Conquest there had been Normandy to defend and, from the accession of the Angevins in 1154, an even larger part of France. Even after most of the French possessions had been lost under John (1199–1216), the remnants had to be defended, and this defence eventually became all-out war against France, culminating in the Hundred Years War from 1337 to 1453.

At first the financing of these wars was very much a hand to mouth process, but ultimately there was no way of evading the issue that wars on the scale of those against France would require a form of national taxation. Indeed, the issue arrived on the political agenda straight after Magna Carta. If Magna Carta stated that the king was beneath his own law and therefore no longer allowed to take his landed subjects' property as he pleased, he had to find a legitimate way of raising money for his wars. This turned out to be the tax or subsidy levied on the value of the subject's goods. The terms of its levy took over a century to work out, in a series of negotiations and confrontations between king and nobles and then between king, nobles and knights or gentry. Most of these occurred within an assembly that by the end of the thirteenth century we may call parliament. By the middle years of Edward III, the process was essentially complete. The king's subjects accepted that this was a legitimate levy on their property, as long as the king asked for their consent in parliament, but they themselves were obliged to consent if a defensive necessity could be shown. It was not usually difficult for the king to do this because 'defence' was taken to include offence against a potential attacker. Parliament also agreed to the imposition of a number of customs dues, in return for the sole right to grant them. Most notable among these was the wool subsidy, which had been a particular cause of dispute. In turn the king himself agreed to regulate, or simply failed to exploit any more, the numbers of older rights (sometimes called 'prerogative rights' by historians) that he had tried to continue to demand while exploiting the subsidy.

The question of how strong the king was financially in the late middle ages has been much discussed and is still debated. In examining the question of the royal finances, it is vital to separate ordinary revenue and expenditure from extraordinary. One of the problems with some pessimistic accounts of royal revenues is that they throw the two together and make it impossible to judge whether kings could make ends meet when they were not fighting wars, or indeed how far they got into debt as a result of war. Ordinary revenue was defined as that which the king normally received, from a variety of sources, and ordinary expenses as his routine expenditure on household and government. The customs, normally granted in peacetime since the 1360s, were regarded as a part of ordinary revenue, and regular defensive commitments – the Scottish border and Ireland and the king's hereditary lands in France, Gascony and Calais – were deemed to be covered by ordinary expenditure. Extraordinary revenue was the parliamentary lay subsidy, taxation which was given only in time of war and for extraordinary military purposes, normally expeditions abroad but also to withstand an invasion. There were also clerical subsidies, demanded and granted under the same conditions by convocation, the clerical equivalent of parliament.

Lord Cromwell's estimates of 1433[3] are a good starting place for assessing the financial health of the late-medieval monarchy. These were intended as a spur to the Commons to grant a tax and are thus unlikely to have underestimated the crown's financial difficulties. On the face of it they show a deficit of £15,892. The largest item, about £25,000 of total expenditure, was for regular defence. Although the customs were intended primarily to subsidise this need, the trouble was that the decline in the wool trade, which was the most heavily taxed item, and piracy in the channel, as England began to lose the French war, had caused the customs revenue to fall. They stood at almost £50,000 per annum earlier in the century but at only about £30,000 in 1433. While £30,000 was sufficient for the defence commitments, the customs also helped subsidise the king's personal expenses, notably over £23,000 on administration and over £14,000 on his household in 1433. So it was the fall in customs revenues while the monarchy still had such serious defensive commitments which was the root of the problem.

However, this did not need to be a disabling difficulty. First, since extraordinary taxation was intended for defence, it was not impossible to ask for taxation to cover mounting defensive debts, as indeed Cromwell did in 1433. Moreover, the king could tax in time of truce, if he could persuade the Commons to make him a grant, and this was obviously a good way of paying off arrears arising from defence. Secondly, since 1399 the monarchy had had the revenues of the Duchy of Lancaster at its disposal. Under Henry V, the clear profit from this, used to supplement the crown's ordinary revenues, was over £6,000. Unfortunately, in 1433

[3] Usefully set out in R. A. Griffiths, *The Reign of King Henry VI* (London, 1981), p. 108. The figure for "administration" includes fees and annuities which may have been paid to people who were not in the king's employ and may therefore be inflated: see *Select Documents of English Constitutional History 1307–1485*, ed. S. B. Chrimes and A. L. Brown (London, 1961), pp. 271–4.

much of the Duchy was in the hands of feoffees to Henry V's will[4] and, except indirectly through loans, did not contribute to the royal coffers, so the Duchy's profits available to the crown had fallen by almost £4,000. Then there was the war itself. If this went successfully, and especially if the king made money from ransoms, booty and financial support from allies, he might well end up with a profit. This, even if it had been made possible by taxation, could be diverted to regular needs with no-one any the wiser. The problem by 1433 was that the war was no longer going particularly well.

This brings us to extraordinary revenue and expenditure. In a discussion of late-medieval and sixteenth-century taxation, it has been rightly pointed out that no government ever has enough money for its large-scale projects,[5] and war must be counted the one major cost for late-medieval governments. Even so, very large sums could be raised, as they were by Henry V in 1415–17 and Edward IV in 1475. A lay subsidy brought in about £30,000 from 1433 and a clerical one between £10,000 and £15,000 by the fifteenth century, even though both had had to be reduced to allow for the fall in population and land values after the Black Death in 1348–9. How much could be raised depended on how many subsidies the king could persuade the Commons to offer. This, and the frequency of taxation, was, of course, not a financial but a political matter. It related to how far the gentry and leading townsmen, whose representatives sat in the Commons, trusted the king and were convinced by his management of the war. What happened under Henry VI, as we shall see, was a downward spiral. There was failure in war, leading to reluctance to grant taxes for it, let alone to cover regular defensive obligations. This was compounded by increasing extravagance, especially after Henry's marriage, which made the Commons still more reluctant to pay, and inefficiency, which led to further falls in ordinary revenue. It was not that financial weakness caused political failure but the other way round; a moderate shortfall, by no means beyond remedy, was turned by political, military and administrative ineptitude into financial disaster. The fact that the situation could be so rapidly brought under control by Edward IV[6] shows how superficial the difficulties were.

In fact, national taxation, as its terms were finally defined under Edward III, meant that when fighting a war the king's access to the nation's wealth placed him potentially in an immensely commanding position. Even as magisterially successful a king as Edward I had met the united opposition

---

[4] This means people who held the land in trust, using the revenues to perform the various religious grants and foundations specified in Henry's will.

[5] See reference to work by Bernard in the bibliographical guidance to this chapter.

[6] See below, pp. 166–7.

of nobles and gentry in the later part of his reign, when he became engaged in large-scale war, because he was unwilling to concede that taxation had a *quid pro quo*. This was the willingness to listen to, if not always to redress, his landed subjects' grievances. After a major crisis over war expenditure and taxation in 1340–1, Edward III found that a less confrontational style of monarchy brought taxation without constitutional crisis. By the early 1360s the terms and conditions of taxation had to a large extent been hammered out. There was plenty of parliamentary dissent concerning taxation in the following century and a half, but it was political. That is, it was about failure in war and allegations of wastage. It was not constitutional, not about the actual principles of whether and on what terms the king might tax. Moreover, despite the existence of a firm theoretical distinction between the king's ordinary peacetime revenue and extraordinary revenue, the fact was that once the king had this money from taxation it was almost impossible to discover what had happened to it. This was why, when there were expensive failures in war, it was often assumed that people around the king were embezzling his taxes.[7] But it also meant that, if the war went well, the king could easily divert taxation to cover gaps in ordinary revenue with no-one the wiser.

However, many historians still deny that a late-medieval king's finances should have been adequate and see the royal finances as a long-term weakness in the monarchy which many date back to Edward III's reign. They see the Hundred Years War, on which Edward launched England, as an impossible financial encumbrance. It can be argued that this view rests on a misunderstanding. Much of the discussion has assumed that 'good housekeeping', that is a balanced budget, or even the creation of a surplus, was what kings throughout the period should have been aiming for. But it has been shown that the whole notion that 'the king should live of his own' did not properly enter into political vocabulary until the fifteenth century. Then the combination of continued taxation with the crown's acquisition of the large and wealthy Duchy of Lancaster led the parliamentary Commons to assert that royal revenues should be enough for a king who was not fighting a foreign war. Until then the only lands annexed permanently to the crown had been the Earldom of Chester (from 1246) and the Duchy of Cornwall (from 1337) and both had been used routinely to support members of the king's family, usually his son and heir, rather than to generate money for the crown. As the government's financial situation worsened in the fifteenth century, so demands that the king make better use of his private resources intensified and, as we shall see, under Edward IV and his successors, exploitation of these became much more central to royal finances. But even then the building up of surpluses was

---

[7] See below, p. 106.

not what royal finances were actually about. As long as the king had enough for peacetime purposes, large-scale expenditure for war would be met by taxation. There are those who maintain that the development of parliamentary taxation placed the king at the mercy of the taxpayers and therefore seriously undermined his ability to levy money, placing him in a 'financial straitjacket'.[8] But we have seen that taxation actually put far greater resources at his disposal than he would otherwise have had. Confidence in the king produced generous grants and we shall see later that the grants went on coming remarkably late into Henry VI's reign, despite increasing failure in war. What the king required above all in wartime was to generate sufficient confidence in his financial management, and in his ability to tax, for financiers to be ready to make loans of the large capital sums necessary for war. It was when credit lines failed that things went badly wrong. Moreover, if there was a financial weakness caused by war, it was certainly not present until well into the fifteenth century, so it can hardly be seen as the long-term consequence of Edward III's wars.

LOCAL GOVERNMENT AND THE LAW

If the king had extensive powers and large financial resources, he could not rule without being able to enforce his commands. By the fifteenth century there was a remarkably extensive system of local government for this purpose, which had developed since before the Conquest. It was based on the ancient administrative units of the shire and hundred. The sheriff in charge of the shire received most of the royal writs and collected a certain amount of royal revenue, while a variety of officials and commissions was responsible for raising the bulk of the revenue, both ordinary and extraordinary. Justices of the peace were the main officials in charge of keeping the peace and, to do the work at the lowest levels, in every village there was a constable answerable to the JPs. Regular commissions of assize and gaol delivery, mostly staffed by professional royal justices, took royal justice into the shires: the former dealt with numbers of private pleas, the latter with the trying of criminals who had already been before a local tribunal, usually the JPs. In the event of a serious outbreak of disorder or rebellion, the king could send out special commissions to enquire and to punish called *oyer* and *terminer* commissions. By now most of the local officials were unpaid local amateurs rather than the direct royal servants who had held the more important local offices from the twelfth until the later thirteenth centuries. Even so, they were the king's officers, appointed by the king.

[8] A phrase used by J. R. Lander, e.g. in *Government and Community: England 1450–1509* (London, 1980), p. 68.

The legal system, of which some of these officials and commissions were a part, was quite as impressive, and an increasing amount of legal business, both criminal prosecutions and private litigation, concerning even the least of the king's subjects, was coming into the royal courts. At its apex were the Westminster courts, of which the most important for our purposes were the Court of Common Pleas and the King's Bench. By the fifteenth century most cases concerning landowners would be likely to proceed in one or other, if not both, of these courts. The Common Pleas dealt with private pleas only, and a large amount of litigation, much of it over very minor matters, such as debt and small-scale damage, went through this court. The King's Bench had a twofold capacity and was a forum for both private litigation and crown prosecution, what we would now call criminal jurisdiction. There were also local courts, but landowners' pleas would by this time not normally be heard before them. The only local jurisdiction of real significance for landowners was that of the JPs, who were judicial as well as peacekeeping officers. Normally a prosecution would start with a hearing before the JPs, before whom a jury would indict, that is decide whether there was a case to answer, just as their lineal descendants, the magistrates, still do. At this juncture defendants with any influence, which tended to mean landowners, would get the case taken into the King's Bench for trial.

There were also equitable courts, which means courts where a certain amount of flexibility could be used in interpreting the strict letter of the law, in the interests of securing its spirit. Since the only person who had the power to dispense with the law in this way was the king, all these courts grew out of the king's personal authority as original creator of the law. They were the king's council, parliament, which had emerged from enlarged meetings of the council, and chancery, a conciliar court which was rapidly developing as the court of equity. This was the result of the king committing much of his equitable authority to his chancellor. As might be imagined from the steps that had been taken to curb the king's power to act beyond the law, equitable jurisdiction was regarded with some suspicion, and its use was quite severely constrained. On the other hand, it was manifestly useful in cases where there was no remedy in the law or when a litigant's opponents were too powerful for the normal legal processes to be open to him, and it was generally speedier and cheaper than the common law.

THE NOBILITY AND THE KING

We now move from the king to his subjects. The subjects who mattered in medieval England are commonly referred to by historians as 'political society', the people with a stake in the world of governance and politics.

Although townsmen had some influence when it came to granting taxes, through their representatives in parliament, political society in late-medieval England consisted essentially of the landowners alone. The greatest of these were the nobles. For much of the fifteenth century there were about eighty to a hundred nobles at any one time, sometimes more, sometimes less, although their numbers fell towards the end of the century. Not all of these would be equally active, some would almost certainly be underage, and the real leaders of political society were the greater nobility, most of them earls, perhaps about twenty families in all at any one time.

The nobles were the key subordinates of the king in the process of ruling. This was not primarily because of any official positions they might hold but because at the heart of all power in late-medieval England lay landed property, and the nobility were the greatest landowners. To understand the relationship between land and power in this period one must first grasp the fact that all governments need a monopoly of force if they are not only to issue orders but to see those orders enforced. As in all reasonably stable countries, the force lying behind a command was by the fifteenth century more usually implicit than explicit. However, it had to be understood that a royal officer if resisted could summon a force to support him, in exactly the same way that a motorist, stopped for speeding, knows that resistance will quickly bring numbers of further police officers on to the scene. Equally, this force that makes it possible to rule has to be non-negotiable: modern governments that lose control of army and police quickly surrender power. It also has to be readily available at the point of enforcement. Now, in medieval England, there was no standing army, much less a police force, and, of course, the government lacked the modern technology that will get troops or police to a disturbance or to the scene of a crime. What kings did have was a landed aristocracy which had control over a non-negotiable force that could be put to use wherever it was needed. These were the peasant tenants of nobility and gentry who rented their lands from the lord and were also under his manorial jurisdiction. For the most part these had no choice but to fight for him. This fact of life is effectively demonstrated by the great political importance attached to the stewardships of the crown estates; whoever held the stewardship of a particular royal property was in a position to call out its manpower, whether on his own or on the king's behalf. What we are dealing with therefore is a realm in which the public governmental authority of the king was based on private force which he himself did not directly control.[9] This intermingling of the private and the public was a crucial factor in the rule of late-medieval England.

Therefore, if it was landowners who made it possible for monarchy to

[9] Exceptions were of course regions where the king himself was the leading local landowner: see below, pp. 69–70.

be effective, through the military force of tenants they could put at his disposal, then the greatest of these, the nobility, lords of the largest acres and the greatest number of tenants, were the fulcrum of his rule. This can be dramatically illustrated from the estates of the duke of Buckingham in the early sixteenth century, on which there were 4,840 tenants who owed him service. If Buckingham was unusually great and, as Welsh Marcher lord,[10] had a particularly large number of tenants (2,766 of these tenants were Welsh), he was by no means unique. To put these figures in perspective, we should note that Henry V won Agincourt with only a part of the force of 9,000 men he took to France and that most of the battles of the Wars of the Roses were probably fought with rather fewer men on each side than that. The nobles, as the commanding figures in the localities, were the essential linking point between command and enforcement. In the hierarchy of power, they were the essential intermediaries between king and lesser landowners. The latter, as lords of men themselves, were not only an indispensable part of the private power that made rule possible but the source of the local officers who administered that rule.

However, the nobility were not merely the purveyors of royal rule into the shires. They faced both ways, bringing the responses of the shires to the king; in a sense they represented the realm to the king. For both these reasons they had an important role in counselling the king. It used to be thought that throughout the late-medieval period there was a formal advisory council but it now seems probable, in the light of recent work, that there was no such thing. Councils of this sort were set up only in periods of minority and of political crisis, when a restraining or guiding council might be forced on the king. A council consisting of the king's senior administrators, assembled to discuss administrative policy across a broad range of issues, had probably existed as long as the king had had a bureaucracy at the centre of governance and it had emerged as a formal body under Henry III. There was also the council in the legal sense of the body which dealt with conciliar jurisdiction.[11] Noble counsel on the other hand was normally something that was offered informally.[12] The nobles had no right to offer counsel but it was foolish for a king to ignore what they had to say or to fail to take their advice. Moreover, a king who was receptive to counsel of all sorts would be less likely to ride roughshod over the susceptibilities of his subjects; for a start he would know what these were. That was why it made sense for the nobles to be able to offer counsel

[10] See below, p. 55 for comments on the peculiarity of these lordships.
[11] See above, p. 34.
[12] There were great councils, which were rather like parliaments without the Commons, but they were very formal occasions and they were not the channel through which noble advice would normally be offered.

to the king whenever and wherever they happened to be with him. If they were given free access to the king on this informal basis, the shires could be sure that their opinions would reach a conscientious ruler, while the ruler himself would know what was going on in his country. If it was always foolish for kings to ignore the nobility, it was doubly foolish if he was at war. Nobles were trained as warriors and, unless too old or otherwise disabled, would almost invariably lead contingents into the king's wars. Many would also act as diplomats and negotiators in time of war. When at war, the king would need not only the weight of noble power, to make possible his heavy military and financial demands on the land, but the actual service of the nobility as generals and recruiters for his army. Usually when the nobility complained that their role as 'natural advisers' to the monarch was being ignored, they meant that the king was either not giving them access to his presence or, if he was, that he was failing to listen to them. The latter they minded less as long as the king's policies worked. But if the policies failed, especially if the king failed in war after ignoring noble advice, and wasted his subjects' taxes, the nobility felt bound to stand up for themselves and for the unfortunate taxpayers who looked to them for redress.

In this business of representing the realm to the king, parliament was less important than has often been alleged. Certainly, representatives of the lesser landowners might have a chance to articulate their grievances to the king in parliament, but parliaments were not called regularly, were mostly rather short and had a lot of business of the king's to get through. The nobles represented the realm to the king on a much more regular and omnicompetent basis than could be achieved by the attendance of the shire representatives in parliament. For the nobility, who could normally speak to the king whenever they chose, parliaments were not usually of any particular interest, which is why they were often rather bad attenders. It was when this informal process of request and response ceased to operate, most notably when the king's presence was monopolised by hated favourites, that kings would find themselves dealing with hostile parliaments. It was then through parliament alone that both nobility and gentry could make their complaints to the king. Noble complaints about exclusion from the king's counsels, or of misguided counsel being taken, especially in war and foreign policy, sometimes associated with a parliamentary crisis, are something we shall meet under both Henry VI and Edward IV. Such complaints were not always strictly true but the way they were used by aggrieved nobles shows how close counsel was to the noble heart.

Indeed, how the nobility got on with the king, especially the higher nobility, who were more likely to be in his presence, was crucial to the entire functioning of the governmental system. The logical corollary of free access to the monarch was that nobles should be not just his natural counsellors but his natural companions. A king would normally share the tastes of his nobles: martial arts, hunting and participating in the chivalric culture that was common to aristocratic Europe. While the king was free to choose his own friends, his close associates were likely to be nobles of his own age. If he took his friends from elsewhere, he would be expected to separate personal friendship from the public business of rule. He had to understand that personal relationships and public rule were to be conjoined only at the legitimate meeting points of private and public power. One of these was the royal court, where nobles and king could mingle, as private individuals who bore huge public authority. Kings who failed to make this distinction, placing loyalty to personal friends above their relationship to the nobility, cut themselves off from the natural modes of ruling. Richard II (1377–99) did this because he did not share the military tastes of his magnates and had no intention of ruling in line with accepted practices. Edward II (1307–27) did it because his tastes were in every way alien to those of landed society, a king who preferred the peasant pursuits of rowing, hedging and ditching to those of the class into which he had been born. In neither case did it prove to be a recipe for successful rule. Nobles would equally have to recognise that their free access to the king did not mean that they might order him about or expect always to have their own individual interests or opinions take precedence over others'.

As Edward II and Richard II apparently failed to realise, the nobility of late-medieval England were not the ignorant 'thugs' who have too often been depicted in histories of the period. They were experienced politicians, spokesmen on behalf of the realm, military leaders, managers of local politics and of broad and often widespread estates. They were well educated for their tasks, literate and well trained for the management of their estates and households. They had an ideology which fitted their authority and responsibility. Certainly this included the military virtues, and it is striking that late-medieval nobles were so often prepared to put up with lengthy waits for payment for war service, simply because they saw it as part of their duty to the crown. However, to suggest, as one historian has done, that the price that had to be paid for the continued existence of such a military nobility was the mayhem they wreaked at home is an oversimplification.[13] As with all social groups, there were some who were naturally violent, but along with the military code went a strong code of chivalry, which included obedience and loyalty to one's lord, who, for the nobles,

---

[13] C. Richmond, '1485 And All That, or What Was Going On at the Battle of Bosworth', *Richard III: Loyalty, Lordship and Law*, ed. P. W. Hammond (Richard III and Yorkist History Trust, London, s.d.), pp. 172–206.

was the king. The nobles were not necessarily terribly nice people on the whole, but they were notably better behaved and more useful adjuncts to royal rule under kings, as diverse as Edward I, Edward III, Henry V and Edward IV, who knew how to get the best out of them, than under rulers who despised or neglected them.

None of this should imply that the nobility were anything but subordinate to the monarchy. They willingly sustained the king's power by placing their own at his disposal because they needed him, his majesty and his authority. Any society whose basis is land is very vulnerable to conflict and upheaval, which can destroy the land and its produce. It will need a system for regulating disputes and dealing with disorder, and in medieval England the system that evolved was the king's. Equally only the king could guarantee the country's safety against its enemies and lead it into foreign war. It has been observed already that once the king's authority was so great it was very dangerous. All landowners had to be sure that no-one but the king could use it, but the nobility needed this security most of all. Only the king could stand above the nobles and prevent them attacking each other. Ineffective rule nearly always resulted in disunity among the nobility. Moreover, as the king's closest associates in peace and war, at the centre and in the localities, they were humiliated and threatened when the king failed. There was in fact a large degree of consensus binding together monarch and ruling aristocracy. To put it very crudely, kings and landowners were a ruling elite. They had a common interest in taking much of the country's surplus for themselves, in keeping a united front against any inferiors who might want to challenge their hegemony, and in maintaining a level of stability which would keep their lands safe. These were far more cogent than most of their passing disagreements over the exact distribution of power between ruler and ruled. Like all ruling classes they were considerably more likely to confront the powerless than each other.

For all these reasons both nobility and gentry were bound to stand up for the powers of the monarchy. An undermighty king was normally a much greater danger to them than an overmighty one. A king who could be controlled by a member of the governing classes was still more dangerous. That was why, as we have seen, the monarchy was supposed to be subject to neither correction nor control. But what was then to happen when kings showed themselves so incompetent or alternatively so dangerous that taking the monarchy's powers into the hands of his leading subjects was to be reckoned a lesser peril? Ever since Magna Carta, it had been the barons who had felt obliged to undertake reform or opposition if the king was not up to his job. But they usually acted only with the utmost reluctance and considerable care was taken both to justify what was ultimately an unjustifiable action and to ensure that none of those who were temporarily acquiring such huge authority should use it for their own ends. Despite these precautions, movements of this sort, as in 1215 against John, in 1258 against Henry III, in 1310–11 against Edward II, in 1386–7 against Richard II, had almost always ended badly. Royal power had been arrogated by a single nobleman or group of nobles, there had been conflict amongst the temporary repositories of royal power, or the recovery of royal authority, or a combination of these. These episodes would only have confirmed the belief that the king's authority had to be absolute.

In 1327, in the face of arguably the worst and ultimately the most dangerous king ever to rule England, a solution of sorts had been found when Edward II had been deposed in favour of his son and heir Edward III. But even then, to avoid irretrievable damage to the monarchy, the deposition had been dressed up in the fiction that Edward was voluntarily renouncing the throne. For the same reason, the deposition was only conceptually possible because by this time there was a distinction in people's minds between the king, the holder of the kingly office, and the crown, the office itself. The king could be deposed if he was entirely unsuitable, but the crown's attributes, essential for the running of the body politic, continued regardless of who bore it and of whether he had been crowned or not: 'The king is dead; long live the king.' On a more practical level, deposition was a most unsatisfactory solution, since, whatever the deposers might say, frequent depositions were bound to weaken the majesty of kingship. More immediately, a deposition could not fail to cause a certain amount of disorder; it might encourage the lower orders to start questioning the nature of authority; it could lead to death and disgrace for failed would-be deposers. Between 1327 and 1330 it led to the rule of Edward II's queen Isabella and her lover Roger Mortimer, which was in some ways worse than what had gone before. If the adult Edward III was eventually to emerge as a most satisfactory outcome, there must have been doubts whether the political community would always be as lucky as this.

The problem was that, if the constitution demanded that the king, with his vast and potentially destructive powers, should be immune to any higher authority other than God, there had to be ways of ensuring that he would use his powers for the common good alone. If there was no satisfactory mechanism for dealing with really bad and dangerous kings, at least there were ways of ensuring that rulers of average or better capacities kept in mind the needs of their landed subjects. It helped that ruler and landed subjects needed one another in equal measure: if landed subjects were really obliged to offer the king unconditional loyalty for their own security, he himself could not rule without the implicit military power of his nobles that made his commands enforceable. Then there was the accepted role of the nobility in counselling the king, even if he had no obligation to listen to them, let alone to take their advice. The theory was that, through counsel and the accumulation of different but expert opinions, a right conclusion would emerge which would be formulated by the king and put into effect by his will. In practice the process is likely to have been less to do with the magical emergence of a general opinion and more a matter of the king formulating policy and his greatest subjects and leading administrators responding, but the theory contained an essential truth. This was that a king ruled best when he used his nobles positively for the good of the realm.

How is it then that some historians have continued to argue that late-medieval kings were weakened by what they see as an unhealthy dependence on the nobility? This is an idea that dates back to Stubbs but has been developed further in recent years.[14] It encompasses the view we have already examined that the late-medieval monarchy had inherent financial failings dating back to Edward III's reign but it ranges much more widely than this in its condemnation of Edward. The argument goes that he valued war over proper governance and as a result England became a 'war state'. This means that it had been so distorted by Edward's achievement in organising his kingdom to fight large-scale and lengthy war that the kingship was fundamentally weakened and unable to operate unless there was a successful war, and that only under these conditions could the nobles be kept quiet. Some of these charges we have examined and discounted already: that the way the nobles raised forces for Edward's wars gave rise to 'bastard feudalism' and rampant disorder; that, in return for the support of the nobility in war, he allowed great agglomerations of noble land to be formed.[15] Another part of the allegation that Edward's wars made the nobility too powerful is that the requirement to seek the consent of the political classes for taxation forced the king, in return, to delegate his local authority to local powers. This not only brought about all the harmful consequences for law and local stability that historians like Plummer depicted but further enhanced the power of the nobles, the masters of the local officers. The need to delegate, it is alleged, was compounded by the 'financial straitjacket'; the use of unpaid local amateurs in local administration is said to have been caused by lack of money to pay a professional bureaucracy, as well as by the trade-off against taxation.

More recently, a slightly different slant has been given to the same charge. It has been suggested that the war enabled the nobles to receive subsidies from the crown that kept them financially afloat in the period of falling landlord incomes after the Black Death. Borrowing a concept and a

---

[14] See above, pp. 8–10.   [15] See above, pp. 19–20.

phrase used for the situation said to exist in France at this time, this has been named a 'budget of noble assistance'.[16] In this sense it would be an earlier version of the conduct of foreign affairs as described by John Bright in the mid-nineteenth century: 'A gigantic system of outdoor relief for the aristocracy of Great Britain.' It is argued that the decline in landowners' incomes resulting from the collapse of the labour and produce markets, after the catastrophic fall in population in the Black Death and subsequent plagues, made them heavily dependent on the wages and spoils of war and on royal grants of land and money. In so far as the war was subsidised by the taxpayer, taxpayers' money was being recycled to end up in the hands of the nobility. Thus, it is said, when the wars became unprofitable under Henry VI, and this development made nobles even more dependent on crown grants, they ended up fighting the king and each other over what the king had to offer.

There are several objections to this hypothesis, which may perhaps fit France in the late middle ages but cannot be applied to England. First, there was no guaranteee at any time in the fourteenth and fifteenth centuries that the war would prove profitable to any noble family. The accidents of war meant that there was as great a likelihood that a noble would be captured and have to ransom himself as that he himself would take a prisoner whose ransom would bring in a vast sum. Whenever there was war, the royal finances were always under strain and nobles quite often had to wait some time for payment of their soldiers' wages. As far as the profits from royal grants are concerned, it must seriously be doubted that, once the king had rewarded his immediate servants and administrators, there was ever enough of a surplus to go round amongst the nobility. When kings were at war, their resources were so stretched that it was even less likely that they would have anything much to offer their nobles. Had the nobles truly depended on the crown for survival in this period, they would have been in a parlous state. In any case, studies of noble estates and finances have shown fairly conclusively that they were not in serious financial difficulties if they exercised proper management, and there are mismanagers in all periods of history. Certainly, incomes from the Welsh marcher lordships, drawn principally from the lords' judicial power, fell badly in many cases in the fifteenth century, under the combined assault first of the Glendower rebellion and then of the lords' inability to demand

---

[16] C. Given-Wilson, *The English Nobility in the Late Middle Ages* (London, 1987), pp. 154–9. Given-Wilson seems to say that the process of 'buying' the nobles in this way was entirely financed by taxation (see p. 159). This clearly would not have been possible, since, however cunning they were, kings could not routinely divert large quantities of tax into the hands of objects of patronage and, if they were thought to be doing so, there was always a parliamentary outcry (see above, pp. 29–31, 37).

what had been paid before from tenants who were now numerically scarce. However, even this diminution of income has been shown to be surmountable, especially in the case of the great lords, like York and Buckingham, who suffered badly but had large enough incomes elsewhere not to need royal hand-outs.[17] The only real loser from the economic conditions was the king, in that times of plague or agrarian disaster, as, for example, in both England and Normandy in 1439–40,[18] would make it harder to gather taxes for war, but, as we saw earlier, the whole issue of taxation has to be judged more in political than in economic terms.

But the real problem with the 'budget of noble assistance' is the same as that with the whole 'war state' hypothesis: it assumes that the nobles had to be bought and that the system collapsed when there were no longer suffficient funds for this. Indeed, the 'war state' hypothesis contains the lingering Stubbsian sub-text that anything that benefits nobles must be bad for kingship and vice versa. There is a failure to understand that the cake of power does not stay the same size in the later middle ages but is growing. Kings have to delegate more, to both nobles and local gentry, because they are doing more. This chapter has demonstrated how the basis of governance was co-operation between kings and nobles and how difficulties were caused not by nobles being too powerful but by the power of the kingship. This made it theoretically impossible to oppose a king and extremely difficult in practice to do so. As soon as historians deny that there was a natural unity of interest between kings and nobles, a completely different account of the medieval polity has to be found. No historian has yet succeeded in offering one that is coherent, that takes into account all the work done by McFarlane and his successors and that is not largely dependent on Stubbs.

It is in this context that we must place another idea whose omission so far may seem puzzling to some readers. This is that it was patronage above all that was the essential lubricant of government. Historians have emphasised its importance in tying the nobles to the crown, but many also believe that it enabled the nobles to bind the gentry to themselves by handing on the benefits of royal bounty.[19] Although the importance of patronage was one of McFarlane's central ideas, we have seen already that it does not go well with the rest of the 'McFarlanite' approach.[20] In fact the same objections apply as have just been given for the notion of fatal weaknesses going back to Edward III. First, it assumes that the nobles have to be bought, rather than being the king's natural allies. It should be noted also

---

[17] See also above, p. 36, below, p. 55.   [18] See below, p. 95.

[19] There is a further aspect to the patronage thesis, concerning the judicial favour of the crown; this is discussed below, pp. 63–4, in the context of the governance of the shires.

[20] See above, pp. 21–2.

that, with very few exceptions, nobles did not need grants from the king to make them great; their status came from their existing lands. The 'court nobles', who did, were, as we shall see, exceptions who proved the rule. For the magnates, the security of their lands through effective kingship was far more important than the possibility of securing a little more. Secondly, it assumes a level of royal largesse that was simply not possible. Until the dissolutions of monasteries and chantries in the sixteenth century brought large quantities of land into royal hands, there was just too little patronage available to the crown, especially since so much had to be employed in the reward of the king's unsalaried professional servants.[21]

It would just about be possible to argue that, if patronage was essential to late-medieval monarchy and there was not enough to go round, then the polity was fatally incapacitated throughout the fourteenth and fifteenth centuries. Such an approach would certainly help support the view that the monarchy was gravely affected by financial weakness: although most patronage was in the form of land grants, clearly an impoverished monarch would need all his land to support himself. However, if this line is to be taken, then we have to ask why the monarchy was able to function most of the time, even in periods of exceedingly bad kingship. Furthermore, as we shall see in the next chapter, just as the nobles accepted the king's authority without bribes, so the gentry had their reasons for accepting the authority of both nobles and crown. They too did not need to be bought. We should also note that some of the greatest kings were very stingy and do not seem to have suffered for it. Edward I was especially ungenerous, while Henry V on his accession curbed his father's generosity, to ensure the kind of royal frugality which would encourage parliament to make him large grants for war.[22] What is quite clear is that only kings who had forfeited the instinctive support of the nobility, and usurpers who did not yet have it, had to buy the nobles. Usurpers had to go on buying them until they themselves became accepted as 'real' kings. And for both it could be only a temporary expedient because, as we shall see, most notably under Richard III, there was no end to the price of loyalty if it had to be bought. It is instructive that the only work on this period which makes a convincing case for the importance of patronage in ruling is on this arch-usurper's reign.[23]

THE BOTTOM OF POLITICAL SOCIETY: GENTRY AND COMMONS

The gentry have already featured in this discussion because the importance of their role in governance and politics by this time has made it impossible

---

[21] See above, p. 30.   [22] For more on Henry V, see below, p. 72.

[23] This is Rosemary Horrox's work on Richard III, for which see the bibliographical essay to chapter 10.

to keep them out of accounts of both crown and nobility. Their role in relation to both will receive lengthier consideration in the next chapter but, in the context of political society, they need some introduction now. Well before the fifteenth century, political society had been enlarged to include these lesser landowners. They had first emerged as a political force in the thirteenth century, under Henry III. By the later fourteenth century, their importance and expertise in local government and as taxpayers for the crown's wars had made them an indispensable part of the political and administrative world. It was understood from the end of the thirteenth century that the nobles could no longer grant taxes on behalf of the rest of the realm. Thenceforward, it was the parliamentary Commons – the representatives of the shires, usually joined by those from the boroughs – that had to consent to taxation and, by implication, be responsible for its collection. During the fourteenth century it became routine to summon them to parliaments and they began to deliberate separately from the nobles, or Lords, as the latter began to be known in a parliamentary context. A lot has been written, on the whole inconclusively, about how far the Commons were independent of the Lords or merely their lobby-fodder, but it is clear that the Commons learned to protect their own interests in parliament during the fourteenth and fifteenth centuries, notably against the peasants and the crown.

However, since parliaments did not usually last very long, and, except in times of crisis, parliamentary politics were rarely significant, it was in the shires, which they administered and where their political allegiances were forged, that the real importance of the gentry lay. Within these local societies, they were beginning, by the fifteenth century, to make differentiations of wealth and status among themselves. Once the lesser landowners had ceased to think of themselves collectively as 'knights', probably in the late twelfth and early thirteenth centuries, there had been no obvious title for those who chose not to be knighted. The appearance of titles to dignify the gentry who were not knights reflects to some extent the gentry's growing sense of their own importance. These titles were 'esquire' by the late fourteenth century, followed by 'gentleman' in the first decades of the fifteenth, for those below the esquires. By 1436, although the terms 'esquire' and 'gentleman' were still used ambiguously enough for there to be doubts about the precise status of these, there were perhaps some 7,000 men who could be called gentry.

There is now some discussion of how far beneath gentry and wealthy townsmen political consciousness was to be found. As long ago as 1964 McFarlane wondered whether the commons, in the social rather than the parliamentary sense, were more politically committed and aware than had been assumed. Some recent work has begun to take up these questions. There can be no doubt of the lower orders' involvement in the various rebellions of 1450–1, which were in many ways similar, in their combination of political, fiscal and economic grievance, to the Peasants' Revolt of 1381. Equally, the northern rebellion of 1489 and the western one of 1497, both caused by taxation, can be classified as popular revolts, even if that of 1497 had considerably more strands to it. While the northern risings of 1469–70[24] may seem to have had more obvious noble or gentry instigation, the popular input should not be discounted, any more than it has been in the rather similar Pilgrimage of Grace of 1536. Despite all this, what can be said with certainty is that the landed classes, if ready on occasion to exploit popular resentment in the cause of their own rebellions, were not yet ready to allow the populace to consider itself a part of the political world. Even the duke of York, who was mentioned with approval by the Cade rebels and took his political stand in the 1450s upon the common weal,[25] found it politic not to be seen as the defender of low-class rebels.

However, the growing political awareness of the lower orders, like the political education of the gentry in the late twelfth and thirteenth centuries, reflected the lengthening reach of the government of late-medieval England. In turn it had brought each of these social groups under the king's law and made them taxpayers and in some cases local officials. It is an indication of quite how great the powers and responsibilities of the fourteenth- and fifteenth-century kings were. If the relationship between crown and nobility was crucial to this governance, implicit in it was something that has already been touched on at various points: the magnates' ability to harness the support of the gentry for the rule of the shires, the real coal-face of government. It is to these linked themes, of nobility, gentry and local governance that we shall now turn.

---

[24] For all these, see below, pp. 173–8.   [25] This term is explained below, p. 120.

3

THE GOVERNANCE OF ENGLAND IN THE FIFTEENTH CENTURY II: NOBILITY, GENTRY AND LOCAL GOVERNANCE

The outlines of local government and local society have already been delineated, but we have yet to see which aspects of local government were of vital concern to landowners or how they worked in practice. In this chapter we shall look at local government and society and then, having looked at governance and politics both at the centre and in the localities in these two chapters, we shall summarise the qualities required by a king for successful rule.

In so far as there was broad agreement amongst the ruling classes that the lower orders should be kept in their place and that taxes should be collected once they had been agreed to, the routine tasks of government were to a large extent uncontentious. Unsurprisingly, in view of what we have already seen, conflicting interests appeared most often in relation to litigation amongst landowners. These were usually disputes over land or matters associated with land, such as marriages, which often involved the movement of property between families, or wardship of underage heirs. We should remember that land is a very tangible commodity. Leaving aside the complexities of inheritance, it is likely to give rise to dispute, most obviously in the sort of conflict between neighbours over boundaries and nuisances which still keep solicitors employed and, even in the late twentieth century, have occasionally led to assault or murder. In the middle ages there was additionally a host of sources of tension related to agriculture. These included grazing rights on communal pastures, attempts to enclose allegedly communal pastures and woods, animals straying on to others' lands, the intermingling of the lords' lands, both demesne and tenancies, in villages where there were open fields belonging to the entire village but more than one lord (a common occurrence). When personal injuries, which might be prosecuted as crimes, were inflicted, these also occurred most often in the course of land disputes.

Although litigation and prosecution in affairs of this kind would be going through the Westminster courts, that did not mean that they were divorced from local government. That a prosecution could not proceed without the acceptance of the JPs has already been observed.[1] Then, all pleas at Westminster, whether private or crown prosecutions, had to be administered in the county where they had begun. That meant, for a crime, the county where the indictment had been made or, for a private plea, where the offence had been committed or the land at issue lay. Above all, the defendant had to be got into court, for, with few exceptions, no case could proceed without his or her presence. To secure this, writs were sent out to the sheriff, first to take the defendant and then to summon him or her to appear at the appropriate court. If the defendant did appear, the sheriff was instructed by writ to summon a jury and send their names, and eventually the jury itself, to Westminster. Finally, if a guilty verdict were eventually reached, it was the sheriff's duty to execute the verdict, normally a fine to the king in a criminal case and damages to the offended party in both civil and criminal cases.

Since sheriff and JPs were all local landowners, wrapped up in the system they were supposed to be administering, it will be readily appreciated how great were the possibilities for bringing undue influence to bear. This was especially true from the later fourteenth century, once the crown had more or less given up the all-powerful supervisory commissions, staffed with the king's own men, that it had formerly sent out to the shires: the eyre, and its successors, the general commissions of *oyer* and *terminer*. If the sheriff in particular refused to co-operate there was little the offended party could do other than resort to one of the equitable courts.[2] But the problems with the system went considerably further than this. In practice it was not far off impossible to get a gentry or noble defendant into court. Failure to appear led ultimately to outlawry, but this once fearsome penalty now held few terrors, least of all for the country's political and social elite. Jurors were understandably reluctant to go to Westminster and, by the fifteenth century, it was becoming increasingly the rule for verdicts to be given locally before visiting commissions of justices, by special delegation from the central court. The possibilities for bringing local influence to bear on their verdicts are obvious. But not only was it most unusual for a verdict to be reached; it was still more unusual for this to be a verdict of guilty or one in favour of the plaintiff. This is almost certainly why influential defendants in criminal pleas took steps to get the case transferred to the

---

King's Bench. In most cases the defendants would eventually turn up in court, having purchased themselves a pardon from outlawry and often from the offence itself.

It is in fact apparent from the three surviving correspondences of gentry families in the fifteenth century, Paston, Stonor and Plumpton, that the outwardly formalised and bureaucratic legal system was in its local functioning what one writer has called 'a riot of mutual back-scratching'.[3] Even cases concerning the lower orders could be drawn into this morass. For example, the JPs' powers to detain criminals or suspicious characters until they had made security, rarely used against the upper classes, could be deployed to harass the tenants and servants of an enemy. In all this the power of the local nobility can be seen at work: in attempting to ensure that the majority of important local officials were their men; in proceeding to exploit such control to pursue the litigious interests of the rest of their gentry followers; in leading little armies to take by violence for themselves or their followers what they could not be sure of getting by lawful means; in protecting their men, gentry and non-gentry, against the lawful consequences of such actions.

This account seems to confirm all the worst opinions of late-medieval England: we have seen already that it is this combination of noble protection of the gentry and apparent abuse of the law that has come to be known generically as 'bastard feudalism' and has got the late-medieval period such a bad name. But historians are now revising these views. First, as we have also seen, they are beginning to realise that they may have misunderstood the nature of the relationships between nobility and gentry which they christened 'bastard feudalism'. At the same time it was mentioned briefly that this is related to a re-evaluation of the feudal ties that preceded the arrival of 'bastard feudalism' and a realisation that, in dealing with both, we are talking, not about institutions that can be precisely defined, but about social relations among landowners.[4] We should now pursue the implications of these changes in interpretation further. Above all, both 'feudalism' and 'bastard feudalism' need to be looked at in the context of local societies to understand how our interpretation of social relationships among late-medieval landowners and of local politics is changing.

First, it is now understood that, far from being the unchanging social system of a settled society, 'feudalism' was introduced into England almost as the by-product of the need to defend their conquered territories by William I and his fellow Normans. It did not arrive 'complete' but developed over the next century and a half and was never simple – each knight holding land of a single lord – but right from the start there were

---

[3] C. Carpenter, 'The Beauchamp Affinity: a Study of Bastard Feudalism at Work', *English Historical Review*, 95 (1980), p. 525.   [4] See above, p. 17.

tenants holding of more than one lord and tenants with fractions of fees. Moreover, this relationship was never a purely military one; military service was only one aspect of what was essentially a social and political tie, binding together the greater and lesser landowners in a bond of mutual benefit. The tenant received the land and could then expect the lord's protection of the land, in return for which he gave all sorts of support and services. The lord protected the land partly by force, for this was a world in which law was a less all-pervasive influence than it was later to be, and partly through his own feudal or honorial courts, where he did justice amongst all his knightly tenants. As society became more complex, and especially as a land market developed, there was yet more fragmentation of fees and dilution of lordship. This was accentuated by the growth of royal law we have already looked at in another context, for it took cases concerning knightly tenants out of the lord's court and into the royal courts, so the lord lost jurisdictional control over the lands that he or his ancestors had given. Thus, there was a need for a social system that conformed to new social realities, above all in not being based on land tenure.

Consequently, it is not surprising that money, a much more negotiable commodity, not land, should loom large in the new social system that was emerging at some unknown point during the thirteenth century. But it would be a great mistake to suppose that it was money that made it work and that we are here entering a world of commercial transactions in which loyalty had no meaning. What remained at the heart of late-medieval political society was the need for a binding tie between greater and lesser landowners. As with all countries at all times, government could not have functioned at all unless there was a social imperative, far deeper than either commerce or contracts enforceable in a court of law, enabling those with a political stake in society to co-operate in the interests of governance. In sum, what was required was something that, in protecting the lands of the lesser landowners and providing cohesion within the landowning hierarchy, was performing the same function as the defunct ties of 'feudalism' had done.

Indeed, in analysing the groupings formed around noblemen in the 'bastard feudal' period, historians have found a large measure of continuity from the 'feudal' period. In the wake of McFarlane's work historians have firmly shifted their focus away from the household, allegedly full of retained thugs, to retaining as a link between the lord and the gentry in the locality and they have found themselves dealing with very much the same kind of relationship. If most retainers or other feed men were no longer the feudal tenants of their lords – even when they were, the relationship had become virtually meaningless – they were likely to be gentry resident in the areas where their noble lords had their lands, so there is no question of what might be called a free market in lordship. The geographical determinants of the relationship were so strong because its core remained one of mutual need, and a lord would neither require support from the local gentry in a region where he had no land nor be of any use to them. Since the whole relationship was so much grounded in the realities of local tenure and local politics, if men served more than one lord, it was not because there was a free and unstable market in lordship but rather because such service was usually compatible with loyalties to both lords. It was in any case only professional administrators and lawyers who had numbers of lords and this usually reflected wide professional employment rather than political promiscuity.

The lord still protected the lands of his men, but now he did it by the pressure he could bring to bear on the royal legal system, rather than through mere force or his now defunct feudal courts. As we have seen, many of the officers of that system in the shires were probably the lord's own men. His men still provided military support, both themselves and their peasant tenants, whether the lord required it to back up royal rule, to make a local show of force on his own account or as the core of a royal army for foreign war. But in this also there was nothing new, as we can see from the origin of the 'feudal' relationship in William the Conqueror's need for military service to hold down a conquered land. It was not contract armies that subverted feudalism, but the decay of feudalism that made it necessary to raise royal troops by contract armies. The money that the lord paid was no more than a small addition relatively speaking to the income of the man, except in the case of professional estate servants and lawyers. Even these would benefit more from the lord's help in finding lands to buy, or to marry into, than from the money itself. Nor would most lords in the fifteenth century on average spend more than about 10% of their income on retaining. As for the contract itself, a contract was in fact made between feudal lord and man when homage was done for the land. What was new was that the late-medieval world was one where the law-courts and a more word-conscious society demanded that such agreements be written down and their terms clearly specified. All in all, it was less the relationship itself that changed than its context.

It is therefore considered more important to examine the dynamics of the landed society within which these ties between nobles and gentry developed than to look at surviving indentures of retainer or to study the legislation on retaining. Although giving livery was circumscribed by statute under Richard II and, more severely, under Henry IV, and retaining was first forbidden in Edward IV's statute of 1468, such legislation was only dealing with the outer forms of what was an inescapable part of social organisation. It is small wonder then that legislation had little effect on the way in which gentry associated themselves with nobles; it would indeed have been astonishing had it done more, since legislation by the modern state, with all its powers and resources, is unable to change society. It is apparent that these statutes were not by and large intended to effect fundamental changes but were rather the product of particular periods of disorder or of regimes which desired to have a means of coming down hard on the nobility.[5] There is a similar story with the indenture itself, whose form is now realised to reflect less the tie which it formalised than external conditions. For example, if England was in the middle of a long-running war, there would have to be provision for the details of war service in the indenture. Furthermore, the legislative context was bound to have considerable influence on the wording of the indenture. In fact, formal retaining itself probably increased as a direct result of Richard II's statute of 1390, since this prohibited the giving of livery to men who were neither permanently resident in the household (the actual household men would normally be menial serving-men) nor retained for life. Indeed, the focus of study is moving from the indentured retainer to what is called the lord's affinity.[6] By the affinity, we mean all those lesser landowners connected to him by anything, from indenture and contract to nothing more tangible than a sense of loyalty or obligation which might be called on at need. The altered perspective recognises the fact that we should place less emphasis on money, on indenture, retaining and military retinues, and more on 'bastard feudalism' as the key social and political link between nobility and local gentry in late-medieval England.

This re-evaluation of the ties of 'bastard feudalism' necessitates a re-examination of its local effects: the role played by lords and followers in the royal administration as it operated in the shires, especially with respect to the potentially contentious legal system. There can be no doubt that, on the face of it, the king's law did not work, nor that there was a lot of manipulation of the law and outright violence in this period, much of it linked to the activities of lords and their affinities. All those possible causes of disagreement enumerated earlier suggest that it would be odd if this had

---

[5] However, Henry VII may have had more far-reaching intentions (see below, pp. 227–8).

[6] A lingering 'institutional' approach is still current in some quarters. It focuses on the form of the indenture and relates its development to the fief-rente (a cash payment from the lord) of the 'feudal' era. As the payment was made to members of a lord's household, this account ignores all the recent work which has placed 'bastard feudalism' firmly in a landowning context. The fullest version is J. M. W. Bean, *From Lord to Patron: Lordship in Late Medieval England* (Manchester, 1989).

not been the case. But this is only part of the story. Land could easily cause conflict but it could be seen equally as a powerful reason to reach compromise and agreement. Potentially disputes of this kind were far more damaging than, for example, fire damage to a factory in the present century. For a start there was no insurance and thus no possibility of recouping the loss. Secondly, an agricultural economy has to work with the rhythms of the seasons: if a crop was trampled under horses' hooves, it would take a year to replace it; cattle or sheep rustled away could be replaced by purchase if the owner had sufficient funds but even that had to wait on the breeding seasons; tenant rents which could not be paid because tenant animals or crops had been taken or destroyed would have to be waived for that year. This was not a good period for landlords; the population had been falling since the catastrophic losses in the Black Death of 1348–9 and it reached its low point about the middle of the fifteenth century. That meant a shortage of labour and of tenants, and therefore higher wages and falling rents, and the collapse of the markets for the produce of the lords' lands. By careful administration of what was now mostly a rentier economy, both gentry and nobility could avoid bankruptcy, but it was certainly not in their interests, at this of all times, to engage in mindless conflict which could inflict severe damage on their incomes.

It is in fact important to realise that there is no evidence to support the often-expressed opinion that England was more disordered in the fourteenth and fifteenth centuries than it had been before. What we have is, simply, more evidence, which comes from fuller records. To a large extent this is due to innovations in the king's handling of crime made in 1305. In that year he began to take a serious interest in trespass, an offence which had hitherto been largely the subject of private pleas and which carried fines rather than the death-penalty. He also introduced the criminal trespass of 'conspiracy', an offence which covered the sort of activities that landowners might engage in in relation to the law. Only then did it therefore become feasible for the king to prosecute landowners for anything less serious than treason. Given the increase in means of litigation as an alternative to violence, it is indeed highly probable that the late-medieval period was a less violent one. Indeed, it has been rightly pointed out that, in so far as there was concern about the administration of the law in the later middle ages, this was due not to a retreat of direct royal involvement in peacekeeping but to its advance and the fact that it therefore affected more people than ever before.

What we must realise in any case is that it was not primarily the king's law that kept the peace amongst landowners. The law itself was a relatively recent innovation; what had kept the peace long before its arrival, and was to be the mainstay of the law long after, was the network of relationships among the landowners themselves. It is clear that it was these ties among the gentry that lay at the root of local stability. First, as we have seen, it was private force and the co-operation of the local landowners who controlled that force that made it possible for government to happen at all. Secondly, it was the magnates' ability, using the ties of 'bastard feudalism', to harness the support of the gentry for the king's rule and to help build cohesion among the gentry that played a large role in creating the circumstances in which local government could occur. Thirdly, and most importantly, if there was truly a sense of mutual trust among local landowners, the need for conflict or for the king's law to regulate conflict would be considerably reduced.

There is now some debate as to how far it was the nobles who were the key figures in binding local societies together in this way. Clearly, there would be local and regional variation: the more concentrated the lands of a noble in a particular area, the more likely he was to dominate it, as long as he was neither a child nor an incompetent. Conversely, there were certainly areas, often encompassing just part of a county, where cohesive gentry networks existed independent of noble dominance. This might be because of their inaccessibility, or because of the lack of noble lands or of resident nobility, or for all three reasons. We should also remember that, although England was remarkably unified by contemporary European standards, it was not a homogeneous whole. In particular, there were regions where noble authority was notably strong. Even within the impressive framework of royal government and law, there were still franchises. These were analogous to the present-day policy of contracting out public services: they were areas where it was still the king's law that was administered, but the administration, and whatever profit was to be had from it, was in the hands of private subjects. The three great late-medieval franchises were the Palatinates of Durham (owned by the bishops) and of Chester and Lancaster; Chester was not even represented in parliament until 1543. But, since the latter two were now the possessions of the monarch, they cannot be seen as threats to royal power, and it was the king who usually had the largest say in the appointment of the bishop of Durham. But there were lesser franchises scattered throughout England; for example, some of the indictments which reached the King's Bench in the fifteenth century, although they certainly ended up in a royal court, were initially made within the private jurisdictions of franchise-holders. As it happened, most of these were by now confined to ecclesiastical institutions, which were unlikely to seek to wield great local power through a privilege, and its main benefit to them was probably financial.

However, in two particular regions there was a large concentration of independent jurisdictions combined with an unusual concentration of noble power. These were the Welsh and Scottish Marches. In both instances the circumstances were related to problems of defence and to the necessary degree of defensive delegation which arose from their exposed position and their distance from the centre of government. The Welsh Marcher lords had mostly acquired their powers before Wales was subjugated by the English and, even after the conquest was completed, had managed to hang on to them. They were to all intents and purposes independent rulers of their lordships. During the fifteenth century they found it increasingly hard to extract the potentially lucrative financial rewards of their private authority,[7] but the fact remained that they alone of all the English nobility had access to military force over which no-one else could claim authority. Most Marcher lords were among the greatest English nobles: for example, the Staffords of Buckingham, whose lordships included Newport, Brecon and Hay, and Richard duke of York, who owned, amongst others, Montgomery, Wigmore and Usk. The number of tenants they could raise from these lands has already been mentioned.[8] It may well be men raised from these lordships that enabled some of the participants to fight the Wars of the Roses.[9]

In the north of England the situation was similar, although not identical. Here too franchises curtailed the crown's direct authority: not just Durham but, for instance, the Liberty of Hexham of the archbishops of York, which, with other franchises, took a large slice out of the county of Northumberland. Unlike the Welsh Marches, these were principally held by clerics, and the lay nobles by no means had the solid blocks of landed power to be found on the Welsh borders. Nevertheless, there was in the north a combination of much greater concentration of individual noble estates than was mostly to be found further south and constant warfare with the Scots. Together, these conditions gave northern nobles a more dominant local position than was normal outside the Welsh March. Like the Welsh Marches, the north may also have been a principal source of men for the battles of the Wars of the Roses. If the number of men that the duke of Buckingham could raise on his estates in the early sixteenth century is startling enough, much more so is the 11,241 that the earl of Northumberland's bailiff thought could be produced from his master's tenantry against the Scots in the same period. On the northern border there was a more militarised society, where regular raids and counter-raids across the border, punctuated with more official campaigning, may well have made local landowners less frightened to use violence against one another, since a certain amount of destruction of property and produce

---

[7] See above, pp. 42–3.   [8] See above, p. 36.   [9] See below, pp. 151–2.

could almost be regarded as routine. Moreover, the wardenships of the Scottish March, one for the west and one for the east, which were usually held by the great northern border families, the Percies and the Nevilles, enabled the wardens to raise forces for defence at the crown's expense which could be turned to other purposes. For example, between 1411 and 1436, the warden of the West March of Scotland was paid £2,500 in wartime, and of the East March £5,000. It seems indeed that this was the only part of England where the old argument that forces raised for war and paid for by the crown were later used against the crown might hold good. Another aspect of the more central role of the nobility and of military affairs in the north is that, although part of the money spent on retaining by these lords may have come from the wardenship, the northern lords mostly expended far greater sums on retaining than the average 10% that has been mentioned. The earl of Salisbury was using 25% of his Middleham revenues for this under Henry VI and the Percies seem to have paid out still more.

There has been a lot of recent interest in the whole subject of the borders of England, not just those of England itself but also of the English possessions in Ireland and even in France. It is being suggested that these border regions, especially those within the British Isles, may have had more in common with each other than with other parts of England, and that perhaps generalisations about how late-medieval governance worked in England have been based too exclusively on the southern parts of England closest to London. It seems, in fact, that in the fourteenth and fifteenth centuries the far north, especially the north-west, was actually becoming less like the rest of England. The pressure of constant war with the Scots, the need to develop ways of living with the enemy just over the border, the emergence of the 'law of the March' to help cross-border dealings: all these tended to create a cross-border Marcher region, with its own ways of doing things. This is an interesting body of work but there is a danger that some of these ideas may be taken too far. The fact is that the whole of England had a uniform administration, which set it apart from other realms where there were English settlers, despite the fact that, on the ground, this administration worked in different ways in different parts of the realm. Even the Welsh Marcher lordships, independently administered as they were, and Wales itself were becoming assimilated to the political and cultural world of England. Furthermore, most of the nobles who had lands in the Welsh or Scottish March, and all the greater magnates of the Marches, had property in other parts of England, often scattered over several different areas. They could therefore hardly look at government from an exclusively Marcher perspective. While they might regard destruction in the north with a greater degree of equanimity, they could not fail to be concerned about what happened to their own lands and those of their local gentry followers further south.

The truth is that, within the parameters we have been examining, power structures throughout England were very varied. Certainly, the generalisation will mostly work that, under normal circumstances, the closer to London and the easier to reach a region was, the less likely it was to become dangerously disordered. Thus, we move from areas like East Anglia and the Thames Valley which were easily accessible and close to London, through more distant ones like the south-west, to upland areas that were both relatively distant and relatively inaccessible, like parts of Staffordshire and Derbyshire, to the distant and defensively exposed northern border. Accordingly, if a region in the category of accessible and close to London was seriously destabilised, as happened with East Anglia in the 1440s and Kent in 1450, that could be seen as a major failure of governance. Up to a point, it is also true that noble power tended to be more concentrated and society to be more militarised in the more distant, inaccessible and militarily vulnerable regions. But even that generalisation quickly breaks down when we remember that the Welsh Marches were usually no longer militarily vulnerable; that in the south-west (Duchy of Cornwall) and Staffordshire and Derbyshire (Duchy of Lancaster) there was a powerful noble possessed of a lot of land, but he was the king; and that Cheshire was in some ways the most militarised of all English counties, but only because the combination of ownership by the crown since 1246 and a poor economy had made it a major recruiting ground for the king's wars. More generally, it must always be remembered that the power structures and governance of counties where the crown was the leading noble are likely to be different from others which are similar in other respects.

However, although all historians accept that there would be local variation, some historians would like to argue that the norm of local power structures was not noble leadership. They believe that it was instead independent county 'communities', on the model first postulated by historians working on seventeenth-century local societies, in which the gentry regulated their own affairs and the nobles had little direct influence. It is pointed out that there were very wealthy members of the gentry who were at least as well off as the less wealthy lords. For example, in Lancastrian Nottinghamshire, Sir Thomas Chaworth had an income assessed at £320 in 1436, while in the same year several minor lords were assessed at similar or lower levels. However, it must be said that knights as rich as Chaworth were not that common, and his income fades into insignificance beside those of great noble families like Stafford, Beauchamp of Warwick or York, all of whom had incomes of £3,000 or more. A more telling objection to the 'noble' model of local societies is the fact that in any county the gentry were likely to own something between 60 and 75% of the land, and thus to constitute collectively far and away the most powerful group. This fits much better than the financial argument with the fact that it is the number of tenants on an estate, rather than its income, by which power in this period can be measured. All the same, the contention that the gentry would therefore be able to dictate the terms of local politics and administration skips a stage in the argument, because it assumes that they would be able to act together without direction from above. In most counties there were one or two nobles, who were *individually* absolutely dominant in territorial terms, who were the obvious figures to give direction and who can be shown to have done so, even if with varying degrees of success; for example, the earls of Warwick in Warwickshire and Worcestershire, the earls of Stafford, later dukes of Buckingham, and the duke of Lancaster (who was also king) in Staffordshire.

This point is driven home by figures taken from the income tax returns compiled by the government in 1436, from which Chaworth's income was taken. There is some debate about their completeness and reliability but what is unequivocal is that they indicate the gap between nobility and gentry: according to the returns, 7,133 gentry landowners owned £151,000 worth of lands, while a mere fifty-one nobles owned £45,000 worth. One historian has used these global figures to minimise the gap between nobility and gentry but, even with the proviso that wealth did not necessarily equal power, they seem rather to emphasise it. The same historian has suggested that it was mathematically impossible for a noble to dominate the gentry in a county, for there were simply too many of them for him to be able to retain more than a small proportion of them.[10] This also represents a misunderstanding of how noble power operated in the shires. It is clear that noble authority was not normally exercised directly over all the gentry. There might occasionally need to be direct intervention or a show of force, but mostly it was a matter of attracting the most significant and influential local gentry (not always the most outstanding in landed terms), through whose associates the lord's influence would percolate through local society.

Indeed despite this great variation in the extent to which nobles were in practice locally dominant in England, it has not so far proved possible to establish the existence of independent county communities of gentry. Attempts to do so have foundered on insufficient research, on the fact that most county boundaries to a greater or lesser extent ignored the bound-

[10] S. Payling, *Political Society in Lancastrian England* (Oxford, 1991), chapter 1 and pp. 105–8.

aries of noble and gentry lands, and on some historians' failure to note that counties which seem to have no nobles were actually dominated by the crown in its capacity as nobleman, as duke of Lancaster or Cornwall, or as earl of Chester. There are indeed now serious doubts as to whether 'county communities', as envisaged by earlier historians, existed in the Tudor and Stuart periods. In the later middle ages, there seems little question that the model that has been put forward here of a hierarchical system of power, in which the nobles functioned as the essential pivot between king and localities, was, notwithstanding all the local variations, the one which obtained. That the nobility expected, and were expected, to be the ruling powers in the areas where their lands lay – what they called their 'countries' – can be seen in the fact that they would normally be named JP, at the head of the list, in all those counties to which this applied. All this leads to the conclusion that it must have been the nobles who would, under normal circumstances, be the focal point of local societies.

This is the structural background against which we now need to examine the safeguarding of land which was the centre of local politics. As has been made clear by the emphasis on the key role of private power and private relationships in the operation of royal authority, land was protected by informal processes as well as by formal, legal ones. We shall start with the informal methods. Associates for the myriad transactions, from family settlements to sales, that put a landowner's property at risk could be found among local contacts. Transactions would be grounded still more firmly if the lord validated them, either by putting his own name to the deed or by encouraging other members of the affinity to do so. This was why a nobleman did not need to retain or reward more than a relatively small number of the local gentry; if there was general acceptance of his authority among the local gentry, then, directly or indirectly, all these associations would ultimately be linked to him and he would be understood to be the ultimate guardian of the gentry's compacts with each other. If this was not enough to prevent disputes, minor disagreements among the gentry could be ironed out by neighbours, who themselves had a considerable vested interest in the maintenance of local peace. More substantial ones might need to go to the local lord – or lords, if the antagonists belonged to different affinities – for formal arbitration or even for the simple expedient of knocking heads together.

Only when local and informal peace-keeping devices had failed would it be necessary to use formal means, in the shape of the law. And then the object of litigation, as with much litigation today, would be less to get a verdict, producing a winner and a loser and then probably the reopening of the conflict by the losing side, than to force the opponent back to the negotiating table. Following on an arbitration, the parties would usually be

placed under recognisances or bonds. This meant that each party undertook to keep the peace in general, and specifically towards an opponent,
on pain of losing a punitive sum of money, usually secured on the
bond-maker's lands. Not infrequently friends would also put their lands in
jeopardy for the principal pledge. These agreements were enforceable in
the common law courts, so that private and public processes worked
together to maintain the peace. In fact, disputes amongst landowners in
this period were almost never concluded by a verdict in the law-courts; if
there was one, it was probably because, behind the scenes, one party had
agreed, as a clause in a negotiated agreement, that the case might be taken
to a conclusion. This would be a means of obtaining a written confirma-
tion in law of the other party's agreed tenure of the property. What did
bring a suit to an end was the restoration of amicable relations, or at least
the semblance of them, among the parties concerned. Indeed, the very fact
of a case appearing in the courts is a fairly safe indicator that relationships
amongst local landowners have broken down. In both the breakdown and
the restoration local magnates would often have played a large role.

All this being the case, it is hardly surprising that, when the law was
employed among landowners, for criminal prosecution or private litigation, cases rarely reached what we would regard as a conclusion. Nor is it
to be wondered at that the law was subsumed into these private mechanisms for dispute avoidance and dispute settlement, its local officers sometimes favouring one side or the other and private violence being used in
pursuit of claims to be made good in the public courts. This is not a cause
for disapproval on our part but for recognition that a system that looks so
much like our own was actually different. Law was a late addition to a far
older process of private peace-keeping and settlement that still had a large
role to play in preserving local stability. All the same, we must not assume
that there were no limits to interference with, or disregard of, the law. This
was a society that had its own standards, and its own muddled thinking
about the boundaries between acceptable and unacceptable behaviour, just
as we have ours. Complaints were made by the Commons in parliament,
where the gentry were represented, about the excesses of lordship. But it
would be a mistake to suppose, as has sometimes been done, that these are
the beliefs of 'independent gentry', outside this system of lordship; lordship was simply all too pervasive for this. What they do convey is a sense
that what was an acceptable amalgam of public authority and private
power had become unbalanced, and the use of private influence or private
violence had gone too far. After all, we must not forget that this was a
society that put a tremendous premium on the impartiality of the law, for it
was the law that was the last and firmest defence against both the king and
other landowners.

What is significant is that these complaints nearly always occurred when there was inadequate kingship. Similarly, although there are as few adequate statistics as there are many confident generalisations about levels of lawlessness, it seems that the worst periods of conflict and disorder among landowners occurred at times of excessively bad kingship, such as the reigns of Edward II, Richard II and, as we shall see, Henry VI. This gives us a clue to what may seem a puzzling question in the light of this new account of the legal system: what, if any, was the king's role in this, if landowners were still relying primarily on private powers and relationships to resolve their differences? The answer is that it remained a large one, even if in a more complex way then has been generally understood. The king's law was not supposed to deal with every minor conflict or infraction of the peace, not even those committed by landowners: no government had the resources to do this for several centuries to come. Thus, to condemn the legal system for failing to do this is to miss the point. This was in any case a more violent society than our own, in which the law itself might be violently enforced and a certain level of disorder, although probably much lower than has often been supposed, was routine. What the king could do was act as the ultimate guarantor of both private and public means of redress, precisely because he alone could stand fearlessly above all parties. He was head of a public system of law and administration but he was also at the apex of the unofficial hierarchy of landed power that made the public system work at all, and in this sense he was indeed 'the lord of all lords'.

This intermingling of private and public in the person of the king can be seen most obviously in the relationship with the nobility that has already been examined; it was a personal one that had immense public repercussions, affecting the way the country was ruled. Indeed conflicts amongst the nobility were rarely dealt with in the law courts: the king, as he had ever done, acted informally as peacemaker among them. Where the rule of the shires was concerned, the king could intervene in a variety of ways, both official and unofficial. He could send special commissions to disturbed areas, as for instance was done by Henry V in the early years of his reign or by Edward IV in 1468 for a bad outbreak of violence in Derbyshire. He could make loud declarations, to be heard by those around him and then relayed to the rest of landed society, on his desire to have his laws obeyed. He could make examples of those who disobeyed him. This was often done by summoning the parties formally before him, and the result of such a summons might be to impose a settlement on them. Like the formal arbitrations performed by the king's subjects, this would normally be enforced by bonds or recognisances. Both declarations and examples were used by Edward IV in the early years of his reign when he had inherited a serious problem of disorder from Henry VI, as the Paston letters tell us. The king could show himself personally in disordered parts of the country, sometimes using his presence to reinforce the official power of a special commission.

What was most important was that he should maintain a good working relationship with the nobility, something which could demand disciplinary measures as well as reassurance and reward. If that relationship failed then everything else failed. The magnates lost confidence in the king and in each other; there was no trust at the top of the ruling hierarchy and this mistrust was transmitted down to the gentry who ceased to believe in the ability of either king or nobles to keep order. As in all societies, once that vital confidence in the forces of order had been lost, order itself was lost, for there would be a premium on being the first to strike against an enemy. At times of acute disturbance and division, as in 1381 (the Peasants' Revolt) and 1450 (Cade's Rebellion), even the lower orders in town and countryside began to question the power of authority. To repeat, this was a form of government essentially founded on private power and private relationships; in the king government and power met in a single figure who embodied the pinnacle of both the public and the private. However devolved local government had become, and however peripheral new work on the law seems to make the king's part, it was all premised on the existence of an effective active monarch.

Inevitably, as in all societies, there were causes of strain. One region might lack a single controlling magnate to order it, and the local nobility might find themselves unable to achieve a workable local equilibrium. There could be a hiatus in local power caused by a minority in a dominant noble family or by such a family coming to an end through lack of a male heir. The leading local noble could quite simply be too often absent or not up to the job. It is clear that, despite the use of trusted gentry to administer their estates and see that their will was done among the local gentry, noble rule in the shires required careful personal attention to detail; not least to ensure that the lord's authority *did* percolate out from his closest gentry associates to the wider local society. For example, in the later fourteenth century, John of Gaunt, duke of Lancaster, was both too bound up in national and foreign affairs and too neglectful to look after his 'countries' properly, and the result was serious disorder. Much of it was caused by Gaunt's own minor officials, who abused their master's authority in his absence. Minorities or failure of heirs in numbers of important gentry families could have the same result on a smaller scale. Ambitious social climbers, usually administrators or lawyers, could disturb a society, especially since these were often pursuing the landed estates which would give them a stake in the society of lords. Paradoxically, at a time when agricultural land was a glut on the market, estates with lordship over peasant tenants were in short supply. These rising professionals are the only significant exception to the rule that the gentry were normally reluctant to get involved in the law, for they knew their way round the law, their noble employers gave them connections in high places and often the only estates available for purchase had more than one claim to them. The Pastons were a family of this type, and areas like East Anglia, home of the Pastons, that were full of families like this, were more likely to be under strain. This is why historians need to be more careful than they have sometimes been about generalising from such an obviously attractive source as the Paston letters.

Late-medieval society was undoubtedly a highly competitive one, in which each family strove to maintain the family name and estates and, if possible, to increase the estates, and was prepared to use violence where necessary to do so. On the other hand, the dangers of unmitigated conflict and disorder were all too evident. This was especially true of the gentry, whose lands, unlike those of the nobles, tended all to be concentrated in one or two areas, and who could not live in a state of constant attrition with families whom they had to meet and deal with on a day-to-day basis. The gentry wanted the best of both worlds: freedom to pursue their individual interests and the assurance that, if they went too far, a higher authority, a noble or the king, would step in to save them from themselves. What was less essential to the gentry was patronage of all sorts, either direct from their noble patrons or from the king through the intervention of a patron. Largely on the evidence of the Paston letters, it used to be thought that the lord's ability to reward his followers, either from his own resources, or by access to the king's, was central to the bonding of nobles with their gentry followers. Now, in the wake of the studies of local societies published in the last twenty years, it is realised that the Pastons are not only atypical in themselves but give us a very atypical view of late-medieval local politics. For the gentry, as for the nobles, it was not getting more but hanging on to what they had already that mattered most.

Since this was the case, it might be supposed that the view that patronage was important in cementing the tie of nobles and gentry *did* work with respect to the law: that nobles were valued in proportion to their ability to get the king to bend the law for their men. But this argument fails on two points. First, the whole point of the legal system and the way it operated within this very devolved form of government was that its ultimate guarantee was a level of impartiality that the king alone could provide. Kings might have the latitude to offer the occasional favour to a close and deserving servant but too much of this would bring about all those inequities which subverted local government and the law. The line that a king was supposed to take is well summed up in the statement by Edward IV reported by John Paston III to his brother, John Paston II, when the king was urged to see justice done to the Pastons: 'The king answered ... that he would neither treat nor speak for you but to let the law proceed.'[11] Secondly, the devolution itself meant that the king had insufficient direct control over the legal processes to be able to manipulate them on a regular basis on behalf of his subjects. A noble did not need to purchase the loyalty of his gentry affinity either with material reward or with getting them royal favours. A lord who could protect his followers and their land, by the means we examined in this chapter, would have their life-long loyalty.

Much of historians' concentration on grants and favours can be traced to the assumption that the model of Tudor politics, about which we know much more, can be applied to late-medieval England. Under the Tudors there was indeed a political system in which grants and judicial favours played a large part in enabling nobles to build up followings among the gentry, but it was not the same system as that which obtained in the later middle ages. It was more centralised and so there was more lobbying of central government for special treatment. There was also much more to grant. Now that late-medieval England, particularly government and politics in the shires, is beginning to be studied thoroughly, we are learning that this may be an inappropriate comparison. In fact, patronage, in the sense of either judicial favour or reward, was only a political issue in late-medieval England when politics were malfunctioning: in the majority of Henry VI for example. We shall see that there may be a case for arguing that what we think of as Tudor rule, complete with 'patronage politics', was starting to emerge towards the end of the century, but not before then.

So, finally, what qualities did an effective king require? Landowners at all levels wanted, if possible, charismatic leadership in both peace and war. A king who could give this would be in a particularly good position to exploit their underlying hunger for stability in order to curb destabilising ambitions for aggrandisement. But, even without exceptional qualities, kings could usually rely on the wish for stability dominating their landed subjects' ideological landscape. Perhaps not surprisingly, most of the other desirable qualities turn out to be those advocated in the advice literature of the day: justice, mercy, evenhandedness, the knowledge of when to be firm and when pliant. Much of it could be summed up in the modern phrase 'man-management', particularly the all-important dealings with the nobility. Not a great deal had to do with learning either to play off nobles against each other or to give and withhold favour and reward. Late-

[11] *Paston Letters and Papers*, ed. N. Davis (2 vols., Oxford, 1971–6), i, p. 545; also in *The Paston Letters*, ed. J. G. Gairdner (6 vols., London, 1904), v, p. 32.

medieval kingship was not about buying support in any way, but about fostering the natural ties that bound landowners to the monarchy; about balancing rigour against mildness, discipline against co-operation, favour against impartiality; about making private relationships and powers work in the interests of public authority and using public authority to secure the safety of private power; about respecting the landed hierarchy that made rule possible and exploiting it to make governance work. Some of the worst rulers of late-medieval England were very rich; notably Edward II and Richard II. But it was the ways they had made themselves rich, their ruthless exploitation of their landed subjects, which caused their downfall. Money could not then save them because it could not buy support from the people they had alienated and, England being essentially an island, they could not bring in hired mercenaries from a neighbouring country to make war against their own people.

What is important to remember is that kings at this time were naturally in a very powerful position. To say, as is sometimes done, that there had been so much devolution of power under Edward III that kings were now at risk unless they were very able[12] is to confuse delegation and loss of authority. It was the enormous increase in royal authority in the thirteenth and fourteenth centuries that made delegation necessary, and this increase meant that the monarchy controlled what went on in the kingdom, through its local agents, to a remarkable extent. This, to turn the point on its head, certainly meant that a great deal was expected of the king, and that failure to do his job had such devastating consequences that some action would have to be taken, perhaps deposition. Indeed the single main reason for the cluster of depositions in fourteenth- and fifteenth-century England was paradoxically this mighty authority. The king had such great influence, for good or ill, that malfunctioning could not be ignored, or a substitute system found. It had been possible to do this under Stephen, between 1135 and 1154, but it was no longer. By contrast, in Scotland in this period kings were relatively rarely attacked or deposed, but that was because their role was so limited that a dreadful king could be left in place. The problem of the late-medieval monarchy in England was that its power was so great but that there was no constitutional means of dealing with an inadequate or overbearing king.

There was, however, no single recipe for rule. Good rulers came essentially in two types: the disciplinarians like Edward I, who mostly got on well with his nobles but was always jealous for the rights of monarchy, and the enablers, like Edward III, who, although by no means pliable, concentrated on getting the best out of his nobles in both peace and war.

---

[12] See above, pp. 23, 41–3.

In the later middles ages, the huge degree of landowning co-operation needed to run a government as financially and legally ambitious as this one meant that the Edward III model was generally the more apposite. But there were plenty of variations on these two themes. As long as the king knew and did his job, there were as many ways of doing it as there were kings. The period from the late 1430s to 1500 must be seen primarily as a crisis of kingship; either kings did not do their job or circumstances made it impossible for them to do it. The cutting edge of our analysis must be why this was and what happened as a result.

4

THE LANCASTRIAN KINGS TO
c. 1437

The deposition of Richard II in 1399 was in some ways more of a watershed than that of Edward II in 1327, for it placed a new dynasty on the throne rather than the king's own son, as in 1327. Richard indeed had no direct heir but his nearest heir was Edmund Mortimer earl of March, great-grandson through the female line of Edward III's second son, Lionel of Clarence. However, if, as was arguable, the throne was to descend to the heir male, then Henry IV, as eldest son of John of Gaunt, duke of Lancaster, Edward's third son, had the superior claim.[1] Whatever the exact rights of the situation, the fact that the ruling house was no longer unrivalled had implications that we need to examine.

We have seen that the belief that the Wars of the Roses were retribution on the House of Lancaster for the removal and death of Richard is no longer taken seriously, but it lingers in the view sometimes expressed that the Lancastrians were always under threat if they faltered. It is undoubtedly true that for the first part of the reign Henry IV was seriously at risk, especially from the Percies who had helped put him on the throne and demanded rewards that in the end Henry was not prepared to give. At this time, he had insufficient support among the nobility to be sure of survival and was heavily reliant on forces he could raise from his own Duchy of Lancaster. But, having survived revolts in 1399–1400, 1403 and 1405, by about 1406–7 he was reasonably secure, a point exemplified by the abject failure of the last Percy rebellion in 1408. By then a group of young nobles was emerging, including the Beauforts, Henry's legitimised half-brothers

---

[1] See genealogy, pp. 82–3.

(the sons of John of Gaunt by his mistress, later third wife, Katherine Swynford), and the earls of Arundel and Warwick. Of the loyalty of these to the House of Lancaster there was no doubt. Indeed in Henry's later years the serious threats to his position came from his own son and heir, the future Henry V, who took charge of government in 1410–11 and may have tried to force his father to abdicate in 1411. This may not have been a comfortable matter for the king but did at least demonstrate that the succession was assured.

The reign as a whole shows how relatively easy it was to be a king in late-medieval England as long as you obeyed a few basic rules; principally respecting landed property and showing no outrageous favours to anyone. Henry IV, for all his promise as a young noble under Richard II, was not an outstanding king, the first part of his reign wrecked by constant revolt, the second by illness and difficulties with his heir. But, against pretty severe odds, the system of governance was maintained and he was able to hand over to his son a kingdom which still needed a lot of work done on it, but which did seem prepared to be ruled by the Lancastrians; that was the real achievement.

Apart from this central issue of survival, most of the principal themes of the reign were to resurface under his son and grandson. There were first the royal finances. Henry had a number of military obligations, including internal rebellion, Glendower's rebellion in Wales, which began in 1400–1 and continued for most of the reign, French raids on the coasts and, within France itself, the defence of Gascony, the last remnant of the lands held by earlier English kings, and of Calais, a later acquisition. Calais was particularly important because nearly all the wool trade, with its revenue-creating customs, passed through it. The theoretical position with regard to financing these obligations was not clear-cut.[2] There had been a truce with France since 1396 but, as there was no absolute peace, the king was still allowed to ask for taxes. On the other hand, none of these needs could be construed as foreign war; either they were purely defensive or, in the case of the rebellions in England and Wales, they were strictly speaking internal. Whether the king could successfully demand taxes for these military expenses would depend a lot on how he handled the parliamentary Commons and how much faith they had in his financial management. Of his right to levy the various customs duties in peacetime there could be no doubt, but he still needed consent for them. This he did get throughout the reign, but only by tedious negotiation. As far as the lay subsidies were concerned, the Commons were hardly in co-

---

[2] See above, p. 30.

operative mood. One of the reasons for this was that, having been pillaged by Richard in the period leading up to the deposition, taxpayers were not disposed to be generous when, although there was no absolute peace, there was also no large-scale war. But there was also lack of confidence in Henry's ability to order his finances, concern at the way revenue was being pledged before it had been collected and a feeling that the large and wealthy Duchy of Lancaster estates that Henry had brought with him should be used to subsidise royal expenses and relieve the taxpayer. Henry himself had encouraged the Commons to take this line, as he had initially, and very unwisely, promised to 'live of his own'. This was before he knew much about how the royal finances operated and while he was still very anxious to differentiate himself from his deposed predecessor. Subsequently he took the view that the Lancastrian revenues were his private property, quite separate from crown revenues, and used most of their profits to increase further the large expenditure in annuities he inherited from his father. These gave him crucial military and political resources in the early part of the reign. He was also using royal revenues to make generous grants for the same reasons.

Then there was the matter of foreign policy, inseparable from the royal finances. In 1411 civil war broke out in France between the Burgundians and the Armagnacs, or Orléanists. This was an ideal moment for English intervention in France. The Prince of Wales wanted an expedition to support the Burgundians, but the king was against it, probably as much as anything because he feared the financial consequences. Characteristically, during his period in control from 1410–11, the Prince tried to restore a measure of order to his father's finances, to some extent because this was a precondition of any kind of adventurous foreign policy. In the event, he launched an expedition in late 1411. It achieved a victory but did not prevent the Prince being removed by his father from his leading position in government soon after. In fact, in 1412 the king did authorise an abortive expedition, but it was in favour of the Armagnacs and was probably against the Prince's wishes.

The third theme with implications for the future is the place in English government of the Duchy of Lancaster now that the Lancastrian usurpation had annexed it to the crown. We have seen already that there were financial implications which Henry IV was not prepared to accept and military ones which proved vital to his survival in the first years of the reign. There were also longer-term political and governmental consequences. In the previous chapter we saw that in the later middle ages the nobility were the key figures in the rule of the shires, and that kings had come to rule in a less directly interventionist way, relying more on delegation to largely unsupervised local powers. The accession of the

Duchy to the crown meant that there were large areas of England, including Lancaster itself, Yorkshire, the north midlands, Leicestershire, Northamptonshire, Norfolk and Sussex, where the king was either one of the leading landowners or the leading landowner. Hitherto, in so far as the crown had possessed a permanent landed estate in England, it had been mostly confined to two rather peripheral areas, Cheshire (the earldom of Chester) and Cornwall and parts of Devon (the duchy of Cornwall). Until recently it was assumed that the crown's acquisition of the Duchy was a source of political as well as military strength but recent work by Helen Castor has raised grave doubts about the validity of this assumption. Naturally possession of the Duchy of Lancaster considerably enhanced the king's capacity to control the shires directly, but it also carried serious responsibilities; it was not so easy to be simultaneously the ruler of England and the directing local magnate, especially over so much of the realm.

Henry IV seems to have been jealous of his personal authority as Duke, and there is evidence that in some counties, such as Staffordshire, Warwickshire and Yorkshire, he used his power as king to extend his dominance beyond what he could have expected as mere duke of Lancaster. As Helen Castor has pointed out, this raised the issue of whether the king could really be simultaneously the chief public authority in the realm, acting without favour to anyone, and, as duke of Lancaster, the private lord of some men, with a duty to protect their particular interests. Favouritism and abuse of Duchy authority seem to have been the cause of violent attacks on the Lancastrian affinity in Staffordshire from 1408. However, over much of England there was accelerating disorder from this time, or soon after, which arose less from over-use of royal power than from neglect. The cause was the king's illness, which afflicted him from 1405, shortly after the suppression of the rebellion of that year, and in some respects the instability was simply a demonstration of the fact that monarchy required 'hands-on' direction. But it was most marked in those areas where the king himself as landowner should have been most responsible for order, that is Duchy areas in the north and east midlands, the southwest where the controlling power was the Duchy of Cornwall, and Shropshire, which bordered Chester, Staffordshire and the royal Principality of Wales. What all these areas had in common was their particular relationship with the king. In most of them, illness had deprived them of their natural lord, and, because he was also king, no-one else had the power or the temerity to intervene effectually. In Shropshire, the great local noble was the earl of Arundel, a close associate of the House of Lancaster. In this case, Henry's illness meant that he was unable to act, from his position as leading magnate in the neighbouring counties, to restrain Arundel. This left the earl to abuse his authority, unhindered by the king, within his own 'country'.

If Henry IV's reign shows how little a king needed to do to achieve a modicum of rule, and conversely how much more was demanded of the king where he was also a great noble, his son's demonstrates just how far the whole system could be pushed. It also tells us that, even with a king of this level of ability, experience and maturity (he was twenty-five at his accession in 1413), a new dynasty, however well established, was in danger again when it passed the crown on for the first time. This is a point to which we shall return in 1483. In the first two years of Henry V's reign there were a number of conspiracies and rebellions, involving supporters of the deposed Richard II, the Scots and the Lollards, the latter led by Henry's former friend Sir John Oldcastle. These culminated in the South-ampton Plot of 1415, revealed as Henry prepared to set sail for France. The conspirators aimed at the death of Henry and his brothers and at placing the earl of March on the throne. Amongst those executed for their part in the plot was the earl of Cambridge, younger brother of the duke of York and father of Richard, the future duke of York of the Wars of the Roses. If, with hindsight, none of these threats seems very grave, notably not the Southampton Plot, which was revealed to the king by March himself, we should remember that the king could not see into the future and that he had a major crisis of order to deal with while all this was going on. When Henry left England, Oldcastle was still at large and the focus for rumours of conspiracies; it is worth considering what might have happened had Agincourt been lost.

Henry was certainly anxious to be conciliatory, especially at the start of his reign. He reburied Richard's body in Westminster Abbey and over the course of the reign brought to a fruitful conclusion his father's policy of restoring the heirs of dispossessed traitors. These included the Percies and another participant in the rebellion of 1405, Mowbray of Norfolk. Like all successful kings, he handled his nobles well, and, during the course of the reign, the completion of the restorations and the widening circle of nobles around the king assured the dynasty at last of the wholesale allegiance of the nobility. It was at this time that it ceased all together to be a usurping dynasty and became the natural ruling house. This meant that the purchase of loyalty, so alien to the normal process of rule, was a thing of the past. It had been to some extent necessary under Henry IV, especially in the early part of the reign, and its dangers can be seen in the rebellion of the Percies when they thought their price was being set too low. Like all English monarchs in normal conditions, Henry V could assume the loyalty of his subjects unless he himself did something to lose it. This was therefore no pliant rule, for the magnates were expected to obey and to earn their

rewards. For example even the king's own brother, the duke of Gloucester, was once penalised financially for mustering a contingent for war that
was two men short.

There was also greater stringency with regard to the Duchy of Lancaster. In some ways Henry's rule, especially in its early years, can be seen as a
commentary on his father's. The very act of war, particularly in alliance
with the Burgundians rather than the Armagnacs, was a defiance of Henry
IV's policies, and it was clearly going to be impossible to raise the huge
sums needed for the French war without tackling the financial issue that
Henry IV had so consistently evaded. As king, Henry V pursued much the
same financial measures he had tried to implement in 1410–11. These were
a combination of ensuring the maximum collection of all revenues, both
ordinary revenues and extraordinary taxes, and severe curtailing of expenditure. Besides the obvious advantages of thrift, there was the added
benefit that it encouraged the Commons in parliament to believe in the
king's concern for their pockets and to be generous with their grants.
Royal and Duchy of Lancaster annuitants were among the principal
victims of this policy; at his first parliament Henry authorised a cut of
£10,000 in annuities. He was clearly alert to the notion that had been
gaining ground since 1399 but had been strenuously resisted by his father,
that crown estates should help sustain royal revenues. Yet, although the
personal link between crown and Duchy was to be more distant than
under Henry IV, and the new king was to be more willing to share power
with others in the Duchy regions, the Duchy remained locally and
nationally a major source of military and political support.

Henry V was also aware that it was his father's failure to fulfil the
fundamental royal obligation of keeping the peace that had contributed to
the Commons' reluctance to subsidise his father's rule. There were other
obvious incentives to take hold of a deteriorating situation: it was just as
much his duty, as both king and duke, as it had been his father's; and to go
to France leaving the country in a state of major upheaval was out of the
question. Henry's manner of dealing with the now widespread disorder is
an object lesson in late-medieval kingship. We must remember that the
shires had contradictory views on direct royal intervention. Mostly they
wanted to keep it out, believing that their own peace-keeping arrangements, whether they made use of the king's law or not, worked better than
external interference, which produced winners and losers and adjudicated
without respect to local power structures. On the other hand, the impartiality and absolute quality of royal justice were also valued. What Henry
gave the shires was the best of both worlds. He sent powerful centralised
commissions to the areas of greatest disturbance and these made large-scale
enquiries covering the whole of his father's reign. Some of the commis-

sions he accompanied himself. Even the earl of Arundel, one of the king's most trusted associates, and the major cause of the troubles in Shropshire, was unable to keep the king's commission out of that county and had to accept the indictment of several of his retainers. But this almost Edward I-like display of royal wrath was followed by the other kind of justice: the offending parties, having been thoroughly scared by these official proceedings, were dealt with more informally, by a mixture of fines, of forcing them into bonds to keep the peace and of pardons in return for war service in France. There they could vent their violent instincts on the French and make a new start, which several are known to have done. Thus, royal interference was used to restore local equilibrium.

By 1415 Henry had done all the preliminary work necessary before embarking on the war with France. His handling of parliament, his attention to the royal finances, and his demonstration that he understood the king's obligation to provide good government in return for subsidies, assured him an almost unprecedented level of taxation for the rest of the reign. There was a string of successes in France, including the reconquest of Normandy, lost under King John, culminating in the Treaty of Troyes in 1420. There it was agreed that the English king would succeed Charles VI of France and a dual monarchy of France and England be created. This was an ambition that had been pursued since early in the reign of Edward III but never achieved. While abroad, the king kept a careful eye on internal order in England and the all-important defence of the north against the Scots. In general, there was no question of the kingdom being neglected while he was away, and this was a major reason for his success in getting further taxation from an anxious Commons. The reign showed that a king of this extraordinary ability could harness the administrative, financial and political resources of his kingdom to a remarkable degree. This was a king who understood that his relations with his nobles should be fundamentally consensual, and that the gentry, who provided him with his taxes, were highly sensitive to aggressive interference in their affairs by the crown. At the same time, he managed to assert his authority and exploit England's resources with a ruthlessness which is in some ways reminiscent of Edward I.

It is indeed arguable that this combination of old-style direction from above and new-style co-operative rule marked the highpoint of kingship in medieval England. It is important to make this point because some historians explain away such an outstanding reign, in a period they believe to be one of crisis for the monarchy, as a matter of 'papering over cracks'. But no ruler could have managed this level of achievement if the foundations had been flawed. What the reign shows is what could be done by a truly outstanding ruler. By the same token we must stress that, when

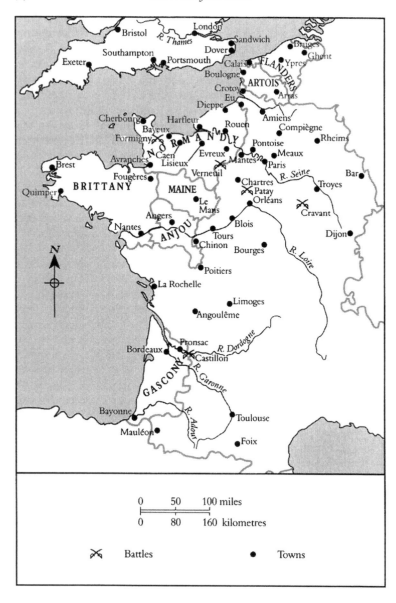

Map 2   Lancaster and Valois in France

Henry V died unexpectedly in 1422, at the age of thirty-four, he did not leave his infant son an impossible inheritance. On the contrary, he left him a legacy that was the main reason for his survival for so many years of incompetent rule. The dynasty was securely established. This is unequivocally demonstrated by the unquestioned accession of a nine-month-old baby at a time when active personal rule, always the essential basis of medieval monarchy, was made yet more urgent by the war. The existence of a successful war was always an advantage to the crown, for it gave it all those financial powers we have noted and the enthusiastic loyalty of a ruling class trained for war. Henry V left his son a reunited nobility, bound together in common service in peace and war to a great leader, and committed to preserving his legacy at home and abroad for his son. He left a country that had shared in, and been willing to support, militarily and financially, all the glories the king had brought them. He left the great Duchy following, for he had shown that, whatever his father's problems in handling the Lancaster lands, they could still be a significant military, political and financial adjunct to monarchical power if carefully supervised and absorbed into a national kingship.

The only questions hanging over Henry V's achievement concern the future of France. The French monarchy had been acquired but France had yet to be conquered, and south of the Loire, apart from the existing English territory of Gascony, it was untouched. In particular, there was the future Charles VII, the Dauphin, who unsurprisingly had not accepted the terms of Troyes. Indeed, the French throne itself had been achieved by accident: 'Through the hole in the duke of Burgundy's skull',[3] as a contemporary noted wittily, meaning that it was the assassination of John of Burgundy in 1419 that brought about the Burgundian alliance with England which made possible the Treaty of Troyes. So, to a great extent, the long-term future of the English in France depended on continued division amongst the French, above all on the survival of the alliance with Burgundy against the Dauphin. Even without this unknown factor, there was the question of the English government's ability to finance a large-scale war of attrition and occupation. By the end of Henry V's reign parliament was expressing anxiety about further taxation, especially about the possibility of having to subvent what had become an English government in France. It secured a statute that it would never have to support the English king as king of France. This was not unreasonable, but it meant that, as king of France, the king of England would have to raise taxes in France to fight his rebellious subjects; not an idea that would have

---

[3] J. H. Wylie and W. T. Waugh, *The Reign of Henry the Fifth* (3 vols., Cambridge, 1914–29), ii, p. 286.

appealed to the French. There was the larger question of whether the tax system, which had not been updated since 1334, before the substantial demographic decline and social and geographical redistribution of wealth which followed the Black Death, was adequate for demands of this sort. It had in any case been the pattern during periods of prolonged and heavy taxation for the sums actually collected to fall, and there was no reason to suppose that post-Troyes things would be any different. Whether Henry himself, had he survived, could have achieved reforms that were in fact to be delayed until the wars of William III with France is a debatable point, but the government of his son had to work within the *status quo*.

Thus, inevitably, the dual monarchy would prove a chimera once French resistance was organised, but we must not leap from this point to the conclusion that the English were doomed to failure in France. We must remember that Troyes had also marked a victory for England in other areas that had been major concerns since the thirteenth century. For example, the ancestral Duchy of Normandy, lost under King John, had been won back. The Duchy of Aquitaine, acquired by Henry II's marriage to Eleanor of Aquitaine, had been threatened throughout the thirteenth and fourteenth centuries with dismemberment at the hands of invaders and by France's claim to feudal suzerainty. Indeed, Gascony, the remaining territory that the English kings had been struggling to defend during this period, was no more than part of Aquitaine. Only under Edward III, at the Treaty of Brétigny in 1360, had the English Duchy been returned to almost all its former glory, and the restoration had not lasted long. The Treaty of Troyes restored to Aquitaine the borders of 1360 and, although there was ambiguity in the Treaty, it seems that it was to be held by the English kings in full sovereignty, henceforward permanently attached to the *English* crown. Thus, lesser goals, such as the retention of Normandy and Aquitaine under the terms of Troyes, might have been achieved, and the French crown could have been used as a bargaining counter for these. Normandy, in particular, seems to have been not unhappy to be ruled by the English king, a more distant power than the king of France in Paris. As we shall see, it was mismanagement more than inevitability that brought about the final débâcle.

Taken as a whole, the situation in 1422 was a good one, and the success of the minority government, against all the apparent odds, was an indication of the strength with which Henry V's reign had imbued monarchy and realm. However, some sort of substitute would have to be found for the personal rule without which the realm could not function, for as much as thirteen years or more. An added complication of minority rule at such a crucial moment in the war was that it was always easier to persuade the king's subjects to offer financial and military support for war when the king himself led expeditions. Yet there would be no king to act as military leader for many years to come.

To a large extent the minority of Henry VI can be seen as the continuation of Henry V's rule in the absence of the king himself, rather as if he was abroad on a prolonged campaign. Many of the commanders, like the earls of Warwick and Salisbury, remained unchanged, the organisation of war went on much as before, and the unity among the nobility that made all this possible was very much Henry's legacy. Interestingly, Henry's last instructions may have been to give his second brother, Humphrey of Gloucester, a leading role within England during the minority. If the codicil to his will can be interpreted in this way, then the magnates and leading churchmen deliberately chose the path of co-operative rule, against the wishes of their revered master, rather than run the risk of a substitute king taking too much power to himself. Instead, Gloucester was given the rather imprecise titles of Protector, defender and principal councillor. There was to be no official regent of the realm, and when John duke of Bedford, oldest of the late king's younger brothers and heir presumptive to the throne, was in England, Gloucester's titles were to lapse.

In France there was no risk of a single noble abusing his authority, while the military situation made a unitary authority essential. Here Bedford was made regent and for most of the decade the war went remarkably well. Conflict was now between the Dauphin, whose father had just outlived Henry V, and the English. In 1424 a crushing defeat was inflicted on the Dauphin at Verneuil, on the south-eastern border of Normandy. By 1425 Normandy and Maine had both been secured; by 1428 there was growing economic and political stability in Normandy, an essential precondition for the Normandy Estates' continuing acceptance of the need to shoulder much of the financial burden of the war. In 1428 a major campaign to open up France south of the Loire was begun with the siege of Orléans; the fortunes of the Dauphin had now reached their low point. It was only the intervention of Joan of Arc in 1429 that saved the town, but this marked the beginning of the recovery of France and there followed the coronation of the Dauphin as Charles VII at Rheims, the ancient coronation place for the kings of France. Even so, although the English were never again to be as close to total conquest as they had been at Orléans, all was far from lost. In response to events at Rheims, the young Henry VI was taken for the first time to France in 1430, as nominal leader of an expedition which culminated in his coronation in December 1431, although this had to be in Paris, as the English had no access to Rheims. From 1432 to 1435 English forces were able to repulse a series of French attacks on Normandy and Maine.

It was only in 1435 that things began to go badly wrong. First, an attempted peace conference at Arras produced not peace but a *rapprochement* between Charles VII and the Burgundians that removed one of the main planks of the English success in France. Then the death of Bedford deprived England of the only leader with the authority to bring unity to the prosecution of the war. By the end of the year there was intense military pressure on Normandy, which was now considered too poor to contribute to its own defence. As the French advanced, the Norman region of Caux rebelled, an event which confirmed the view that Normandy had been taxed to the point of exhaustion. In early 1436 the duke of Burgundy launched an attack on Calais and in that year Paris was lost to the French. The young duke of York, son of the executed earl of Cambridge, was sent to France in Bedford's place. But he was clearly too youthful and inexperienced to step into his shoes, and the real saviour of Normandy, in 1437, was the great soldier Lord Talbot.

Reflecting the fairly steady progress of the war until 1435, its financing had not yet turned into the major problem it was later to become. Certainly, parliament had initially held to its intention not to pay the expenses of the French kingdom, and this hampered the government in borrowing the capital needed to fund the war, but the gap had been filled by loans from Cardinal Henry Beaufort, bishop of Winchester, the king's half-great-uncle. The sudden realisation in 1429 that all was not well in France had produced considerable generosity on the Commons' part in 1430, on a scale not seen since 1416, and they were to remain in this mood for the rest of the decade. On the other hand, the wool custom, a major source of royal revenue, particularly for the defence of Calais, was falling rapidly, as wool exports were outstripped by cloth exports, which were less highly taxed. However, despite some serious concern in 1433, after the heavy war expenditure of 1430–2 – the occasion of Cromwell's estimates[4] – until 1439 the government remained just about able to pay its way in the war. This means that it could repay most of its loans, and that loans did not yet outstrip anticipated revenue. But the situation was already beginning to deteriorate and the breach with Burgundy disrupted the English wool trade, bringing a fall in customs revenues. At the same time, by 1433 the Estates of Normandy, hitherto a generous provider for the war, was beginning to voice reluctance, leading eventually to the decision not to tax it in 1436. It was of course particularly important not to alienate the Normans if English rule was to last there.

However, the real problems for the minority government were to do with internal politics, although they often arose from the war. Political

---

[4] See above, p. 30.

divisions at home frequently turned on, and even gave rise to, divisions over foreign policy. In so far as the war was mismanaged in these years, it was because of conflicting policies. The problems with both war and internal division stemmed from the impossible attempt to square the circle of monarchy and rule by committee. The minority council was both representative and committed to preserving Henry V's legacy at home and abroad, but there were certain things with which only a king could deal. In keeping a strict brake on grants during the minority the council was by and large successful. Where it found itself in difficulties was in the related areas of making decisions over the war and preserving peace among the magnates. The principal confrontation throughout the minority was between Gloucester and Cardinal Beaufort. Gloucester's failure to secure more than the most limited powers in relation to the young king's person seems to have rankled. Beaufort was in a notably strong position during the minority. Not only was he, like Gloucester, a relative of the king, but, as we have seen, it was his loans that were to a large extent keeping the war effort afloat, especially in the 1420s. His influence was enhanced by his position as the most prominent of the Duchy of Lancaster feoffees.[5] They had held a large part of the Duchy since the death of Henry V, principally to use the proceeds to pay off his debts and fulfil the provisions of his will. These revenues were therefore not at the government's disposal but could be made available by loans from the feoffees. It was in any case inevitable that control of the council should increasingly devolve to churchmen like Beaufort and Archbishop Kemp of York, for they would not be fighting in France, nor had they the lay magnates' need to be periodically in the shires for the sake of their local political standing. It was from leading clerics that the great officers of state had traditionally been drawn and they were used to being continually about the king's person. It is unsurprising therefore that, for much of the minority, the council was dominated by the Cardinal and a group of lesser associates, principally churchmen, like Kemp, or lesser nobles who had built their careers in royal service, like Cromwell and Hungerford.

Warfare by committee, especially if the committee is often unable to draw widely on the expertise of the leading warriors, is likely to lead to contradictory policies and the minority was no exception. One instance is the decision to besiege Orléans which led to the first serious reverse for the English. Bedford was for following a more cautious advance on Anjou but he was over-ruled by those who sought a dramatic breakthrough into central France. But most of the dispute over the conduct of the war was between Gloucester on the one hand and Bedford and Beaufort on the

---

[5] For these, see above, p. 30 n. 4.

other. Broadly speaking, throughout the period up to 1435 Cardinal
Beaufort and Bedford were agreed on a conservative foreign policy,
initially aimed at fulfilling the legacy of Henry V through the gradual
reduction of France to submission to the English monarchy. As events
turned against the English in 1429, it became apparent that the legacy
would not easily be realised, and it then became a matter of holding on to
what they had until the king was of age and could take charge. Gloucester,
by contrast, favoured more dramatic campaigns, usually in other areas. In
1424 he launched an expedition into the Low Countries to secure the
lands of his wife, Jacqueline of Hainault, which risked alienating England's
crucial ally, the duke of Burgundy, and he did not give up this hope until
1428, when the marriage was annulled by the pope. In 1434 he claimed
that the war had been mishandled and demanded to lead a large and
extremely expensive force to France, which, he claimed, would decisively
defeat the French. Gloucester also favoured making Calais the highest
priority. In 1433, amid French threats to Normandy, Maine and Paris, he
tried to persuade Bedford to concentrate on defending Calais and north-
eastern France. In 1436, when both Calais and Normandy were at risk,
Gloucester, as the man who had always argued for the defence of Calais,
was able temporarily to steal a march on Beaufort. Gloucester's willingness
to attack Burgundy, one of England's trading rivals, and enthusiasm for
defending Calais, the centre of the English wool trade, made him popular
in London, where he was able to bring out crowds to demonstrate in
support.

Gloucester's feeling of being passed over was thus intermixed with
personal dislike of Beaufort and opposition to his war policy. The fact that
Bedford, nominally the neutral in all this, in practice sided with Beaufort
over the war was not calculated to improve Gloucester's confidence in the
minority government. In 1425 relations between Beaufort and Gloucester,
never good, became explosive and climaxed in armed confrontation in
London. Significantly it proved necessary to request Bedford's return to
settle matters, which he did in 1426, although the dispute was to rumble
on until 1428. Bedford was here acting as if he were king: he was the heir
presumptive and, as an outsider, he could take a more impartial stand
between the two enemies. In 1431–2, Gloucester launched a major attack
on Beaufort while the latter was with the king in France. He accused
Beaufort of committing *praemunire*, the offence of taking into an ecclesiastical court a matter that belonged in the royal courts, and seized his very
large treasure. As it happened, Gloucester had over-reached himself and
was unable to carry parliament with him to condemn the cardinal. But it
was again Bedford, returning in 1433 to ask for men and money for the
war, who cut Gloucester down to size and, after he had done so, it was

requested that he stay longer. In 1434, when Gloucester made known his grandiose ambitions in warfare, it was Bedford himself, the object of his criticisms, whom he openly confronted. Later that year, after Bedford had left, it seems that Gloucester tried to seize the king from control of the minority council, and Beaufort and the other councillors had to go to Cirencester, where Gloucester had taken him, to reassert the power of the council.

The truth was that, if planning war and foreign policy collectively was problematic, the one thing that only a king could do was referee amongst the nobility. Bedford might act as king to compose the differences between Gloucester and Beaufort but he himself was not entirely exempt from Gloucester's incessant quarrelsomeness. Similarly, there was an urgent need for a single undisputed authority to deal with the local conflicts that were in themselves often related to tension amongst the magnates. As early as 1424 there were parliamentary complaints of disorder and requests that something be done, and further comments on the same lines in 1433 led to notables throughout the shires being asked to make oaths to keep the peace. Even so, there is little doubt that support for Gloucester was limited amongst the nobility. However overbearing and exploitative of his financial power over the crown Beaufort may have been, Gloucester was unforgivably irresponsible. One instance of this is the delay in sending reinforcements to Bedford in 1432, occasioned by parliament's inability to decide on how the expedition was to be financed until it had dealt with Gloucester's attack on Beaufort: had the parliament found Beaufort guilty, his wealth could have paid for the army. The resulting late arrival of the troops led to Bedford's failure to take Lagny, a key fortress east of Paris.

However, what is perhaps most notable about the rule of the great magnates and leading clerics in the 1420s is the remarkable extent to which, without a king to lead them, they managed to maintain a united front. Gloucester's various efforts to place himself in a position of authority were nipped in the bud and, when confrontations between Gloucester and Beaufort threatened the peace, they did not on the whole bring in other nobles as they might have done. For example, in 1425 a dispute over precedence between John Mowbray earl (soon to be duke) of Norfolk and Richard Beauchamp earl of Warwick came to a head. Beauchamp was very much identified with the Beaufort interest, so Norfolk sought Gloucester's help. There was then a risk that Beauchamp's dispute with Lord Berkeley over the Berkeley inheritance, which had been settled temporarily, largely in Beauchamp's favour, in the previous year, would be drawn into the affair: Berkeley had recently married Norfolk's aunt, in the hope of obtaining Mowbray support for his claims. And there were other tensions among the nobility which could have contributed to a broader

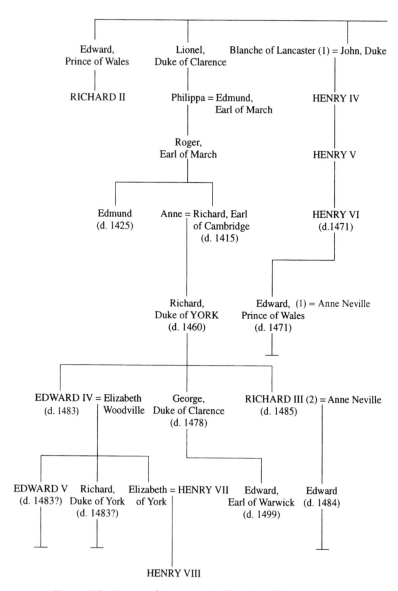

Fig. 1   The Houses of Lancaster, York and Beaufort

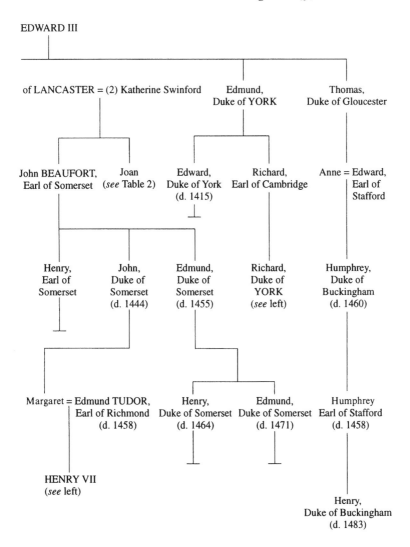

EDWARD III

of LANCASTER = (2) Katherine Swinford   Edmund,   Thomas,
                                       Duke of YORK   Duke of Gloucester

John BEAUFORT,   Joan   Edward,   Richard,   Anne = Edward,
Earl of Somerset (*see* Table 2) Duke of York Earl of Cambridge   Earl of
                            (d. 1415)   Stafford

Henry,   John,   Edmund,   Richard,   Humphrey,
Earl of   Duke of   Duke of   Duke of   Duke of
Somerset Somerset Somerset YORK   Buckingham
          (d. 1444) (d. 1455) (*see* left) (d. 1460)

Margaret = Edmund TUDOR, Henry,   Edmund,   Humphrey
       Earl of Richmond Duke of Somerset Duke of Somerset Earl of Stafford
          (d. 1458)   (d. 1464)   (d. 1471)   (d. 1458)

HENRY VII
(*see* left)

                                                  Henry,
                                           Duke of Buckingham
                                           (d. 1483)

polarisation between Gloucester and Beaufort and no doubt would have done so in very different circumstances thirty years later. The fact that Bedford was able to compose the differences between Beaufort and Gloucester in 1426 was a reflection not only of his own personal standing but also of a situation in which potential deep internal division, which would have made his task much harder, was voluntarily contained among the nobility. It is significant that at the parliament of 1426, when Bedford was attempting to act as arbiter between Gloucester and Beaufort and needed the full endorsement of the nobility for such a settlement, the Lords, usually rather reluctant to attend this assembly,[6] came in large numbers. It is also noteworthy that in 1428, when Gloucester sought widening of his powers as Protector, the noble councillors who rebuffed him included none other than the duke of Norfolk, whose grievances Gloucester had exploited against Beaufort in 1425–6.

By about the mid-1430s there was a mounting sense of urgency about English politics as it became apparent that the minority was drawing to a close. In November 1429 Gloucester's Protectorate had already been brought to an end with the king's coronation in England; the one in France, two years later, confirmed his nominal adulthood. The implications of these actions had already been demonstrated by Gloucester in 1432, when, in pursuit of his vendetta against Beaufort, he used Henry's authority to fill the principal household and state offices with his own men. Even though he failed, it was now clear that either Henry himself, once he felt ready to rule, or anyone else on the king's behalf, was at liberty to start using the authority that the coronations had formally given to the young king. We have seen already that Gloucester tried to do so again in 1434. There was also anxiety that the adult king might rescind grants made in his name and punish those, like the earl of Warwick, his personal guardian from 1428 to 1436, who might later be perceived to have offended the royal person. These matters became all the more urgent when Henry began to make grants on his own authority in 1436. There was also, it appears, a dawning sense that whoever was close to the king when the minority ended might prove to be exceedingly powerful. This is a point to whose implications we shall return in the next chapter.

Meanwhile, the number of problems that really only the king could deal with was growing. There was increasing disorder in the shires. This was typified by events in Bedfordshire in 1437. Here the dominance of Lord Grey of Ruthin was being challenged by the new power of John Cornwaill, recently created Lord Fanhope. Grey was able to ensure that the members of the commission of the peace remained predominantly his men and so failed to reflect, as they needed to, the changing balance of local power. Fanhope, who was closer to the group that was beginning to emerge round the almost adult king, responded by suing out a special commission to enquire into local disorder, which could override the peace commission. The special commission, accompanied by an armed force, then proceeded to try to sit at Silsoe in Bedfordshire, a town which was Grey's but was not far from Ampthill, Fanhope's main seat in the county. Hearing of this, and fearing that the main object of the commission was to indict his men, Grey arrived with a fairly large armed force and the two sides faced each other in the middle of Silsoe. By mediation, armed conflict was avoided on this occasion, but this could not obscure the fact that the episode had arisen from disunity at the centre that came precisely from rule by committee. It was up to the king, after listening to his nobles, to judge how the local offices should be distributed to represent the realities of local power. The Bedfordshire case is a particularly interesting one, because it shows the locally divisive effects of inaction at the centre. However, significantly and ominously, the drift towards lack of direction and disorder in the shires could be seen most clearly in the mid to late 1430s in areas of the royal estates where the king was both ruler and magnate, such as Derbyshire and Nottinghamshire.

Then there was the French war, and the problem of the deteriorating situation after 1435, and the related issue of the royal finances. The war and its financing remained very much at the centre of politics. If the thrust of the minority policy had been to hold on to Henry V's gains until his son was in a position to decide what to do next, the time had come for an urgent reassessment of the situation. The main reason for the English failure at Arras was that nothing could be surrendered on the king's behalf while he was underage. Even though Henry V's last instructions to Bedford had been to hold Normandy at all costs, no-one but the king was in the position to make the decision to abandon some parts of the Treaty of Troyes, especially the throne of France, in return for securing others. Moreover, in the face of constant campaigning from 1417 – the lengthiest period of sustained warfare in the later middle ages – enthusiasm for fighting and for paying the taxes which sustained the war was diminishing. By 1435, most of the men who fought in France were veterans who had been given lands in the Norman settlement: other Englishmen were now showing great reluctance to participate in the war. It was however undeniable, and confirmed by the expedition to crown Henry in 1430–1, that the king's presence produced both more soldiers and greater willingness to grant taxes. That was why it was originally intended that Henry should lead the expedition of 1436, mounted in the face of the danger to both Calais and Paris after Arras. This seems to be the reason for the first signs in this year, the grants made personally, that the king really was ruling.

Royal leadership was all the more urgent because Bedford's death had allowed a greater degree of disunity in foreign policy. Principally, it had taken Beaufort off the leash and turned his enormous contribution to the royal finances into the power to dictate. The most notable result was the expedition to Maine in 1438 of Edmund Beaufort, marquess of Dorset, the cardinal's nephew. This, an unnecessary diversion of English force, especially at a time when the need was to concentrate on Normandy, was designed primarily to create a landed endowment in Maine for Dorset. Like most of the other lay Beauforts, he did not have lands commensurate with his title and relationship to the king, because the family did not have a claim on the Lancaster lands; the cardinal's great wealth had come from his being bishop of Winchester, one of the richest sees in England, and from his financial acumen. At home there was the problem that, with the defection of Burgundy in 1435, the English coasts were exposed to raiders from the continent as they had not been since Henry IV's reign. The fleet built up by Henry V had been allowed to decay and what was needed was either to rebuild it (which required money) or to secure allies along the channel coast. It was, on all counts, time for the king to take command of the war. Throughout the minority the first priority had been to thrust personal responsibility of every sort on Henry VI as quickly as possible. The time had now come for him to take it.

5

HENRY VI'S ADULT RULE: THE FIRST
PHASE *c.* 1437–1450

————— · —————

We are far from certain of when Henry VI really began to rule without any formalised guidance. That is a highly significant fact, for a major debate about the reign in recent years has been the extent to which Henry himself ruled at any time. It used to be thought that the answer was not at all. As K. B. McFarlane put it succinctly, 'In Henry VI second childhood succeeded first without the usual interval.'[1] The standard interpretation followed contemporary descriptions of the king, notably that of his confessor, John Blacman. Much was made of his lack of interest in worldly affairs, his consequent neglect of the business of rule and his wholesale commitment to spiritual matters, which was seen most spectacularly in the great foundations of Eton and King's College, Cambridge, Henry's only worthwhile legacy. Then B. P. Wolffe wrote an almost deliberately provocative piece, followed by lengthier treatment of the same hypothesis in his book, proposing that Henry was less inert than has been supposed and that, like Edward II, he himself made his own positive contribution to the disasters of his reign. He suggested that all the evidence that had been used to support the traditional view was tainted, in that it post-dated the reign, and that Blacman was especially suspect because he was writing under Henry VII when moves were afoot to canonise Henry VI. For instance, for Wolffe, the inconsistencies in foreign policy in the 1440s were due not to the divided policies of the men who were running the kingdom but to the king's capricious changes of mind and susceptibility to others' influence.

As so often with historical controversies, an uneasy compromise seems to have been reached. The outrageously interventionist king of Wolffe's

---

[1] McFarlane, *Nobility*, p. 284.

work has not found general acceptance but there is fairly widespread agreement that Henry's wishes may be seen at work in some of his over-generous grants and pardons and in the foreign policy of the 1440s. Contrary to Wolffe, this is now interpreted not as royal interference of an inconsistent nature but as a steady desire for peace, in line with the king's allegedly pacific character, while deviations away from this are attributed not to royal changes of mind but to the interference of others, notably Cardinal Beaufort. On the other hand, Blacman has been rescued from Wolffe's dismissal and shown to be a much earlier witness than he supposed, and no-one, not even Wolffe, has tried to make much of a case for Henry being in control of events after the second Protectorate ended in 1456. Indeed, only Wolffe seems seriously to believe that Henry was any kind of a force after his first bout of madness in 1453–4. However, the whole question of Henry's active role as king is one that will bear re-examination, for there are some quite serious problems with the new orthodoxy.

First, leaving aside Blacman's rehabilitation, there are comments suggestive of Henry's 'lifelessness' that do predate his deposition and even belong to the 1440s, when, according to the new perspective, he was at his most active. All educated contemporary comment has to be treated with care because so much of it is conventional. On the face of it, Henry was the 'perfect' medieval king of the advice manuals for monarchs: receptive to advice, peace-loving, generous, religious. But this is only one side of kingship and, not surprisingly, it was the one that was stressed by the mostly clerical authors of the manuals. It was taken for granted that there would be a very powerful royal will,[2] which would be the essential vehicle for the central royal tasks of keeping internal peace and external defence. That was really why the manuals were so emphatic about the king's need for more pacific, receptive qualities: to mitigate the faults of egoism which they assumed to exist in a normal medieval monarch and which could not be contained except by self-restraint and responsiveness to counsel, because the king could not be subject to external restraint.[3] When confronted with a king who seemed to have no will at all, they could only laud the qualities which were the platitudes of their writing. This makes it very dangerous to go through these comments, as one historian has done, taking them as a literal account of the king's character, but at the same time their existence is an interesting indication of the one-sidedness of Henry's adult kingship, the lack of a royal will at the heart of it.

Then there are more specifically focused observations, among both the

---

[2] See above, p. 41.   [3] See above, p. 28.

educated and informed and the uneducated and less informed. For example, the chroniclers John Hardyng and John Capgrave, both writing in the 1440s, made comments suggesting a lack of energy in Henry's rule, precisely in those areas of defence and justice where the king's will was so important in activating governance. Alleged treasonable statements of the period, although sometimes exceedingly wild and doubtless usually delivered under the influence of drink, make the same kind of implication: that the king was a child or a fool. Naturally, they have to be handled with care, but they do reveal a wider apprehension of the quality of Henry's rule; it is improbable that such comments would have been made about Henry V or Edward IV.

There are also conceptual objections to the present orthodoxy. We must realise that, whatever conclusions we come to about the king's personal role in governance, the evidence of activity is of the same kind in every sphere of his rule. Once the king was an adult, all governance would come from him, and all governmental directives that were not entirely routine would be made in the king's name. The 'Henry VI' entry in the index to Wolffe's book shows how Wolffe has assumed that anything which bore the king's personal imprint was actually done by him. It is, however, a dangerous assumption to make. In the last years of Edward II, for instance, it is almost certain that a large proportion of the orders from the king came in fact from the Despensers, his favourites, who were using the king's powers to their own advantage. But that conclusion itself relies not on hard evidence but on probabilities, on what we know about the respective abilities and previous behaviour patterns of Edward and these last two favourites. It is highly improbable that Edward, having shown an extreme distaste for any kind of serious involvement in government for the first fifteen years of his reign, would suddenly display the most tremendous energy and ability in the last four or five years. At the same time, most of what Edward did in these years was for the benefit of the Despensers, who were his closest advisers and companions in these years. With Henry VI, we are dealing with the same kind of evidence, all of which shows the king as the origin of all significant governmental activity. As with Edward II, how we choose to interpret it is another matter: we may decide that he was personally responsible for some parts of his rule and not for others, but the evidence itself is all of a piece and can only lead us to believe that he was doing everything, or, if we prefer it, nothing.

In weighing up the balance of probabilities in this regard we also have to be conscious of what we are saying. It is generally agreed that the king was inert enough to leave a series of key policies in the hands of his advisers: appointment of local officers and hence the rule of the shires, settlement of conflict amongst his magnates, the general oversight of law and order, most major grants, the management of the royal finances, with all their implications for foreign policy. In that case we must surely assume that these advisers were in a position to prevent him taking an active role in any aspect from which they chose to exclude him. We must therefore consider what those spheres where Henry is now thought to have intervened meant for those around the king. The odd minor grant or pardon may not have been of any great significance, and we shall see that there may be grounds for suspecting some kingly involvement in some of these, although not necessarily as an act of personal will. The war, however, was absolutely central to the domestic politics of England in the 1440s, a fact that became all too plain when disaster in war in 1449–50 brought nemesis to those who had been closest to the king in the 1440s. It is scarcely conceivable that they would have allowed the king to dictate a policy on which their very lives depended when they seem to have been able to dictate to the king on everything else that mattered.

Ultimately, conclusions resting less on supposition and more on hard evidence are most likely to come from analysis of the reign itself. This is one of the reasons why it is so necessary to consider structures of rule and the consequences for them of Henry's failings as king; once we can diagnose the symptoms, we are in a better position to evaluate causes. Accordingly, much of the argument that we should return to the older view of Henry will grow out of the discussion of his adult reign, in contrast to the recent trend, which has generally been to make assertions about Henry's character and from that to deduce the consequences for his rule. We can begin conveniently where this chapter began, with the sequence of events leading to Henry's majority. From 1436 there is evidence in the documentation of government that the king was beginning to play a larger part in rule, taking joint responsibility with the minority council and making some grants on his own.[4] In November 1437, when Henry was rising sixteen, there was a declaration of the council, which has been taken to mark the formal ending of the minority, but in fact did no more than confirm a state of affairs that had developed over the previous year or so. This was to the effect that the king would deal only with matters of grace – essentially pardons and grants – whilst matters of state remained within the purview of the council, now in conjunction with the king. From about the middle of 1439 the influence of the council began to diminish and that of courtiers, as they moved into prominent positions around the king, to grow. This latter group included major household officials like Ralph Boteler, soon to be created Lord Sudeley, and William Ayscough, the

---

[4] See above, p. 84.

king's confessor, bishop of Salisbury from 1438, and nobles who were to become closely indentified with Henry's court such as Viscount Beaumont, John Sutton, Lord of Dudley and Lord Fanhope. The latter's influence over those around the king we have already seen at work as early as the Bedfordshire dispute of 1437.[5]

In constitutional terms there was nothing sinister about this process; we have seen that it was more normal for kings to take advice from their nobles on an informal basis than on a formal one. Once the king was active as an adult there was no longer any need for a formally constituted council. Indeed the existence of one was antithetical to effective monarchy, which depended on free access for all major subjects, not just those who had been made members of a formal body, at all times, not just those of formal council.[6] With an adult, active king, the focus of rule would be expected to move from the council, which would wither away as a formal body, to the household and court. It was in these that the king was in daily personal contact with those most important to the management of the realm. But what began to happen at an early stage of Henry's nominal adulthood is that those who had access to the king were able to dictate his actions. So much was this the case that by late 1441 a decision seems to have been made to return to a more careful delimitation of the king's powers. This was chiefly because of the welter of grants being made in his name, now that his majority had opened the floodgates, something which was already causing unease as early as 1438. Towards the end of 1441, a formal council seems to have taken control again of a large measure of the king's authority.[7] But this could not be a permanent remedy once the king was recognised to be of age, for in effect the council was accroaching the king's powers. Moreover, as soon as the king was undeniably adult, power would drain inexorably to his person and therefore to anyone disposed to remove him from such formal oversight. There was the added incentive that all along the magnates had been trying to thrust rule upon the king as soon as possible, and there would be reluctance to rescind his personal rule, which was now so badly needed. By late 1443 evidence of conciliar activity is already fading away and by 1444 the adult reign of Henry VI had truly begun.

[5] See above, pp. 84–5.   [6] See above, pp. 36–7.

[7] There is clear evidence of a revived conciliar authority from autumn 1441. This may be associated with a document which it has not been easy to date. The most recent historian to have looked closely at it is John Watts, and in his most recent statement, in *Henry VI and the Politics of Kingship* (Cambridge, 1996), having earlier suggested that it may date to 1441, he offers more support for the more traditional date of 1444. However, he concludes that it could belong to any period between the late 1430s and late 1440s. Whatever the dating, it shows an attempt to bind the king to conciliar authority which would be altogether strange if the king was an adult.

But what was this rule? The impossibility of naming a date at which Henry formally took control, in contrast to Henry III, Edward III and Richard II, who had all been under tutelage of some sort, and all announced its ending with some force, is very telling. So is the revival of the minority council in 1441, as if it was realised that the king was as yet unable to cope with adult responsibilities. Perhaps most striking is that in 1437, for the first time, Duchy of Lancaster stewardships were given in numbers to members of the nobility. In each case it was to locally dominant nobles: for example, the Nevilles in Yorkshire and Lancashire, Lord Beaumont in Leicestershire, Lord Cromwell in Nottinghamshire, the earl of Stafford in Staffordshire and Derbyshire.[8] In Norfolk, the same principle held but on slightly different terms. The stewardship was confirmed to Thomas Tuddenham, a Duchy official of considerable seniority, but by this time he was coming within the political orbit of the earl of Suffolk, who had recently been granted some of the major offices for the Duchy as a whole. Even the most ardent proponent of noble greed must acknowledge that this is too early for the nobility to be falling on a helpless king and dividing up his resources. What is much more likely is that they were aware of the growing problem of order and were anxious to hold the line while the king still failed to show any signs of emerging from childhood. Accordingly, they decided to make use of the king's private power in the localities, in conjunction with their own, to buttress his absent public authority. As it turned out, they had to continue to do so.

And yet Henry should have had no difficulty in assuming authority centrally and locally, especially as he was surrounded with such experienced and loyal advisers. Boys grew up early in medieval England; Edward III threw off the rule of Mortimer at eighteen, Richard II had been given almost unsupervised rule of England at thirteen, Henry V had won his first battle, at Shrewsbury, at fifteen, Edward IV was to fight his way to the throne at the age of eighteen. By the late 1430s Henry VI, in his late teens, should have been more than ready to rule. However, one of the problems for those responsible for the country's welfare was to determine whether they were dealing with the inexperience of youth or with something rather more serious. That would explain the temporary resuscitation of the minority council in the early 1440s, when it may have been thought that events had been moving too fast for the young king and he needed a little more time to grow up. It can only have been gradually that the realisation dawned on those around the king that he was never going to grow up.

This has some far-reaching implications for historians' interpretation of the internal rule of England in the 1440s. Here, despite Wolffe's efforts to

---

[8] Stafford had these offices from 1435 but it is perhaps significant that they were converted into life-grants in 1437.

turn Henry into an active king at home as well as abroad, the long-standing orthodoxy has prevailed until very recently. Conventionally, the decade has been seen as one in which an inert king allowed a group of grasping courtiers to take hold of his government. These men took great quantities of royal patronage for themselves, seriously undermining the crown's financial position. Their personal profligacy at the crown's expense reduced parliament's willingness to grant taxes and the taxpayers' to pay them. They exercised a stranglehold on appointments to local office in the counties where they were major landowners, which allowed them to manipulate the legal system at will against all those who were not under their protection. This was reinforced by a wholesale control over the monarch at the centre which cut off the established nobility, like Gloucester and the duke of York, from offering advice or receiving favour, and litigants worsted in the shires from taking their plaints to the king. The transparent partiality of their rule in the king's name and their consequent inability to deal with magnate conflict caused a spiralling level of violence which was to erupt in 1450 in an extreme form, bringing well-deserved retribution on the worst of the villains.

There is in fact much truth in this litany of evil but there may be grounds for re-examining its causes. It used to be universally held that the same group of men was responsible for the disastrous foreign policy, but we have seen that most historians now take it for granted that the king had some role in foreign policy. It will, in fact, be suggested here, on the basis of some very recent and revolutionary work on the reign by John Watts, on which much of this chapter and the next two is based, that Henry VI was not responsible for any part of the rule that occurred in his name during the 1440s, either at home or abroad, but that the consequence of this was not the triumph of 'evil counsel' but rather a concerted effort to put a semblance of monarchy in the void created by the absence of an active king.

It is hard to believe that it did not dawn quite soon on those closest to the king, as they struggled to turn him into an adult, active monarch between 1436 and 1444, that the essential royal will which made monarchy possible was entirely lacking in this king. But the next stage of reasoning need not have been that this was a wonderful opportunity for certain people to enrich themselves at the monarchy's expense. We should remember that essential to the self-image of nobility was a sense of public service, without which they were little more than local power-brokers, but with which they shared at second hand in all the public authority of the monarchy. As we have seen, this sense of service had received additional nurture under Henry V and in the minority of his son. During the latter period, a surprising degree of unity had been preserved where direction by a king was most required: that is the conduct of the war and the securing of internal order, especially peace among the nobles themselves. It has accordingly been suggested by Watts that the nobles' overwhelming response to an alarming situation was to accept, in the words of the duke of Wellington, that exemplary public servant of the nineteenth century, that 'the king's government must be carried on' and to take responsibility for this: both external war and internal peace.

The man who emerged as the power behind the throne, the earl and eventually duke of Suffolk, had all the credentials for the job. His father had died at the siege of Harfleur and his older brother had been killed at Agincourt; he himself had fought in France under Henry V and VI and had even been made captive. He had thus shown his commitment to the French war and was not likely to surrender France without a struggle. It is certainly true that Suffolk was linked to a group whose focus was the household of the king, for, now that access to the king meant access to the real source of power, the household was assuming the central role that it always had under an adult king. This group included Sudeley, Beaumont, Dudley and Bishop Ayscough of Salisbury, whom we have already met, and John Lord Beauchamp of Powick, close associate of Sudeley, James Fenys, later Lord Say, and Adam Moleyns, later bishop of Chichester. Yet Suffolk had married into the Beaufort kin and many of his circle were Beaufort connections. Although he may therefore to some extent have usurped Cardinal Beaufort's position, and, as we shall see, there may have been friction between the two over foreign policy on occasion, he was in many ways heir to the Beaufort political interest. This we have seen to be identified in foreign policy with the respected and responsible Bedford interest. Beauchamp and Sudeley too had been active upholders of the English position in France and had only recently returned to England. Moreover, a detailed analysis of connections between those we think of as courtiers shows that the 'ancient nobility', far from being excluded from a tiny controlling clique, were almost all knitted in to what became an all-encompassing political connection. Even Gloucester was not isolated at first.

To understand how this 'front' for the king might find general acceptance among the political classes, we must look again at the way the monarchy was supposed to work. If the theory was that the king would listen attentively to advice, and then pronounce, Henry VI was on the face of it an admirable ruler. He listened, and, if he lacked the essential royal will to pronounce, then someone else could do it for him. As long as the outward forms of monarchy were preserved, it was not inevitably apparent that it was someone else's will and not the king's. Government went on much as before, its aims basically identical, and any differences could be assumed, as they are sometimes by historians in relation to foreign policy, to result from the ideas of the adult king. Those who had readiest access to the king, who are likely to have included most of the nobles and the members of the royal household, could hardly have failed to realise that what they had was a royal façade covering the actual rule of Suffolk, not the real thing. But the nobility may have been happy to persuade themselves that all was well, since that would relieve them of yet another period of immediate responsibility for the monarchy. Those who knew full well what was happening may have preferred to let Suffolk take the burden he was apparently prepared to shoulder. Anyone further away from the hub of government, which means all the non-noble population without direct access to the household, probably thought that it was royal business as usual (although the treasonous words that were cited earlier suggest that some at least were unconvinced). What is more, it can be shown that Suffolk's policies in France found acceptance amongst all the lords, with the exception of Gloucester: the greater nobility who were in England were involved at every stage of the process that was to determine the fate of the English in France.

It was France that remained the first priority and, in connection with France, the royal finances. These were showing signs of serious wear and tear by the end of the 1430s. Debts were mounting, troops and commanders unpaid, and Cardinal Beaufort's financial assistance was still more in demand. Moreover, in 1437–40 there was a serious agrarian crisis and famine in both England and Normandy which reduced the ability of both to pay for the war. Parliaments in 1439 and 1442 granted taxes, but grudgingly and with efforts to force the government specifically to set aside money for some of the king's financial needs, especially his household. In 1442 there was further intervention from the Commons, although the new power of the household may have lain behind it. This concerned the Duchy of Lancaster feoffment, made to implement the will of Henry V.[9] Instead it had been used chiefly to make advances to the crown of over £50,000. We have seen how Cardinal Beaufort, as one of the feoffees, and a very rich man in his own right, had been able to control virtually all the credit offered to the king for the French war. In 1442 the speaker of the Commons, William Tresham, who was an esquire of the household, successfully requested that the feoffment be finally wound up. Presumably it was hoped that freeing the Duchy from the feoffees' control would, as under Henry V, make its funds available for the subvention of the monarchy and relieve the taxpayer.

There may also have been an element of jealousy on the part of the

---

[9] See above, p. 30.

Suffolk circle of the control over the war that Beaufort's monopoly of loans had given him. However, it is important to separate Beaufort's attempts to advance his family through the war from any more generalised differences with Suffolk over foreign policy, especially the movement towards negotiation, on which the two were in principle agreed. In 1437 a peace policy was first mooted and in 1439 the direction of English foreign policy began overtly to change, from the all-out conquest that had been at its heart throughout the minority, towards negotiation. This was made all the more urgent by the worsening financial situation. In fact, in some ways, the move towards negotiation was less an alteration than an adaptation of prevailing policies to the new circumstances of growing French strength and English financial weakness. The Bedford/Beaufort line had always been to pursue a gradualist and, where necessary, defensive strategy. It had been Gloucester who had been the odd one out in urging grandiose and expensive campaigns and there had been a more or less united front among the minority government to resist his demands. Even as the government began to espouse a peace policy, the financial difficulties were highlighted by the large expedition sent to Guyenne in Gascony under John Holland earl of Huntingdon in 1439, to strengthen the military position, and therefore the negotiating position of the English. Anticipation of revenue from lay and clerical taxes granted for 1437–9 made Huntingdon's campaign so difficult to finance that several crown properties had to be sold to Cardinal Beaufort to pay for it.

Indeed, once the realities of international diplomacy and national finances had come firmly into view after 1435, it is hard to see that any sober observer of the scene could have come to any other conclusion than that serious negotiations with France had to be opened while England was still in a position of comparative strength. One does not need the rise of an anti-Beaufort group in the household, still less a pacific king, to explain this shift in policy, especially as it was less a shift than a change in direction. The gradualism that had been espoused by Beaufort himself remained. It was a long-overdue recognition of the facts of life. It was delayed until the later 1430s by the obsession with preserving the young king's inheritance until he was of an age to decide for himself and by Henry's increasingly evident inability ever to make such a decision. What the new policy may therefore represent is the moment at which Suffolk, and perhaps other nobles as well, concluded that there never would be any decision and he would have to make it for the king.

In mid-1439 the peace policy began to move forward with an inconclusive conference at Calais, where the English delegation was led by Cardinal Beaufort. Beaufort seems to have had wide powers to try to secure a general settlement aimed at salvaging as much as possible of the English conquests.

It was suggested that the duke of Orléans, held in captivity since Agincourt, be released to act as intermediary. This itself is highly significant because Henry V's last instructions had been that no major prisoner was to be released until his son was of age; it seems to show that those around Henry had made the decision to act as if he were of age, even though their continued supervision of the king at home shows that they knew this was not the case. The council in England, urged on by Gloucester, rejected the proposed terms, although it was eventually decided to release Orléans in 1440. The failure of the conference has been seen as the turning point in Beaufort's public career. On his return, he was subject to a blistering attack by Gloucester, which included allegations concerning the sales which had financed Huntingdon's expedition. Gloucester was not, however, the beneficiary of the cardinal's partial eclipse. It is from this time that the council became dominated less by old Beaufort associates like Lord Cromwell and Archbishop Kemp and more by Suffolk and those linked to him through the king's household. Nevertheless, if Beaufort's failure at Calais was the occasion for the start of his political decline, the fundamental cause was the impossibility of sustaining an official minority once the king was deemed to be of age. As Beaufort's power-base was the minority council and that of the Suffolk group the royal household, authority could only move towards Suffolk once the king was held to be active on his own account, and the household was thus the new centre of authority. That however did not prevent Suffolk absorbing much of the old Beaufort circle, including Lord Cromwell, into his new household nexus.

Moreover, Beaufort and Suffolk remained in agreement on foreign policy at this time. Characteristically, it was Gloucester who opposed the first serious attempts at peace in 1439, and his wholesale attack on Beaufort, which included rejection of the release of Orléans, suggests that, in the eyes of its chief opponent, the cardinal was as compromised by the peace policy as anyone. Gloucester was gagged in 1441 when his wife, Eleanor Cobham, was most conveniently implicated in a scandal involving necromancy and the prediction of the king's death. He does not seem to have found anyone to run to his defence. Throughout the reign he had shown lack of judgement at home and abroad. Whether his wife was framed or not, her behaviour would have been seen as consistent with her husband's waywardness at home, while his continued attempts to sabotage negotiations abroad reflected his wild foreign ambitions and were likely to be welcomed by few. York's further appointment as Lieutenant in France from 1440 to 1445 indicates his own acceptance of the policy being formulated under Suffolk's leadership: he was not the ally of 'Good Duke Humphrey' in an aggressive foreign policy, as was later to be implicit in his political platform.

However weak the support for Gloucester, such differences over foreign policy reflect further the divisions that were likely to appear in the absence of an effective king, and they surface again in respect of the Beauforts' efforts to use the French war for their own ends. It is in this instance that we do see a division between Suffolk and Cardinal Beaufort, and it came about because, as in 1438, Beaufort deliberately chose to sacrifice the national interest in the French war to the advancement of his family. The problem, as before, was the need to create a substantial landed endowment for the family and, as before, the hope was to do it in France. From 1436 grants of office and land in Normandy to both Beaufort nephews, Edmund of Dorset and John of Somerset, had been growing apace. The ransoming in 1438 of Somerset, who had been in French captivity since the battle of Baugé in 1421, had accentuated the problem of the family's underendowment. In 1442 Cardinal Beaufort proposed a large-scale attack on France, to be led by Somerset. The justification for the campaign was this: while debate went on over whether it was better to defend Normandy or the lands in Gascony further south, both of which were under serious threat, the solution was to attack the space between the two. In practice the real beneficiaries were the Beauforts. Immediately, the terms of service, in giving Somerset 600 marks' worth of land and waiving the king's rights to a percentage of any war profits, were to help restore Somerset's finances. In the longer term, there were aspirations to carve out a patrimony for the Beauforts from hoped-for conquests in Anjou and Maine.

The whole expedition was an almost deliberate insult to the duke of York, the overall commander in France. Somerset was permitted to have a command that was entirely independent of York's authority and, because of its scale, the campaign used up almost the entire exchequer funds for the war for 1443. Moreover, he was made a duke to give him parity with York. But it was hard to reject the Beaufort plan, for the simple reason that the cardinal's loans had become even more vital to the royal finances. Somerset landed at Cherbourg in Normandy in August 1443 and moved on Maine and Anjou. After a series of rather pointless sieges and raids, he retreated to Rouen and returned home, a broken man, in spring 1444, to die in May, possibly by suicide. Not only had he taken much-needed funds from York's command, but large numbers of troops had joined him from Normandy, with the result that in August 1443 Talbot was unable to continue with the crucially important siege of Dieppe in Normandy.

Here we can see very clearly the results, in inconsistent policies, of lack of royal leadership: this is not intermittent interference by the king but an absence of royal input which led to decisions dictated by whoever had the loudest voice at any one moment. Somerset's expedition was antithetical to the cardinal's own previously unwavering belief in avoiding over-ambitious plans. It was still more hostile to the new peace policy, a situation that Charles VII cunningly exploited by suggesting further nego-tiations just as Somerset was rather aimlessly plundering Anjou. This pattern of attacking when negotiation and retrenchment were required and failing to fight when aggression was the better course was to be the undoing of the English in France. It came about because there was nobody with the authority to formulate and force through a clearly thought out policy, that would enable the laudable plan of withdrawing with as much honour and land as possible to be effected. Only the king had this and he was not using it. Furthermore, as we have seen, royal leadership in itself was always an enormous inducement to subjects of all kinds to lend military and financial support,[10] and its absence in the 1440s, as in the minority, partly explains the diminishing enthusiasm for fighting or paying for the war.

Internally the impact of the Beaufort expedition may not have been as great as some historians have suggested. It is sometimes seen as the turning-point in York's relations with the court, souring them beyond retrieval. And it is certainly true, as we shall see, that Yorkist propaganda in the 1450s was to make a lot of the dishonour of the Beauforts' loss of France. It is also suggested that the elevation to dukedoms in 1443 and 1444 of nobles related to the royal house, who could be seen as possible heirs to Henry VI should he die childless, was a deliberate slight to York. Somerset's, from earl to duke, has been mentioned, and there were also John Holland earl of Huntingdon to duke of Exeter (both of these were descended from Henry's own great-grandfather, John of Gaunt) and the earl of Stafford (descended from Thomas of Gloucester, son of Edward III) to duke of Buckingham. It could be argued that none of these should have been put on a par with York, who was heir male of Edward III's fourth son Edmund Langley duke of York, and therefore had a strong claim to be considered heir presumptive to the throne when the childless duke of Gloucester should die. He was also descended through the female line from Edward III's second son, Clarence, which could arguably give him a better title than the reigning king, whose claim came from Edward's third son.[11]

But these arguments do not bear close scrutiny. The fact remains that York continued as commander in France until 1445 and that the person who had every reason to be most annoyed by the consequences of the Beaufort expedition was Suffolk, supposedly York's main enemy until 1450. The Beauforts' efforts had first halted his attempts to negotiate and

---

[10] See above, p. 85.   [11] See the genealogy above, pp. 82–3.

then weakened his negotiating hand. York apparently agreed to the decisions made in the subsequent negotiations with the French and indeed to almost every step in the foreign policy of the next few years whose consequences he was later roundly to condemn. It was the Beauforts who were to be the real losers from the collapse of the English position in France; the Beauforts who were excluded from the new feoffment of the Duchy of Lancaster in 1443–5; the Beauforts who lost one of their family titles, previously held by Cardinal Beaufort's brother, Thomas, who had died without heirs in 1426, when Holland was raised to his dukedom of Exeter. On the other hand, the Beauforts had better success than York in getting their war arrears paid. All this emphasises again that we should not look too soon for permanent divisions amongst the nobility. As before, the one isolated figure was Humphrey of Gloucester. It may well be that one of the reasons for drawing attention to some of the king's closest relatives by giving them dukedoms – a policy that, apart from the sop to Somerset's *amour propre* before the expedition of 1443, has still to be satisfactorily explained – was to undermine Gloucester's own position as heir presumptive.

Significantly, the greatest contradictions in foreign policy disappear from 1444, the time when all attempts to reconstruct the minority government ceased, and it could well be argued that the greater consistency evident from that year was due to Suffolk's unchallenged mastery of a nominally adult king. It seems highly improbable that it could be due to the sudden engagement of Henry in foreign affairs, since, at the age of twenty-two, he should long before have become an active force if he was ever going to be one. In May 1444 negotiations with the French were opened at Tours, with Suffolk as the English representative. Before leaving he made great play of his reluctance, a point that has been used to stress that the embassy was very much the king's personal policy. But, bearing in mind that only the king could renegotiate Troyes, and knowing the consequences of failure, or of success built on unacceptable surrenders, Suffolk was bound to maintain that he went at the king's personal command. In any case, as we have seen, militarily and financially, it was by now the only possible course. The king's finances were in such a parlous state that non-payment of military commanders was becoming the norm. Recovery would only be possible with a long period of peace. At last, the negotiating position was taken which should have been espoused nearly a decade before: Normandy and Gascony in full sovereignty in return for surrender of the French throne. But it was now too late. Suffolk could extract no more than a truce, the Truce of Tours, concluded at the end of May, to last only from July 1444 until April 1446. However, he did manage to make an agreement for a marriage between Henry VI and

Margaret, daughter of René of Anjou, hoping probably that he would be able to get the truce extended on the strength of this union. It seems that he may also have made a secret verbal promise to surrender Maine, on which the English still maintained a precarious hold.

In December 1445 the agreement on Maine was formalised, although still secret, the French reciprocating with no more than a twenty-year alliance between England and Anjou. This undertaking to surrender Maine was given in a secret letter under the king's signet, and the use of this most personal of the royal seals and the fact that it mentions the entreaties of his wife (who had arrived in England in May) have been seen as evidence that Henry really was acting on his own initiative. But this assumption rests on taking the letter at its face-value. Given Suffolk's known influence in the royal household, there is every reason to suppose that anything sent by the king would be vetted, if not drafted, by Suffolk. Suffolk may have made the secret promise to surrender Maine. He was certainly committed to a policy of gaining breathing-space through truce, to the point where it could not be reversed, even if it meant that Maine had to go. Since the marriage of Margaret had been made with the specific purpose of securing a peace, the mention of her name need not be more than a piece of diplomatic courtesy.

This concession is another piece of evidence which undermines the idea that York faced a uniformly hostile court in which Suffolk and the younger Beauforts were prominent. It was in fact a serious blow to the Beauforts, whose landed future was so bound up with Maine, even if it was later agreed that the new duke of Somerset was to have a substantial pension in compensation. There are also other indications that Suffolk was not prepared to allow Beaufort interests in France to stand in the way of negotiations. Conversely, for the moment the truce guaranteed the security of Normandy, where York was the greatest English land-owner, and where he had been given more land late in 1444. When York, his command having come to an end in 1445, was replaced in France in December 1446 by Edmund Beaufort, now earl of Somerset, it would again be unwise to use hindsight and find here the cause of York's later conflict with the Beauforts and the court. Given the amount of favour York had been shown by Suffolk, and the reverses the Beauforts had had to endure, it was sensible enough to try and right the balance a little and it would have been petty-minded of York to take umbrage. Above all, there was the need to placate Beaufort for the forthcoming surrender of Maine, which would bring to an end hopes for the perma-nent establishment of his family there. Perhaps more damaging to York's self-esteem and his loyalty to Suffolk were the charges of peculation while in command in France levelled against him by Adam Moleyns about this time: these may have been intended as justification for not renewing his commission.

All the same, if the evidence of all York's dealings with the court in the 1440s is read without prior knowledge of the 1450s and of York's self-justifying claims then, it does not look as if he was a hated outsider. Negotiations to marry York's eldest son to a daughter of the king of France, first suggested in 1445 by Suffolk, continued, if fitfully. York was present at several discussions, including those which dealt with the surrender of Maine. He was at the Bury parliament in March 1447 where Gloucester was arrested for treason and derived some territorial benefits from Gloucester's death, which occurred, probably from natural causes, soon after his arrest. In 1445 York had already arranged to marry his daughter, Anne, to the heir of the duke of Exeter, one of his supposed dynastic rivals, and in July 1447, after the Bury parliament, York was given the wardship of his son-in-law, Exeter's underage heir. It is telling that, after his return from France in late 1445, he seems to have secured payment of quite a substantial amount of the nearly £40,000 still owing to him from his time as lieutenant there, for the exchequer was nearly bankrupt and there were many other claims on it. Nor should York's appointment to the lieutenancy of Ireland in July 1447 be seen as a ploy to get him out of the country. He was allowed to serve by deputy and did not in fact leave until June 1449. His distinguished ancestor, Lionel of Clarence, through whom he had inherited substantial property in Ireland, had spent much of the 1360s fighting for his father Edward III in Ireland, and indeed had died there. It was a logical appointment, not a malevolent design, and York was given wide-ranging powers with the lieutenancy. Meanwhile, apart from the pension to compensate for Maine, Somerset received nothing between 1443/4, when he was given grants to sustain his new title of marquis, and 1451, when he obtained full control of the king's government.

Perhaps the most significant piece of evidence against the conventional view that York was progressively estranged in the 1440s by a ruling faction dominated by Suffolk and the two dukes of Somerset is an action of 1448 that ranks very low on the political Richter Scale. A piece of land in Essex, disputed between minor local landowners, was twice in that year given in trusteeship for its protection jointly to York and Somerset. It is inconceivable that this would have been done had the two been at odds with each other. Paradoxically, the rival claimants used Suffolk for the same purpose, which certainly shows the lack of a united Suffolk/Beaufort front against York, but equally, given the other evidence that has been cited, cannot be used to demonstrate that York and Suffolk were moving towards confrontation. Most likely, both sides were trying to obtain special protection from men they believed to be close to the king. Again, it must be stressed that Gloucester was the noble who was on his own. Doubtless the charges at Bury were fabricated and doubtless the arrest was made to prevent Gloucester speaking at the first parliament held after the agreement to surrender Maine was becoming public knowledge. But the duke had exhausted the patience of his peers. Furthermore, any repetition of his earlier history of whipping up Commons opposition by a display of aggressive righteousness against the French was most certainly not needed at this juncture. A breathing-space had been won and money, in the form of permission to take loans, was to be requested from the Commons to make the most of it. Amongst those who arrested Gloucester was the earl of Salisbury, the close ally of York in the 1450s in opposing the court and perpetrating the myth of 'good Duke Humphrey'.

Over the next three years the military collapse that was now inherent in the inequality in the French and English situations ground to its inevitable conclusion. The English bought extensions of the truce with renewed promises to surrender Maine but, partly because of English resistance in Maine and partly perhaps because of divided counsels, the surrender was not made. In February 1448 the French launched an attack on Maine, beginning with its capital, Le Mans. This at least had the effect of galvanising Somerset, the king's lieutenant in France since late 1446, into actually preparing to go there. But, even fortified with the dukedom given him on 31 March, he did not arrive until a little while after the loss of Maine. In March, after the fall of Le Mans, at the Treaty of Lavardin, Maine was handed over to the French. Thereafter interest shifted to Brittany. This French Duchy had often been a participant before in the Hundred Years War, especially when rival claimants to the dukedom sought the support of the kings of France and England respectively. This was the state of affairs in 1448, compounded by the fact that the English in Maine who had lost their lands moved into the borderland between Brittany and Normandy. Protracted negotiations for a more lasting peace kept on foundering on the Brittany issue: its allegiance to the king of England in his capacity as king of France and the English occupation of the borderlands.

Then in March 1449 the border fortress of Fougères was seized by the English, an action designed to secure the release of the 'English' claimant to the Duchy which, it seems, had been approved some time before by both Suffolk and Somerset. Surprisingly, negotiations with France continued even after the English had unilaterally broken the truce in this way, but an appeal to Charles VII, king of France, by the French-sponsored duke of Brittany meant that Charles could legitimately attack the English, in alliance with the Bretons. At the end of July Charles announced that he was no longer bound by the Truce of Tours; by early 1450 most of Normandy, including the capital, Rouen, had been overrun; on 15 April

1450 at the Battle of Formigny English resistance in Normandy was effectively ended. On 12 August Cherbourg, the last English bastion, fell. Somerset as commander had done little to avert the disaster, receiving a safe-conduct out of Rouen on its surrender at the end of October in return for humiliating terms, including the surrender of several more fortresses. A combination of indecision and endemic lack of funds ensured that none of these dearly bought extensions of the truce had been used constructively to restore the English position in France.

Why was the fall of Normandy so sudden? Partly, it was the result of years of growing reluctance to fund or fight in the war and of lack of purpose in organising the defence of the Duchy. It is noticeable that the actual sums of money raised from taxes for war fell under the pressure of incessant taxation and military failure: in the eight years from 1428 to 1436 the total was £207,821, while in the seventeen years from 1436 to 1453 it was only marginally higher: £239,500.[12] Moreover, only in 1429–30, when, uniquely, the expedition was led by the king, and 1436, when there was the first real crisis in France, anger against Burgundy and the promise of royal leadership, were taxpayers as generous as they had been under Henry V. In 1449, in the face of a similar, but more serious, crisis in France to that of 1429, the parliamentary Commons were far less generous. It is also significant that in 1449 parliament seemed more concerned with the Scottish border than with the imminent loss of Normandy. If less money came from England then more had to come from France, and the loyalty of the native Normans was sorely tried by the growing burden of demands. There was also a surprising lack of urgency in the military response. From York's first lieutenancy onwards, English commanders had been slow to take up their duties and the government had been slow to replace them. Perhaps an energetic, active king would have had a more galvanising effect. Both defence and its financing became harder as the military front lengthened under French attacks in the years after Arras. Lack of military enthusiasm also undermined the war effort, not just in depriving France of troops but also in placing increasing weight for the defence of the French possessions on the English settlers, which meant that there were not enough influential people in England who cared about what happened on the other side of the channel.

However, the immediate cause was the failure of the English to make good use of the hard-bought truce from 1444. Theoretically, the breathing space of 1444–9 should have given the English the opportunity to re-establish their position in Normandy. Above all, because it was a truce and

---

[12] These figures are from G. Bernard, *War, Taxation and Rebellion: Henry VIII, Wolsey and the Amicable Grant of 1525* (Sussex, 1986), p. 127. There are useful figures for individual taxes from 1437 in R.H. Britnell, 'The Economic Context', *The Wars of the Roses*, ed. A. J. Pollard (London, 1995), pp. 60–1.

not a peace and because annual taxes had already been voted for 1445–9, there should have been an annual surplus of about £30,000 for these years to spend on defence. But, despite the best efforts of Marmaduke Lumley, bishop of Carlisle, who became treasurer in 1446, this money was not used effectively. This was partly because Lumley concentrated on repaying the crown debts, to rebuild lines of credit which had failed badly after Beaufort's death in 1447. That meant that in the emergency of 1449–50 there was no large surplus to draw on. The unavailability of loans from Cardinal Beaufort may have guaranteed somewhat greater consistency in foreign policy but it also meant that there was no substantial source of funds for an emergency. But an added difficulty was that in 1444–5 £4,000 of Duchy of Lancaster lands, enfeoffed between 1443 and 1445, was diverted to pay for Henry VI's foundations of Eton and King's, while substantial lands from the Duchies of Lancaster and Cornwall were assigned to Queen Margaret. Thus funds that had been used to pay much of the costs of the royal household were no longer available. Moreover, with the arrival of the queen, household costs rose rapidly. The result was that from 1444 the annual amount the exchequer had to find for the household increased from £8,000 to £27,000. The exchequer was likely to have to look to taxation for this shortfall, and that both reduced its capacity to fund the war and made taxpayers ever more reluctant to pay taxes which seemed to them to be disappearing into the household. By 1449 the Calais garrison was owed nearly £20,000 in wages. Meanwhile, in Normandy itself, as the delayed arrival of Somerset indicates, the truce was not being used to employ such money as there was to organise better defences. It has indeed been suggested that the discipline of the English troops collapsed during the truce, as soldiers were left unpaid and any semblance of leadership disappeared. To sum up, the lack of leadership in England was the prime cause of the lack of forward planning for France from 1444–9. It also led to the confusion of negotiating positions which hampered the efforts to secure a more permanent peace and to the confusion of policy which produced the breaching of the truce when the English were least ready to defend themselves against the French. Indeed, right through the reign, policy and diplomacy had vacillated between defending Normandy and defending France, until it was too late to defend either.

Before examining the momentous consequences for the king's chief advisers of these disastrous events, we must look at the other charges that have been made by historians against the group around Suffolk. In this account so far, it has been suggested that the government of England in the 1440s should not be seen in these narrow terms, but rather as a determined attempt to find a substitute for a non-operational king. In this the rest of the nobility apart perhaps from Gloucester were fully complicit in one way or another. This explains why the decisions made in foreign policy which we have been examining, flawed as they were, were accepted by all the magnates but Gloucester as the only option, while much of the misjudgement and inconsistency came from the unavoidable differences caused by lack of royal leadership. If that is the case with regard to external affairs, then, by extension, it is likely to apply internally as well; a nobility badly divided by internal feuds could hardly have co-operated over the war. Indeed, the way the Duchy stewardships were handed out amongst the nobles in 1437 indicates that there was an acceptance of corporate responsibility within the realm, as well as outside, even if at that stage they could hardly have foreseen how long it would last. However, there were undeniably serious flaws in the internal administration of England in the 1440s which may seem to fit uneasily with this new interpretation. First there is the matter of royal grants. Too many of these were made, it is said, given the parlous financial circumstances of the monarch, the need to conserve money for war and to impress the Commons with governmental good housekeeping when they were asked for taxes; and too many went to the same people. Mostly this is true, although the scale of grants perhaps seemed especially monstrous because it contrasted with the poverty of the king, who could increasingly barely pay for his own household. Equally, what produced particular hostility was that a small number of donees did spectacularly well. These included Suffolk himself and the king's chamberlain, James Fenys, esquire of the body and later royal chamberlain, created Lord Say in 1447.

All the same, this is only one side of the story. First we must note that others outside the Suffolk circle were in receipt of grants, including most of the great nobility, amongst them York, Buckingham, Warwick and even Gloucester. This we would expect, since we have seen already that there was no gap between the court and the nobles. It is indeed unclear whether one can speak of a court nobility on the one side and the great hereditary families on the other. We have already seen that Buckingham himself owed his dukedom in 1444 to the elevation of nobles related to the royal house. The young Henry Beauchamp earl of Warwick, also made duke in 1444, despite the absence of any blood relationship to the crown, was favoured in his brief period of adulthood from 1444 to 1446. He was also closely linked to some of those most notoriously associated with the court, for example the esquire of the body, John Norreys. Further complexities are revealed by the fact that in local politics, in the centre of his 'country', the west midlands, Warwick was in fact in conflict with Buckingham.[13] We have seen equally that the Duchy stewardships were divided among the nobles in a way that undermines conventional beliefs

---

[13] See below, p. 112.

about divisions between court and country, ins and outs. Then, from the point of view of someone like Suffolk, there was some justification for his rewards. Good service to the crown was meant to bring such benefits, and he himself was neglecting his local interests in East Anglia and the Thames Valley, and probably putting in a very large number of hours, to do something that needed to be done and no-one else was prepared to do. The same could be true of, for example, Sudeley and Lord Beauchamp and possibly even the reviled Adam Moleyns. This was of course a dangerous attitude to take, because the king, not his servants, was supposed to judge the merits and rewards of his servants and it could easily lead to justifying naked greed, but, if there was no king, who was to discriminate?

There were other dangers to Suffolk's system of alternative kingship. These were the household men, often quite meagre, who could exploit the situation purely to their own advantage. Suffolk was exposed in two ways. First there was the very fact of the king's nullity. In medieval England the system for making grants was that would-be recipients drew up the authorisation and got the king to sign it. Unless Suffolk was to put a permanent guard on the king, there was no means of stopping others, beyond those who were authorised, getting to the king and persuading him to append his sign. Even a permanent guard could be suborned because the rewards were so obvious and so easy to obtain. An instance of a relatively lowly household employee who rose rapidly at this time is Thomas Daniel, henchman in 1440, king's esquire by 1444 and recipient of large numbers of grants. Probably using Castle Rising in Norfolk as his power-base, by the later 1440s he was even alleged to be challenging the power of the duke of Suffolk in Norfolk. That in itself shows how it was possible to construct an independent power-base through access to the king. Instances of the grant of the same office or piece of land to two different people are another indication of the ease with which almost anything could be obtained from the king. A notable example, which helped start a major local feud, was of the stewardship of the Duchy of Cornwall. This was given to Sir William Bonville, a prominent west country knight, in 1437, as part of the parcelling-out of stewardships on royal lands in that year. But in 1441 the earl of Devon obtained a rival grant, probably after interference by his Beaufort relatives. Another example is one of Daniel's grants; he was given a fine owed to the crown by someone who had founded a chantry without the royal licence required for making all grants to the church. When Daniel discovered that the money had already been paid to someone else, he was able to obtain reimbursement from the financially hard-pressed crown to the tune of £100.

It may even be that Henry VI's most lasting contribution as king, and the only one which there has been almost consistent agreement to attribute to him personally, the foundation of the colleges[14] of Eton and King's, has to be seen in the same light. Eton was founded in 1440 and King's in 1443, the new feoffment of Duchy lands being made between 1443 and 1445 to support these new foundations. On the face of it this seems a clear-cut case of the pious but otherwise inactive ruler of earlier historiography diverting revenues from urgent necessities to religious self-indulgence. However, there is an intriguing body of evidence suggesting that here too interested parties may have been exploiting royal revenues and grants to their own purposes. For much of the reign the higher clergy were in an unusually pre-eminent position around the king. We saw, in the context of the minority, that this was a likely outcome when the king was inactive, because it was clerics who could afford the time to be constantly about the king, but the point would hold equally good for Henry VI's majority. There was in fact a rash of collegiate foundations, several of them in the 1440s, made and supported by a close-knit group of clerics associated with the household and with Suffolk, and some of these were dominant among the Duchy feoffees of 1443–5. The group included William Wainflete, the first Provost of Eton and Cardinal Beaufort's successor as bishop of Winchester, who founded Magdalen College, Oxford, and Henry Chichele, the Archbishop of Canterbury, who founded All Souls College, Oxford. Both were responsible for several other foundations. Suffolk himself helped with the establishment of both Eton and King's and set up his own college at Ewelme, Oxfordshire in 1437. It is thus perfectly possible, if the interpretation of Henry's nullity offered here is accepted, that these clerics were using the king and his realm's resources on behalf of the church, in the same way as the lesser household men on behalf of themselves. Suffolk may have been actively assisting them but it is difficult to see that he can have had much enthusiasm for the way Duchy revenues were taken, given his problems in financing the war. It may be in fact that Suffolk had no choice but to give these men their head: clerics could not only afford to stay close to the king but the nature of their jobs, as confessors and spiritual guides, could give them undue influence over him. That Henry's household clerics did very well out of him can be judged by the unusual number who obtained bishoprics during his majority.

This brings us to the second reason that Suffolk was to some extent at the mercy of even relatively menial people within the household. If he was to make his rule work, he needed the backing of the lesser administrators and servants, and could not afford to hold out against their demands for

---

[14] A 'college' at this period meant an institution to commemorate and pray for its founders and their families while often providing education for poor boys.

offices around the king or grants for themselves or their friends. He was *not* king and therefore did need to purchase the support that came to the monarch naturally. There was undeniably a considerable expansion of the royal household in the 1440s; for instance, there were 176 esquires and valets of the king's hall and chamber in 1437–9, which had risen to 256 by 1451–2. At the same time, the coherence of retaining by the crown diminished. This was particularly noticeable in the Duchy of Lancaster regions. In several of these there was a rebuilding of the Duchy following, which had tended to languish during the minority, but it proved impossible to recreate the effective local networks focused on Duchy retainers of the first two Lancastrian kings. Former Lancastrian stalwarts were often absorbed into the followings of the nobles, like Buckingham and Cromwell, who were now taking up the Duchy's regional authority and, although some of them were also retained by the Duchy, there was no directional force from the king/duke. We shall see shortly that this absence of local leadership could have disruptive consequences.

A second accusation that may reasonably be made against Suffolk's rule is the perversion of justice, notably by using control of the king to concentrate local offices in the hands of the courtiers' friends and associates. Lack of justice led to disorder, as victims took the law into their own hands. The two best-known examples are East Anglia and Kent. We know about the first from the Paston letters, which show particular concern about the activities of Suffolk's men in Norfolk and Suffolk. We know about the second from the Cade rebels of 1450, who lynched the prominent courtiers, James Fenys Lord Say and William Crowmer, sheriff of Kent in 1444–5 and 1449–50, for their alleged part in local misgovernance. Other evidence includes charges in parliament against William Tailboys, a friend of Viscount Beaumont, for malpractice in Lincolnshire, and, allegedly, protection of Tailboys by Beaumont and Suffolk against investigation; and a number of petitions made after Suffolk's fall, claiming the direct abuse of royal power at the centre and in the shires by men close to the king like Ayscough.

It would be foolish to deny the force of this evidence, but we should all the same exercise care in its use. Petitions in parliament and chancery against men who have fallen from power must be treated with a certain amount of circumspection. That does not mean that they are all to be disregarded, for it would not be possible for some of the lowlier victims to protest until their enemies were powerless. But lying behind the articles against Tailboys is Lord Cromwell, a careerist royal official, who had been part of Cardinal Beaufort's circle, and had then, like others linked to the cardinal, moved into the new power structures based on the household.

Here we have an example of the caution required in handling the evidence against Suffolk and his associates and an indication of a further problem already touched on in relation to Henry Beauchamp duke of Warwick and the duke of Buckingham. This was the inevitable tendency for those around the king to divide among themselves when there was no effective monarch to do the essential job of wielding authority over his influential subjects. It is, moreover, worth noting that Cromwell himself had been as formidable a manipulator of the law as any of those accused in 1450 and that the crisis of that year gave him the chance to succeed Lord Say as the king's chamberlain and recover any ground he might have lost at court. We await a full study of Kent in the 1440s, but must assume that the commons of Kent would not have gone to London nor turned into a lynch-mob without good reason. They did however have plenty of others, in taxation and neglect of coastal defences, and whether the gentry of Kent felt as outraged as the commons by the rule of Crowmer, Say and others remains to be seen.

The Pastons in their letters give us the most graphic account of what it felt like to be on the wrong side in a region where the friends of Suffolk were all-powerful. As Margaret Paston wrote, probably in 1449, 'Sondery folks have seyd to me that they thynk veryly, but if ye have my Lord of Suffolks godelorchyp, qhyll the werd [world] is as itt is, ye kan never leven in pese ...'[15] This seems to endorse the long-held belief in the version of events offered by the Pastons: that Suffolk usurped the traditional power in the region of the dukes of Norfolk and used it dictatorially to the benefit of his own friends and the undoing of Norfolk's. But here again we need caution, for it has now been shown that this is a one-sided view and much of it was brought to public attention after Suffolk's fall. It is true that the power that came from the Duchy of Lancaster lands in Norfolk was exploited to give Suffolk and his affinity dominance of that county. It is equally true that John Heydon and Thomas Tuddenham, Suffolk's principal local agents and Duchy officers, exercised formidable control over East Anglia, and that the local administrative offices were by and large filled with Suffolk's men. However, it is now apparent that there was a long-standing crown connection in East Anglia, built up under Henry IV and V, consisting of the Duchy interest, of nobles closely related to the king, notably Henry V's half-uncle, Thomas Beaufort duke of Exeter, and of other nobles and leading gentry who served the king. Suffolk, as leading Duchy officer, royal servant and local nobleman, was in many ways legitimate heir to this power-base. Similarly, the reviled Tuddenham and Heydon were long-serving Duchy officers long before they came into

---

[15] *Paston Letters*, ed. Gairdner, v, p. 75. The letter is here dated to 1463 but more convincingly attributed to 1449 in the Davis edn (i, p. 236).

Suffolk's orbit. The interlopers were actually people like the socially climbing Pastons, Sir John Fastolf – the returned soldier, using his war profits to purchase lands – and the duke of Norfolk, whose family, despite the title, had never had any real influence in the region. Moreover, a careful analysis of events reveals that much of the reason for Suffolk's dominance was the crass incompetence of the duke of Norfolk. Certainly, all the principal victims and opponents of the Suffolk circle that we meet in the Paston letters in the 1440s, notably the Pastons themselves and their employer Sir John Fastolf, were under Norfolk's protection, but the duke himself was too ineffectual to help them. The feebleness of his lordship is shown by the fact that for much of the 1440s he himself was at odds with two of his own closest supporters in East Anglia, Robert Wingfield and William Brandon. We should also note that Fastolf, like Cromwell, had been no mean exploiter of the law, and that his troubles over his property could be seen as another case of the biter bit.

What is noteworthy is that the received picture of East Anglian politics throughout the 1440s really only applies to the very last phase of Suffolk's rule, from about 1448. It was then that the Suffolk group began to get a complete stranglehold on the region. This coincides with the attempt by Robert Hungerford Lord Moleyns to make a most dubious claim to the Paston manor of Gresham with the full weight of the government behind him. He was a Wiltshire landowner with no interests in East Anglia, but a close associate of the court. It also coincides with the main series of attacks on Fastolf's properties which Fastolf attributed to Suffolk and his East Anglian associates, including the queen's household official Sir Edward Hull. Similarly, in Lincolnshire the more extreme activities of Tailboys, under the protection of Beaumont, also date to this time. Here we indubitably see the unacceptable face of Suffolk's rule, but it may not be entirely the norm. It is possible that it was around this time that Suffolk began a panic-stricken effort to secure his power-bases in England, should he be called to account. This would have been because he sensed that foreign affairs were moving beyond his control; that some of the nobility were getting extremely cold feet in the wake of the refusal to surrender of the English in Maine, and were neither leading expeditions nor participating any more in decision-making; that there was more generally a growing division in his power-base around the king, caused by unease over foreign policy and the progressive effects of absence of royal rule. This may have been particularly urgent if Suffolk had been unable to exert influence personally in the shires because of his almost constant presence at the court. Thus, he may have felt obliged to support men like Moleyns, or Tailboys, with his powerful protector, Lord Beaumont, or to allow too many grants. This was perhaps the price to be paid for their backing for

Suffolk's governance of the kingdom on the king's behalf, and especially so when the duke felt under threat.

Although we still know all too little of what really happened in the shires in the 1440s, it is significant that most of the evidence we have suggests a lack of local stability rather than overbearing control from the centre exercised by Suffolk. That would be in keeping with the source of government, for, as the minority had shown, the one thing only a king could do was bring order to the realm. His role in this respect began of course with the resolution of disputes among the nobles. Henry VI's principal contribution to the avoidance of noble conflict in the 1440s was one of the absurd duplicate grants that has been mentioned, giving Thomas Courtenay, earl of Devon, effectively the same Duchy of Cornwall stewardship that had already been granted to Sir William Bonville in 1437. This was the immediate catalyst for the Courtenay–Bonville feud, which had been threatening for some time and was to rumble on right through the 1440s, reaching crisis proportions in the following decade.[16] Both parties jockeyed for position with the duke of Suffolk, so more peaceable behaviour could be forced on neither, and in 1446 and 1449 the judicial records reveal rising levels of local violence. In the north, for most of the 1440s, the Percies, the family of the earls of Northumberland, were in conflict with Cardinal Kemp, archbishop of York and former chancellor. In Bedfordshire, the local tension between Grey and Fanhope that had caused the near-riot of 1437 culminated in 1439 in an actual riot, when, in a similar situation to that of 1437, Fanhope and his men gatecrashed the sessions of the peace in Bedford town hall and eighteen people were killed. In Warwickshire there was a power vacuum almost throughout the 1440s, caused by a series of minorities in the family of the Beauchamps, earls of Warwick. This led to conflict for control of the shire among a group of magnates who were all in some way connected with the court, with all the attendant disorder among the gentry one would expect. The Courtenay/Bonville feud also reflects the failure of the king in the regions where he was a great noble as well as king. In the Duchy of Lancaster regions things seem to have been as bad as in the Duchy of Cornwall. The failure of Duchy rule can be shown in Nottinghamshire, Derbyshire and Staffordshire. Attempts to fill the vacuum in Duchy regions by magnates like Cromwell in Nottinghamshire and Buckingham in Staffordshire and Derbyshire seem to have caused only further local division, violence and political confusion. The royal duke of Lancaster, the natural ruler, was not there, but ironically, without reinforcement from either the duke of Lancaster or the king, no-one could properly take his place.

---

[16] See below, pp. 126, 139.

Arguably, much of the perversion of royal justice and favour should be seen in these terms: a collapse of kingly direction which made impossible demands in terms of both probity and command on those who were trying to provide a proxy authority. What the 1440s shows is why a king was needed and, by implication, that there was none, not even the half-hearted and periodic interferer of the present orthodoxy. It also shows the impossibility of acting to remedy the defects of an adult ruler for, once accepted as such, he could be judged by God alone and no-one therefore had the right officially to stand in for him. In this case there had been collusion to pretend there was a king, but in 1449–50 the fiction was exposed. It was at this point that the nation woke up collectively to what had been allowed to happen. The common people, along with the gentry and greater townsmen represented by the Commons in parliament, all of whom seem to have assumed that this was a responsible government directed by the king, suddenly found that it was not what they had supposed. They had been voting, and paying, taxes in huge quantities that had led to ignominious defeat and they wanted to know why. They had in some cases been enduring a level of disorder and abuse of the law that was not acceptable, and the failure in France led them to ask why this too had been allowed to happen. The parliament summoned in February 1449 to grant a tax in face of the impending crisis in Normandy was dismissed in July, having offered little financial support. Later that year, when the full extent of the débâcle was being revealed, the nation went for the most obvious culprits. The parliament that met in November 1449 named Suffolk as the cause of the French disaster. In January 1450 Adam Moleyns, despite being a bishop, was murdered by soldiers at Portsmouth. In February the impeachment[17] of Suffolk began. In spring and summer there was a series of risings in southern England, culminating in Cade's rebellion in June and July, when London was taken over by the Kentish mob and Say and Crowmer met their ends. The objects of the rebels were the 'fals progenye and affinite of the duc of Suffolke',[18] who were held responsible for the loss of France. Demands included that the king take the great nobles into his counsels, that the crown revenues that had been granted away be restored and that local abuse of office by household men be punished. There were other disturbances over much of southern England. In June Ayscough, bishop of Salisbury, had been murdered by a mob in the capital of his diocese.

The nobility were also having to re-evaluate the 1440s. It seems that, despite the evidence for their increasing concern from 1448 about what

[17] This was the form of parliamentary trial by which the Commons acted as accusers and the Lords as jury.

[18] *The Politics of Fifteenth-Century England: John Vale's Book*, ed. M. Kekewich, C. Richmond, A. Sutton, L. Visser-Fuchs, J. Watts (Stroud, 1995), p. 206.

they had agreed to in foreign policy, the outbreak of popular feeling at all levels took them by surprise. This does not speak well for their listening abilities in the shires during this decade, but they may have been so overwhelmed by the cares of government and war, and so determined to ignore the ill-effects of the rule they were endorsing, that they did not wish to know. Above all, they were confronted by the fact that they had made a series of decisions, or at least agreed to them, each one inexorably dictated by the last, that had led to total disaster in France, and that the nation was now calling for heads to roll. The evidence is that they decided to make Suffolk the sacrificial victim, protecting others like Ayscough on whom vengeance was demanded, and doing no more than sending Suffolk into exile under the king's protection. They then had to rewrite the history of the 1440s, something which York himself was to do in the 1450s and the Yorkist chroniclers were to complete after 1461. York himself was singularly fortunate, for he had at last left for Ireland in June 1449 and was therefore untainted by the revelations of governmental perfidy that began with the attack on Normandy the following month. The myth that it was Suffolk and his men, not the ancient nobility, of whom York was the greatest, that had led England to ignominious failure can already been seen at work in the choice of speaker for the parliament of November 1449. He was Sir John Popham, York's annuitant. The myth gained ground, in parliament and in the popular consciousness, during the momentous events of 1450, above all in the constant iteration that York should be the king's chief adviser. For the nobility who could free themselves from the association with Suffolk it was the perfect let-out and deflection of popular wrath. Suffolk, saved from impeachment and sent into exile, was intercepted as he sailed from England in a ship named the 'Nicholas of the Tower', forced to land and then and there beheaded with a rusty sword. His executioners, who had evidently been reading some constitutional history, rejected the king's safe-conduct, saying, 'they did not know the king, but they well knew the crown of England, saying that the aforesaid crown was the community of the said realm, and that the community of the realm was the crown of that realm'.[19]

That was the trouble: the truth, that there was no king, was now out and the question was what was to be put in his place. Searching for a solution was to be the central matter of the politics of the 1450s. Suffolk, not a great man, and doubtless by no means immune to the temptation that had been put in his way, should be rescued from opprobrium and given credit for taking on an impossible job. We can sum up what has been said about his difficulties by noting the constitutional impropriety of his position. In

---

[19] Quoted in R. Virgoe, 'The Death of William de la Pole, Duke of Suffolk', *Bulletin of the John Rylands Library*, 47 (1964–5), p. 499.

directing affairs from the centre and in exploiting his local authority, he was both a noble, a man who expected to argue for his own interests and those of his followers, and king, the man who was supposed to contain noble ambitions, so that none could use his power to destroy another. Acting for the Duchy in East Anglia, he was also a king trying, like Henry IV, to reconcile his impartial public authority to his private and partial authority as a noble. It was an insoluble situation that carried the seeds of its own destruction even before the failure in France precipitated the crisis. Looked at from this perspective, it can be maintained that there is no evidence that there was anything at the centre of power all through the 1440s but a vacancy. New work on the decade has certainly shown that foreign policy was known and approved by the nobility and was not the private creation of Suffolk; that there was no clear distinction between a courtier nobility and an excluded 'ancient' nobility; and that there is a radically different reading of East Anglian politics from the one offered us by the Pastons. Taken together, all the evidence points to the idea that, some time between 1437 and 1443 or 1444, it was realised that the king would never become an adult except in name, and that the nobles, directed by Suffolk, decided to shoulder the burden of rule, just as they had done under Bedford in the minority. After the momentous events of 1450, the new candidate to take up the vacant royal authority was to be the duke of York, but he was not the only one, and politics were to move from the precarious preservation of unity under a sham king to total disunity under a king about whom there was no pretending any more.

6

THE ROAD TO WAR: 1450–1455

On the face of it, the 1450s seem quite simple: growing internal violence and a steady descent into civil war concluded by the deposition of Henry VI and the accession of the Yorkist Edward IV in 1461. But closer examination reveals rather less coherence. The seeds of confrontation were already there in 1450, and we must therefore consider why they took so long to germinate. Then, although the Wars of the Roses are normally thought to have started with the first battle of St Albans in 1455, there followed four years of uneasy truce. Arguably the Wars did not really begin until late 1459, with the encounter at Blore Heath. Indeed, during the 1450s, politics seem to have progressively less coherence. More baffling still is the mode of deposition. On both previous occasions, 1327 and 1399, the king's military power had just melted away, exemplifying royal dependence on landowners' support for military security. In this instance, however, Edward IV had to make good his claim to the throne in battle and even then his position remained under threat until the Lancastrians were finally disposed of in 1471. All these facts require explanation and all of them have their roots in the events of 1450–5.

The period from 1450 until the first battle of St Albans in May 1455 was dominated by the deteriorating relations between the dukes of York and Somerset. We have seen that it now seems to be unwise to date this situation to the 1440s. Although York later made great play with Somerset's loss of France and more generally with the misconduct of the war in the 1440s, it is clear that he neither resented Somerset's succession to his command in 1446 nor resisted the inexorable progress towards the surrender of Maine. It is equally clear that in the 1440s Somerset was far from identified with Suffolk in either internal politics or the conduct of the war. What York was doing from 1450, apart from taking care to distance himself from the disasters of the 1440s, was to ally himself retrospectively with what was becoming the cause of 'good duke Humphrey' of Gloucester.

To understand why this should be, and the larger issue of the York–Somerset animosity in the 1450s, we need to start not in the 1440s but in 1450. We must remember that York was in Ireland when he first heard of the occurrences of 1449–50. In its combination of overwhelming opposition in parliament and violent rebellion in the country at large, this was one of the worst crises in the history of medieval England. All the nobility must have felt shaken to the core, especially in view of the fact that we must now accept their acquiescence in the governance and policies that had caused it. What would have made it particularly humiliating and alarming for them is that it showed that, in their anxiety to maintain unity and the semblance of rule in the 1440s, they had lost their ability to act as links between the centre and the provinces. They, who should have spoken for the gentry, had allowed themselves to be led into a course of conduct that was being rejected wholesale by the rest of the political nation. That this rejection was shared by the lower orders, and indeed demonstrated in their own way, made it even more alarming, since all landowners were normally at one in not allowing those at the bottom of the social hierarchy an independent voice.

York may have been especially embarrassed at his co-operation with the government of the 1440s because of the nature of his political following. Because his estates were so widespread, many of them in France, and he had been in England for so little of his adult life, he had never built up a strongly localised affinity based on his lands in England. Unusually, several of his leading retainers, including Sir John Fastolf, Sir Edmund Mulso and Sir William Oldhall, had either come to him through service in France or hitherto been primarily employed by him in France. Not only was the defeat personally humiliating to them but some had lost lands and offices in France and so it behoved York to stand as the defender of English interests there. Consequently, York found himself unable to resist when his name was bandied about as the saviour of the realm. According to the mythology that the nobility were rapidly finding themselves obliged to endorse in 1450, it was York who would restore the rule of 'the trewe lordis of his [the king's] roiall blood of this his reaume'.[1] If it could henceforth be openly admitted that someone would have to stand in for the king, York

---

[1] This is a quotation from the Cade manifesto: see *John Vale's Book*, p. 206.

was ready to elect himself to such a position. He would take over Gloucester's place as heir presumptive and Gloucester's self-proclaimed political position as the man who might have saved France.

It is not necessary to see York as 'greedy' or 'self-seeking' or in some way using ideas concerning the need for better rule as a cloak for personal ambition. To argue in this way, as many historians have done, is to forget two things. One is that it is very rare for human beings to be moved by a single intention; usually, even if they have strong personal motives for their actions, they take pains to provide justifications for themselves, let alone for the outside world. The other is the nature of the fifteenth-century body politic. It demanded an active king; as a nobleman York would have been perfectly aware of this and, as a landowner, he, as much as anyone, needed the internal order that effective kingship alone could bring. As a nobleman he would have inherited beliefs grounded on education, on awareness of the mutually beneficial relationship with the gentry, on a sense of the importance, even self-importance, given the nobles by their key role in the polity, that would lead him to believe in his duty to intervene. No doubt much of this was self-deceiving, but what matters is the fact of the deceit and the language in which York's case was put. In the end we cannot see into the hearts of people long dead – it is hard enough to see into the hearts of the living – but what we can do is ask why they took up certain political positions and used certain kinds of political language.

If we do this in the case of York, it is apparent that he was taking what might be called a 'populist' stand, just as Duke Humphrey, with his appeals to the Commons in parliament and his popularity with the commons of London, had done. York's constant harping on the loss of France in the attacks on Somerset should be seen in this light, rather than as the root cause of the animosity. In a sense France was less a rallying-point in itself than symbolic of the wider anti-household stance inherited from Glouces-ter. This is evident in the fact that York was unable to retain the allegiance of several of the veterans of France, many of whom predictably believed loyalty to the crown should take precedence over personal outrage. But his reason for accepting this political inheritance must in large measure be seen as the response to the calls made in 1449–50 for vengeance for the loss of France and 'good governance' at home. It was for this reason that, unlike Duke Humphrey, whose opposition was always focused on France, he espoused both causes. It is arguable indeed that, apart from the dishonesty of the rewriting of his role in the 1440s, the real charge against York should be the self-importance that led him to believe he must be the natural and only arbiter of the nation's destinies.

Unfortunately both for York and ultimately for the realm of England,

Somerset had already claimed that position for himself even before the duke could return home. Somerset also had a perfectly valid platform. He was in fact the king's closest relative through the male line, and, had the family not been barred from succession because of its illegitimacy, he, not York, would have been the heir presumptive.[2] He and his family had a strong tradition of loyalty to the Lancastrians, which was more than could be said for York, the son and nephew of traitors.[3] If York had served in France, so had the Beauforts, in numbers, not to mention the loans from Cardinal Beaufort that had kept the whole affair afloat. And Somerset had one priceless asset over York, the lack of a large landed estate that was otherwise the bane of the Beauforts. If the cynic might suspect that this was good reason to control a king on whose grants this magnate was so unusually dependent, it also meant that, unlike York, he could afford to give the king constant personal attendance. This was essential to the maintenance of consistent policies and could usually be achieved only by clergy and professional administrators. York, on the other hand, would have to spend at least part of the time on his estates if he was to prevent mismanagement on his lands and assure himself of a local power-base. York was also in the very dangerous position that his cause, including the identification of the duke himself with good governance, had first been espoused by the mob, from whom he would have to distinguish himself. Although the cause was endorsed by the respectable element represented in the Commons, influential people were unlikely to forget its origins. To the landed interest, when he returned from Ireland, as if in answer to the mob's call, he looked potentially traitorous right from the start.

Perhaps the most persuasive argument in Somerset's favour is that it was he who stepped into the breach in 1450 when for anyone to take responsibility for government, not least the man who had just lost Normandy, was a major act of courage. The king, who had fled from the Kentish rebels, did not re-enter London until the end of July. Somerset was in the king's counsels by the middle of August, a fortnight after returning to London with his defeated troops. During the period before York's return efforts were made to restore the still greatly disturbed country to some kind of order. Commissions were issued to investigate the abuses alleged against the household, and the Paston letters suggest that there was some real hope that they might be effective. The trouble was that, like Suffolk's,

---

[2] This is on the assumption that, as was the case with York, the claims of females and claims through females to be heir presumptive were, if possible, to be ignored, on the grounds that they raised embarrassing questions about the rights of the reigning Lancastrians (see above, p. 67). If they were not, then Margaret Beaufort was the Beaufort heir to the throne.

[3] His uncle, the duke of York who died at Agincourt, had been involved in a major rebellion against Henry IV at the start of the reign and lucky to escape punishment.

Somerset's substitute rule had to be dependent on the household; that was where the seat of power lay and where the actual administrators were to be found. And like Suffolk he found there was a price to be paid, in allowing the members of the household to continue to receive rewards and to use the judicial system for their own ends. It was the same situation as in the 1440s: if the king was ruler in name only but was nevertheless still officially in command, it was impossible to prevent some degree of free-for-all with royal authority.

The recovery of the household as a political force after its collective shocks can be seen at three levels. First there was the Act of Resumption of May 1450. This bill, designed to cancel all royal grants made under Henry VI, was the condition of any further taxation. Money was still needed urgently to try and salvage something from Normandy and to preserve the remaining English possessions in the south of France. However, it proved impossible to prevent the act being weakened by a huge number of exemptions, mostly of household men, such as Sudeley and Lord Beauchamp. Secondly, further grants, including some of those just resumed, went to members of the household. Thirdly, we can see in the Paston letters the disappointment of the politically excluded of the 1440s as their opponents began to recover power by early 1451 and the reformatory commissions issued during 1450 were shown to be toothless. In September 1450, Lord Moleyns, the Pastons' enemy, was given a special royal protection to preserve him from the Pastons' vengeance, on the dubious grounds that he was serving elsewhere as a special judicial commissioner. The Duchy interest remained the most considerable political force in East Anglia, and, after the initial shocks, its leadership was taken up by Suffolk's widow and by Lord Scales, an associate of Suffolk in the 1440s.

By September therefore, before York had even returned to England, two rival poles of authority had been set up as alternatives to replace the defunct authority of the king. Somerset's was very much the inheritor of Suffolk's, not just in personnel but also in its location in the royal household, at the very seat of power. It stood, ideologically speaking, for the ancient and conventional virtue of obedience to the ruler and, even if there was no active kingship behind Somerset's rule, his overt justification for his actions was always the king's personal authority. York's was something new. It was founded on the notion of the common weal, or common good, and represented the legitimate opposition of the non-household nobility and of the lesser ranks of political society, gentry and townsmen. In taking this stance, he had to be careful to separate himself from the illegitimate opposition of the mob, something he took pains to do as soon as he arrived back in England. He stood for financial probity and good management as a precondition of taxation, and therefore for continued support for the war effort, and for proper enforcement of law and order. Much more than Somerset, who generally was able to hide behind the king, York stood for collective conciliar action. We shall see that in some ways this made his approach better suited to times of extreme crisis, but his programme had a fundamental weakness. Whatever his professions of obedience and assertions that he was attacking 'evil men' around the king rather than the king himself, he could not disguise two truths. First, by opposing the site of authority in the realm, he was risking the creation of still greater disorder, and secondly it was almost as difficult to claim that he was not opposing the king himself.

The trouble was that it was far from clear that most of the nobles really saw York as the country's saviour, once they had got over the shocks of 1449–50, unless they believed themselves to be excluded from power and reward. The Nevilles, for instance, were happily linked in to the court at this stage, just as they and all the magnates except Gloucester, including York, had been in the 1440s. That York was standing on a platform initially erected by the feared common people must have made it yet more unappealing. It is also probable that the only way to proxy rule, as long as the king was nominally in charge, was Somerset's, via the household. On the other hand, York made it very difficult for Somerset to rule. He was espousing the cause of all those who resented the rule of the group round the king and of those who, for personal or simply patriotic reasons, deplored the loss of France, and were prepared to blame Somerset for it. This was a far from insignificant constituency. With hindsight we can see that substituting for the king could only be done if there was an unspoken agreement not to break ranks, as there had more or less been among the nobility in the 1440s. It also helped that during that decade there had been ignorance in the rest of the country about the true state of affairs in relation to the king, which had largely protected the alternative rulers. Now there was neither unanimity nor ignorance. It is arguable that the loss of unity was the real significance of the loss of France. The driving force behind the generally united façade of the 1440s had been the need to prevent dissension while France was to be defended. Once it had been lost, there would be recrimination over the cause and a diminishing requirement to submerge conflict in the name of the general good. Both York and Somerset claimed the right to rule and neither could deliver total dominance of the country. By the time York arrived in England in early September 1450, both dukes had argued themselves into corners from which neither could escape without either unacceptable loss of face or the destruction of the other. Meanwhile, the nobility were in most cases caught between the two, unwilling to see either destroy the other but finding it ever harder to resolve differences in a situation which positively invited disharmony. That is the basis of events up to St Albans.

Partisan positions were immediately taken up when York's return was met by the appointment of Somerset as constable of England. According to York, household men were sent to waylay him as he passed through the royal territory of north Wales in early September. Whether this was really the case or whether, as is more probably true, a delegation was simply being sent to establish the cause of his return is immaterial, if York thought he was under threat. This region and the adjacent royal earldom of Chester had come very firmly under the control of household men in the later 1440s, notably Beauchamp of Powick, Sudeley and the Stanleys, a prominent Cheshire and Lancashire family. It could therefore seem to York quite dangerous territory to cross on his return. The fact that William Tresham, a Northamptonshire esquire, was actually murdered later in the month while allegedly going to join the duke as he journeyed towards London would have given substance to York's suspicions.[4] It seems most likely that there was a general air of alarm among both the followers of York and the members of the household, especially as the latter were still on the defensive in the aftermath of the events of 1450. By the time York reached London in late September, with a retinue numbering perhaps several thousand, he had committed himself to an anti-household stance. At first the bills that he submitted to the king as he moved towards London were purely defensive, denying the traitorous intentions that he claimed were being alleged against him. If such allegations were indeed being made, there was every reason for them. He had returned without permission, had taken it upon himself effectively to imprison a leading member of the household, Sutton of Dudley, in his own castle at Ludlow and was gathering a threatening force as he rode to the king's capital. His third bill, circulated widely in London, initiated the attack on the governance of those around the king and was effectively a Yorkist manifesto. It was not, as his biographer has said, that he 'posed as the champion of "reform"';[5] he *was* the champion of reform. As we have seen, he had no other political constituency. An interview with the king brought no more than a vague promise to establish a means of taking proper counsel.

York left London and, as the capital grew increasingly disturbed, his next attack was launched through parliament. This reconvened in London early in November, largely to give an answer to the increasingly urgent request for funds for Gascony. The speaker was York's chamberlain, Sir

---

[4] Tresham was a household man and the murder was caused primarily by a local feud, so his widow's claim, made to parliament in 1450–1, may reflect her efforts to incite antagonism towards her murderers rather than the actual truth.

[5] P. Johnson, *Duke Richard of York 1411–60* (Oxford, 1988), p. 85.

William Oldhall, an indication that the duke's appeal to the country at large was having some effect. Another is the Commons' request to have a number of people, the list headed by Somerset, removed from about the king's person. Towards the end of the month York arrived in London for the parliament with a large force, and it is probable that it was his arrival that precipitated the violent anti-household outburst in the Commons and on the streets of London at the beginning of December. This was essentially a protest at the loss of Normandy, directed especially at the duke of Somerset, who was put in the Tower for his own safety. If York had any deliberate hand in these events, as he may have done in the Commons' contribution, he was most unwise. London and much of the country around it was ready to erupt again and the new developments threatened to bring things to a head. They also tarred him further with the brush of traitorous incitement of the commons. It seems that most of the rest of the nobles were now regarding York with the suspicion previously reserved for Gloucester: a rabble-rouser whose egoism made effective corporate rule impossible. A newly discovered fourth bill presented by York on his original entry into London in September had been specifically designed to allay such fears by making the 'reformist' case to the Lords, but this parliament was only strengthening them. Even before parliament dispersed for Christmas and York lost his power-base in the Commons, he was placed on a commission to execute justice on the Kent rebels, an appointment which must surely be seen as a means of forcing him to declare his abhorrence of the lower orders' actions. Significantly, this commission apparently failed to act. Once parliament had recessed, the lords were able to regain the initiative. Somerset was released soon after and in January 1451, not long after parliament had reconvened, the king and most of the nobles departed.

Their destination was Kent, where there had been an attempt at another rising, which some believed to be York's creation. After a period in which there seem to have been two rival sources of authority for governmental directives, York had to admit defeat and there began what has been seen as a personal effort at effective rule by the king. Leaving aside the extreme improbability that Henry, at the age of almost thirty, would suddenly have discovered an appetite for government, what was done in his name reflects Somerset's necessary response to York. In January Somerset went to Kent as leader of a commission, accompanied by the king and a large and armed following, which finally did exemplary justice on the rebels. It was followed by others in the other rebellious southern counties. Household men were saved from the commissions of the previous year, by pardon or acquittal. The commission in Kent was actually used to indict the household's principal adversaries in East Anglia, including the Pastons, for improper maintenance of the investigatory commission in Norfolk. The object of this was to force them to abandon their own litigation. In May, an attempt by York's attorney, the MP Thomas Yonge, to have the duke officially named heir presumptive was rebuffed. This should not be seen as an indication of York's ambitions regarding the throne, but rather that he realised that official recognition of this sort would greatly have enhanced his case to be put in charge of the government. Rejection shows the strength of Somerset's position. Somerset was not only successfully disciplining those who might have looked to York for leadership, both commons and gentry, but also stealing York's reformer's clothes and hence his political constituency. Parliament's request for an Act of Resumption with teeth was finally granted in June, when a limited amount of banishment of non-noble household men was also agreed to. On the basis of this new financial prudence, attempts were made to get an expedition to Gascony, where Charles VII, having finished with Normandy, was ready to complete his conquest of the English. Here the government was unsuccessful, because it was still not possible to raise enough money from either loans or taxation. By July 1451, there was little hope for Gascony and increasing concern about Calais.

Nevertheless, the extent of Somerset's achievement can be seen in York's response, which was to stay away on his estates while engaging in acts that were openly defiant of royal authority, either himself or by proxy. During 1451, if we are to believe the charges later made against him, Sir William Oldhall became engaged in what look like near-treasonable activities in London and at York's castle of Fotheringhay, in Northamptonshire. York himself took it upon himself in September 1451 to intervene unauthorised by royal commission in the further dispute between Courtenays and Bonvilles in Somerset. In a sense his action was quite proper, in that something had to be done, and for York it was a means of demonstrating that he could still make a stand for good rule. But it was impolitic, especially if Oldhall really was guilty of such dubious exploits, for such unofficial intervention intensified the belief that York was really a rebel, just like the Kentish men. And it gave Somerset the chance to show that he too could restore order. In the same month he took the king and an imposing gathering of nobles to Coventry, where he dealt with Bonville and other major disturbers of the peace, acting in his case with the proper authority of the royal government.

By February 1452 York felt in some danger and decided to mobilise his considerable military forces and march on the king to demand the removal of Somerset. In anticipation of what York might do, Oldhall had already been forcibly removed from sanctuary in London where he had fled. The king, also accompanied by a considerable force, moved to meet York. On

1 March the two sides encountered one another in Kent, the royal forces at Blackheath and York's a few miles away at Dartford. York submitted to negotiation and agreed to dismiss his forces on the understanding that he would be allowed to make his charges against Somerset to the king. These consisted of an unconvincing wholesale denunciation of Somerset for all the losses in France and, after delivering them, York was taken back to London, effectively a prisoner, under escort with the king. There he was made publicly to swear allegiance. This was followed by a commission to Kent, led by the earl of Shrewsbury,[6] to deal with risings linked to the confrontation in Kent. In April 1452, a general pardon was issued to draw a line under all the events of 1450–2. The implication that there would be a return to normality was clear and this was emphasised by the announcement already made earlier in the year that the king himself would lead an expedition to save Gascony.

Although the expedition came to nothing, the semblance of active kingship continued. Despite the pardon, much of the rest of the year, from June onwards, and the early part of 1453 was taken up with a royal judicial progress concentrated in the main regions where York had lands: mostly the Welsh border counties and eastern England. Whatever the truth of the accusations of treason against the duke's men and others implicated in the confrontation of 1452, the object was clearly to demonstrate the inviolability of the king's authority. Like the plan to lead the army abroad, this was kingship from Henry as it had never been seen before, and must surely be interpreted as Somerset's response to the challenge of York. To make York's claims even more untenable, an expedition that had finally been despatched to Gascony under the earl of Shrewsbury in October 1452 had had remarkable and unexpected success in recovering lost territory. That York had lost the very people whose interests he claimed to represent is evident in the enthusiastic and remarkably generous parliament which met at Reading in March 1453. Besides granting a large amount of taxation, the gathering made its hostility to attacks on the royal household quite plain, not least by attainting William Oldhall, who lost his estates, although not his life.

York had been wholly unable to deprive Somerset of the position of stand-in for the king. So convincing had Somerset been that York, finding no legitimate grounds for opposition, had been forced to resort to means that merely emphasised the illegitimacy of his whole position. The continued endorsement of Somerset by the nobility, including the 'great and ancient' houses allegedly damaged by his rule, was exemplification of the situation. Nevilles, Staffords and others were happy to co-operate with

---

[6] This was the war hero Lord Talbot, who had been promoted to an earldom in 1442.

Somerset and with 'courtier nobles', like Viscount Beaumont and a new force on the scene, the earl of Wiltshire. The latter was the heir of the earl of Ormond and thus an Irish landowner but he also had lands in England. He had a previous history of allegiance to York but in 1453 he was given York's lieutenancy in Ireland. Of the major nobility only the duke of Norfolk and earl of Devon had shown any disposition to follow York. Neither was an asset nor a constant ally; Norfolk was motivated solely by his abject failure to make anything of his position in East Anglia, even after Suffolk's fall, and Devon by the long-running Bonville affair. What broke this noble unity, and was even beginning to do so by this time, was the Achilles heel of rule by committee or proxy, conflict amongst landowners, especially the nobility.

There is evidence from several counties of growing division and disorder in the early 1450s. In Derbyshire, for instance, the duke of Buckingham was finding it difficult to keep peace even among his own affinity, and a large-scale conflict involving numbers of prominent local landowners, including the Blounts, the Gresleys, the Vernons and the Longfords, was getting out of hand. In Warwickshire there was a new earl of Warwick, Richard Neville, 'the Kingmaker', son and heir of the earl of Salisbury, the head of the great northern Neville family. Warwick was unable to re-establish the former dominance in the county of the Beauchamp earls and there was a series of violent incidents. In East Anglia the vacuum left by Suffolk's death was only partially filled by the efforts of Lord Scales and Suffolk's widow to take over the combined Duchy/de la Pole interest, and division and disorder continued. Indeed, even on the basis of the limited amount of research that has been done for these years, the tendency for Duchy areas to be disrupted when the king was ineffective is noticeable. This is particularly marked in Derbyshire, where all the leading antagonists came from families with long-standing Duchy associations and Buckingham's difficulties were caused to a large degree by being obliged to take on responsibilities in a county where he had insufficient territorial power.

But the worst disturbances arose from feuding amongst the nobles. As we have seen, the Courtenay–Bonville feud had broken out again in the south-west. Bonville, a peer since 1449 and thus a still greater threat to Devon, had found a substitute ally at court for the duke of Suffolk in the earl of Wiltshire. The earl of Devon, frustrated by his lack of influence in high places, launched a private campaign in 1451 that ranged through the county of Somerset and was only brought to a close by York's unauthorised intervention. In 1450–1 an inheritance dispute between the Talbots and the Berkeleys was causing what has been likened to a private war in Gloucestershire.[7] From 1452 the duke of Exeter was at odds with

Lord Cromwell over Ampthill Castle, Bedfordshire, which Cromwell had bought from Lord Fanhope,[8] and this was leading to serious disturbances in that county. But the most dangerous affairs were those that led to the Nevilles' alienation from those around the king. The first of these was the confrontation between the new earl of Warwick and Somerset over parts of the Beauchamp of Warwick inheritance. Warwick had acquired his earldom by marriage to the principal Beauchamp heiress, sister of Henry Beauchamp duke of Warwick. She, however, had three half-sisters by Richard Beauchamp's first marriage; they also had some claims on the estate and one of them was married to Somerset. The estate had been divided, apparently amicably, among all four in 1449–50 but certain contentious issues remained. Notable among these was the custody of half of the Despenser part of the Warwick estate, an inheritance shared between Warwick and the underage Despenser coheir, Warwick's cousin George Neville, later Lord Bergavenny. Conflict over various other aspects of the division that had rumbled on since 1451, without reaching serious proportions, became confrontational in mid-1453. Then custody over George Neville's lands was awarded to Somerset and private war between Somerset and Warwick broke out within the Despenser lands in south Wales.

Meanwhile, events in Warwickshire had been driving a wedge between Warwick and Buckingham and pushing the latter towards Somerset and Wiltshire. Here, the *cause célèbre* of the 1450s was the dispute over the Mountford estate. Sir William Mountford, the greatest gentry landowner in Warwickshire, had been a close and loyal associate of Richard Beauchamp earl of Warwick. In the 1440s, during the minorities after Beauchamp's death, he had played a major part in the royal custody of the lands and, in this capacity, had become part of the court grouping. At this time he had formulated a plan to disinherit Baldwin, his heir by his first marriage, in favour of Edmund, the heir of the second marriage. To this end, he had ensured that Edmund also found a place in the royal household. Between 1450 and 1452, when William died, Baldwin began to look to Warwick to advance his claim and Edmund and William to Buckingham, Somerset and Wiltshire. From 1453, when the real contest for the lands began, these positions became firmer.

---

[7] This was a development of the Warwick–Berkeley feud of the 1420s (see above, p. 81): the first earl of Shrewsbury had married one of the daughters of Richard Beauchamp earl of Warwick by his first marriage to the Berkeley heiress (see immediately below), and so had acquired a share in the Beauchamp claim to the Berkeley lands: it was to have further repercussions later on (see below, p. 175).

[8] This is the same man who had been at odds with Lord Grey in Bedfordshire in the late 1430s: see above, pp. 84–5, 112.

Also in 1453 Warwick's family, the Nevilles, were embroiled on another front. In the north, relations between Percies and Nevilles, the two
great families of the region, were deteriorating. The Nevilles had been
steadily advancing as a power in the north and had somewhat eclipsed the
Percies but until 1453 this seems not to have troubled the latter sufficiently
to make them resist. What proved too much for them was apparently the
marriage of Salisbury's younger son to one of the heiresses of Lord
Cromwell, because Cromwell had some Percy estates that the family was
trying to recover. As one historian has put it, 'Until 1453 Neville aggrand-
izement had taken place at the expense of others: this was the first time that
Neville was to gain directly at the expense of Percy.'[9] Neither royal letters
to enforce the peace nor special commissions had much effect, and in
August the Nevilles were waylaid by a large Percy force as they returned
from Cromwell's castle of Tattershall in Lincolnshire, where they had
been celebrating the marriage. There was a small battle at Heworth in
Yorkshire, for which more than 700 men were later indicted. Further
large-scale armed demonstrations followed. By October there was almost
civil war in the North Riding. Since governmental handling of the affair
was so ineffective, each side looked round for powerful allies. The events
in Wales disposed the Nevilles to abandon their hitherto almost impeccable loyalty to the Lancastrian crown and move towards York. Cromwell
was finding himself heavily on the defensive against Exeter at this juncture:
he was even accused of treason in the Kentish rising that followed York's
fiasco of 1452. The Neville match was probably designed as much as
anything to provide him with effective allies and it had the inevitable effect
of driving Exeter towards the Percies. The earl of Devon had already
responded to Lord Bonville's protection by the court (despite the discipline briefly imposed on Bonville in 1451) by being almost the only noble
to join York in 1452. York's humiliation in that year was followed by a
period of disgrace and eclipse for Devon in which Bonville's dominance in
the south-west grew apace, so it is not surprising that Devon was to be one
of the first to endorse York's claim to be Protector.

As in the 1440s, all the drawbacks of government without a king were
evident. There was no impartial figure powerful enough to constrain
feuding magnates; no one who could insist on the king's law being obeyed
and peace restored in the shires. There was no authority to hold back those
disposed to abuse their proximity to the throne. Above all, Somerset was
unable to restrain himself when the opportunity presented itself of using
his position to get his way against Warwick over the Despenser custody.
Thus by mid-1453 it was becoming apparent that the magnate unity that

⁹ A. J. Pollard, *North-Eastern England during the Wars of the Roses* (Oxford, 1990), p. 256.

had so far been shown against York's largely illegitimate campaign was in jeopardy. However, what immediately proved the death of Somerset's rule was Henry VI's madness. In August 1453, while on a progress to the west country, he went into a state of catatonia that lasted eighteen months. He may have lost his reason when he heard of the defeat and death of Shrewsbury at Châtillon in Gascony, which had occurred on 17 July and sealed the defeat of the English in southern France. However, it may well be that a constitution that seems never to have been notably effervescent was destroyed by the hard travelling to which he had been put over the last year. By late in the year Henry's illness could no longer be kept secret. Moreover, some kind of properly constituted authority was needed to deal with the growing and apparently uncontainable conflict among the nobles. It seems that, with or without an officially sane king, Somerset was now unable to offer this.

York was at last summoned to attend the deliberations of the lords. He arrived in London in November 1453 and another fierce attack on Somerset was launched, this time by Norfolk. It focused as before on the loss of France. Somerset was placed in the Tower and, in recognition that no-one could now pretend there was a king, by early December conciliar rule had been re-established. The question was then who was to lead the council. Complicating the issue further was the birth of a son and heir to the king in October 1453, and it was doubtless this that prompted the queen's attempt, resisted by almost all the lords, to claim the regency at this time. There seems all the same to have been disagreement among the nobles over York's suitability to be Protector. Since the Nevilles constituted the core of his supporters, his candidacy could be seen as a partisan scheme to promote the interests of Nevilles and Lord Cromwell against Somerset and Exeter. Even the Commons of the parliament that reassembled in early 1454 seem to have been uncertain about York's impartiality were he to be made Protector. However, on 15 March, the creation of Henry and Margaret's infant son as Prince of Wales indicated York's recognition of him as Henry's heir and brought the nobility together behind the duke. On 27 March he was named Protector, to be succeeded if necessary by the Prince of Wales when he was old enough. Soon after, the great offices were filled with York's nominees, including the earl of Salisbury as chancellor. This most unusual appointment – throughout the middle ages, chancellors were almost invariably churchmen – perhaps indicates how little support there was for York among the higher clergy, many of whom had been recruited from the royal household in the 1440s.[10]

---

[10] See above, p. 108.

York had at last attained his end. Three points should be noted. First, the 'Yorkist road', eschewing control of the household, was possible only in a situation like this when no further pretence need be made that the king himself was ruling. Secondly, a precondition was the neutering of Somerset. Thirdly, it was York's claim to speak for a broadly based constituency that made him the appropriate person to lead when Somerset had shown his inability to deal with magnate feuding and when the king's madness had made rule by council essential. As before, the unfortunate nobility were caught between Somerset and York. Nevertheless, as ever, there was a will to keep the show on the road. In April household nobles, including Sutton of Dudley and Sudeley, were added to the council, and the deputation sent to examine the king before the Protectorship was formalised even included Viscount Beaumont, the only noble prepared to endorse the queen's claim to the regency. In February York had already shown his sensitivity to the need to ensure wider acceptance of his rule when, in an effort to force the nobility into wholesale complicity in the setting up of a Protectorate, lords absent from parliament without licence were fined. Once Protector, he made some serious efforts to put his programme of reform into effect. If there was no longer any French war, there was extensive opportunity to display probity, evenhandedness and the capacity for restoring order. The king's household, even though it was Somerset's power-base, was barely purged. Grants were few in number and distributed more equitably than before and there is certainly no evidence of their going wholesale to the Protector's friends. Some efforts were made to enlarge the king's income, for instance by collecting the subsidy on aliens granted in 1453. However, serious endeavours to economise by reducing the households of both king and queen had to wait until York's rule was well established towards the end of 1454. But the real and urgent need was to deal with the worsening disorder.

In the north Exeter had joined forces with the Percies against their joint enemies Lord Cromwell and the Nevilles. By May 1454 Exeter's behaviour had got completely out of hand. The younger Percies and younger Nevilles had been particularly violent during the whole affair and Exeter and Lord Egremont, a younger Percy, began rebellion throughout the north against the Protector and attacked Neville properties. Exeter claimed the right to rule during the king's illness and, according to the admittedly government-inspired indictment, he acted in alliance with the king of Scotland and took it upon himself to distribute the duke of Lancaster's livery. He ignored a warning letter from the Protector. York and Cromwell went to the city of York, where Exeter and Egremont had been gathering an army, but these two fled and continued to incite rebellion and disorder and allegedly plotted to kill York. Finally in June the Protector, now in command of a large force at York, was joined by other lords and began proceedings against Egremont's and Exeter's men. Exeter fled to sanctuary in Westminster Abbey and was removed from there in July and imprisoned. In November at the 'battle' of Stamford Bridge in Yorkshire, the Percy leaders, including Egremont, were captured. If York's proceedings in all this could be seen as favouring the Nevilles, it could undoubtedly be said that Exeter, and arguably the Percies as well, had gone way beyond the boundaries of acceptable behaviour. Moreover, the action taken against the ringleaders was exceedingly mild compared with their crimes: many were pardoned, and the punishment meted out to the Percies themselves was essentially the payment of heavy fines to the Nevilles, who had, after all, suffered serious damage to their property. And York had displayed exemplary dynamism in handling a dangerous episode. He showed yet more statesmanship in dealing with the latest round in the Courtenay–Bonville feud. The earl of Devon evidently decided that York's Protectorate was an outstanding opportunity to launch attacks on Bonville and Wiltshire, and the county of Devon became seriously disturbed during the spring and summer of 1454. But, although the earl had been one of York's few early supporters, the Protector was rightly not prepared to take a partisan position. Neither Bonville nor Wiltshire was removed from authority in Devon. In April the earl of Devon was placed under a bond of £1,000 to keep the peace towards Bonville and, when he broke it, in July both he and Bonville were put under still more punitive bonds.

There is some evidence that the Protector's rule was beginning to have some effect in the shires, although this is a subject on which we are still inadequately informed. In Warwickshire, where Richard Neville wisely used the control the Protectorate gave him to broaden the base of his support, rather than to get at his rivals, there was a general slackening of tension. Perhaps more remarkable is the way the divisions among the midland nobility that were beginning to harden during 1453 can be seen to ease. This is especially true of the region formed by east Warwickshire and the west of Leicestershire and Northamptonshire, where there had long been a very cohesive gentry network. Leading magnates here included York himself, Wiltshire and Beaumont, but they and their followers, as well as clients of Warwick's, can be seen acting together in 1453–5 and even as late as 1456. The reason is that the local networks, from which the gentry drew their friends and associates for doing the business connected with their lands, were immensely complex and often included the intertwined affinities of several magnates. For the gentry, real division among the nobility was therefore immensely dangerous, as former friends, who might be key witnesses or feoffees, could become enemies.[11] There would thus always be pressure from the gentry on magnates to come to terms with each other, whether in the normal context of local politics or the abnormal one of near-civil war. For their part, the nobility had no way of knowing when the king would recover and so it was best to acquiesce in the status quo if it could be made acceptable, something which York tried hard to do. Perhaps above all, there remained the longing for unity, common to almost all landowners, if it could be achieved.

Arguably, the Protectorship was the best possible solution for the hard-pressed English polity; for the first time since the minority, it gave a legitimacy to governance on behalf of the king. But even this was ultimately no solution to internal conflict. We have seen that, however legitimately conceived, York's actions against the Percies and Exeter were bound to be taken as preferential treatment of the Nevilles; a king might have done the same, but York was a subject and a friend of the Nevilles. In Derbyshire his efforts during 1454 to deal with the Longford–Blount feud by summonses before the council came to nothing. The reason was that Walter Blount managed to manoeuvre him into a position in which, despite all his attempts to act with a kingly neutrality, he was, in the eyes of the Longfords, too closely identified with the Blounts. The summons to the Longfords, sent in May, was rejected because the latter refused to accept the authority of a royal writ from York; they identified the sheriff's officer who tried to deliver the writ not as the bearer of the supreme royal authority but as the lackey of the noble with whom their enemies were linked. The unfortunate officer was told to eat the writ, seal and all, and when he refused the Longfords' men spat on the king's command, made the bearer tear it up and then put him in the stocks. Later that month, the Longfords gathered a force of about a thousand men, alarmingly full of important Derbyshire families, and sacked the Blount manor of Elvaston. Significantly, they quartered a tapestry with the Blount arms, claiming that Blount was a traitor because he served the Protector.

The whole episode is a perfect demonstration of the weakness of York's position when it came to ending internal conflict. He might claim to have the unassailable and universal authority of the king, upheld by full parliamentary sanction, but in the last analysis, like Suffolk in the 1440s and even his rival Somerset, he was only a noble, part of the partisan political world over which the king was supposed to maintain a commanding impartiality. At the same time, he was constrained by uncertainty about the future. In June 1454, he tried to get the nobility to try Somerset but they refused to co-operate. When the king recovered, Somerset would be released and then, if Somerset retrieved his former position, York would

---

[11] On these gentry associations, see above, pp. 53–4.

be in serious danger. For this reason, however impartial he wished to be, he could not wholly neglect allies like the Nevilles and the Blounts, especially as he had been so isolated before the onset of Henry's madness. This is dramatically evident in the case of the earl of Devon, who responded to his treatment at the hands of the Protector by changing sides; he, who had been York's earliest committed noble ally, actually fought with Somerset at St Albans.

That York was not the king also hampered his efforts in foreign affairs. Here the only outstanding issue, now that the English had been driven from France, was the payment of the Calais garrison, where the last English foothold was maintained and where Somerset had been captain since late 1451. The legacy of inadequate governmental funding resulting from nearly two decades of failure in war and financial mismanagement was still all too apparent. It was seen most clearly in the rush in late 1453 to get preferential treatment at the exchequer by those who had been unable to obtain payment of money owed them by the crown while Somerset was still in power. Calais needed to be defended against what was thought to be impending attack from France. Furthermore, the presence there, in charge of a large body of troops, of Lords Welles and Rivers, Somerset's deputies and allies, was a threat to York's own security in England. York's aim with respect to Calais was threefold. He intended to have the castles around Calais and all the town's offices put into his hands; to find regular payment for the soldiers, whose wages were nearly always overdue; and, to accomplish this, to secure loans from the Staplers, the merchant company which managed the wool trade to Calais. To achieve the last of these objects, the Staplers were promised the repayment of the 12,000 marks owed to them by the government from previous loans. In May 1454, in the midst of these negotiations, the unpaid soldiers mutinied but at least this persuaded the Staplers to make a large loan to York's government. In July, now that Calais had an annual income, York could take Somerset's place as captain. But, even though steps were taken to make the promised repayments to the Staplers, the garrison's wages remained unpaid and York was unable to enter the town before the Protectorate ended. Mindful of the importance of control of the Channel to both the security of Calais and the wool trade, with its regular royal income from the customs, York also tried to restore the neglected navy. But here again policy foundered on lack of money and only one naval expedition was sent out during the Protectorate, in the summer of 1454.

The great weakness of York's position all through was that the nobility remained anxious about his treatment of Somerset and unwilling to see the latter destroyed – just as they had not allowed Somerset to destroy York earlier on. That meant that, as soon as Henry recovered, Somerset would be able to achieve again a position based on the person of the king and that is indeed what happened. On Christmas Day 1454 the king did begin to recover his wits and in February 1455 Somerset was released and the Protectorate was ended soon after. In March York's nominees to the main offices of state, including the earl of Salisbury, were relieved of their posts. In the same month, Exeter, whose punishment had been no more than imprisonment, was also released. This decision must have cemented the alliance for self-preservation of York and the Nevilles, and they withdrew from court. The mishandling of the Nevilles was a mistake on the government's part. The nobles, if perhaps reluctantly, had been prepared to accept the return of Somerset's authority and so York as sole naysayer could have been isolated, as in 1452. York was now another matter. He was allied with the hugely powerful Nevilles, earls of Salisbury and Warwick, both of them convinced that there was a court faction, led by Somerset, including Wiltshire, Beaumont, Exeter and Northumberland, and that it was bent on their destruction. This is the first moment when we can see clearly the confrontational pattern of the rest of the decade. There could be no battles if neither side could find enough men to provide an army, which, of course, meant winning over members of the nobility. Until 1455 the determination of the greater part of the nobles to remain neutral had isolated York whenever he tried to remove Somerset from the presence of a nominally active king. But the absence of any kind of real rule, except when York was officially Protector, ensured that there would increasingly be unresolvable conflicts among the nobility. By 1455, once York was no longer Protector, these conflicts, especially those involving the Nevilles, were violent and intense enough for the participants to be prepared to line up on opposite sides. The king was always likely to find nobles ready to fight for him, just because he was king; now York had an army as well.

A great council was summoned to Leicester for 21 May. This was very much in the heart of the king's private power as duke of Lancaster, and York and his friends feared the worst. They would remember what had happened to Gloucester at Bury in 1447. They gathered their forces in the north and rode to intercept the king on his way to Leicester. Those with the king had also armed themselves. They were still in the majority. This was because it was not just the nobility closely identified with Somerset and hostile to York and the Nevilles, like Northumberland, that stayed with the king, but men like Buckingham. Buckingham was sympathetic to Somerset but not yet fully committed to him, but he could not countenance an attack on his sovereign, whoever happened to be pulling his strings. The only reason York was able to make such a large show of force – perhaps 3,000 men or even more – was that he had the power of the Nevilles on his side. The only other noble of any standing to fight with him was Viscount Bourchier, half-brother of Buckingham but brother-in-law of York. At St Albans the two sides met, and here another precedent came into play; this was Dartford, where York had been persuaded to disarm and then humiliated.

Negotiations, conducted for the king by Buckingham, foundered on the refusal to deliver to York 'suche as we wull accuse',[12] doubtless a code for Somerset chiefly. This underscores the fact that it was now principally fear which was driving the Yorkists on. What followed on 22 May was no more than an affray and few were killed, but those few included some rather important people: Northumberland, Clifford – another northern lord with the king – and, most significantly, the duke of Somerset. The Yorkists emerged victorious, and control of the king and the death of Somerset opened the way to yet more comprehensive Yorkist rule. St Albans was a watershed, not just because it was the first occasion when confrontation between the Yorkists and those with the king took on a military dimension. It marked the point when the fact, openly apparent since 1450, that whoever controlled the king ruled England became absolutely explicit. It also marked the moment when the narrowing down of the broad base of nobility that had co-operated to make government work since 1422 made a return to consensus still possible but extremely problematic. Too many magnates had aligned themselves with either side, too few were left in the middle. Of those that were still just about able to hold a middle position, most, like Buckingham, were being drawn inexorably into confrontational positions. It was local disputes that undermined unity, but the root cause lay in the failure of kingship, without which those disputes could not be resolved.

[12] *John Vale's Book*, p. 191.

7

THE END OF LANCASTRIAN RULE:
1455–1461

Historians are still very uncertain about what happened in these years, in both high politics and the country at large, and equally uncertain about why exactly Henry VI was deposed and why the deposition took the form it did. The best way into the problem is to abandon the idea of two rival camps formed by 1455.[1] Instead, the nobility should still be seen as trying to maintain an ever more precarious unity around the king and regrouping around him whenever possible. Those who were pared away from this neutralist centre to either side – and gradually they came to be in the majority – were in some cases firmly committed to one side or the other. In most cases, however, it was immediate circumstances that forced them to take sides, and they were not necessarily averse to taking up common ground again. As in the immediately preceding period, divisions among the nobility, which only a king could have healed, were usually what impelled nobles into a partisan position. However, it will be apparent that increasingly, as the decade drew to a close, partisanship was forced on them. In practice, because loyalty to the king was the single issue that could unite the nobility, whoever had control of the king would be likely to be the focus for magnate unity.

After St Albans this was patently York. The victorious Yorkists took Henry back to London where a parliament was immediately summoned for July. In a sense it was business as before. York, although not yet Protector in name, made a second attempt to convince the country that he could provide the good and impartial rule he had promised and to rally the nobility round him, and through them the rest of political society. How-

---

[1] This follows the work of John Watts, as referred to in the bibliography to chapter 5.

ever, there were two major differences. The first, which made things easier, was that Somerset was dead. Although his son Henry inherited the estates and title, the latter was a minor until 1457 and seems to have been a less rebarbative figure. Crucially, he had not compromised himself by setting out to be a rival source of authority. At this point, for the first time since York's return from Ireland, there was only one authority and that was York. The second difference, which made things more difficult, was that enmities were now out in the open, in some cases had led to deaths which could never be erased from political memory. Thus, the process of creating a solid noble foundation for rule was going to be even more problematic than before. In fact, the whole tone of politics was becoming more violent. Even before St Albans, there had been armed demonstrations in London, notably when numbers of nobles came armed to the capital in the tense atmosphere of early 1454. After, the growing mistrust at the highest political levels led to nobles habitually turning up at meetings with large armed retinues.

York's conduct at the start of his second period of rule makes it clear that he was trying to construct a workable basis for governance from among the nobility. He had no choice, for the Nevilles were still the only substantial noble family prepared to support him in opposition, although Viscount Bourchier remained with him and was appointed treasurer and, as ever, the duke of Norfolk blew hot and cold. The reason for the lukewarmness of the rest of the nobility is that nobles and opposition to the monarchy – as York's antagonism to Somerset had had to be conceived, however much he disguised the fact – did not mix. There was no 'loyal opposition'; it could only be disloyal, treasonous, as York had found all along. Magnates who tried to take power from the king were always suspect, even if they were really removing him from the control of others. They were doubly suspect when they did it by force. The single outstanding problem of Henry VI's adult rule remained; that there was no legitimate way of coping with an inadequate king. York's particular problem since 1450 was compounded by the fact that ideas about the king's freedom to have men of his own choice around him still lingered, despite the king's inability to make any kind of choice. These made Somerset's method of managing the king seem more legitimate than York's. Somerset's rule could just about be construed as business as usual, although it was conducted on behalf of a sham king. On the other hand, York's appeal to the common weal and attempt to rule through councils representing this general good hinted at illegitimate control.

York's efforts to achieve legitimacy after St Albans by restoring unanimity began with the summons of all the peers to parliament; even as antagonistic a figure as Wiltshire and the heirs of those who had died

fighting against York at St Albans. The exception was the new duke of
Somerset, who was in any case underage. The efforts continued with
attempts to prevent any future exploitation of the divisions of St Albans. As
after Dartford, a full pardon was issued, reinforced by a parliamentary
pardon for those who had fought with York. Responsibility for the battle
was assigned where it did least harm: to Somerset who was dead and two
minor household figures. Although this judgement has often attracted
derision, it made very good sense if the battle was to be taken off the
political agenda. Buckingham, the leader of the royal forces at St Albans,
was put under bonds but not otherwise punished and he was among the
lords summoned to parliament. Councils seem to have been attended by a
reasonably broadly based group of lords. As in York's first period of rule,
there was no Yorkist monopoly of grants. In February 1456, after protracted negotiations, York was finally able to get a settlement with the Calais
merchants and the unpaid garrison, which enabled the merchants to make
advances guaranteed by control of the customs revenue. The agreement
also made it possible at last for a Yorkist, the earl of Warwick, to become
captain of Calais, an appointment that was to have momentous consequences later in the decade. To emphasise that York's rule still rested on
what Yorkist propaganda now defined as an honourable tradition, the
post-St Albans parliament petitioned that Humphrey of Gloucester be
formally rehabilitated.

As in the first Protectorate, there are indications that conciliation was
seeping down to the shires. In September 1455 Buckingham was able to
effect an arbitration between the Vernons and the Gresleys in the north
midlands.[2] Both parties had been encouraged to settle by being called
before the council in July: it was precisely this kind of informal pressure on
litigants that kings were supposed to provide. In Warwickshire the progress towards stability continued, as did the functioning of the cross-
factional networks, scarcely interrupted by St Albans. There was especially
notable restraint on Warwick's part in the Mountford dispute which had
been one of the conflicts driving a wedge between the Nevilles and the
court.[3] Even though Warwick stood behind the heirs of William Mountford's first marriage, while Buckingham, aided by Wiltshire, gave assistance to those of the second, during this period the estate was rather
remarkably divided by negotiated settlement.

Unfortunately there were also less optimistic similarities with the earlier
period of rule. Above all, there were still major disturbances in the realm.
In the north, the death of the earl of Northumberland at St Albans seems to

    [2] See above, p. 126, for their dispute.   [3] See above, pp. 127–8.

have had a calming effect but elsewhere there was serious trouble. Wales had been badly neglected for most of the king's adult reign and there was disorder over much of the Principality itself and the Marcher lordships. In particular, the crown's inactivity had enabled certain members of the Welsh gentry to become almost independent powers within the Principality. One of these was Gruffydd ap Nicholas, who exploited his local offices for his own financial ends and carried out criminal actions with impunity. The creation of the earldom of Pembroke for the king's half-brother, Jasper Tudor, in 1453 had failed to curb Gruffydd, and York's efforts as Protector to remove him and his family from office in the Principality and the March in 1454 were no more successful. It has been said of Wales at this time that 'It was a society coming adrift from its former loyalties', and we have seen already that it was in the Welsh March that noble incomes were collapsing most spectacularly in this period; many were in fact becoming uncollectable.[4] But the worst instances of local violence were in Devon, part of the unfinished Courtenay–Bonville feud. This now took a new turn, the main protagonists having changed sides: since Devon had fought with the king at St Albans, Bonville subsequently hastened to associate himself with the Yorkists. From October to December 1455 the Courtenays went on the rampage in Devonshire. The most appalling among an array of excesses was the abduction and murder, preceded by the ransacking of his house, of Nicholas Radford, an elderly lawyer who had served Lord Bonville. There followed a mock inquest performed by Devon's men over Radford's body, at which a verdict of suicide was recorded, after which the body was thrown naked into a grave and crushed by stones in such a way as to make a real inquest impossible. Exeter was taken and held as if it were a conquered town. There were other enormities, principally directed against Lord Bonville. Nothing was done.

The whole affair raised the question of York's authority in England. While doubts about this had been an obstacle to his governance during his first Protectorate, it was worse now because he had no real title to rule. Accordingly, when parliament reassembled in November 1455, York was made Protector again, explicitly to give him power to deal with these outrageous acts. The procedure on this occasion suggests that the king had not experienced another collapse, was indeed no more comatose than usual, and this was potentially undermining of the basis of York's authority. It is noteworthy that a new form of minority council was apparently established about the same time, with York as chief councillor. This implies that it was at last admitted openly that Henry would never be a real

---

[4] R. A. Griffiths, 'Wales and the Marches', *Fifteenth-Century England 1399–1509*, ed. S. B. Chrimes, C. D. Ross and R. A. Griffiths (Manchester, 1972), p. 156; above, pp. 42–3.

king, but also perhaps that there were some quite serious constraints on York's freedom of action. Steps were taken from December to bring the earl of Devon to order, but with no very great urgency, principally because York's rule was beginning to founder on a still greater test of authority. This was the Act of Resumption that the Commons had demanded in 1455 to re-establish the finances of the royal household. This one was intended to have real teeth and it is most probable that York was committed to its effective implementation. Even the queen was to have her expenditure limited, albeit to the large sum of 10,000 marks a year, and the Duchy of Lancaster was not to be used any more for the fulfilment of the royal wills, which meant for a start the abandonment of Eton and King's. In the event almost all these laudable aims came to nothing. In early 1456 York was trying to persuade the Lords to agree to further resumptions, but without success.

He had never been able to achieve a broadly based government after St Albans. Wiltshire, for example, had refused to co-operate; Exeter had had to be kept in prison; all York's major officers had been men whose loyalty he could count on. The nobles were as a body reluctant to come either to councils – for example in the immediate aftermath of St Albans – or to parliament. In some instances this was because they were simply opposed to York's rule, in others because they were unwilling to commit themselves to a side that might lose power to its rivals. In these circumstances York could not hope to force warring nobles into amity, for this was a hard enough task for one who was not the king at the best of times. Nor could he expect the nobles who were not clearly committed to his cause to make self-sacrificial gestures like the Resumption. Their reluctance would have been accentuated by the fact that this particular Resumption involved a radical restriction of the crown's power to make grants. It is not surprising that the Lords should refuse to accept so fundamental a proposal by a government that had so limited an authority for its actions. The Lords' withdrawal of support over the Resumption enabled power to return to the king and this could happen with particular speed because York had so little command within the royal household. 'The king' meant whoever had inherited Somerset's position within the household, together with his claim to authority based not on the common weal but on proximity to the king. The person now emerging as Somerset's successor was Queen Margaret.

In February, York resigned the Protectorship. He remained for the moment in charge of the government but there was now no formal bar to anyone else assuming his place. From then until mid-August there was something of a vacuum at the centre of power. In May York was still sufficiently in command to respond to the king of Scotland's threat to invade. In July and August there were renewed outbreaks in Wales and its March, this time involving William Herbert and Walter Devereux, both York's men, and Edmund Tudor, the king's half-brother. Tudor seized the royal castle of Carmarthen from York's custody. It seems improbable that he would have done this without the encouragement of someone close to the king. In August Devereux besieged and took the castle, and took Tudor prisoner with it; Tudor died soon after his release later that year. Meanwhile, by the end of April the queen and the Prince had moved to the heartland of the Duchy of Lancaster in the midlands, but it was the king's departure from London to join her in August that marked the moment when Margaret assumed control of the government and York had to give way. The coup was completed between September and October when York's nominees in the major offices were replaced by men deemed to be loyal to the queen. These now included the second earl of Shrewsbury, son of the 'great' earl who had died at Châtillon. Coventry, a town under the lordship of the Prince of Wales as earl of Chester, at the centre of the midlands, where the Duchy was so powerful, became the royal capital. Devereux and Herbert were summoned to a great council there in September and imprisoned, although Herbert escaped and fled back to Wales.

This should have been the moment from which there was a rapid descent into civil war. Why this was not so is not clear, but there are indications. First, we must return to the fundamental point that there were still enough nobles who, while far from endorsing York's position, nevertheless set their faces against partisan rule in the name of the king. Buckingham, for example, was reported to have objected to some of the dismissals among the great officers. Even the earl of Shrewsbury may have been another who was uneasy about Margaret's conduct. Both were in different ways committed not only to the principle of defending the crown but also to the benefits that it might bring them – Buckingham, for instance, in his power struggle with Warwick in Warwickshire – but that did not mean that they wanted an outright assault on York. To turn to the other side, the Nevilles may have believed that, with the death of Somerset and Northumberland, their two arch enemies, they had no further reason to take up arms for York. They may even have hoped in the long term to return to their previous position as loyal servants of the crown. What this meant was that neither side was militarily strong or determined enough to destroy the other and so stalemate ensued.

Throughout this stalemate there are reasons to believe that efforts were being made by the nobles committed only to the king, not to York or the queen, to bring both sides together. These were focused on the quasi-minority council established at the same time as the second Protectorate.

Remarkably, this council continued to function, even if only after a fashion, throughout this period. In 1456 it remained much as it had been during York's rule, and included a substantial Neville presence. In a sense it still represented the authority of the king, as opposed to Margaret's or York's, and it certainly represented the continuing aspirations of many of the nobility towards unity around the king. It is therefore significant that it seems possible to identify certain non-partisan measures in 1456–7 with the council or with the nobility as a group. These include politically balanced special commissions; resistance to the queen's efforts to have York and his adherents punished at a great council at Coventry in October 1456; and the forcing of bi-partisan policies on the queen at a further council at Coventry in March 1457. The lords also took the lead in preparing for a threatened French invasion in mid-1457 and, again, representative commissions were issued for this. Another indication, both of the residual power of the lords and of the Nevilles' successful identification with this, is that Warwick was able to enter Calais and take up his potentially enormous military authority there in July 1456, some time after York had lost the Protectorship. Indeed, his position there was strengthened when he was commissioned to keep the sea late in 1457. This enabled him to engage in some dubious privateering enterprise against foreign merchants in 1458 and 1459, which, while they did nothing for trade in the narrow seas, enhanced his standing with the Calais garrison and gave him an international reputation.

Meanwhile the queen was establishing her own power-base. Its focus was her son Edward, Prince of Wales, and it was located in the midlands, the Welsh border and Wales. It was built on twin foundations: the Duchy of Lancaster lands in the midlands, where she herself held the Duchy honors of Tutbury and Leicester, with the Duchy castle of Kenilworth, Warwickshire, which was to become the crown's principal military bastion; and her son's earldom of Chester and Principality of Wales. The Prince had already been taken on a tour of the crown's midland estates and of Cheshire in 1455–6. A household was established for him, packed with men she could trust, and his newly appointed council included Wiltshire, Beaumont and others closely connected with the queen and the royal household. Among those who were gathering at Margaret's side were also the heirs of men killed at St Albans, such as Somerset, Northumberland and Clifford; troublemakers who had fallen foul of the Yorkist government, notably Devon and Exeter; and, rather ominously, some of those who had approved the Yorkist Protectorates, such as Jasper Tudor, earl of Pembroke, and, as we have seen, the earl of Shrewsbury. Pembroke is a good example of the threats to noble unity from unresolved quarrels, for he, like his brother Edmund, had been badly damaged by the exploits of

Herbert and Devereux in Wales. Shrewsbury probably felt he had no option, since the geographical basis of the queen's power so closely matched his own. In 1457–8 two marriages indicated that the duke of Buckingham was now increasingly to be identified with the nobles around the queen. These were between Margaret Beaufort, cousin of Somerset and widow of Edmund Tudor, and Buckingham's second son, and between Shrewsbury's heir and Buckingham's daughter.

However, like York's, Margaret's authority remained narrowly based and insufficient as long as the lords exercising the authority of the council were able to continue to act in the king's name, and in 1457 she achieved little beyond the judicial punishment of Herbert and Devereux. A commission of *oyer* and *terminer* sat at Hereford in April, bringing a host of charges (not all necessarily true) against these two and their followers. In the event, Herbert submitted and was pardoned and Devereux was released from gaol in early 1458. At the same time, Jasper Tudor was becoming the king's main lieutenant in central and southern Wales. In April 1457 the constableships of Carmarthen and Aberystwyth were taken from York and given to Tudor and he began to rally south Wales on the king's behalf. But in England the queen was making less headway. It appears that it was the council that forced the court and its opponents towards a reconciliation at the 'Loveday' in London in March 1458. However, it was then that the queen was able to set aside the aspirations of the council itself. The Loveday was intended to be a general reconciliation and restoration of magnate unity under the king, and it followed the post-St Albans dispensation in refusing to rake over the battle itself. Probably at the queen's instigation, it turned into specific shows of amity between the Yorkists and the heirs of Lancastrians killed in the battle. This was a formal recognition, which the lords had all along avoided, that there were two opposing camps. What is more, it was done not under the aegis of king and council but of king and queen. This was really the end of the noble/conciliar attempt to ignore the emergence of rival camps and it is perhaps at this point, ironically at the most overt moment of conciliation, that the Wars of the Roses can be said to have begun.

Nevertheless, after the Loveday, York and the Nevilles remained in London once the king and queen had left, still trying to keep a form of rule based on noble co-operation and conciliar authority. Since the king was now firmly under the queen's command, this was in fact the only kind of authority open to them. They directed such activities of the council as we are able to trace, acted in foreign policy and even tried to summon a broadly based council for the autumn. But their very success caused the queen to return to London in autumn 1458 and seize control of the government that remained there. Steps were taken to deprive members of the Neville family and other Yorkists of offices and grants, and Yorkists were attacked in other ways. Notably there was an attempt in London to murder Warwick, who was proving impossible to eject from his office in Calais. It was evident that so many lords were now gravitating to the queen, either in fear or because she did represent royal authority, that the Yorkist lords were highly vulnerable to an attack of this kind. Accordingly York, Salisbury and Warwick left London, Warwick moving to his stronghold of Calais.

It was at this point that the real confrontation began, for it was from that moment that both sides had enough force to try to destroy the other; the centre could no longer hold. Margaret probably already felt strong enough by this time. What changed on the other side was that the Nevilles now felt sufficiently threatened once again to take the field for York. This is indeed made explicit in a meeting of Salisbury with his counsellors at his seat of Middleham, Yorkshire, in November 1458, where it was decided 'to take full party with the full noble prince the duke of York'.[5] Had York and the Nevilles been in close political and military alliance since St Albans, as is commonly supposed, it is hard to see how the decision could have been put in those terms. What prompted them to make it? First, we have seen that there were clear threats, of the most violent kind, against Warwick as Captain of Calais. Secondly, the Nevilles may have been increasingly uneasy about the power of the Percies and challenges to their own position in the north. The new earl of Northumberland was now firmly allied with the queen. Offices and favour in the north were beginning to go pronouncedly to the Percies and to members of the senior Neville line. These were the earls of Westmorland, sometimes known as the Nevilles of Raby, after the family seat. Their territorial interests had been ruthlessly subordinated to those of the younger line ever since Henry IV's half-sister Joan Beaufort had married an earl of Westmorland as his second wife and become the mother of the famous Nevilles, including Salisbury. An additional concern would have been that in 1457 Lawrence Booth, one of the queen's household officers, became bishop of Durham, the diocese that covered much of the region of Neville power, and proceeded to withdraw most of the annuities that his predecessor, a Neville, had granted to members of the family. The Nevilles were ready to fight.

In May 1459 king and queen returned to Coventry, the centre of the power being built around the queen and the Prince of Wales. Letters were sent to the shires summoning their military forces to Leicester for the same month and a great council was called to Coventry in June. Those who failed to come, which included most of those sympathetic to York, were allegedly indicted for this. Fearing the worst, the Yorkist lords gathered with their forces at Ludlow in Shropshire, one of York's main residences, Warwick bringing part of the Calais garrison. On 23 September Lord Audley tried unsuccessfully to intercept Salisbury's men at Blore Heath in Staffordshire as they went from Middleham to Ludlow, and he himself was killed. On 12 October the royal forces arrived at Ludlow and found the Yorkists at Ludford Bridge, to the south, but overnight the Yorkist forces melted away. Significantly the reason appears to have been the reluctance of their soldiers, especially the Calais men under Warwick, to fight against an army commanded, at least nominally, by the king. Their captain, Andrew Trollope, led their defection. This shows again the immense power conferred on whichever side controlled the king, and the innate respect for monarchy, which had survived nearly forty years of Henry VI's kingship.

The Yorkists fled, York to Ireland and Warwick, Salisbury and York's eldest son, the earl of March, to Calais. The latter were helped on their way by John Dinham, a Devonshire esquire of whom we shall be hearing more. In October, Somerset, now appointed Captain of Calais in rivalry to Warwick, and using the neighbouring castle of Guisnes as his base, tried to take the town from Warwick. In this he made use of the forces from Calais under Trollope that had defected to the king at Ludford. He had no success, but this was really the only comfort for the Yorkist lords. They were now exceedingly isolated; the queen had not just the king but the real Yorkist claim to legitimacy, the support of most of the lords. This was partly because, in the name of her husband, she demanded that loyalty be shown to her, rejecting noble neutrality, and partly because the Yorkists' resort to arms against the king, however they tried to dress it up, had alienated all but the most committed. In effect, the first had caused the second, since Margaret's deliberate destruction of the neutral centre had forced the Yorkists into fighting for their lives. At the parliament summoned to Coventry for November, Queen Margaret's position was greatly strengthened, both practically and theoretically. Parliamentary attainders, depriving them of their lands, were issued against all the major Yorkists and several of their minor followers, and the lands were handed to loyal subjects of the king. At the parliament, and in a contemporary tract, the *Somnium Vigilantis*, the Yorkists were condemned for their behaviour throughout the decade and, momentously, the victorious Lancastrians deliberately set out to steal York's propagandist clothes. They asserted that he could not pretend to represent the common weal because the king alone could do this. Thus the queen's government claimed to unite the rival poles of authority that had existed since 1450, in the person of the king, under a rule validated by the lords and led by herself in the interests of her son. The price she paid was that she had to accept the possibility of submission and reconciliation that, even at this late stage, was contained in the parliamentary proceedings. Margaret's period of rule shows that, attaintees apart, there was still room for all the lords; even the duke of Norfolk is found on commissions. If she wanted a truly effective government based on all the remaining magnates, she would have to exploit this by relinquishing both total vengeance and wholesale reliance on the faction that she had constructed around herself and the Prince.

Whatever those magnates who still hoped for such an outcome may have thought, it is very difficult to see that the Yorkists could now submit. In the unlikely event that they managed to regain their lands, they could no longer trust the queen and her followers; if she chose to sacrifice unity to vengeance, even without carrying the majority of the nobles with her and as leader of a faction, she was still too strong for them to take a chance on her good faith. It may well be that by this time the logic of their position was forcing itself on them all. They had no practical basis for power unless they could capture the king, and that was dangerous and potentially reversible by a counter-blow, and no theoretical basis now that the queen's side had appropriated the Yorkist notion of the common weal. There is evidence that York may have begun to contemplate an attempt on the crown itself as early as 1455, although there are certainly no signs of this in his actions or those of his supporters, but by 1460 this possible way out had probably occurred to both York and the Nevilles. In any case, whether they chose to capture or to replace the king, they were going to have to use force with all its attendant risks.

Efforts to starve the Yorkists out of Calais in 1459–60 failed and in January they had two considerable triumphs over the government. First, Warwick raided Sandwich, where a fleet was being prepared to assist Somerset against Calais, and then Dinham descended on Sandwich and kidnapped the lords who had been set to guard the fleet and prepare an expedition to Guisnes. It is a nice ironic touch that these included Lord Rivers, Edward of March's future father-in-law, and his son Anthony Woodville, both of whom were 'rated' by the Calais earls for their common birth. In June 1460 the Calais earls arrived in Kent, no doubt encouraged by the support, in men and supplies, they had been receiving from that county while in Calais. It seems they were made welcome, which may be further indication of diminishing enthusiasm for the queen's rule in the south-east, caused perhaps by the royal household's move to the midlands. They were admitted to London within a week and then went out to meet the royal army. The two sides met at Northampton on 10 July and the Yorkists won. The king was taken and Buckingham, Shrewsbury and Beaumont were amongst the dead. But after the victory the Yorkists were in the same position as Margaret after Ludford: total revenge on their enemies was not possible unless they were prepared to forfeit the support of the uncommitted or those who could be persuaded to leave the queen. As throughout the 1450s, if in a rapidly diminishing form, there remained a body of nobles who, whether they veered towards one side, the other or neither, were still dedicated to the recovery of unity under the crown and would not countenance either side's destruction of the other.

All this was thrown into turmoil by the duke of York's return from Ireland in early September. Very soon it became clear that he had come to claim the throne. He arrived in London early in October and, as he entered, he was displaying the Clarence arms: for the first time he was making the point of his superior hereditary right through the Mortimer line by descent from Lionel of Clarence. He was also acting like a king. On 16 October, in the parliament summoned by the victorious Yorkists, he claimed the throne. Arguably he now had no choice. But it was a very dangerous thing to do. His enemies could claim, as subsequent historians have done, that this out-and-out treason was what he had been intending all along, however much he had cloaked his designs in the respectable garb of legitimate opposition. The resistance of the assembled lords, possibly even of York's closest allies, tells its own story of the power that monarchy still held after so many years of misgovernance and of the risks of cutting off the vital support of the nobles that York was running. It is noticeable how few major lords fought for the king at Northampton, before York claimed the throne, and how many more fought at Wakefield and St Albans, after he had done so.

The settlement that was subsequently negotiated, and announced on 31 October, to some extent restored York to a more broadly based position, for it upheld the rule of the king, probably with York as Protector, while naming York as his successor. York now had the legitimacy of both the existing ruler's authority, vouched for by the lords, and the promise of his own personal authority in the future. What he also had was the undying enmity of the queen, and with the queen were Somerset, Northumberland, Pembroke, Devon,[6] Wiltshire and other, mainly northern, lords. From now onwards, it would be even more dangerous for a noble to try and stay neutral without having the queen to reckon with. This of course helps explain why so many more of them fought for Henry from this stage, but, like the nobility's own hesitancy to endorse York, it was itself the result of York's attempt to make himself king. The fact is that, even as the

---

[6] This was the son and heir of the earl who had caused so much trouble earlier in the decade: the latter had died in 1458 but his son espoused the 'Lancastrian' cause that his father had eventually chosen.

nobles found themselves obliged to choose between one side and the other, those who chose York included very few great nobles beyond the Nevilles and York's own family. As the Lancastrian troops assembled in the north, York went to deal with them. On 30 December he was surprised outside his castle of Sandal near Wakefield and heavily defeated. Amongst those killed were York himself and his second son, Edmund of Rutland, and Salisbury was executed after the battle. While this was happening, Edward earl of March had gone westwards to raise troops from the lands of Warwick and his own family in the Welsh Marches. On 2 February, at Mortimer's Cross near his own castle of Wigmore in Herefordshire, he attacked and defeated an army led by Pembroke and Wiltshire.

Meanwhile the queen had put herself at the head of the victorious Lancastrians in the north and was coming south towards London, her men pillaging as they came. Warwick went north from London to intercept them, taking the king with him, but in the second battle of St Albans on 17 February he lost both the battle and the king. As soon as the news reached Edward he made a dash for London, meeting Warwick in the Cotswolds along the way. Their course was now self-evident: with control of the king lost and a vengeful Lancastrian army descending on the capital, unless Edward took the throne the Yorkist cause was finished, but he had to get to London before the queen. In the event he was too late, for St Albans had already left the way clear for the queen and her army, but the Londoners, terrified of the excesses of the northerners, were reluctant to admit the queen. There has been some debate as to why this should be so. One historian has argued that London was never particularly pro-Yorkist in the 1450s and that it was only fear of Margaret's soldiers that drove the City authorities to keep the queen out. And it is certainly true that the small amounts of money that the government was able to raise from loans in this decade came mainly from London. It is equally true that a series of affrays and near-riots in London from 1456, such as the attempted murder of Warwick that has been mentioned, meant that 'at times the capital was like an armed camp',[7] and that there would have been deep reluctance to let in the rampaging army of either side. However, it is now suggested that there was a significant group of London merchants, mostly Staplers, who resented the way the government allowed foreign merchants, especially Italians, to evade the regulation that wool be shipped via Calais. It is thought that they may have provoked the anti-alien riots of 1456–7, which were also anti-government. It was indeed after the punitive commission into these in April that the queen and Prince left London for Coventry. These merchants may therefore have constituted a 'Yorkist' faction in the

---

[7] J. L. Bolton, 'The City and the Crown, 1456–61', *The London Journal*, 12 (1986), p. 15.

City throughout the 1450s and seized the opportunity to resist the government and then to allow in a rival claimant who, they hoped, would represent their interests better.

As the queen hesitated outside the City, she heard of the approach of the Yorkists. She withdrew with her army and on 27 February Edward, Warwick and their forces entered London. On 4 March Edward became king, but a rival power still existed, for the Lancastrian army had yet to be defeated. The new king and his army went north and met their antagonists at Towton in Yorkshire on Palm Sunday, 29 March. The battle was fought in a snowstorm and was the bloodiest and possibly the largest of the war; some contemporary estimates of the number of deaths put it at 29,000 or more, although we must always allow for the medieval tendency to inflate numbers. Amongst the Lancastrian dead were Northumberland and Clifford, while Devon and Wiltshire were captured subsequently and executed. Unfortunately for the Yorkists, several important Lancastrians were able to flee to Scotland, including Exeter, Somerset and, most seriously, the entire royal family. On 28 June King Edward IV was crowned. The crisis of legitimacy through which the English polity had laboured since 1450 had ended at Towton – but not entirely. An anointed crowned king and his son and heir still awaited their opportunity in Scotland. Why the resolution took so long to happen, why it occurred at all, why it was in favour of the Yorkists, and why it was only partial are problems that we must now examine.

Some part of the solution to all four is to be found in the response amongst landowners, the gentry particularly, to the conditions of the 1450s, especially the years 1455–60. To understand these, we need to place them in the context of the structures of local governance and society that were described in the third chapter. It has already been observed that division amongst the nobility was potentially extremely damaging to the gentry, because it forced polarisation within gentry networks, which often consisted of the intertwined connections of different lords.[8] For national politics to dictate that a former friend, whose affairs were intimately bound up with your own, was suddenly an enemy was wholly undermining of the system of mutual favour and obligation which held local societies together. We have seen, in the activities of the network in east Warwickshire, west Leicestershire and west Northamptonshire in 1453–6, that pressures of this kind could restore consensus at a local level after it appeared to have broken down irretrievably in the national arena. These pressures were exerted on the magnates as much as on anyone; they could hardly ignore the promptings of their own affinities and connections. This

[8] See above, pp. 131–2.

was especially true if the disintegrating tendency of national politics suggested that the affinities' military support would be required, in either local conflict or national confrontation. When we talk of nobles being conscious of the need for unity, we must bear in mind that quite a lot of this came from their sense of what the gentry were prepared to accept.

Another aspect of this necessary sensitivity on the part of the nobility to the needs of the gentry was awareness of the much greater effect of local disorder on lesser landowners. If the nobility had their feet in a local world as well as a national one, they moved on a far greater stage. Their estates were large and widespread; the destruction of one, or part of one, was the loss usually of only a small part of their income, and localised instability affected only one of probably several centres where they had lands. Even diminution of income on a larger scale could be absorbed by the great noble families, as the ability to surmount a large fall in their Welsh revenues on the part of York, Buckingham and others demonstrates.[9] Most of the gentry on the other hand had properties concentrated in one, two, at most three centres. They could not afford to be at loggerheads with their neighbours in the very small-scale world in which even the greatest of them moved, nor, since they had narrower margins of financial safety than most of the nobles, could they as easily absorb the loss of even a small proportion of their income. To manage their areas of local power, nobles had to show themselves effective peacemakers amongst all the possible destabilising influences. To this end, they had to give careful attention to local needs; they were expected not to take short-cuts to dominance by stirring up trouble and putting too much weight, military or otherwise, behind their own men.

In the 1450s it may well be that circumstances forced the magnates to break most of these rules. As national figures they were highly exposed and, as the decade progressed, their own feuds, or pressure from the queen, or both, obliged them increasingly to take sides. They were therefore trying to force on the gentry crude choices where complex local loyalties were the norm, demanding commitment where it was impossible to give it and threatening to create unacceptable disorder with an undesirable civil war. What made this worse was that the extreme urgency of high politics took magnates away from the shires – in the Yorkist case into exile – and, in doing so, not only deprived the provinces of their natural leaders but proved an incitement to the nobles to take disruptive measures in the shires. They had to be sure of their clients if it came to war, or at least sure that they would not follow anyone else. Thus, on the one hand they needed to be absolute masters of their regional power-bases, where a form

---

[9] See above, p. 43.

of power-sharing had often been acceptable before. On the other, under the pressure of national events, they no longer had the time for the involvement in the minutiae of local affairs which was the essential precondition for proper local management. Short-cuts could well become the order of the day.

This is certainly true of Warwickshire, where, from the time of the queen's ascendancy, Buckingham set out to dominate the shire against Warwick by the single-minded and increasingly illicit pursuit of the claim of 'his' side of the Mountford family, and it may well have been happening elsewhere. In this case the response of the Warwickshire gentry seems to have been refusal to countenance what they felt to be unacceptable perversion of the law or to recognise the victorious heir. This is especially remarkable because he was closely attached to the queen, whose temporary capital, Coventry, and military arsenal, Kenilworth, lay within Warwickshire itself. It was also probably this affair that pushed Buckingham ever closer to the queen, even though it is not clear that that was where he wanted to be. The whole episode demonstrates how attempts to prepare for confrontation actually brought confrontation closer, while alienating the gentry whose military power would be necessary in a fight. We shall see shortly that in the Duchy of Lancaster region of the north midlands Margaret's similar short-cuts, her efforts at rapid reconstitution of the Duchy retinue as a ready-made army, fell largely on deaf ears. In East Anglia division among the nobility produced more obvious polarisation from the second half of 1456. Although Norfolk, despite fighting against the court at Northampton, did not commit himself to the Yorkists until early 1461, there was nevertheless a redrawing of the antagonistic lines of the 1440s, in which Scales now stood for the court/Suffolk/Duchy of Lancaster interest, supported by men like Heydon and Tuddenham. The predictable result was that conflicts that had gone into abeyance, like that between Heydon and the Pastons, blew up again. It was not an outcome that was necessarily seen as satisfactory by the majority of the local landowners.

None of this can have made the gentry very happy, either about the lords they looked to or about the government itself. Thus, if the gentry may have played a large part in restraining the lords, they may also have made a substantial contribution to the nature of the confrontation when it came. They were in fact in a position to disregard calls from the lords, since it was the latter who were willing to fight while most of the lesser landowners were probably not. Forcible conscription of a politically aware and locally powerful social group and their tenants was not on the agenda. It is quite possible, although an issue as yet largely unexplored, that the forces that fought the battles of 1455–61 came largely from towns, from the Welsh Marches, where the lords' control of the tenantry was almost complete (this would include the royal bastion of Cheshire) and from the north of England.[10] Here also lordship was more concentrated territorially and it was an area where warfare and border raids were endemic, and the gentry may have been less reluctant to disturb the peace.[11] That would certainly fit with the landowning and recruitment pattern of many of the protagonists.

A further and, in the long term, more important point is that politics as they developed in the 1450s were simply inappropriate for the gentry's way of life. Because these families were highly competitive and yet forced to get on with each other, they needed the reassurance of a firm single authority at the centre, which would make possible the functioning of the complex interweaving powers that ensured the peace. Only thus could they attack others or defend themselves when necessary, confident that matters would not get out of hand. Significantly, in so far as it has been traced, the level of localised violence seems in some areas to decline from 1455, not because the country was becoming more peaceable, for this was the time of descent into civil war, but because it had become too dangerous to pursue these quarrels. If conflict was to some extent ruled out by these conditions, so, much more seriously, was the daily business of gentry life. If a friend of today could be an enemy of tomorrow because his lord had changed sides; if a change of power at the top could suddenly make a lord, whose associates were closely implicated in the security of your estates, *persona non grata* to the government or, worse, a traitor; if government became partisan; if there was no consistency in who ran the government and in whose interests; if all this happened, then the gentry were deprived of much of the basis of their way of life. Not everyone had the courage or the connections to follow the example of Sir Thomas Harrington of Hornby, Lancashire. In 1458 or 1459, knowing that his master, the earl of Salisbury, was about to make potentially fatal cause with the duke of York, he deliberately gave his lands in trust to a group of enemies, on the grounds that by this means he would safeguard them whoever won. It is more than possible that during the later 1450s the gentry passively withdrew their support, not only from their lords in many cases, but from the king as well. So, by 1460 there was a dwindling constituency for the rule of Henry VI in any form, whoever ran it, leaving two opposing factions to fight it out, the Yorkists and the Lancastrians. The two sides may rightly be given these titles at this stage because neither represented the broad mass of landowning society, any more than either was able to stand for the

[10]   See above, p. 36, for numbers of tenants who could be raised from lordships in the north and on the Welsh Marches.
[11]   For the Welsh and northern Marches, see above, pp. 55–7.

authority of the king as a whole. Unless he had lost the natural loyalty of a large number of his subjects, Henry could simply not have been deposed, and it seems that this was how he did it with regard to the gentry. Why then did the Yorkists win rather than the Lancastrians? Partly this was a matter of luck and of Edward's good management. On a number of occasions in 1461 the victory could have gone the other way; had Edward been defeated at Mortimer's Cross, for example. But we should not neglect the rule of the queen, which was openly partisan, in the way it was built on private Lancastrian power, located in a Lancastrian capital at Coventry rather than in the national capital, and in the way her enemies were treated, except when she was restrained by the lords. It is noticeable that in the periods of Yorkist rule, between Northampton and Wakefield and between Edward's entry into London and victory at Towton, we can trace in some of the transactions of the gentry a move to seek protection from the new power. For instance, Thomas Tropnell, a Wiltshire esquire, who had been quite intimately bound up with local 'Lancastrian' nobles like the Hungerfords and the earl of Wiltshire, hastened to seek Edward of March's protection in a land dispute after the battle of Northampton, while his opponent was simultaneously enfeoffing the disputed land to all the leading Yorkist lords, including Edward himself. This is, of course, an illustration of the gentry's problems in protecting their interests at such a difficult time, but the evidence as it stands at the moment suggests a more pronounced sympathy for the Yorkists when they were in command than for the royal government.

A case has been made that in the late 1450s the queen was seriously trying to reconstruct the Lancastrian retinue that had been destroyed under Henry VI by neglect, incompetence and too much concentration of too many Duchy offices in too few hands. Attention has been focused especially on the queen's recruitment in the Duchy regions in the mid-lands and on the appointment of household sheriffs to several counties at this time. However, the theory does not bear investigation. For a start, Margaret's efforts were concentrated in her dower lands and in the lordships of her son the Prince of Wales, so they did not affect the whole Duchy. Then, there is no evidence that even in these areas Margaret had anything like the wholesale gentry commitment that had previously been evident in some Lancastrian areas. It was an openly partisan policy which was unlikely to garner wide support. That it existed at all is an indictment, for it was only a new usurper like Henry IV who needed this kind of private military power; real kings were given the power of their subjects with open hands. Margaret's efforts to recreate the Lancastrian constituency in the midlands and to add to this the force of the oldest royal lands, in Cheshire, had the effect of turning Henry back into a private subject, the duke of Lancaster, the very status that his two predecessors had worked so hard to rise above. So had her attempts to extract money as well as men from the regions of the crown's private landed power, Lancashire, Cheshire and north Wales. It is clear that this hastily patched-together following, even though buttressed by Lancastrian nobles with midland estates like Shrewsbury and Beaumont and by the royal presence in the region, never had the breadth of local allegiance of the Duchy network at its height. This is apparent in the lack of a significant showing of midland gentry on the Lancastrian side in the battles of 1459–61. Even at Blore Heath, which was fought in Staffordshire, north midland nobles and gentry seem not to have been greatly in evidence and most of Margaret's army appears to have come from the neighbouring county of Cheshire.

In the same way, an established king had no need to appoint local officials from his private following: his power was public and all his subjects were bound to uphold it. Indeed, the appointment of household men as sheriffs in the later 1450s represents less a household policy than an act of desperation, which can be seen in other appointments to local office. The queen's government was less and less able to trust the gentry, while the gentry were less and less willing to commit themselves. The government had to resort to the appointment of increasingly unsuitable local officers, including men who did not even meet the official qualifications and household men who had often become cut off from the places of origin where they were now trying to enforce the king's rule. In the end, Lancastrian or not, loyalties were largely decided by whether the gentry had any faith in the regime. It is noticeable, for example, that three prominent Nottinghamshire gentry, William Babington, John Stanhope and Robert Strelley, all household men, from impeccable Lancastrian backgrounds, rapidly accommodated themselves to the Yorkist government as early as October 1460.

By the end of the decade, landowners, especially the gentry, must have been desperate for some way out of the impasse, even if many were not ready to fight to achieve it. Perhaps many did not care whether it was a Lancastrian solution or a Yorkist one, as long as it meant the strong unitary rule that could only be achieved by the destruction of one side or the other. This was no longer two rival forms of authority acting in the name of an ineffective king but a war to the death between two equal factions. But the more partisan approach of the queen could well have tipped the scales in her rivals' favour. Of those who were prepared to fight, perhaps marginally more wanted to fight for Edward by 1461, especially as the descent of the northerners aroused the fears of the south as a whole. What seems sure is that no-one was particularly keen on deposing poor old Henry VI; his deposition was merely incidental to getting rid of the queen.

The deposition of Henry VI took an unprecedented form. Both Edward II and Richard II had been deposed peaceably because no-one would fight for them. In fact, loyalty to the monarch was so strong that it required appalling behaviour on the ruler's part for him to be deserted at a stroke by all his subjects. So, the need to go to war to decide the succession is partly explained by Henry's extreme limpness, and is further evidence of that limpness. He had done nothing wrong – in fact he had done nothing – and he was king, so some nobles and gentry were still ready to defend his throne, especially as he was Henry V's son. But it also arose out of the circumstances of the 1450s which in turn arose out of the peculiar nature of Henry's rule, or lack of it. If there were alternative sources of authority, then one of them had to defeat the other. Unfortunately for Edward IV this was only a partial defeat and the rival power was there throughout the 1460s. There was also the legacy of the decade for the gentry. There is evidence that, left to their own devices by the magnates, or unwilling to be pushed around by them, they had begun to manage affairs among themselves with far less direct reference to the magnates; this development has been traced in both Warwickshire and the north midlands. What it might mean for the balance of power within the shires and the country had yet to be seen.

8

EDWARD IV'S FIRST REIGN: 1461–1471

Edward began his reign under difficult circumstances. The war had left the country divided and disordered. Beyond the battlefields themselves, the absence of any real central authority in 1460–1 was the occasion for the reopening of old quarrels and the opening of new ones. The king did not yet control some of the peripheries of his kingdom, notably Wales and the north of England. Amongst the nobility he had little support. When it came to a choice between Henry VI and a usurper, several major figures had in the end committed themselves to the king. We have seen that the royal forces at Towton included the earls of Northumberland, Devon and Wiltshire and Lord Clifford, all of whom met their end there; amongst many other peers with the king in this battle were the dukes of Somerset and Exeter, the earl of Shrewsbury and Lords Roos, Dacre and Scales. Lord Hungerford had not fought at Towton but went into exile with the Lancastrians. The Nevilles had remained the Yorkists' only substantial noble allies, although at Towton, when he himself was already king, Edward was joined by a larger body of peers, including the Yorkists' unpredictable ally the duke of Norfolk. There were also the Bourchiers, whose head was Henry Bourchier, count of Eu, Edward's uncle by marriage. While this family had never committed itself wholesale to York in the 1450s, its members had tended to uphold Yorkist periods of rule and some of them had held office in both Protectorates.[1] They were of middling rather than great noble status but, like the Nevilles, there were several of them, and one of their number, Thomas, was archbishop of Canterbury.

[1] See above, pp. 135, 137.

But, taken as whole, Edward's support among the nobility was no better than Henry IV's had been after the rebellion of Richard II's nobles in 1400. Like Henry IV he needed therefore to build bridges between himself and the magnates, including those who had fought for the previous king. This was even harder for him than it had been for Henry IV because of the existence of the rival power in exile in Scotland. Magnanimity would have to be shown to his former enemies, especially the more powerful of them, if he was to be secure and be able to create a proper basis for the governance of his kingdom. But there was always an alternative master for Edward's old antagonists to return to. If he was unable to enlarge his power-base he would, like Henry IV, be at the mercy of the family that had helped him to the throne, in Henry's case the Percies, in Edward's their northern rivals the Nevilles. Between them the Nevilles controlled two large earldoms – Warwick and Salisbury, both now in the hands of the earl of Warwick – and three minor peerages, while the female members of the family, who included the king's own mother, gave them connections with most of the noble houses. On Edward's accession another Neville, Warwick's brother John, was raised to the peerage as Lord Montagu. The king was young (he had his nineteenth birthday not long after Towton) and, although he had already proved himself a formidable warrior, was very inexperienced. His older and much more experienced cousin, the earl of Warwick, was more than likely to try to dominate him. An indication of how much influence Warwick expected to have over the king is that the earl attested no fewer than forty-one of the forty-six charters issued by Edward between 1461 and 1464. This does not necessarily mean that he was with the king on nearly every occasion on which a charter was issued, but it certainly suggests a close degree of proximity. Only Hastings, the chamberlain of the king's household, whose job demanded that he be with the king much of the time, attested more.

The story of Edward's first reign is one of gradual conquest, literally of parts of his kingdom, and figuratively of the obstacles to his rule. Then, his very success brought about his temporary downfall, when it became apparent to Warwick that the king meant to be master in his own kingdom and would soon be in a position to be so. In Edward's first year there were dangers from several quarters in addition to the more serious problems in Wales and the north: in the west country, in Hampshire, in Somerset, Dorset and Wiltshire. All this disaffection along the south coast was compounded by the threat of a French invasion in favour of Queen Margaret. In February 1462 it was necessary to send a formidable commission to deal with treason and disturbances over much of the country. In the same month the earl of Oxford, one of the few major nobles who

had contrived to remain essentially neutral throughout the period up to
1461, was tried and executed for taking part in a Lancastrian plot, along
with his son and heir. There was also serious local disorder; in Warwickshire, for example, where a number of feuds broke out in 1461–2, and in
Norfolk, where the coroner Thomas Denys was murdered in August
1461, possibly on the orders of the duke of Norfolk, and where the
elections to Edward's first parliament were accompanied by mob violence.

The king took all this very seriously. Immediately after Towton, as he
returned to London to be crowned, he perambulated through parts of the
north and midlands. In July 1461 he mustered an army for Wales, where
Jasper Tudor was still at large and where several castles were still held by
the Lancastrians. The army was led by one of the principal Yorkist
adherents in Wales of the 1450s, Sir William Herbert, and the son of the
other, Sir Walter Devereux, also called Walter; in September Pembroke
Castle in the south was taken and in October the Lancastrians under Tudor
and the duke of Exeter were defeated outside Caernarvon in the far north.
The north Wales stronghold of Harlech remained in Lancastrian hands,
however, and the whole country was still only exiguously held by the new
dynasty. In late summer and early autumn of 1461 Edward himself perambulated through the south of England to the west country, and thence
northwards along the Welsh border to his castle of Ludlow. Meanwhile,
the earl of Warwick was trying to complete the Yorkist conquest of the
north. Before examining how he did this, we must look at how Edward
established his rule once the immediate crisis of accession was over.

There were obvious rewards for Edward's major allies of the war, of
whom Warwick was the greatest. He received numbers of offices on the
royal lands and a collection of confiscated estates, including Percy properties in Yorkshire and Clifford ones in Westmorland. Other Nevilles were
also rewarded, for example Lord Fauconberg, who was made earl of Kent,
and John Neville, whose grant of a peerage has been mentioned. Edward's
kinsman, Henry Bourchier, was raised to the earldom of Essex and there
were grants to Essex's younger brother, William, Lord Fitzwarin. Edward
also ennobled Humphrey, one of Essex's sons, as Lord Cromwell, by
virtue of the fact that Humphrey had married one of the previous Lord
Cromwell's nieces and coheiresses. However, the Nevilles were the only
great noble family to be favoured on the grand scale, and others, including
John duke of Suffolk and the earl of Arundel, brothers-in-law respectively
of the king and the earl of Warwick, did much less well. In fact, the
rewards handed out to 'old' nobles and their families in the early part of
Edward's reign were very much for those who deserved well for their
loyalty to the Yorkists between 1459 and 1461.

There were two reasons for this. The first was Edward's laudable aim of winning over former enemies. That meant limiting the number of attainders of Lancastrians. In 1461 there were a mere fourteen attainders of nobles, all of whom had either died on the Lancastrian side in the violence of the previous two years, or were still in arms against the king. A remarkable degree of mercy was shown. For example, the duke of Buckingham's property was not confiscated; instead it remained with the duke's widow during the minority of Buckingham's grandson and heir. In 1467 she married Walter Blount, the Derbyshire man who had been linked to the Yorkists in the mid-to-late-1450s. Similarly, the estates of the earls of Shrewsbury were preserved for the heir, who was twelve years old at Edward's accession. Other lesser nobles, like the Stanleys of Lancashire and Cheshire, were pardoned their own involvement in the wars on the Lancastrian side. A large measure of mercy was shown towards gentry participants: of the ninety-six non-nobles attainted, many were beneath the rank of gentry or had already died in arms, or were to do so in the next three years, or were irreconcilable. This display of mercy, although necessary and laudable, restricted the number of grants available.

The second reason for Edward's limited generosity to existing nobles was that much of what did come to the crown was wanted for other purposes, the establishment of a new 'Yorkist' peerage. All of these new peers were from the gentry retainers who had served Edward's father faithfully, and at some considerable personal risk, between 1459 and 1461, and in some cases earlier. They were Humphrey Stafford of Southwick and Hook in the west country, made a baron in 1461 and given a large part of the confiscated Courtenay estates; Sir John Dinham, another westcountryman, the Yorkist hero of 1459–60, who received much of the Hungerford estate and was raised to the peerage in 1467; Sir John Wenlock, another recipient of confiscated Lancastrian estates, made a baron in 1461; Sir Walter Blount, created Lord Mountjoy in 1465 and, as we have seen, married to the Stafford dowager in 1467; Sir Walter Devereux, given lands in the Welsh Marches and elsewhere and created Lord Ferrers of Chartley in 1461 (he had married the heiress to the title some years before); and the two greatest, Lords Herbert and Hastings. Herbert had served both Warwick and York in Wales in the 1450s, and we have seen how, with Devereux, he had upheld Yorkist interests (as well as their own) with considerable violence in Wales in that decade. As a result of confiscations (chiefly of Jasper Tudor earl of Pembroke), minorities (Buckingham, Shrewsbury and Norfolk, who died in late 1461) and the king's personal possession of the Principality and the Lancaster and York estates, Edward was in a position to deal with the Welsh problem by reallocating power on a massive scale. Nearly all of this went to Herbert, first in south Wales, then, after 1463, as Edward's control of the country grew, in north Wales as well. Even Warwick's ambitions in south Wales had to give way to Herbert. Herbert was given considerable lands elsewhere, was made a baron in 1461 and in 1468 became earl of Pembroke. William Lord Hastings became Edward's greatest friend and ally. A man of impeccable loyalty, even unto death, he came from a family located in the midlands and Yorkshire that had served the March/York line since the early years of the century. He was made the king's chamberlain in 1461, the year he became a baron, and kept this office, which gave him constant access to the king, for the rest of the reign. Most of his grants were in the midlands – Leicestershire, Lincolnshire and Rutland – and were from the confiscated estates of Lord Roos, one of the Lancastrians in exile in Scotland, Viscount Beaumont and the earl of Wiltshire.

One other major recipient of confiscated lands was Edward's younger brother George, created duke of Clarence, eleven years old when Edward came to the throne. Between 1461 and 1465 he was given a large number of forfeited estates. These included the Honor of Richmond, formerly of Edmund Tudor earl of Richmond, who had died in 1456, now held by Edmund's widow, Margaret Beaufort.[2] This was not confiscated but, as a crown property, taken back in the Resumption of 1461. Nevertheless, it was tantamount to confiscation, since it is doubtful whether it would have been resumed had its previous owner not been perceived to be an enemy of the house of York, while his brother, Jasper, was still very obviously hostile. In 1464–5 Clarence also received large tracts of Duchy of Lancaster lands in the north midlands, including the Honor of Tutbury. As is suggested by these grants of royal lands and the way royal lands and offices were handed out to Warwick and in Wales, it does not seem that Edward was yet ready to take the disordered regions dominated by royal estates personally in hand.

It was this combination of old and new nobles that formed the basis of Edward's rule, but he also needed the unregenerate Lancastrians, and most of those were in Scotland or resisting the new king in the north. All the major castles in Northumberland were held by Lancaster, and the king of Scotland was threatening to intervene over the border. In July 1461 Warwick was granted complete control of the northern March: hitherto, the Nevilles had usually had the wardenship of the West March and the Percies, now disgraced, of the East March. It was also Warwick who was given overall command of the campaigns to bring the region under control. By August 1462, despite some previous reverses, the Northumbrian castles of Alnwick, Bamburgh and Dunstanburgh were in the king's

---

[2] This effectively excluded all the Yorkshire lands of the Honor, except for the castle of Richmond itself (see below, pp. 184–5).

hands. However, in October Queen Margaret, who had been pleading for help in France without much success, arrived in the north with her husband. All three castles either defected or fell; in a paradigm of Edward IV's predicament with respect to the pardoning of former Lancastrians, Sir Ralph Percy, who had surrendered Dunstanburgh to the new king the previous year and been pardoned and allowed to remain constable there, handed it over to the Lancastrians. The situation in the north was particularly tricky because of the strong local allegiances, notably to the Percies but also to other northern lords. Many of these lords, among them Clifford, Dacre, Roos and Fitzhugh, had fought for the Lancastrians. Edward badly needed to win over northern landowners and especially members of the earl of Northumberland's family and their associates. Even so, in 1462 few local gentry rose in Henry's favour and, as Warwick and then the king himself went rapidly north, the Lancastrians returned to Scotland by sea, most of them suffering shipwreck on the way.

Just after Christmas Dunstanburgh and Bamburgh surrendered. With Bamburgh came the duke of Somerset who had commanded it on behalf of the Lancastrians. He was pardoned and restored to his lands and titles. This was by no means as foolish as has been suggested, but was all of a piece with the need to bring Edward's former enemies to his side. If Somerset came, then many others might follow. In the same vein, Sir Ralph Percy was pardoned again and given command of both castles. Somerset himself helped to take Alnwick early in 1463, although a relieving army of Scots enabled the garrison under Lord Hungerford to escape. By now it seemed that Edward was master of his whole kingdom apart from Harlech Castle. But this was not yet the end. In March 1463, after first Edward and then Warwick had left the north, Sir Ralph Percy once again let an army of French and Scots into Dunstanburgh and Bamburgh. At Alnwick, Sir Ralph Grey, a northerner who had actually helped Hastings take the castle in 1462, allowed Hungerford to return. In May, in recognition that a resident commander was needed in that area, especially now that Warwick was less continuously in the north and more constantly about the king, Lord Montagu was given command of the East March, which covered the problem region of Northumberland. Nevertheless, Warwick went north, only to find a threatened invasion by Margaret and the Scots. Fortunately it was easily repulsed, and a punitive raid over the border discouraged the Scots from any further adventures in England. Margaret and her son set sail for France. In September a major expedition to the north was mounted by land and by sea, paid for by the first parliamentary grant of the reign, and led by the king. But although Edward did go to York with an army and lingered in Yorkshire until the following January, there was no campaign. This infuriated the taxpayers but, before the expedition fizzled out, Edward had secured a major diplomatic triumph: in October 1463 a year's truce between England and France was agreed through the good offices of the duke of Burgundy. It ended for the moment French assistance to either Scotland or the Lancastrians.

That, however, was still not the end of Lancastrian resistance in the north. The duke of Somerset, despite being showered with signs of affection by the king, had defected at the end of 1463 and escaped to Bamburgh, in Lancastrian hands since the previous March. This was a bad moment for the king, for the fact that he had taken a tax but had not fought was causing some unrest. In Wales, Lancashire and Cheshire the unrest took a treasonable form, some of it possibly fomented by Somerset who had fled to Bamburgh from Wales. In the event these troubles were laid to rest but there was a more serious crisis in the north-east. In early 1464, Somerset began to use Bamburgh as a base for raids into the surrounding area. Amongst the leaders of his force was the renegade Ralph Percy and Humphrey Neville. The latter, a nephew of the earl of Westmorland, was another who had been pardoned by Edward. They began to take a number of places in Northumberland. Meanwhile another northern castle came into the hands of the Lancastrians, as the disgraced Cliffords took back their castle of Skipton-in-Craven in Yorkshire and declared themselves for the former king. Montagu was sent to escort the Scottish ambassadors who were coming to York to negotiate with the English. At Hedgeley Moor, north of Alnwick, he was attacked, albeit unsuccessfully, by an army that included Somerset, Sir Ralph Percy and other Lancastrian leaders.

Edward was now organising a massive expedition to deal with the north, and peace between England and Scotland looked imminent; the Lancastrians needed to act quickly if they were to have any chance at all. They moved south towards Newcastle, Montagu's base, taking Henry VI with them. On 15 May, at Hexham, Montagu attacked them and secured a quick victory. Somerset was taken and executed, along with Lords Hungerford and Roos and numbers of other Lancastrians, including the egregious William Tailboys of the anti-Suffolk petitions of 1450.[3] Montagu was rewarded with the title, and some of the lands, of the earldom of Northumberland and in late June he and his brother Warwick took the fortresses of Alnwick, Dunstanburgh and Bamburgh, the first two without resistance, the third after the only siege of the whole northern campaign. In May and June Edward completed negotiations for a fifteen-year truce with the Scots at York. In mid-July he left the north, his work there now largely complete. In July 1465 Henry VI, who had gone into hiding after Hexham, was captured in Ribblesdale and put in the Tower. A significant

---

[3] See above, p. 109.

indication of the progress that Yorkist governance had made in the north was that Henry was betrayed by local gentry.

Nevertheless, Edward had had in a sense to admit defeat; he had hoped to palliate local powers, which meant not just the gentry who had been pardoned and in some cases revolted again, but the Percies, the other great power in the north. This was desirable both to ensure that it was the whole of the north that was on his side, not just the Neville parts, but also to restore the natural brake on Neville power, and it was why he persisted with pardoning hostile northerners like Sir Ralph Percy and Sir Humphrey Neville. It had proved impossible and a Neville had been made earl of Northumberland. Thus there remained question-marks over the loyalty of the north and over the Nevilles' ability to keep the allegiance of the entire region. Edward's wider attempts at conciliation, seen most notably in the treatment of the duke of Somerset, had also come to nothing. The restoration of the heir to the earl of Oxford in 1462 proved similarly abortive, although not until six years later.[4] The trouble was that, as long as the rival Lancastrian power existed, the policy of forgiveness of former enemies and obliteration of their past was if not unworkable at least unpredictable in its outcome. There was always a way out for restored but discontented former Lancastrians, and in the end this, with the related problem of the north, was to prove Edward's temporary undoing. It would have been best had he killed Henry once he had him in captivity. It has been argued that this had little point until Prince Edward had been taken, but there was a real difference between an anointed crowned king who was Henry V's son and a Prince of Wales who was Margaret's. That Henry VI, uniquely among deposed kings, was allowed to live was a misjudgement, but it is further evidence that he was entirely ineffectual and undislikeable. It also indicates a refreshing lack of vindictiveness on Edward's part.

All the same, considering the extremely unpropitious circumstances in which he began to rule, Edward had made considerable strides by the end of 1465. The very fact of survival, emphasised by the successful suppression of Lancastrian resistance and the recognition of Edward by England's foreign enemies who might have helped the Lancastrians, strengthened his hand. Once he had shown he was here to stay, his rule could become the basis for a return to normal relations in the shires and that in itself gave a vested interest to all landowners in its continuance. Very little is known as yet about the state of order in the provinces under Edward IV, although ignorance has not deterred impressionistic generalisations. We do know that Edward took his duties regarding the law extremely seriously, as well

⁴ See below, pp. 173–4.

he might given his father's political tradition, the state of the realm and the need to show he could do better than his predecessor. Several declarations early in the reign make his determination to enforce the law absolutely clear. We have already had a glimpse of his promptitude in visiting disturbed areas soon after he came to the throne, in contrast to Henry VI's normal inertia. This pattern was to be particularly marked in the early years of the reign, when the king went, for example, to the east midlands in 1462, to Cambridge in 1464 and to Gloucester in the same year. Some of these visits were made in the company of judicial commissions. Other activity included legislation right at the start of the reign to strengthen the restrictions on giving liveries, and in 1468, for the first time, most forms of retaining were made illegal. In the event, a certain amount was allowed by royal licence but that gave the king the means to control the process. However, since the links between nobility and gentry, of which retaining was merely a part, were fundamental to the functioning of government and society, such ties did not disappear. The legislation, made in response to a serious outbreak of disorder in Derbyshire,[5] was essentially propaganda to show that his heart was in the right place and an immediate weapon to be used against men who were abusing the law too obviously.[6]

Ultimately of course enforcement of the law depended not on machinery but on the country's faith in the king's ability to make his law work. That, as we saw when examining the system in general, depended to a large extent on the king demonstrating his concern and his impartiality, and on the nobility reposing their trust in the king. Henry VI's reign is an exemplary demonstration of how loss of faith in the king produced a collapse of order which went downwards from the nobility to the gentry and then even into the lower orders. Thus, the energy displayed in the early years and throughout the decade was one part of Edward's work to re-establish confidence in his law and the retaining legislation another. Then there were the statements, clearly designed to be heard and passed on, reported in the Paston letters, in which the king made explicit his intention to have his law obeyed and to act against all who resisted it. Practical action reinforced his words, as in 1461, when John Paston was put in the Fleet prison for failing to obey the king's command to appear before him in his quarrel with Sir John Howard. But what is more remarkable is that, despite the series of denunciations of Paston to the king by Howard, who was one of his own household men, and by others, Paston was eventually released and it was Howard who was put in prison. As this episode suggests, there is evidence that Edward was beginning to make systematic use of his council to deal with powerful offenders in a

---

[5] See below, p. 165.   [6] As it was used in 1469 (see below, p. 165).

summary manner that avoided the delays and political infighting associated with the common law. This is another area that still needs proper study, but it is evident that in Warwickshire, where the earl of Warwick was not making a very satisfactory show of imposing his presence on a county where he was now all-powerful, the king was bringing some of the worst offenders before him and forcing them to make bonds for their good behaviour.[7] It is indeed more than likely that bonds and recognisances were used more frequently under Edward IV. As for regaining the confidence of the nobility, there was much that must have helped to do this: the success of the early campaigns; the lack of vindictiveness towards former enemies; the return to all the monarchical virtues of listening to counsel and complaints, rewarding virtue and, perhaps above all, displaying energy in all aspects of his rule, must have given them the assurance to do their job in the shires.

However, until Edward was in uncontested control of his kingdom, he could not be as hard on some of his more powerful subjects as he might sometimes have wished to be. This can be seen in East Anglia, where the Pastons were engaged in a ferocious dispute with the duke of Suffolk over part of the inheritance of Sir John Fastolf. Although it is arguable that the Pastons were the real destabilising force in this affair, Suffolk behaved with the most appalling ferocity in sacking one of the properties at issue and should have been brought to order. This did not happen, and the reason was probably that the duke, who was Edward's brother-in-law, was too important to him to be harshly disciplined. Equally, although, as order deteriorated in East Anglia in 1469, the dukes of Norfolk and Suffolk and a large number of their followers were indicted under the retaining legislation of 1468, the reward for the dukes' relative loyalty during the major crisis of 1469–71 was pardons for themselves and most of their men. There is a similar story in Derbyshire where, later in the decade, there was the violent feud that occasioned the retaining legislation. This was between the Vernons, a prominent gentry family, and Lord Grey of Codnor, a lesser Derbyshire noble. In response Edward sent a powerful commission in 1468, but it was hampered by the fact that Clarence and Hastings, its leading members, were increasingly locked into confrontation over their favouring of either side, and the earls of Shrewsbury and Warwick were also behind the Vernons. All efforts to restrain the parties, including the legislation to forbid retaining, were to no avail because the participants were too powerful and Warwick and Clarence on the verge of rebellion. It is only in the second reign that Edward's true ferocity towards delinquent magnates is to be seen.

[7] See above, pp. 59–60.

The issues we have looked at are the ones that really mattered in the establishment of Yorkist rule. Much less attention needs to be given to the royal finances, which often assume too large a part in the discussion of whether a stable monarchy was created under Edward IV. We must remember that, under normal circumstances, ordinary revenues just about matched ordinary expenditure, the exception being the cost of the various garrisons, notably Calais.[8] The latter was meant to be financed by the customs but these were declining because of the fall in wool exports and, during the 1460s, remained at an annual average of £25,000, slightly less than the average figure of about £30,000 between 1441 and 1452. Nevertheless, the extreme financial crises of the 1440s and 1450s were most unusual. They were due to a combination of mismanagement, prolonged expenditure on war, which increasingly outstripped the taxation that was meant to pay for it, and finally growing doubts about whether Henry VI would stay on the throne to repay his creditors. The real problem, especially after the death of Cardinal Beaufort, had been that lack of confidence in the crown's ability to pay its way had led to collapse of credit. Without credit no government can achieve liquidity while it waits for revenues to come in.

Under Edward in the 1460s confidence and therefore credit, from London merchants, the Staple and Italians, were restored. This was despite the fact that he had internal campaigns to finance, initially without any taxation beyond the customs. We saw that when he finally got a grant in 1463 his failure to fight the promised campaign produced resentment and some unrest, and he had in fact to remit £6,000 of the £37,000 he had been promised.[9] The second tax he was granted, in 1468, ostensibly for an invasion of France, was pocketed in the same way. Doubtless these dubious arrangements helped pay off past debts, and they could just about be justified by the fact that many of the debts had been incurred in warfare. Moreover, there were other levies, such as the demand in 1464 that all recipients of royal grants above a certain value contribute to the northern campaign and a clerical tax of the same year, nominally for a crusade, most of which probably went to Edward. Then, in 1466, by the Act of Retainer, he was finally able to resolve the problem of the payment of the Calais garrison: the Staplers undertook to pay the soldiers, recovering their money by taking the profits on the wool custom levied at Calais. As we have seen, customs, if they did not grow, at least remained stable, so the arrangement worked. Although there are records of unpaid royal debts in

---

[8] See above, p. 30.

[9] From 1445, it had become customary to remit £6,000 of the normal £37,000 that a tax brought in, to allow for exemptions for poverty, but in 1463 Edward was promised this extra £6,000 and it was this that he had to give up.

the 1460s – in 1468 Walter Blount Lord Mountjoy complained he had been waiting three years for almost £3,500 expended for the king – there is nothing on the scale of Henry VI's indebtedness, and it has been pointed out that complaints about the royal household's failure to pay its debts disappear from the rolls of parliament from 1461.

Although political stability and the absence of war were undoubtedly the main reasons for the restoration of financial stability in the 1460s, there were nevertheless some changes in financial policy that need to be considered, especially those that are thought to be significant in the light of later developments. First, Edward did come to the throne with a 'Yorkist' programme of financial reform. Central to this were a more stringent control of household expenditure and the related resumptions, to take back over-liberal grants. The very fact of there being an active king in command was bound to reduce the number of household hangers-on, although the necessary costs of administration and maintaining the king's person, his family and a suitably grand life-style and following could not be reduced below the level of £11,000–£12,000 a year. This was still substantially less than the £24,000 a year which the household was said – perhaps with some exaggeration – to cost in 1449. By 1450–1 there were over 800 men in the royal household but by 1463–4 this had been reduced to about 550, and in 1466–7, even after an increase in the 'above stairs' household, the part that was significant to the king's political following, there were only 630 or more. Another telling contrast is in the incomes reserved for the households of the two queens: Elizabeth Woodville had £4,500 in 1466–7, while in 1452–3 Margaret of Anjou was receiving £7,500. Efforts were made to ensure that the household was not only financially restrained but sufficiently endowed to pay its way. For example, from 1462 all fixed payments to the exchequer worth 40 shillings or more were to be reserved for the household and from 1466 the profits of the Cornish mines were similarly reserved. Acts of Resumption were passed in 1461, 1465 and 1467 but, although they doubtless helped with the necessary slimming after the excesses of the previous king's adult reign, their purpose was less to reduce the household and the costs of governance than to allow the reallocation of royal lands for political purposes. We have seen how that of 1461 made possible the return of the Honor of Richmond from Edmund Tudor's widow to the crown, so that it could be given to the king's brother, George. Those of 1465 and 1467 were also important to the endowment of the royal family. The 1467 act had the additional purpose, in common with most of the resumptions and attempted resumptions of the 1450s, of encouraging the Commons to grant the tax of the following year.

Secondly, it has been suggested that in this decade Edward began the

'Yorkist land revenue experiment'[10] that was to develop during the Yorkist period and finally be brought to magnificent fruition under Henry VII.
This policy is held to comprise two elements. First there is said to have
been intensive exploitation of royal lands for the first time, so that they
made an increasingly important contribution to the royal finances. Secondly there is said to be a gradual shift away from using the exchequer as
the principal place of account for the royal finances to the chamber, the
main financial agency within the king's household, starting with lands but
eventually moving on to the bulk of the royal revenues. The question will
be examined further in relation to Edward's second reign and to Henry
VII, but, on the face of it, there are certainly signs of such a policy in the
1460s. From 1461, steps were taken to create a special administration for
the various royal lands, which now included those of York and March, as
well as Lancaster and the older crown lordships of Cheshire and Cornwall
and the lands in Wales. This was staffed less by exchequer-trained men
than by experienced estate administrators, many of whom had learned
their trade on noble estates or crown properties. These officials accounted
not to the exchequer, which kept only a rather delayed watching-brief on
them, but directly to the chamber. That meant that the performance and
probity of the local estate officials was checked not from Westminster but
by personal visits to each property by the auditor or a deputy. The same
process applied to some of the lands more temporarily in royal hands, like
those of the underage Buckingham and the attainted Wiltshire.

This all sounds very impressive, but whether, in the 1460s, it was
intended as a 'land revenue experiment' or made a substantial difference to
the royal finances is open to doubt. First, we should remember, that, as a
former noble, such practices probably came naturally to Edward. It would
have seemed entirely sensible to continue to administer his Yorkist estates
outside the exchequer, especially as the exchequer was an office for the
receipt, payment and accounting of funds; it was not and never had been
designed to run the king's private estates. In fact, there had been no
permanent royal estate, apart from Cornwall, Chester, the lands of the
Principality and some other Welsh properties, until the Duke of Lancaster
became king in 1399, and the first three had normally been given to the
king's eldest son and placed under a separate administration. In the same
way, the Lancastrian kings had always kept their own Lancastrian properties separate from the rest of the royal finances and audited by their own
officials. In 1461, when the addition of the Yorkist lands made the
permanent royal estate very large indeed, it must have seemed logical to
bring them all together in a more or less centralised administration.

<hr />

[10] The phrase is B. P. Wolffe's in *The Crown Lands 1461–1536* (London, 1970).

Furthermore, to a former nobleman, it must equally have been sensible to make them all subject to a form of audit and management that had long been routine on noble estates. At the same time, Edward had witnessed the apparent incapacity of the exchequer during the 1450s. He himself may not have realised that this had more to do with a general paralysis of the royal finances, arising from heavy demands and lengthy mismanagement, and of government, arising from the absence of real kingship. Even if his diagnosis was incorrect, it is true that the central government had been so inert for so long that close personal supervision of its financial management from the royal household was probably desirable at this stage. Thus, the policy in its origins has much more to do with immediate circumstances than with long-term revolution. We have seen, in examining the establishment of the Yorkist regime, that the lands temporarily in royal hands were in many cases soon granted out and others eventually returned to the heirs of the original owners. This was as it should be, for the king did not need the lands to finance the royal government, which, if properly run, had no requirement for financial exploitation on this scale. He did need them to ensure the stability of the government. This would be done by the creation of the Yorkist nobility and the reassurance to the country at large that came from the restoration of some of the heirs of Edward's former enemies. It is very difficult to judge the contribution of the royal lands to the king's finances in the 1460s. There are no chamber accounts for this period to tell us how much the king received directly from the lands and for the whole reign there is a record of payment from the lands to the exchequer for the years 1462–5 alone. This tells us that the maximum they contributed then was £2,000 in any one year. Thus, while allowing for the lack of evidence as to the full value to the king of the royal lands in this decade, it seems unlikely that the lands were in any way crucial to Edward's financial position at this time.

The years 1465–6 are the high point of the first reign. Edward had been learning on the job and had made some mistakes but he had done remarkably well. It is significant that at this time he was able to settle a number of long-running noble disputes, dating back to the previous reign and even earlier. These included one which had started in the 1450s, between the earls of Shrewsbury and the first earl's second wife, over this second family's claims on the Talbot inheritance.[11] The king was showing himself to be rather more than Warwick's tool, for example in his intervention in Warwickshire and in the strategy in the north, designed, even though it failed, to make the Nevilles share power there. He showed his

[11] This second wife was Margaret, daughter of Richard Beauchamp earl of Warwick, who had quarrelled with Warwick the Kingmaker over the Warwick inheritance (see above, p. 127).

independence famously in the marriage to Elizabeth Woodville in 1464, completed secretly and hastily before he went north on campaign, which cocked a snook at Warwick's plans to have him marry a French princess. Even as Warwick came triumphantly south with the captive Henry VI in 1465, he must have wondered how long it would be before Edward was ready to jettison him, or at least to curtail his power severely. There was an inevitability about the collision of these two if Edward was to be in full command of his kingdom, just as there had been between Henry IV and the Percies. In each case, a great noble, in most unusual circumstances, had helped a usurper ascend the throne. In each case, once the usurper began to turn himself into a proper king, he would cease to be reliant on his 'kingmaker' and the latter's power could only wane. We must now look at the causes and progress of the confrontation between Edward IV and Warwick the Kingmaker.

It is not very likely that Edward allied himself with Elizabeth Woodville in order to build up an independent power-base; he already had a much firmer one in the new Yorkist peers than anything he could hope for from the formerly Lancastrian and, as it turned out, politically rather lightweight connections of the queen. The main motive behind what was in many ways a very unsuitable match for a king of England was almost certainly youthful impetuosity, impelled principally by Elizabeth's desirability, with perhaps the added attraction of flying in Warwick's face; after all, the king was still barely twenty-two at the time. However, there were substantial political implications to the marriage, for Elizabeth had a large number of relations, all eager to make the most out of this extraordinarily fortunate alliance. These were kin both of her father, Richard Woodville Lord Rivers, who had been a staunch supporter of Henry VI, and of her former husband, Sir John Grey, heir to Lord Grey of Groby, who had been killed on the Lancastrian side at St Albans II. Indeed it had been Elizabeth's efforts to secure her widow's portion from another part of the family after his death that had first brought her to the king's attention. She already had two sons by this marriage, and there were plenty of other Woodvilles and Greys waiting to benefit. Neither family was territorially outstanding and Elizabeth's father was the first Woodville to be raised to the peerage.

Sensibly, since grants of land were reserved for his complex balancing act between old enemies and friends and new Yorkist peerage, Edward, although he gave high office to one or two of them, endowed his rather grasping collection of in-laws principally by securing them good marriages, and thus at not a great deal of cost to himself. Elizabeth's brother, Anthony, the heir to Rivers, was already married to the heiress of Lord Scales and had been recognised by this title since late 1462. Now followed a cascade of fortunate matches. For example, two of the queen's sisters were married respectively to the young heir of Buckingham and the heir of Lord Herbert; Edward's step-son, Thomas, heir to the Groby title, was married to Anne Holland, heiress to the duke of Exeter, although she died soon after; rather shockingly, even to contemporaries, the twenty-year-old John Woodville, the queen's brother, became the fourth husband of the wealthy dowager duchess of Norfolk, then in her late sixties. Most families seem to have been happy to ally themselves with the queen's family; the one person who was apparently offended by these marriages was Warwick. This was partly on personal grounds, notably that Anne Holland was already betrothed to his nephew, George, son of John Neville, the newly promoted earl of Northumberland. He may also have objected to the use of his aged aunt, the duchess of Norfolk, in the Woodvilles' matrimonial aggrandisement. There was the added fact that he himself had two daughters and coheirs, and it has been argued with some justice that these marriages were taking away potential partners for them. Probably most significant was that the marriage itself was a declaration of independence by the king and that it resulted in the appearance of a group of court nobles who made it harder for Warwick to get to the king and were no doubt not very tactful about their presence near the throne. Symptomatic of the way things were going was the elevation to an earldom of the queen's father in 1466: the man whom Edward and Warwick had 'rated', with some justice, for his low birth in 1460. It must be true however that the real powers around Edward remained men like Hastings and Herbert and indeed Warwick himself. The only Woodville to hold important office in this period was Rivers, appointed treasurer in 1466, and he was a man with governmental experience under the Lancastrians.

It was in foreign affairs that Edward showed the most marked resistance to Warwick's plans at this stage. The marriage itself had been a rejection of Warwick's planned French marital alliance. By 1465 the duke of Burgundy was growing exceedingly suspicious of the French king Louis XI's plans to carry further the integration of the great ducal provinces of France into the realm; the recovery of Normandy and Aquitaine from the English under Louis' father had already been a stage in this process and Burgundy feared that it was next on the list. Indeed, the duke of Burgundy led a group of great French feudatories in the War of the Public Weal against Louis in that year. Together with the dependence of the English cloth trade on markets in the Netherlands, these constituted good grounds for resuscitating the alliance with England that had died at Arras in 1435, and from 1466 the countries began to move closer together. In 1466–7 both France and Burgundy were vying for English support but Edward showed himself considerably more enthusiastic about the Burgundian plan and largely left Warwick to deal with the French. Warwick's efforts climaxed in 1467 when he led an embassy to France but, in his absence, the Bastard of Burgundy, who had come to joust with Edward's brother-in-law, Lord Scales, was received with great grandeur. The death of Duke Philip of Burgundy in June broke off both sets of negotiations, but when a French embassy arrived in England later that month it was coldly and inadequately received. The envoys left unsatisfied in July and in November a commercial treaty between England and the Netherlands was signed. In March 1468 a marriage treaty was agreed with Burgundy, by which Edward's sister Margaret married Charles, the new duke. In 1468, as the tax of that year shows, Edward was beginning to think about a renewal of the French war, although possibly not very seriously. In fact, in October 1468 Charles of Burgundy agreed in the Treaty of Péronne not to aid the English. Even so, the French riposte to the signs of possible belligerence in England was ominous; in July of the same year Louis sponsored a Lancastrian expedition under Jasper Tudor to west Wales, where Harlech was still in Lancastrian hands. The capable response by the Herberts brought it to nothing, but it was a warning of what could happen if internal division in England opened the way to French intervention.

The timing of the actual breach between Edward and Warwick is obscure; Warwick was still being offered substantial favours as late as early 1469 and the rumours about his impending treason, circulating as early as 1467, may have had no basis in fact. How personally Warwick had taken the rejection of his foreign policy is also not clear and, in general, it is easy to read events back too early. However, as early as June 1467, while Warwick was on his grand embassy to France, his brother George, erstwhile bishop of Exeter and recently promoted archbishop of York, was summarily dismissed from the office of chancellor. He had been in this post since the Yorkists returned from exile in 1460. Perhaps the most direct evidence of Warwick's disaffection is his suborning of Edward's younger brother, the duke of Clarence. Clarence had come of age in 1466 and was beginning to assume political responsibilities. He had no reason to turn against his brother; we have seen that he had done well out of the relationship. But he seems to have been one of those unstable spirits – another was Duke Humphrey of Gloucester – for whom proximity to the throne brought unrealistic delusions of grandeur. By early 1467 a marriage between Clarence and Isabel, one of Warwick's daughters, had been suggested and firmly sat on by the king. Nevertheless, steps to obtain the papal dispensation, required because the two were within the prohibited degrees of consanguinity, continued.

Warwick and Clarence remained prominent around the king in 1468, although Edward may already have been suspicious of his brother. It is quite possible that Edward hoped that Warwick would see reason and accept a position as greatest magnate under the king rather than persist with his grandiose view of himself as arbiter of England's destinies at home and abroad. In January 1468, Warwick, still angry about the Burgundian visit while he was away in France, refused to come to the king as long as Herbert, Rivers and Scales were with him, but did then agree to attend a great council at Coventry, a city symbolically at the centre of the midland domain of both earl and king. There Archbishop Neville and Rivers presided over an accord between Warwick and, amongst others, two of Edward's own creations, Herbert and Stafford of Southwick. If Edward did indeed hope that Warwick would eventually see reason, that would explain the continuing favour towards him alongside the clear demonstration that the king was now master. Unfortunately neither Warwick nor Clarence was disposed to settle for half-measures where their own ambitions were concerned.

Compounding these political uncertainties was a growing incidence of internal instability in 1468–9. Some of this was largely a response to the king's embezzling of the tax for the non-existent French war; some, like the Derbyshire conflict, occurred chiefly because Edward was beginning to feel sufficiently unsure of himself to be extremely hesitant about disciplining powerful nobles. Moreover, Jasper Tudor's attempted invasion of Wales of that year, despite its failure and the subsequent surrender of Harlech Castle, must have added to the king's unease. Then there were the alleged Lancastrian plots of 1468, including that associated with Sir Thomas Cook, the London mercer, and others linked with the earl of Oxford (grandson of the earl executed in 1462) and the heirs of Courtenay of Devon and Hungerford. All three of these had been pardoned by Edward in his policy of reconciliation, while Oxford had been restored to his estates and title. Oxford was temporarily imprisoned in 1468 but, as one historian puts it, 'talked his way out of trouble'[12] and was pardoned in early 1469, while Hungerford and the Courtenay heir were executed in January 1469.

But it was the north that brought Edward down. Starting in April 1469 there was a series of risings in Yorkshire. How far these were genuinely popular, resulting from the tax and the commercial disadvantages of the Burgundian treaty, and how far they were from the start orchestrated by the Percy interest – to restore the family – or the Neville one is not clear. The first two risings were led by men calling themselves respectively Robin of Redesdale and Robin of Holderness. Both were put down by John Neville, the new earl of Northumberland. But in June the Redesdale

[12] C. Ross, *Edward IV* (London, 1974), p. 123.

rebellion started up again. In its new form this seems to have been a Neville-led affair. The bearer of the leader's pseudonym, on this occasion at least, was probably a member of the family of Sir John Conyers, Warwick's kinsman by marriage and his steward of Middleham in Yorkshire, the centre of the earl's northern earldom of Salisbury. Sons of three minor nobility, all of them connected with Warwick, were involved: Fitzhugh, Latimer and Dudley. Many of the other participants were Neville tenants or connections. But it was also a substantial popular rising. Suspecting nothing seriously amiss, Edward went north in a rather leisurely way to deal with it. At Newark in Nottinghamshire he learned of the size and threat of the rebel army that was coming south towards him. He retreated to Nottingham to await reinforcements and there he heard that Clarence was about to marry Warwick's daughter, despite the king's prohibition.

In July Warwick, Clarence, the earl of Oxford (despite his pardon) and Warwick's brother the archbishop of York had crossed the channel to Calais, where Warwick was still captain, and there on 11 July the archbishop performed the marriage. The next day a manifesto which was essentially that of the northern rebels was issued from Calais. Evidently designed to be within the 'Yorkist' tradition of demands for good governance, especially with respect to the royal finances and the proper execution of the law, it made great play with the tax, the disorder and the fact that Edward had 'estranged the grete lordes of [his] blood'.[13] It also complained of evil counsellors, amongst them the Woodvilles and the newly created earls of Pembroke and Devon, that is, Herbert and Stafford of Southwick. However, it is self-evidently a rather spurious document; while the tax may have been felt as an oppression by the northern commons, deteriorating order was more the result than the cause of Warwick's and Clarence's disaffection, and they seem to have had little support outside the Neville clan for claims that the king was led by evil counsel. It is not likely that the Woodvilles, although doubtless very irritating, were as powerful as alleged, and the closest of the king's counsellors, William Hastings, was not mentioned, because he was so manifestly not guilty of 'fals and disceyvable purpos'.[14] It is noticeable also that throughout this first phase of the rebellion Warwick's own brother, the earl of Northumberland, remained on the king's side.

Arriving in England from Calais in mid-July, Warwick and Clarence went first to London and then to meet Robin of Redesdale's forces, while the king still waited at Nottingham for forces from Wales, under Pem-

---

[13] The quotation is from the actual 'Robin of Redesdale' manifesto (*John Vale's Book*, p. 213). For what was issued from Calais, see J. Gillingham, *The Wars of the Roses* (London, 1981), p. 162.   [14] *John Vale's Book*, p. 214.

broke, and others commanded by Devon. Near Banbury the two arms of the king's forces became separated, for reasons that are unclear, and on 26 July at Edgecote in Northamptonshire the rebel army attacked and overran Pembroke's force; Devon's men, arriving later, were unable to prevent a defeat. Pursuing his private vendetta against those he perceived to have supplanted him in the king's favours, Warwick had Pembroke executed after the battle. In the same vein, Lord Rivers and John Woodville, the queen's father and brother, who were captured later, were executed at Coventry in August. Edward himself was taken at Olney in Buckinghamshire, on his way to join his troops, unaware of what had happened, and placed first in Warwick's castle at Warwick and then at Middleham. In August the earl of Devon was lynched by a mob at Bridgwater in Somerset.

None of this solved any of the rebels' problems. It has been suggested that there was a measure of support for their actions in 1469, and it is true that the nobles, even Hastings, did not resist Warwick and Clarence while the king was under their control, but Warwick and Clarence could not hope that this situation would survive any fiercer attack on the king and his associates. The trouble was that Warwick had no authority to rule and dared not attempt radical restructuring of the political status quo for fear of giving too much offence. This in itself shows how little his complaints about Edward's rule were echoed in the public consciousness. The predicament of Warwick and Clarence was similar to Richard of York's, except that at least York could base his case on the fact that the king was unfit to rule and the kingdom was falling apart. England did in fact show signs of falling apart under Warwick but that was largely because of the hiatus caused by his own actions. Norfolk laid violent siege to Caister castle. The Berkeley and Talbot families, still at loggerheads over the rival Beauchamp and Berkeley claims to the Berkeley inheritance, engaged in private war in Gloucestershire, which culminated in the 'battle' of Nibley Green in early 1470. There were further alarming conflicts in Lancashire and Yorkshire and disorder in Cheshire, while the Londoners rioted, and up and down the country various opportunities for private vengeance were taken. In August Sir Humphrey Neville, the untiring Lancastrian of the northern campaigns, who had gone into hiding after the battle of Hexham, started a revolt in Henry VI's favour along the northern border. At this point the king had to be released from Middleham to suppress it. Edward was then able to call loyal nobles to his side, including his youngest brother the duke of Gloucester, Suffolk, Arundel, Northumberland, Essex and Hastings, and make off to London.

He returned in mid-October, but in the months from then until early 1470 declined to punish the rebels, confining himself mostly to replacing his lost lieutenants. Gloucester became the major successor to Herbert in south Wales and Dinham to Devon in the south-west. Steps were taken to assure the king of a broad basis of support should Warwick and Clarence challenge him again. But the most momentous decision was to begin the process for the restoration of the Percy earl of Northumberland. The compensation for John Neville, the displaced earl, was ample: the marquisate of Montagu; marriage to Edward's eldest daughter Elizabeth for his son and heir George, combined with elevation for George to the dukedom of Bedford; the substantial Courtenay estates in Devon, made available by the earl of Devon's death, for himself. Even so, the treatment of Montagu turned out to be an error on Edward's part. The reasoning was sound; that the whole decade had shown that only the Percies could hold the Eastern March in check and it had been rebellion here that had been Edward's undoing. But Montagu had been the one loyal member of his family and it was unwise to cross him by depriving him of one of the great northern titles, however well he was recompensed. The Percy restoration also cost Warwick the former Percy lands which had helped sustain his wardenship of the West March and cost Montagu the wardenship of the East March. Moreover, at the same time, there were signs that Edward was contemplating the restoration of the heir of Lord Dacre, as another northern lord who might help settle the region, and this would have created a rival to Warwick's diminished power in the north-west.

The next phase started in Lincolnshire, with another of those local disturbances that had become so common during this crisis of governance. Here the main protagonists were Sir Thomas Burgh, one of Edward's more important household men, and Richard Lord Welles, a Lincolnshire noble. Again it is uncertain how early Warwick and Clarence became involved, but when in early March Edward, accepting his responsibility for his own man, announced his intention of coming to Lincolnshire with an army, Welles and his associates went to Warwick and Clarence for assistance. At the same time, rumours – possibly started deliberately – spread through Lincolnshire and Yorkshire that the king was going to punish the rebels of 1469, despite the general pardon that had been issued in its aftermath. Sir Robert Welles, Lord Welles' son, raised the common people of Lincolnshire in rebellion, possibly with Warwick's and Clarence's support, claiming that Edward was coming to destroy them. Welles was to join Warwick at Leicester, cutting Edward off from London, but, by capturing Lord Welles and threatening to execute him, Edward forced Sir Robert to attack him immediately. On 12 March near Stamford in Lincolnshire the rebels were routed at a battle which was named 'Lose-Cote Field' because so many of the participants fled leaving items of clothing behind. After the battle, captured papers and interrogation of captives revealed the extent of Warwick's and Clarence's involvement, despite the assurances of allegiance that Clarence had given his brother beforehand.

When Edward reached Grantham on 14 March, he learned of a Neville-inspired rising in Wensleydale, the heart of the earldom of Salisbury, and of another in Cornwall. The Cornish rebellion was led by several Courtenays, the family of the attainted earls of Devon, but probably set off by Clarence, who had estates in the region. Both rebellions collapsed at the news of the king's victory in Lincolnshire. There followed a number of letters between the king and his two main adversaries, who were now moving northwards. These two were almost entirely isolated – even Montagu had stayed loyal to Edward although the restoration of Percy was completed in late March – and when they failed to get any help from Lord Stanley in Lancashire they fled south, with the king in hot pursuit. In April they left the country, but Sir John Wenlock, Warwick's own deputy at Calais, where he was still captain, refused them entry, and they were forced to land in Normandy. Before this, Warwick, as in the 1450s, was able to accomplish some piracy in the channel, this time at the expense of the Burgundians. He was helped by ships commanded by the Bastard of Fauconberg, natural son of Warwick's late uncle, William Lord Fauconberg, earl of Kent, which defected from the king's fleet. The response to the rebellion outside the immediate followers of Warwick and Clarence had been minimal: hopes of support from Stanley, Shrewsbury and others had proved groundless.

However, in July everything changed: under the auspices of the French king, an agreement was concluded between Warwick and his great enemy of the 1450s, Margaret of Anjou. By this Henry VI was to be restored and Prince Edward was to marry Warwick's other daughter, Anne. Despite the formidable blockade kept by the English and Burgundian navies in the Channel, and the fact that Edward had taken steps to secure the Yorkist invasion routes of Ireland and Calais, Warwick and Clarence were able to land in September and declared immediately for Henry VI. They were accompanied by, amongst others, Jasper Tudor and the earl of Oxford. The latter had fled to France at the time of the departure of Warwick and Clarence in 1470. Shrewsbury and Stanley joined the newly arrived rebels, as they had failed to do the previous year. Margaret and the Prince were to arrive later. Meanwhile the king had been in the north since August. Neville-inspired rebellions had broken out at the end of July, one in Cumberland, and the other more serious one in Yorkshire, led by Lord Fitzhugh, Warwick's brother-in-law. Although his allegiances were normally to the Nevilles, he was another who had taken Henry VI's side, if not until the final years of the reign, and been pardoned at Edward's accession. His family had already been involved in Robin of Redesdale's rising. The Fitzhugh rising had substantial support from the Neville affinity and may have been principally the brain-child of Conyers. The king's prompt action led to the rapid collapse of both risings, but he then lingered in the north, perhaps because of growing uncertainty about Montagu's intentions. The rebels had gathered a large army, which was moving steadily through the midlands, but Edward was coming south to join his army at Nottingham, confident of victory. Then, as he waited at Doncaster for Montagu and the northern men to arrive, he heard that Montagu had defected. Edward's troops were dispersed in their quarters in the villages near Doncaster and Montagu's now hostile forces were approaching. The king fled, with Gloucester, Hastings, Rivers (Elizabeth's brother, the former Lord Scales, who had inherited his father's title after his death at Edgecote) and a few others, and reached Burgundy early in October. On 6 October Warwick and the others arrived in London, took Henry VI out of the Tower and declared him king again: the 'Readeption' of Henry VI had begun.

In Burgundy Edward received small welcome from a brother-in-law anxious to renew his alliance with the new regime in England. But Warwick's rejection of Burgundian advances and Louis' declaration of war on Burgundy in December brought Edward the money and ships he needed. In England the new regime was having to make some awkward decisions. It was necessary to placate those major supporters of the old regime who had not fled, such as the Bourchiers, the duke of Norfolk and Lord Mountjoy. At the same time, it would be difficult to restore Lancastrians of the 1450s, like Clifford and the Courtenay earl of Devon, for fear of alienating those who had their estates, including Warwick and Clarence themselves. The dukes of Somerset (Edmund, brother and heir to the duke killed after Hexham) and Exeter, who would certainly expect to be restored to their lands, reached England in February. And then there was the impending arrival of Queen Margaret, who no doubt had ideas on suitable measures against those who had helped Edward to the throne and kept him there. And where did Clarence, whose ambitions were quite probably fixed on the throne, stand when Henry VI and his son were restored? He would already lose Tutbury, according to the agreement made in France, and his Honor of Richmond was in some danger if Henry Tudor, heir to Henry VI's half-brother Edmund, the former earl of Richmond, were restored. All these problems were particularly acute because it was far from clear that the regime commanded general acceptance; that meant that, lacking the natural allegiance of the greater subjects, it would have to buy them over, in a situation where there were likely to be conflicting claims to what the crown did have to offer. Although most of the gentry were realistic enough to accept the status quo, it would be if anything harder than in the later 1450s to find enough of them willing to commit themselves sufficiently to act as suitable officers for the shires. It was harder still to find trustworthy landowners of any kind to defend the country, and commissions for this were concentrated in a very small number of hands.

On 14 March Edward landed at Ravenspur in Yorkshire, where Henry Bolingbroke had invaded more than seventy years before. He had few men with him and was in acute danger, despite his assurances, like Bolingbroke before him, that he came only to claim his dukedom. But neither Montagu nor, crucially, Northumberland moved against him and, as he travelled south from Yorkshire, he began to be joined by large numbers of men; from Lancashire and above all from Hastings' region in the midlands which is said to have provided him with 3,000 soldiers. Those who might have resisted him fled instead towards the earl of Warwick, who was gathering men in Warwickshire. Some of the real Lancastrian loyalists, like Somerset, retired to the south coast to await Margaret's arrival. In the south-west Clarence was raising troops and sending out messages for help but encountering a reluctance to jump either way. Neither Shrewsbury nor Stanley would commit himself now that Edward had returned. Edward himself reached Coventry, to which Warwick had retreated, in late March. Those Lancastrian troops in the vicinity that could have attacked him failed to do so but, despite the ever-present danger of attack, Edward lingered nearby. On 3 April, hearing that Clarence was on his way to join Warwick, Edward went out to meet him and the two brothers were reconciled. Edward then made for London and reached it on 11 April. There he imprisoned Henry VI and Archbishop Neville, who had become chancellor again during the Readeption, and saw the son who had been born in his absence in sanctuary in Westminster Abbey, the future Edward V. His troops came flocking in, as he was joined by nobles, like the Bourchiers, Norfolk and Mountjoy, who had accepted the Readeption but were now anxious to return to their old allegiance, and on 14 April, Easter Sunday, Edward went out to meet Warwick's army at Barnet, north of London. He won; Warwick and Montagu were killed, Exeter was left for dead on the battlefield and subsequently taken prisoner, and Oxford fled.

On that same day Queen Margaret and her son landed in Dorset, where Somerset joined them, while the Beaufort and Courtenay interest in the west helped raise a large force. Edward too was gathering troops rapidly. He was anxious to prevent the Lancastrians getting into Wales, joining with Jasper Tudor, who had gone there on his return, and moving on to Cheshire and Lancashire, where ties to the former Prince of Wales and the house of Lancaster were likely to be strong. At Tewkesbury, where they hoped to cross the Severn into Wales, Edward caught up with the Lancastrian forces. On 4 May he won a great victory there and finally destroyed the Lancastrians by killing Prince Edward, the duke of Somerset and a host of others. A northern rising collapsed as soon as news of Tewkesbury reached it, reassuringly surrendering to the Percy earl of Northumberland, which showed that, a little belatedly, Edward's policy in the north had proved the right one. There remained only the invasion of the Bastard of Fauconberg, who in May had landed with his fleet in Kent, raised the country and marched on London. He was driven off first by forces coming out of London, led by Rivers and others, and then by the arrival of the advance guard of Edward's army on 18 May, followed by Edward himself on 21 May. Fauconberg and the commons of Kent and Essex were dealt with in the summer and autumn. Jasper Tudor and Henry Tudor, his nephew, remained at large and in control of Pembroke Castle, but in September they left for France. The night after his entry into London Edward had Henry VI killed, something he should have done long before, leaving the Tudors, through their Beaufort blood, almost the last representatives of the Lancastrian dynasty. Edward IV's victory was complete. The Wars of the Roses were over.

The curious course of politics in 1469–71 might seem to suggest that the magnates who determined their outcome were utterly lacking in principle and blew only with the prevailing wind, but this is too simple a view. Ultimately, it all came back to the survival of the two poles of authority from the 1450s, with the difference that each side now claimed to represent a legitimate king. Most of the nobles were still caught between them in 1469–71, as their unenthusiastic acquiescence through much of the turmoil of these years shows, but each side had enough significant support to be able to overthrow the other if it caught it off-guard. As in 1460–1, the great arbiters were the Nevilles, for as a family they were so powerful that they could topple a king who did not have the undivided allegiance of his landed subjects, and this was something Edward could not have until he had disposed of the Lancastrian dynasty. Even so, had he been able to solve the problem of the north, Edward might never have suffered any of his reverses, especially the final one which led to Henry's restoration. On the other hand, as long as the dual polarity of power existed, Edward could not resolve the northern issue; he needed to restore the Percies to settle the north-east, but in restoring them he lost the Nevilles' allegiance and that proved his temporary downfall.

Edward did not lose his throne in 1470–1 because he had misgoverned in his first period as king. Inheriting an extremely difficult situation, he had dealt with it with remarkable aplomb, especially for one so young and inexperienced. He had coped expertly with both Lancastrian resistance and the foreign interference which exploited this and secured the northern border. Good management had made his finances perfectly adequate for his needs and the resistance to his rather high-handed use of taxation had only become a serious matter towards the end of the decade because of the participation of other much more dangerous forces. Far from throwing away all the confiscated lands at his disposal on his accession, he had used them astutely to build up a Yorkist nobility, while wisely realising that he had to turn the whole nobility into his men and needed therefore to forgive and restore some of his former enemies or their heirs. The defection of pardoned Lancastrians was simply the price that had to be paid for the only possible policy, as long as there was a rival for them to defect to. Neither Warwick nor the Woodvilles had been allowed to dominate him, and his closest associates in governance had increasingly become his new nobles, Hastings above all. Given the circumstances, he had done well with the problem of restoring order, but that was something that could only be properly tackled once he was in a more secure position with regard to the nobility. There had been the odd error and misjudgement, such as failing to kill Henry VI as soon as he had him in his custody and perhaps being a little casual about the extent of rebellion in 1469 and 1470, but surprisingly few considering his age and lack of experience. What brought him down temporarily was a structural problem. There was a rival monarch and in Warwick a nobleman who could not accept Edward's success, which he saw as his own undoing. Once Edward had shown himself to be his own man, Warwick's determination to exploit the alternative claimant made the king's position temporarily untenable.

As soon as it is clear that Edward's travails between 1469 and 1471 arose not from bad kingship but from one great noble's personal ambition and the conditions that, most unusually, allowed this free rein, the behaviour of the nobility and indeed of the gentry becomes explicable. It is not surprising that most who could keep a low profile chose to do so during these events; they had no stake in what Warwick was trying to do and politics were too unpredictable for a wise man to commit himself. A prime instance is Warwick's and Clarence's man, Henry Vernon, the Derbyshire landowner. Exploiting his geographical distance from his two masters, one in the south-west, the other in Warwickshire, in the crisis of early 1471, he simply failed to respond to an increasingly hysterical series of requests for help from both nobles and only finally put his head above the parapet when he was assured of Edward's victory. This was neither cowardice nor dereliction of duty, but simple common sense in a situation that, for anyone with a landed interest to protect, was simply impossible.

9

THE TRIUMPH OF YORK: 1471–1483

In the aftermath of the Readeption, the first need was to secure the kingdom, the second, related, one to issue rewards and punishments. Fauconberg submitted at the end of May and was pardoned, but was eventually executed for some other unknown offence in September. In July a commission dominated by the Bourchiers, the leading family in the area, dealt with the south-eastern counties that had supported Fauconberg's rising. In the same month Hastings became commander of Calais, which had come under Warwick's control during the Readeption. By offering pardons for Warwick's main supporters there and wages for the garrison, he was readily admitted. He returned with Montagu's heir, the young duke of Bedford, who had been sent to Calais during the Readeption. Wales took longer to deal with and, even after Jasper Tudor had left in September, it remained in a disordered and unstable condition. In 1473 raids from France by the earl of Oxford, who had escaped from Barnet, culminating in the seizure of St Michael's Mount, were the last whimpers of Lancastrian resistance. Oxford capitulated at the end of the year, was pardoned yet again and imprisoned in Hammes Castle, one of the English possessions in France. Now that he was fully in command for the first time, Edward could afford to be free with both vengeance and mercy, and it is typical of him that, as with Oxford, on the whole he chose mercy. Fines were preferred to executions and the number of attainders was small, while there was a large number of pardons, even of those like Lord Stanley who had openly defected during the Readeption. A determined effort was being made to show that the past was buried, that this was indeed a new reign. This was as much to the advantage of the king, who had no cause to remember the 1460s with affection, as of anyone else.

The distribution of spoils was designed not just to reward loyalty in the recent crisis but to replace those who had been killed during it and stabilise regions that had become disturbed, in some cases because they had lost their ruling magnate. The major beneficiaries were the king's family – his two brothers and his in-laws – and Lord Hastings. There was a vacuum in the south-west, caused by the death of Humphrey Stafford earl of Devon in 1469 and the final destruction of the Courtenays and Hungerfords in 1469–71. This was to some extent filled by Lord Dinham, who, on Stafford's death, had been given some of the lands granted to the latter in the 1460s, and by Clarence. Clarence's grant of the Courtenay of Devon lands in Devonshire, taken back into crown hands on Montagu's death, made him, in theory at least, the pre-eminent noble in the region after the crown as duke of Cornwall. But Clarence was a less than effective politician, with very wide-ranging lands, and was in any case to fall from power in 1477 and be executed in 1478. The real power in the south-west in the second reign was Edward's step-son, Thomas Grey Lord of Groby, who had already had expectations in the region from his marriage to the Exeter heiress in 1466. She had died in 1467 but in 1474 Grey married the heiress to the Bonvilles, step-daughter of Lord Hastings. His influence here was further enhanced by offices on the Duchy of Cornwall estates and by the betrothal of his son Thomas to the infant daughter of Edward's sister Anne, duchess of Exeter, by her second marriage, to Thomas St Leger. Anne had been allowed to divorce her inveterately Lancastrian first husband in 1472 and keep his lands. How important a force Grey became in the region can be seen from the fact that, extraordinarily, following on the deaths of Exeter himself in 1475 and Anne in 1476, this St Leger child was declared the heir of Exeter by the king in 1483. Grey's position in the south-west was recognised formally in 1475 when he was made marquess of Dorset. St Leger and his wife, as representatives of the Exeter interest, also had some influence here. For the moment Wales was passed on to Herbert's son, another William, who inherited his father's title of earl of Pembroke, as well as his responsibilities. The earl of Shrewsbury, forgiven his wavering in the crisis, was given office in north Wales but died not long after, in 1473, leaving an infant heir.

But the major distribution was of the earl of Warwick's lands, consisting primarily of the two large earldoms of Warwick, acquired by marriage, and of Salisbury, Warwick's inherited Neville property. Each carried with it massive regional responsibilities, Warwick primarily in the west midlands and Salisbury primarily in the north. The inheritance was divided between the king's two brothers. This was logical, since Clarence was already married to one daughter and coheiress, and in July 1472 Gloucester married the other, the widow of Prince Edward; but there was more serious intent. Both areas needed to be brought quickly under authority, and both needed magnates close to the king to replace the chief rebel of the recent crisis. This was particularly true of the north, which not only bordered an enemy country but had been so disordered and disruptive for much of the 1460s, especially in the last two years. If reliability was not exactly Clarence's middle name, he was at least a useful stop-gap and he was given most of the lands of the Warwick earldom. The west midlands was less of a problem than the north, since it had been moderately disordered rather than treacherous in the 1460s under Warwick's lax rule, and Edward's own interventions in those years had already made it susceptible to royal authority if this proved necessary. The much more sensitive northern earldom was reserved for the ultra-loyal Gloucester. The division was accomplished with some acrimony and not a little legal fraud. This was required to deprive Warwick's widow and his heir male (Montagu's heir, George Neville), on whom some of the estates were settled, and to give the two brothers a secure title despite all these machinations. The unfortunate George was in 1477 degraded from the dukedom which had been part of the bribe to his father when Montagu lost the earldom of Northumberland. This and the proposed marriage to the king's daughter, along with all his landed prospects, disappeared in the wake of his father's treason.

This was the start of the rise to northern 'super-power' of Richard of Gloucester. Partly his elevation was a reward for his loyalty between 1469 and 1471 but it was also a solution to the northern problem that had proved all but insoluble in the 1460s. The north was always a difficult area to rule. It was unstable and there was the constant need to defend the border against the Scots; it was the only part of England which could be described as a militarised region.[1] It needed constant attention, but kings could rarely spend much time there. It therefore required a royal deputy, but he had to have territorial power or he would be ineffectual. That normally meant a Neville or a Percy, with the result that the great military offices along the border were too often turned into pawns in local politics. The best solution was always to use a northern noble who was closely attached to the king and would be acting as much in the king's name as in his own.[2] Gloucester, once he had the Neville lands in the north, was the perfect candidate. He took over the Neville affinity and extended it into Durham. He was given numerous Duchy of Lancaster offices in the north. By 1472 he had all the lands of the Honor of Richmond in Yorkshire except the castle: Clarence had been given the Honor in 1462, but in

---

[1] See above, pp. 55–6.   [2] See also above, p. 20.

practice all the Yorkshire lands but the castle had been in the hands of Nevilles to whom Gloucester had become heir. On Clarence's death in 1478, Gloucester obtained the castle as well. His authority in south Yorkshire, where he had no land, grew through links with retainers of the Duchy of York, part of the crown estate since 1461, and through an agreement with the earl of Northumberland in 1474 which effectively made Gloucester the senior partner in the north. Northumberland, after showing some hostility to Richard in 1473, accepted this situation because he was guaranteed the traditional Percy office of warden of the East March. Gloucester himself was in charge of the West March and in 1482–3 his dominance of the north-west border region was confirmed when he was given the office in heredity, with further crown lands and rights, and the grant of anything he was able to take from the Scots along the West March. These conquests were to be turned into a county palatine, the palatinate of Cumberland, which meant that they were to have their own private local administration, albeit one that still administered the king's governance. The only precedents for this were the palatinates of the bishopric of Durham and of the crown lordships of Chester and Lancaster.[3] In 1480, in anticipation of the king's expedition to Scotland, Gloucester had been made king's lieutenant in the north. All other northern magnates looked to him, including even the Nevilles of Raby, the old enemies of the Nevilles of Middleham.[4] The single exception were the Stanleys whose hegemony in Lancashire was largely protected by the king under the aegis of the royal Duchy of Lancaster.

A similar regional command was created in Wales. Pembroke's continuing inability to keep order there necessitated urgent intervention and the obvious basis was the council of Edward's infant heir, who had been made Prince of Wales and earl of Chester in June 1471. The council created for him to administer the Principality in the minority developed between 1472 and 1476 into a body with wide-ranging judicial powers in Wales, the Marches and the adjacent English counties, centred on the old Yorkist stronghold of Ludlow. At first the aim seems to have been to use the council to oversee co-operation among the Marcher lords and in 1473 the king had a series of meetings with these lords at Shrewsbury, from which emanated a number of ordinances to improve the governance of the region. That these plans changed was due to the numbers of minorities (such as Shrewsbury's) and confiscations, and the manifest feebleness of the new earl of Pembroke and unsuitability of Henry Stafford, the young earl of Buckingham. The latter came into his lands in 1473. He was married to

---

a Woodville and at first it seems that he was to be allowed a role in Wales, where his family had long been a major force. But from 1476 Edward decided to engage in a policy of systematic exclusion from authority of both Buckingham and Pembroke. Buckingham ceased to hold office or to carry any political weight in the region and it is probable that the king had already sensed the personal instability that was to become all too apparent under Richard III. In 1479 Pembroke was required to relinquish his earldom, recognition of the fact that Wales was now in other hands. Although neither the council nor the Prince's household was entirely dominated by the Woodvilles and their close associates in the royal household, in practice the queen and her brother, Lord Rivers, seem to have been the dominant force.

The east and north midlands were eventually put under Hastings' command. This was less all-embracing than those in the north and Wales, simply because the territorial structure and political traditions of the region did not lend themselves to this kind of arrangement. It was nevertheless effective. Immediately after the Readeption, Hastings' existing sphere of influence in Leicestershire, Rutland, Northamptonshire and Lincolnshire was enlarged by the addition of offices in Nottinghamshire. In 1472 Hastings was made Clarence's steward of Tutbury and then, in 1474, came the major adjustment. The Honor of Tutbury, the key Duchy of Lancaster possession in the north midlands, spanning Derbyshire and Staffordshire, was taken from Clarence and, although kept by the king, put under the effective supervision of Hastings, who remained its steward. Hastings then proceeded to retain among the leading gentry of Staffordshire, Derbyshire and Leicestershire on a grand scale, becoming the pre-eminent authority throughout the region. As with Gloucester in the north, the lesser local nobles, such as Mountjoy and Grey of Codnor, became subordinate to his command. Grey had been retained by Hastings as early as 1464 but this was almost certainly in the context of the conflict with the Vernons in that decade;[5] now he was part of the widening sphere of north-midland interest being exercised by Hastings on behalf of the king. The king's control of the midlands was extended with the death in 1476 of the last Mowbray duke of Norfolk, who had substantial lands in the east midlands, and the marriage in 1478 of his infant heiress to Edward's young second son, Richard duke of York. As with the Exeter lands, the king bent the laws of inheritance to have the lands settled on his own family. In this case, the beneficiaries were the heirs of Richard, whether by the Mowbray heiress or anyone else. Further south, there were substantial Duchy properties in Northamptonshire, several of them held by the queen, and her own

[5] See above, p. 165.

family, Woodvilles and Greys, was located primarily in the south-east midlands. But the step that all but completed the dominance of the entire midland region by Edward and his family was the destruction of Clarence in 1477–8.

To place this in context, we should first look at Edward's relations with the nobility more generally. It is sometimes said that, apart from Hastings, Edward rested his power to an unusual degree on his family in the second reign. This generalisation, like so many on the period 1471–83, is too reliant on hindsight. Historians have been looking for causes for Richard of Gloucester's usurpation, and finding them on the one hand in an alleged over-concentration of power in Gloucester's hands, and on the other in the alienation of the rest of the nobility by an alleged small family clique. It is in fact a rather misconceived view, since it was normal for kings with large families to use them. An obvious example is Edward III, who married three of his five sons to the heiresses of major noble families – Clare, Lancaster and Hereford – and used those who were old enough as props to his own rule, while intending that they should all be significant aides to their brother the Black Prince. John of Gaunt, for instance, who married the heiress of Edward's close ally, Henry duke of Lancaster, was given powers that would have enabled him to follow his father-in-law as arbiter of the north, complete with extended powers to the palatinate of Lancaster that had already been created for the previous duke. This was a solution to the northern problem very like Edward IV's with Gloucester. It was only the premature death of the Black Prince and the inability of his son, Richard II, to understand who his true allies were that has prevented historians discussing the 'family policy' of Edward III. In Edward III's case the unexpected intervened; with Edward IV the policy worked.

Secondly, it is not true that Edward omitted to exploit the potential of his nobles outside the immediate royal family. Arguably, he was one of the most effective managers of the nobility ever to have ruled England. Unlike Henry VII, he was their natural ally.[6] This was not surprising in a man who had grown up to be a noble, but it was also an essential attribute of kingship. The constitution of medieval England, as it was described in chapters 2 and 3, depended on both monarch and nobility recognising their mutually beneficial interdependence. Edward showed he understood the need to be accessible, to listen, to reward service. It is worth remembering that, for all Warwick's complaints about the excessive power of the Woodvilles and others around the king, not even Warwick's own brother, Lord Montagu, seems to have felt aggrieved on this score. That Edward valued the great nobles outside his family is shown by the fact that, after his

---

[6] See below, p. 226.

recovery of the throne, rewards were given to most of the leading magnates – for example to Northumberland, Arundel, Suffolk and the Bourchiers – even though some of them had wavered in their loyalty during the previous two years. The nobility remained an important part of Edward's governance, notably the Bourchiers in the south-east. So did the Stanleys in Lancashire and Cheshire, where they continued the rise begun in the earlier years of the century.

However, the picture of the easy-going king, too compliant with his nobility, which is another common version of Edward IV, also needs some revision. Like all kings who knew their job – Henry V for instance – Edward made it quite clear that, while he was happy to trust his nobles, he was equally ready to exact retribution if they misbehaved. One magnate who received no particular reward after Tewkesbury was the duke of Norfolk, who had fought in the battle but, as we have seen, had been too ready to use the breakdown of governance from 1469 to his own violent purposes. Moreover, Edward seems to have been sufficiently aware of the impropriety of Norfolk's behaviour to let the Pastons have Caister after Norfolk's death, even though they had actually committed themselves to the Readeption regime, and even though he may already have had his eye on the ducal estate for his son. What is also clear is that Edward was determined that nobles who acted in their normal capacity as local rulers and intermediaries between the centre and the shires would do it within a framework firmly delineated by himself. This does seem to be something new in English politics. In Wales and the Welsh Marches, for example, the independent power of local magnates was firmly cut out. As under Gloucester in the north, their co-operation was welcomed as long as it was given within a scheme of rule set by the king's own lieutenants. One notable casualty of this highly directed policy was the young Stafford duke of Buckingham. We have seen how he was soon excluded from influence in Wales and the March after he came into his lands in 1473 and there was the same story in the north midlands, another of the Stafford spheres of power. Here Buckingham was firmly subordinated to Hastings. By the end of the reign the nobility were bound to a remarkable degree, by either service or marriage or both, to the ruling house; less a 'family policy' than a family takeover.

The royal family itself was tightly knitted into this rule. The Woodville base in Wales was not their own, but created for his own use by the king, even if he was prepared to give his in-laws a certain amount of latitude in their use of royal power. Most of their servants there were first and foremost the king's men and only secondarily the Woodvilles'. To suggest, as one historian has done, that all the major acts of rapacity associated with Edward in the second reign, even his absorption of the Norfolk lands through his son, were engineered by the Woodvilles implies a misunderstanding of both Edward's character and his method of ruling. Similarly, it has now been shown that Gloucester's northern hegemony was less an independent fiefdom than a regional command subordinated to Edward's authority. Gloucester's central position in the rule of England is emphasised by his tenure of the offices of constable and admiral of England throughout the second reign. It is also worth noting that Edward was quite ready to curb his brother when it suited him, especially in the south where the only hegemonic power was his own. For example, in 1478 Gloucester was made to surrender lands in the west midlands and south-west that he had been granted earlier.

Given his previous history, it was to be expected that the duke of Clarence would not be easy to absorb into such a system. As the events of 1469–71 had foretold, he was both unstable and incompetent. The division of the Warwick/Salisbury inheritance was accompanied with a good deal of acrimony between Clarence and Gloucester. By 1473 this was contributing to a growing amount of instability, especially in the regions where most of the lands lay, the midlands and the north. Continued disorder along the Welsh border, where the new earl of Pembroke was still trying and failing to do his job, made matters worse and Edward had to spend much of the early part of that year in the marches and the midlands. The Resumption Act of 1473 rapidly brought Clarence to heel because it potentially deprived him of nearly all his lands and in 1474 he was forced into a settlement with Gloucester. Despite Clarence's submission, it was in this Resumption that he lost the Honor of Tutbury and it was from this time that Hastings began to take command of the north midlands. There were constant rumours of treason linked to Clarence almost from the end of the Readeption, and in his new base in the west midlands he showed himself quite incapable of taking command. A rising tide of local conflict and disorder in Warwickshire and Worcestershire had to be contained by increasingly active intervention by king and council. However, unlike Buckingham, who could be side-lined, the king's own brother could not. It was possible to remove him from influence in the north midlands, where Clarence's power was based solely on the Duchy estates of Tutbury, and Hastings was already available in the region as a substitute from 1472. In the Warwick earldom, where Clarence had his own lands and there was no effective alternative, there was no such solution.

It may well be that Edward never regarded Clarence's presence in the area as more than a stop-gap; certainly the growing need for royal intervention was in itself undermining Clarence's position. The wrangling with Gloucester over the Warwick inheritance between 1472 and 1474, in which the king was bound to be more sympathetic to the brother who had not betrayed him, would not have made Edward any more forbearing towards Clarence. Whether Clarence really did commit treason is obscure, although it would have been characteristic of him to make treasonable murmurings against his brother. It did not help his cause that in 1477 Thomas Burdet, a Warwickshire esquire with links to Clarence, was executed for treason and that Clarence vehemently declared Burdet's innocence. In any event, there was enough in Clarence's non-treasonable actions to bring him down at the hands of a king deeply committed in his second reign to the upholding of the law. Continuing inability to keep the peace in his 'country' was aggravated in 1477 by violent breach of the law, when he committed the judicial murder of a Clarence family retainer. In June 1477 Clarence was arrested; in 1478 he was attainted and put to death, drowned in a butt of malmsey, as the story goes. The large earldom of Warwick that Clarence had acquired through his marriage was not forfeited but held by the crown in the minority of his three-year-old son, Edward of Warwick, but in practice it had come into crown hands for good. Edward, through himself, his own family, his wife's family and his loyal servant Hastings, was now complete master of the midlands. A king who could kill his own brother, one of the most powerful nobles in the realm, and to all intents and purposes absorb his lands, was a man to be reckoned with, and the well-informed Croyland Continuator observed the awe and fear in which Edward was held at this time. Edward was rarely moved to such ruthlessness but, when he was, the consequences could be devastating for those in his path.

All this should be borne in mind as we move to examine Edward's achievements in the second reign at a deeper level, the actual process of rule in the localities. Looking at the 1460s, we could see that Edward's aims as king were much the same then as from 1471, but it was not until the second reign that he was able to put them fully into effect. Once free to unite the nobility behind him and to make examples where necessary, he found it far easier than in the first reign to restore local stability and respect for law. One historian has noted the sharp contrast in Edward's rather hesitant handling of noble disorder in the 1460s and his firm dealing with the destabilising effects of Clarence's conflict with Gloucester in 1473. On the latter occasion there were the meetings with the Marcher lords, the Resumption act and also the issuing in nearly every county of commissions of the peace strengthened by the addition of numbers of the king's own men.

As in the later years of Henry IV and throughout the reign of Henry VI, the areas where the king himself was the major landowner were most urgently in need of attention. As so often in this period, we are still very ignorant of local conditions, but, for example, we know that north Wales had never been brought under full control in the 1460s, while the damaging feud in Derbyshire in the later 1460s suggests that this was another area of royal territorial power which had not recovered from disorder under Henry VI. Bringing order to the regions dominated by the crown lands was very much at the centre of a lot of the restructuring of power we have already examined, almost as much as it was in the judicial policy of Henry V. The subordination of the lands of the Principality of Wales and the adjacent earldom of Chester to the Prince's council in the Marches is an obvious example. In the north there were substantial Lancaster and York lands, as well as the Honor of Richmond, within Richard III's sphere of rule. Hastings' dominance in the north midlands was clearly designed to enable him to restore stability to this region where the Duchy had for long been the dominant political force. The men he retained were in virtually every case from families whose traditional allegiance to the Duchy had been disrupted by decades of misrule under Henry VI. What is interesting is that, in a period when the legislation of 1468 had in theory made it harder to retain without the king's permission, this very large and powerful retinue was quite clearly the king's. It was the revival of the Duchy retinue in the area, even if it was nominally under Hastings' charge. Hastings' own closest associates were not retained formally.

What little we know about the effects of all this reordering of the crown's personal power suggests that it served its purpose. The north was more stable than it had been for a long while. If there was still the local conflict which one would expect in a militarised area where lordship remained strong, there was a notable absence of either the magnate feuding or the peasant rebellion that had been so marked for over two decades. In 1475 Edward and his brother combined to settle the long-running and violent feud between the Stanleys and the Harringtons in Lancashire. After 1473, Wales also appears to have been more peaceful than at any time since the 1440s. In the north midlands the effect of the Hastings/Duchy retinue was to create a broadly based and broadly unified power structure within which there was considerable scope for freedom of action, as long as it did not disrupt the status quo. This seems indeed to be very like the political configuration established in Warwickshire, after Edward acquired substantial private land there by taking over the estates and affinity of the earl of Warwick. It could well be that both Hastings and Edward ruled with a lighter hand than either Gloucester or the Prince's council in Wales, for, as king and chief counsellor, neither of them could be as permanently present in the areas where they had to act as magnates. Although the king's private territorial power had been rather minimal in Warwickshire before Clarence's fall, Edward had nevertheless been active there as private landowner before 1478. This was because Coventry, a royal town linked with the earldom of Chester, and its neighbour Kenilworth, part of the Duchy estate, were given a close attention which must have owed a lot to their crucial role in the events of 1456–61 and 1469–71. From 1472 there was an intense dispute in and around Coventry which drew in numbers of local landowners and Edward was quick to step in when it began to get out of hand.

The attention given by the king to the areas of private royal power should be placed in the context of a hugely expanding royal political connection. There were the men retained directly by the royal household. Then, by the late 1470s, so many great estates were in the hands of either the king or his immediate family – Chester, Wales, Cornwall, Lancaster, York, Norfolk, Neville of Salisbury, Neville of Warwick, Rivers, Grey of Groby, Bonville, to name only the obvious ones – that a large number of magnate affinities were effectively in crown hands. Finally, it should be remembered that the nobles outside the immediate royal family who were willing participants in Edward's rule had accepted a position in which their own followings were virtually under the king's command. It was rather like a macrocosm of the situation in the north midlands and Warwickshire: independence of action within the constraints of an overarching authority. This is clearest in relation to Hastings, who was very much the king's deputy with regard to the retinue based on Tutbury, and whose attraction for his private following was to a large extent his proximity to the king, for he was still a peer of only moderate territorial means. But it was apparently the case with nobles who were less closely identified with the king, such as Suffolk, the Bourchiers and, in the north, even Northumberland.

It seems indeed that the whole of England south of the Humber was knitted in to a vast royal affinity, while, north of the Humber, the magnates and gentry came under the lordship of Gloucester, the king's lieutenant. The effects of this overarching royal connection can be clearly seen in Warwickshire, Staffordshire and Derbyshire, where nearly all connections among the gentry ultimately led back to the king. It can be seen in East Anglia from the fact that Hastings, the king's confidant, became ever more important to the Pastons, even though he was not a local landowner. It can be seen in the south-east and the Thames Valley, where under Richard III a large number of prominent household men of Edward IV were later to revolt in favour of Edward's sons. Fuller local studies should enable us to trace less impressionistically the household connections in the shires, both those where there were substantial estates in the hands of the king and his family and those where this was not the case. Some of the household members of the royal affinity became powerful local figures in this period, a reflection of the burgeoning power of the crown in the shires. These included Sir John Howard, the East Anglian knight who had tangled with the Pastons early in the reign, survived the disgrace of being raised to the baronage by the Readeption government and became a prominent and well-rewarded royal councillor in the second reign. In East Anglia, he was a frequent royal agent, acting as a regular local officer, as member of special judicial commissions and as the king's direct representative. For example, he was employed to bring people before the council.

The most profound consequence of this enormous growth of the crown affinity in its various forms was that an ever-increasing number of the local men chosen for the office of JP or sheriff were in some sense the king's. But this revival of direct royal power in the shires, on a scale perhaps not seen since Edward I's day, was not confined to areas where the king or his family were major landowners. It is evident right across England; in commissions, particularly the number of commissions of *oyer* and *terminer*, often staffed by household men, and in the supervisory work of the king's council. In fact, while acting in a highly interventionist manner, royal governance was operating at a deeper level than in the hey-day of direct rule in the twelfth and thirteenth centuries because of the enormous expansion of law and financial administration between the mid-thirteenth and mid-fourteenth centuries. What all this meant was that the king was beginning to replace the nobility as the immediate controlling force in the shires and it was therefore the king who would have the greatest say in how, and to whose advantage, the legal system worked. It was accordingly the king to whom the gentry would look for the security of their estates. This can be seen very clearly in Warwickshire, where the king was the major landowner from 1478 and is found intervening in local disputes with growing frequency, far more it seems than was the norm in areas of equivalent royal territorial power earlier in the century. The king's intervention is also evident in regions where he was not the dominant landed power; for instance, in East Anglia, even while there were two great noble houses until the death of Norfolk in 1476 and still one, the Duchy of Suffolk, thereafter. The change in the Paston letters from concern with local magnate politics in the 1440s, 1450s and 1460s to increasing focus on the king and those around him, especially Hastings, in the 1470s is inescapable. Even the perversion of East Anglian politics in the 1440s, which impelled local landowners to seek out friends at court, had not altered the essential pattern of fighting conflicts out in the local forum. The development of the royal affinity in Edward's second reign, with its profound effects on local government, was summed up, if with pardonable exaggeration, by the Croyland Continuator when he wrote that Edward placed 'the most trustworthy of his servants throughout all parts of the kingdom, as keepers of castles, forests, manors and parks', with the result that, 'no attempt whatever could be made in any part of the kingdom by any person . . . but what he was immediately charged with the same to his face'.[7]

If there is every sign that Edward exercised authority in his second reign on a scale that had never before been seen in England, there is good evidence that he used it with remarkable wisdom. This is of a piece with his record in national politics, where common sense and conciliation were almost invariably preferred to vindictiveness. Again, we await more local studies, but we know that Hastings' power in Derbyshire was used for conciliatory purposes. For example, Henry Vernon, despite his attacks on Hastings' protégé, Lord Grey, in the 1460s and his links with Clarence and Warwick, was allowed back on to the commission of the peace. In the north, Gloucester showed some concern in dealing with abuse of power by men connected with him, and his council arbitrated in disputes. In Warwickshire the process of restoring order from a peak at the time of Clarence's fall has been traced in detail. Here, where the king was now greatest noble as well as king, he was firm, even harsh, merciful or conciliatory as the circumstances demanded. Remarkably, he was prepared to change his mind, something he did on at least three occasions, when he decided that he was backing the wrong party, particularly once he realised that he was acting very much against local wishes. When, as happened once or twice, he found himself drawn into conflicts where one of the adversaries was a Woodville or someone connected to the Woodvilles, he was more than prepared to act impartially. Edward's rule in Warwickshire from 1478 to 1483, taken as a whole, is an almost perfect exemplification of how to use royal power to its best advantage. He surrendered nothing that was of any importance to himself, showed himself to be a king not to be trifled with and yet left a contented gentry more at peace with itself than it had been for nearly half a century.

The key to his success in Warwickshire was the enduring contradiction in the gentry mentality between the desire to be left alone to pursue their own ambitions and their own means of keeping the peace, and the fear that if they did so without the restraint of firm, possibly interventionist, rule they would do untold harm to themselves and their lands.[8] Edward gave them the best of both worlds, for he respected their independence and their aspirations but was ready with the firm hand that offered discipline and security. It was the ideal use of the law in late-medieval English society, trusting the shire to regulate itself but acting rapidly whenever it showed it was unable to do so. Since Edward's attitude to the nobility was of the same kind as what we know about his attitude to the gentry, and

[7] J. R. Lander, *Government and Community: England 1450–1509* (London, 1980), p. 50.
[8] See above, p. 63.

since we can be fairly sure he had this level of control throughout the midlands and the south, we may suppose that it was not just Warwickshire that benefited from governance of this kind. Perhaps it might be said that in Wales and the Welsh Marches he was too ready to leave all but the major decisions to the Woodvilles, and consequently allowed acts of dubious legal propriety by his wife's relatives to pass unnoticed. However, as even their most vehement critic has admitted, the Woodvilles had little satisfaction of this sort outside Wales.

Edward's achievement was to realise, like all intelligent kings, that the way to order was by harnessing the orderly instincts of his landed subjects, from the nobles downwards, while being firm with their more disorderly impulses. It was not a question of punishing every breach of the law; he had not the resources of a modern state and, in any case, as we saw in chapter 3, that was not how the system was meant to work. At its best it worked by self-regulation reinforced by monarchical intervention; the latter, by making examples, could be used to impose settlements leading to the recovery of local cohesion. Henry V had shown in 1414 how effectively and forcefully this could be done; it seems that in his second reign Edward IV, or his deputy Gloucester in the north, was able to do it constantly and almost at will. To criticise Edward for not using the law enough to punish privileged wrong-doers and for preferring to use imposed settlements to bring lengthy and violent conflicts to an end is to misunderstand how the late-medieval legal system worked. For instance he has been reprimanded for failing to punish the Harringtons after he had forced them to accept a settlement more in favour of the Stanleys, but punishment would only have prolonged the dispute further. The real accomplishment was not only to get the parties to settle but to absorb the Harringtons back into Lancashire society in a way that prevented any renewed outbreak. What should be stressed is that arbitration was not a sign of weakness; it could indeed not be imposed unless the arbitrator was more powerful than the parties concerned. From his position of strength in the second reign, Edward was able to force opposing parties into peace-keeping bonds strengthened by severe monetary penalties. We shall see that, although Henry VII arguably abused his power in this respect, much of Henry's much-lauded control of his landed subjects came from a similar use of his personal authority to deal with disputes and lawlessness.

Equally, to argue that there could be no local order unless the evils of livery and maintenance were eradicated is to misunderstand the nature of late-medieval society. There is some evidence that fewer men were formally retained by nobles from the 1470s and more evidence that Edward, like Henry VII later, used the licensing system to prevent retaining of his own tenants. However, formal indenture remained only a small

part of 'bastard feudalism'. To take parliamentary complaints about disorder, expressed in 1467, 1472–5 and 1483, at their face value and divorced
from context is equally misconceived. Such an assumption ignores the fact
that throughout the later middle ages requests for tax, made in all three
parliaments, were almost invariably met by demands for 'good government' on the part of the governed. That was why the king's own spokes-
man had stressed the importance of justice when asking for a tax in 1463
and may also be another reason for the passing of the anti-livery legislation
in 1468: in a parliament called to offer a tax, it was a symbolic response to a
symbolic request. Some parliamentary complaints of disorder in the late
middle ages certainly reflected genuine disquiet but they should never be
assumed to do this unless there is other supporting evidence, especially
when taxation was on the parliamentary agenda. Certainly, there were
some changes in the system of law enforcement. Notable amongst these
was that the statute against retaining of 1468 allowed the justices of the
peace to give a summary verdict without the use of a jury, a procedure that
was to be considerably extended under Henry VII. But this was not really
the point: it was not institutional change but political control that was the
key to the enforcement of order and it was the latter that Edward was able
to achieve in this period. If we are looking at the use of institutions in this
regard, of far greater significance is the evidence for increasing employment of the royal council as a means for bringing discipline directly to bear
on influential malefactors and disturbers of the peace. But this was the
product of the king's expanding control of the localities, not its cause.

At last secure and at ease, from 1475 Edward was able to spend less time
chasing about his kingdom and more in the royal palaces in the south,
chiefly in the Thames Valley. It was in the second reign that he set in
motion most of his considerable building works at some of these residences. Interestingly, a lot of these works were at palaces where Edward III
had built – Westminster, Eltham and Windsor – and there are signs that
Edward the fourth of that name felt some affinity with the third Edward,
who had started the Hundred Years War. This is particularly apparent in
Edward IV's interest in the Order of the Garter, founded by Edward III,
and above all in the splendid new chapel of St George at Windsor, the focal
point of the Order. This, one of the great achievements of the perpendicu-
lar style, was built as a monument to the new Yorkist dynasty. It was begun
in 1473 and sufficiently complete for Edward to be buried there ten years
later. That he saw himself as the heir of Edward III can be seen also in his
perhaps misconceived attempt to restart the Hundred Years War during
his second reign, to which we shall now turn.

It must be said that, if there was a weakness in Edward's rule in the years
between 1471 and 1483, it lay in his handling of foreign policy and

taxation. It was in fact only because his position at home was supremely assured that he was able to surmount his mistakes and even to turn some to his advantage. From 1472 he began to think about a renewal of war with France, a project owing much to Louis' endorsement of the Lancastrian invasion in 1470–1. As before, the logical route was via the feudatories who felt threatened by French centralisation, Brittany and Burgundy. Negotiations with the former seemed more hopeful and Edward even got as far as sending some troops in 1472 for a projected invasion of France. However, Brittany was scared off and in 1473–4 there were more serious negotiations with Burgundy which concluded in the anti-French Treaty of London in 1474. In May 1475 Brittany, which tended to blow hot and cold, frightened of the consequences of both mollifying Louis and resisting him, rather unexpectedly joined the alliance. Between 1472 and 1475 Edward was able to obtain consent to taxation on a scale greater than anything he or his predecessors had managed to levy in such a short time since the reign of Henry V. This was despite the deep suspicion that his previous misappropriation of taxes had caused. A total of well over £100,000 was promised. To this should be added nearly £50,000 from the church and probably more than £20,000 by a 'benevolence': 'voluntary' gifts from wealthier subjects who were under-taxed in the normal subsidies.

A large and well-equipped army was assembled and was shipped to Calais during June 1475, to be followed in early July by the king himself. Unfortunately the duke of Burgundy, Edward's brother-in-law, had already exhausted his army and his treasury elsewhere, and was unable to provide the promised help, but Edward decided to invade France anyway and in mid-July he moved his army out of Calais. But it was getting late in the year, the French were responding dangerously and neither Burgundy nor Brittany was offering any help. In mid-August negotiations were opened, and towards the end of the month the two monarchs met on a specially constructed bridge over the Somme at Picquigny near Amiens. The Treaty of Picquigny, concluded on 29 August, provided for a ten years' truce but it also gave Edward and some of his closest advisers handsome French pensions. Because Edward was so conscious of the legacy of Edward III, we must suppose that the campaign was seriously meant and it is unlikely that this was the outcome intended by Edward: it would have been a very roundabout and effortful way of collecting a tax and a pension. But it is more than likely that, once he learned that his allies were unlikely to help him, Edward aimed at no more than a token invasion of France to appease the taxpayers. The remarkable fact remains that he had yet again defrauded his subjects, levying a tax for a campaign that failed to materialise, and had yet again got away with it. His only concession was to remit three quarters of the sums that still awaited collection. Indeed the response in 1475, confined to grumbling, contrasts with the rebelliousness in 1464 and 1468 and is another indication of the firm foundations on which Edward's kingship rested in the second reign. It may not be a morally pleasant story, but to use it as evidence of Edward's failure as king is to confuse morality and the exercise of power.

After 1475 there was no further open war with France. Instead there was a series of negotiations in which, from 1477, the central question was Burgundy's relations with France and England. Because of Burgundy's proximity to England and the importance of the cloth trade to the English king's customs and to the merchants who made loans to him, this would always be a pressing matter. It became considerably more urgent in 1477 with the death in battle of Duke Charles of Burgundy, Edward's brother-in-law, leaving only a daughter, Mary. That Mary was married to the Habsburg, Maximilian, heir to the Holy Roman Emperor, greatly enlarged the potential diplomatic scope of the Burgundian question. In 1480 Edward concluded a treaty with Burgundy which was financially advantageous to himself personally but it was not clear how beneficial for his ally. He prevaricated over the plan for a combined invasion of France, while continuing to negotiate secretly with Louis, until 1482, when Mary of Burgundy was killed in a riding accident. Losing patience with Maximilian, some of the leading Burgundians opened negotiations with Louis XI and forced Maximilian to follow suit. In December 1482, at the Treaty of Arras, a Franco-Burgundian peace was concluded, by which the infant heiress to Burgundy was to be married to the French Dauphin. Ominously for England, parts of the Duchy, including Artois, whose coastline was on the narrowest part of the narrow seas, were transferred to France. England was excluded from the treaty.

This complex and ultimately failed diplomacy had made it difficult for Edward to concentrate on the other major foreign policy issue of these years, Scotland. In 1474 Edward had prevented Scotland getting involved on the French side in his projected war against France. This was done by a treaty which promised the marriage of his infant daughter Cecily to James, the infant son and heir of James III. Until 1479 relations between the countries remained good but in 1480 the Scots began to breach the truce. Edward responded by planning a punitive expedition for the summer of 1481. This was perhaps a bad idea as the Scots king, with troubles of his own at home, was more than anxious to remain on good terms and the crisis occurred just as negotiations with cross-channel rulers were growing in complexity. Edward found himself unable to lead the expedition, as he had planned, because he was needed for the conduct of his other diplomacy. Meanwhile, the impossibility of waging war in France and Scotland simultaneously held him back from both. In the event, the Scottish campaign of 1481 came to little more than a naval raid on the Firth of Forth. However, the arrival in England in early 1482 of the disgruntled Scots nobleman, the duke of Albany, led to the planning of an invasion to place Albany on the throne. At Fotheringhay it was agreed that, in return, the north-eastern frontier town of Berwick, lost during the crisis of 1460–1, would come back into English possession and a large tract of land in south-west Scotland would be handed over to England: it was this land that was to form Gloucester's palatinate of Cumberland. Again, Edward decided not to lead the expedition after all, but in the summer a large English army under Gloucester, accompanied by Albany, invaded. James III was captured and Edinburgh taken, but Albany then defected in return for a pardon for his treason. After some negotiations, Gloucester withdrew to Berwick, which he took after a siege, and disbanded most of his army. Further plans for an invasion in 1483 came to nothing because of Edward's death and Gloucester's usurpation although, as king, Gloucester still hoped to campaign in Scotland again.

The Croyland Continuator was very critical of Gloucester's achievements in relation to the money spent in 1482, but it has been suggested recently that they have been underestimated. The return of Berwick was militarily and psychologically greatly significant and, for the first time for many decades, the north was able to feel that it had the upper hand over Scotland. Moreover, whereas it had been essential to give priority to relations with France and Burgundy as long as Edward felt internally insecure, it is arguable that on this occasion it was Scotland that had to be given priority. But, if the Scottish campaign was a greater triumph than has usually been supposed, there is no doubt that the policy with France and Burgundy was a failure, to which the preoccupation with Scotland in some degree contributed. What is really important is that it was a failure which did not really matter: as long as England was internally secure, there was not a great deal that could be achieved by external manipulation. It was only in periods like 1459–61 or 1469–71 that the enmity of France or Burgundy, or indeed Scotland, had serious implications for England. Paradoxically, the relative failure of Edward's foreign policy in his last years highlights the triumphant success of his internal rule.

As in the first reign, this success had little to do with money. It is in this period particularly that attention has been focused on what we have already met as the 'Yorkist land revenue experiment'.[9] From 1471 to 1483 there is thought to have been an intensification of the policies first noted in the 1460s: centralising the administration of all the royal lands, whether

---

[9] See above, pp. 167–8.

inherited, confiscated or in wardship, under special receivers; keeping
their administration outside the authority of the exchequer; paying the
revenues direct to the king's chamber rather than to the exchequer; the
creation of a skilled bureaucracy to administer the lands; and exploiting the
lands, and the king's private financial powers in general, with greater
intensity. There are serious problems with this interpretation. The first is
that, as we saw for the 1460s, it is another backward reading of history,
which in this case reads Henry VII's exploitation of his financial resources,
which we shall examine later, back into Edward's reign. It is true that
under Edward much of the framework for Henry VII's policies was
created but, as we have seen when examining his land policies in the 1460s,
not necessarily for the same reasons.

However, if a case is to be made for a 'Yorkist land revenue experiment', it can be made much better for the period 1471–83 than for the
1460s. Apart from any other considerations, it was only from 1471 that
Edward had the leisure to turn his attention from crisis management to
financial management. The first substantial estate taken into royal hands
that remained there to be exploited for the king by special officials was the
Clarence lands, in 1478. It was also from that year that the use of
commissions to investigate and exploit the financial rights of the crown
became more assiduous. For instance, in 1479 officers were sent to enquire
into tenants of the Duchy of Lancaster holding by knight service, so that
the financial potential of this kind of lordship could be exploited. Also in
the last few years of the reign, there were exceptional efforts to secure the
payment of tenant arrears of all kinds. The Croyland Continuator, the
informed source who noted how terrifying Edward was after Clarence's
fall, thought that from 1475 the king set his mind to the systematic
amassing of revenue from his lands. As against all this, it is evident that, the
Clarence lands apart, Edward still regarded the property that came into his
hands, as opposed to the crown lands, as political rather than financial
resources. For example, the Shrewsbury lands which he had in wardship
from 1473 were worth over £1,000 a year but produced less than half this
sum for the king, chiefly because he let Hastings have the wardship of most
of them for a mere £300. This was not just a favour to Hastings but it
ensured that the latter would not exploit the estate to destruction to
squeeze a profit from them, and that the young earl of Shrewsbury, when
he came into his estate, would therefore not replicate his father's political
wavering. In short, it was good political management. Similarly, the
officers on the former Clarence estates in Warwickshire and Worcestershire were not pressed hard for their arrears because they were mostly
important former members of Clarence's affinity who were now the king's
men in the region. Global figures are hard to come by but it is not

self-evident that the income of individual royal estates increased markedly under Edward, and in some cases it fell.

And, even while acknowledging the greater stringency with regard to estate management of this period, it has to be said that the whole debate has rested on the false premise that without financial stability there could be no political stability, and that political stability was in some way linked to independence from parliamentary finance. Consequently, the historian who has been most effective at showing that there was no 'Yorkist land revenue experiment' has taken a rather admonitory line, referring severely to 'much slackness and inefficiency'.[10] While he concludes that Edward did achieve solvency in the second reign, he focuses on how this relieved Edward of the necessity of calling parliament and on the fragility of a freedom from parliament which could only last as long as there was freedom from war. However, we have seen in general terms that, even with the fall in customs revenues, there was no insuperable royal financial problem during the fifteenth century. More particularly, we have seen that Edward was already able to get the credit he needed in the 1460s, when he was still coping, mostly without parliamentary subsidy, with the mess left by Henry VI and the demands on his purse of continued internal war and threats of invasion. We have seen also that not even the direst financial crisis would bring a king down, nor the greatest affluence save him. There were plenty of dire financial crises under Henry VI but his downfall came years after the spiralling expenditure for the French war had ended. Whether the king was affluent or in a state of poverty, what mattered was the allegiance of the king's landed subjects and, even when he was taxing them to the hilt, this would be won or lost on other fronts. It was the common people, not landowners, who revolted over taxation, as they seem to have done over Edward's misappropriation of taxes in 1463 and 1468. Unlike the commons, landowners had some control, through parliament, over how much they paid and the conditions under which they rendered it and therefore no need to protest by rebellion. A difficult parliament might be an irritation to a king, sometimes quite a serious one, but it was never going to be a threat.

Over ordinary income and expenditure, parliament had only limited influence, even when it suspected, as was not infrequently the case at times of financial stringency, that taxes for war were going into the king's privy purse.[11] Certainly it was better for a king not to have to call parliament to pay off debts incurred for ordinary expenditure, even for regular defence, and if Edward's solvency has any political importance, it was in that respect. However, so great was his mastery of the realm in the last decade

[10] C. Ross., *Edward IV* (London, 1974), p. 383.   [11] See above, p. 32.

or so of his reign that it is difficult to envisage any parliament proving wholly intractable. It was also desirable, if a king was to ask for large sums of money for war, to show that he was doing his best with his own revenues. Thus, the real significance of Edward's exploitation of his landed resources was probably less what it produced than that, like Henry V's similar care with Duchy of Lancaster revenues, it was a form of good housekeeping which encouraged the Commons to make grants of taxation. It is noteworthy, for example, that in the 1470s Edward returned to a policy which had not been seen since the days of Henry V of using profits from the royal earldom of Chester to help finance his government. But when it came to war only parliament could provide the resources. In 1481, no doubt mindful of the possible response to his expenditure of the only three grants of his reign, Edward tried to go to war with Scotland without a tax, partly by employing the expedient of collecting the tax he had remitted in 1475. Inevitably this drew more criticism than a request for a tax would have done: it was dishonest and it deprived parliament of the negotiating powers which made a tax palatable. He did in the end need a tax for the war, obtained in early 1483 at his last parliament, and got it without undue difficulty. He and Henry VII normally financed wars by the only feasible means, parliamentary taxation, and to imply that this somehow weakened them is to forget that taxation was a source of strength to the late-medieval monarchy and to read even later conditions – those of the seventeenth century – back into the period. Arguably, it was Edward's efforts to do without a tax in 1481 which caused more bad feeling than taxation that used the proper procedures.

During the second reign Edward's finances did in fact improve. The increase in his income was due primarily to three things: first, a recovery in trade, along with greater crown stringency in collecting customs and preventing piracy in the channel, which raised the customs revenues to an annual average of £34,000; secondly to the French pension; thirdly, to the addition of the Clarence lands. However, the improvement in Edward's financial position was due above all to the fact that, more by luck than good judgement, he was able to avoid a major war in a decade when he was reaping the financial rewards of internal peace. The backlog of debt, built up through the incessant borrowing caused by a ruinously expensive and badly managed war under his predecessor, could at last be expunged. He died allegedly very wealthy, despite the ambitious building projects of the second reign. However, if after 1475 he could pay off his debts, that made very little difference to the security of his position, perhaps none at all; it was no doubt a great satisfaction to his creditors but not of immense moment for a king to whom they were prepared to lend anyway. It was during his last years, when some historians see Edward at his most financially sound, that it might be argued that he most misjudged the situation, as Henry VII was to do. The Croyland Continuator attributes the greater intensity of his exploitation of his own lands from 1475 to fear of insurrection if he over-taxed the realm and this may indeed be why he misguidedly tried to manage the Scottish war without a subsidy. If, as a result, he was seen as more grasping in his final years, that can have done no political good to himself or his heir.

There is indeed a general tendency to look at Edward's reign through the wrong end of a telescope, and this is nowhere more evident than in the search for causes of his son and heir's downfall. Edward has been blamed for being too soft on great nobles by a historian who contrasts with approval Henry VII's policy 'of humbling and disciplining the mighty of his realm'[12] and takes Richard of Gloucester's power in the north as exemplification of this failing, bringing deserved retribution on the feeble monarch's son. Historians are very keen on moral lessons of this sort. Yet we have seen first that this is a misunderstanding of the essentially co-operative relationship of king and magnates, and that the nobility were normally remarkably forbearing in the face of awful government rather than eagerly on the alert for a chance to attack a king. We have seen also that Edward was a far fiercer and more powerful ruler than is supposed by the traditional view and that, far from being an independent power in the north, Gloucester was very much the king's lieutenant, in a tradition that stretched back to Henry of Lancaster under Edward III.

An alternative view is that Edward was *too* powerful. He confined authority to too small a group of people, mostly his wife's family, leaving his son an inadequate power-base and creating too many enemies who stood to gain by the fall of his family. There is some truth in this, in that as authoritative a figure as Edward was bound to make enemies; no king could exercise his powers to some purpose without doing so. His most obvious victims were the heirs to the Mowbray estates – Lord Howard and William Lord Berkeley – cut out by the marriage of Richard of York to the Mowbray heiress, and the duke of Buckingham, cut off from his political inheritance, although not from his landed one. All three of these, and some others who had cause for complaint, were to be involved in making the tragedy of 1483. It might also be argued that Edward should not have permitted the Woodvilles so free a rein and should not have allowed his heir to become so closely identified with them. But he could not expect to die at the age of not quite forty-one and nor would it be reasonable to take a boy not yet thirteen from his mother. One must presume that the future Edward V would shortly have been groomed to be

[12] Ross, *Edward IV*, p. 338.

king of England rather than a Woodville puppet. And we have seen that the Woodvilles, although undeniably not well loved, were less rapacious on their own account than is often supposed. Again we have to allow for hindsight, in this case a near-contemporary account of Richard III's usurpation that alleges ill-will between Gloucester and the Woodvilles in the last years of Edward IV.[13] The very fact that Edward could perpetrate frauds with major landed inheritances, as he did with the Mowbray and Exeter lands and with some other estates, and as had not been done on this scale since the magisterial rule of Edward I, shows the extent of his authority, for it was one of the most dangerous things a monarch could do. His ability to constrain or destroy magnates who stepped out of line, although he was wise enough to use it sparingly, is another indication of the majestic heights attained by monarchical authority under Edward. All effective kings make enemies, but none of these enmities need have had any impact on the course of English politics if it had not been that Edward IV died at the worst possible moment and Richard of Gloucester reacted with an ineptitude that beggars belief.

Both these points will be pursued in the next chapter. Suffice it to say for now that the idea that Edward's power-base was too limited has been shown by recent research to be completely without foundation. The comparison of the £24,000 spent in 1400 by Henry IV on annuities alone with the £11,000 or so spent by Edward on fees, wages and annuities of all sorts towards the end of his reign shows not, as has been suggested, that Edward had too narrow a power-base. It shows rather that by this time he certainly did not need to buy loyalty as Henry had had to at the start of his reign, and that he was getting much better value for money. This assertion that his support was too limited comes from the 'patronage' explanation of politics; that men did not show loyalty to the crown unless they received tangible reward. But, if we accept that patronage could produce only temporary loyalty, of the sort that a usurper could command, and that lasting loyalty was far more likely to come from recognition that the king could offer internal peace and stability, we can see why Edward had such a broad base of support. If we realise how closely most of landed society was tied in to his personal following, one way or another, even if only indirectly and without tangible reward, we can appreciate why this base made him so very powerful. Long before 1483, the royal affinity was vast and all-embracing.

In a way, as we shall see, that was the trouble, for England was so unified around the king by 1483 that it could be taken by surprise by a coup at the very centre of government. It is disunited countries that can best resist

13 See below, p. 206.

coups and invasions, for they have more than one location of power. So stable was Yorkist rule in the 1470s that former Lancastrians, such as the heir to Ormond, the brother of the Lancastrian earl of Wiltshire, gave up and returned home, to partial restoration. The official Lancastrian claimant, Henry Tudor, ceased to be any kind of viable candidate and even he was negotiating terms of return towards the end of Edward's reign. Edward exercised a form of centralised authority that replicated the power of Edward I, but, unlike Edward I, he knew how to use it in such a way that his landed subjects appreciated rather than resented it. He had an almost perfect instinct in the second reign for the vital kingly balance between justice and mercy. If he had at times been a little casual during the first reign, he had learned to take greater care, and even the casualness was symptomatic of a tendency to trust and forgive that was essential in a medieval monarch, as long as it was allied, as in his case, with shrewdness and force of character. He should be acknowledged as one of the greatest of English kings. Taking the throne in an almost impossible situation, that remained acute for a decade, he was able to rescue the monarchy and landed society from what can best be described as a shambles and leave his dynasty securely settled on the throne.

10

RICHARD III AND THE END OF
YORKIST RULE: 1483–1485

———— · ————

Edward IV died suddenly on 9 April. Although his death was unexpected, he lingered for ten days and recovered sufficiently after the first attack to make provision for his son's minority. Unfortunately we do not know what this was; the only source, Mancini, on whose version much of the conventional account of the usurpation is based, was written by a foreigner who did not know English and, not having access to the seat of power, had to rely on hearsay from those with whom he could converse. He also wrote after the event, and he is the writer most responsible for the hindsight which has made discussion of the last years of Edward IV and of the deposition of his son so difficult. Mancini alleges bad feeling between Gloucester and the Woodvilles, which led to Edward's wishes that his brother act as Protector being overturned by the queen and her family. There is on the contrary no evidence of tension before Edward IV's death and the author of the Croyland Continuation, the other main narrative source for the reign, who was very close to the centre of affairs, implies that Edward's will, whatever it was, was carried out. Indeed, it has recently been suggested that Edward intended his son to stay with the Woodvilles, and it would have been logical to leave the boy with his family while he was still a minor. The most recent and authoritative account of Richard III's reign argues that what Edward wanted was the continuance of a distribution of power that was already working extremely well, possibly even by the device of giving the king nominal rule from the start with the aid of a continual council, as had been done under Richard II between 1377 and 1380.

The trouble was that the circumstances of 1483 almost inevitably doomed such a co-operative form of rule. This was the first time that the

Yorkist throne had been inherited, always an extremely delicate moment for a usurping dynasty. We should remember the threats and instability that even as able and experienced a king as Henry V had had to contend with on ascending the throne in this situation. For the new king to be underage was the greatest disaster that could have struck the dynasty, for it opened the way to disunity, and that gave opportunities to alternative contenders both at home and abroad. The minority of Richard II had been almost as divisive as that of Edward V proved to be, but it did not occur under conditions that could lead to the questioning of the king's title. What made it worse was the actual age of the king. He was twelve, alarmingly close to the age when the process of transferring the powers of kingship to him might well begin.[1] If he proved in any way as malleable as Henry VI, the last minor to ascend the throne, whoever had control of him then would be in a position to run the kingdom in their own interests, at least until the king was old enough to assert his own authority. The nobility had only just recovered from the two decades and more that had been needed to cope with the consequences of the lack of will of Henry VI. Those who had no direct experience of this time would have heard plenty about it from the survivors of the previous generation and would be aware of those who had lost their lives during that crisis. Even if it now seems that most of the failures of governance in Henry VI's majority were ultimately caused less by 'court cliques' than by the structural problems resulting from the king's incapacity, there is no doubt that the period could be read retrospectively and superficially as a series of struggles for control of the king. And, for those who feared the dominance of such a clique, the Woodvilles, with their close connection to the king, their power in his household and their reputation for high-handedness, must have seemed the obvious aspirants. Moreover, there was a terribly short time with which to work; if the Woodvilles could ensconce themselves rapidly around the throne, they would be awkward to remove and, once the king was of age, could entrench themselves by using his powers to destroy rivals and enemies. Gloucester, with an estate whose legal validity had been largely ratified by parliament and could be undone by parliament, was especially exposed. Unless we understand the atmosphere of panic and its causes in these crucial months, it is impossible to grasp why events turned out as they did.

There is some evidence that Hastings and others feared Woodville ambitions from an early stage in the new reign and that military preparations by some of the family may have given them good reasons for doing

---

[1] Compare Henry VI, who, despite his apparent slowness to take on the regal authority, was being edged towards adulthood at fourteen years old (see above, pp. 90–1).

so. This is the background to the coup at Stony Stratford in Buckinghamshire. Edward was coming to London from Ludlow with his uncle, Lord Rivers. They were met by Gloucester, who had ridden from the north to meet the new king and accompany him into London, and the duke of Buckingham. All three nobles had retinues, although Rivers had been persuaded to reduce the size of his. At Stratford, on 30 April, Rivers and a small number of close associates were arrested and Gloucester took charge of Edward V, dismissing his retinue. On 4 May Gloucester and Buckingham entered London with the king. By 8 May Gloucester was made Protector. The Woodvilles had been unable to gather any significant support and Hastings is said to have approved Gloucester's actions. This lends more weight to the theory that it was a generalised mistrust of Woodville intentions that had led to these events. While almost the entire Woodville family lost its lands, not many others suffered, which suggests both the limited basis of independent Woodville power and the co-operation of Edward IV's own household men in what had happened. The only indication of the more radical changes to come is the huge rewards conferred on Buckingham, largely from the fall of the Woodvilles. For example it was his power that to a large degree replaced that of the council of the Marches. Nevertheless the scene was set for the amicable joint rule of Gloucester and Hastings, the two great upholders of the governance of Edward IV. It may be that Edward intended these two to share power with the Woodvilles and that his plans foundered on mistrust of the queen's family and on Edward's deliberate failure to give them a secure landed base independent of royal power. But there was no reason for that to be more than a temporary hitch.

Events thus far are much more explicable than what was to come. A new date was fixed for the coronation, 22 June, and for several weeks the council seems to have ruled harmoniously; contrary to accounts written afterwards there were no signs of the impending crisis. Then at a council meeting on 13 June Hastings was accused of plotting treason, a group of armed men, led by Thomas, son of Lord Howard, came in from the next room and Hastings was taken off to Tower Hill and beheaded summarily without trial. Hastings' death was the precondition for a usurpation against the family he had served loyally all his life. Even so on 16 June, the queen, who had taken her younger son into the sanctuary of Westminster Abbey, was persuaded to release him for his brother's coronation. However, on 17 June the parliament summoned to meet after the coronation was cancelled, while preparations for the coronation itself were abandoned about this time. Lord Rivers and Sir Richard Grey, respectively the king's uncle and half-brother, who had been sent north after the coup at Stratford, were executed, along with one of the servants of the king who had also been taken at Stratford. On 22, 24 and 25 June Gloucester's claim to the throne was made publicly in London, on the last two occasions by Buckingham. The grounds seem to have been that Edward IV was contracted in marriage elsewhere before marrying Elizabeth Woodville and so his sons were bastards. Leaving aside the fact that, had this been true, the real king would have been Clarence's son, then in Gloucester's custody, the justification was clearly immaterial. What mattered was that Gloucester meant now to be king, would indeed have called the legitimacy of his two older brothers into question, as was in fact alleged against him, if this would help his cause. On 25 June, and again on the 26th, some sort of noble assembly, led by Buckingham and on the second occasion afforced by London notables, begged Gloucester to take the throne, and on the second occasion he graciously assented.

Why did this happen? From the time of the events themselves there has been no lack of speculation but not much that convinces. It is apparent that everyone was taken by surprise by Richard and it is this that led to the Tudor tradition that his previous loyalty was deep dissemblance by a man who was biding his time. But, if that is indeed what he was doing throughout his brother's reign, it was a very misconceived plan since the premature death of Edward IV could not possibly have been foreseen. There are two rather more logical ways of looking at the usurpation; either it was the ruthless act of a man who saw his opportunity and took it, or it was an act of panic. In favour of the first explanation is the fact that Richard had spent much of his life as a soldier and seems to have been a straightforward man who, in gathering together his estate, had certainly shown ruthlessness before. Against this is that his whole behaviour at this juncture seems so out of character, and this is emphasised by the fact that he took completely by surprise experienced politicians and managers of men like Hastings. Nobles in close proximity to the throne whose ambition went to their heads usually showed instability of temperament at an early stage: Humphrey of Gloucester and Clarence are two good examples, and there are others from the fourteenth century. If Richard was really ambitious enough to want to seize the throne over his own nephews he would have been super-human to have concealed so powerful an emotion from everyone until 1483.

It may be more fruitful to explore the implications of this sudden change of character that was taken for dissemblance. The ultra-loyal underling, who owed everything to the older brother he had served for his entire adult life, deposed the brother's sons. We must return to the shortage of time. Once the coup at Stony Stratford had occurred, as long as the

Woodvilles were alive, and as soon as Edward V came into his majority, Richard was exposed to the Woodvilles' revenge and also, as was noted before, to the possible destruction of his landed estate. That he was already in a panicky state may be guessed from his sending for troops from the north on 10 June (although it is also possible that these instructions are a sign that he had made his decision to seize the throne by then). Richard did indeed allege a Woodville plot against himself and Buckingham in the letter in which he sent for this force; whether there was or was not is immaterial if he believed there to be one. If he was disposed to panic, he had Buckingham, the *éminence grise* throughout the affair, to egg him on. Buckingham had no cause to welcome the perpetuation of the status quo under Edward IV, and the demise of the Woodvilles and of Hastings opened the way to undreamed-of supremacy for him in both the areas in which the rule of Edward IV had denied him the traditional authority of his family, Wales and the north midlands. Possibly at the back of his mind lay the notion that Clarence's children were disgraced, Richard's only son was a weakling, who did in fact die before the end of the reign, the Lancastrian claimant, Henry Tudor, was in exile, and only Edward IV's disturbingly healthy sons lay between Buckingham and a viable claim to the throne. If this is too far-fetched, he must nevertheless be judged to be an unstable and deliberately destabilising influence. If Richard is seen less as a down-to-earth soldier and more as a born subordinate who could not cope with independent command, a man susceptible to misleading advice, the events of May and June may begin to make more sense. There were others too to urge him on, like Howard; his son commanded the ambush of Hastings, and he had a vested interest in the death of the young duke of York, who stood between him and his share of the Mowbray inheritance.

As king, it cannot be denied that Richard did his best, especially in continuing the Yorkist traditions of active supervision of the country, attention to justice and public order and careful husbanding of the royal finances. All this was aided by the propensity of the lower echelons of royal bureaucracy, as had long been the case in medieval government, to accept the new regime. Richard made several declarations of his intention to provide justice for all and he seems to have had an unusual interest in offering remedies for those who could not afford the law's usual expenses, establishing conciliar measures to deal with these which were to develop into the Tudor Court of Requests. Much of the legislation of his only parliament, of 1484, was concerned with minor reforms of legal procedures. Moreover, he was personally active, travelling the country more extensively than Edward in his second reign, although it could be said that, given the near-continuous political crisis that obtained for much of the reign, he had no choice. His involvement in the administration of the crown estates can be traced particularly closely because of the survival of a docket book, or entry book, of the signet office which issued orders from the chamber. Instructions to local officials, determined efforts to get payments out of officers and tenants and concern with even the minutiae of tenant terms and conditions testify to the energy of Richard's officials, behind which presumably lay the king's initiative, if only in general terms. All in all, as a king going through the correct motions of doing the job at a governmental level, Richard can hardly be faulted, but that was not really the point; what he lacked was the political mastery without which the job was ultimately impossible.

The trouble was that the usurpation itself, if designed to make Richard secure, fatally undermined his position. This is the only deposition in English history of a monarch who had done no damage at all, the successor to one whose second reign had been an almost unqualified success. It was hard enough to justify deposition of a king who was bad at his job, impossible to do so with respect to the as yet uncrowned son of one who had been so good at it. Richard, aware of this, claimed to be taking the throne to preserve the rule of his brother against the machinations of the Woodvilles and against the possible dislocation of a minority, but it was a fairly threadbare justification, especially since he himself had been the major cause of discontinuity and dislocation. At first there was acquiescence, even from the core of Edward IV's household and affinity, perhaps because they felt that that was the best way to protect Edward's political and governmental legacy – and indeed his sons – but it was unlikely to last long.

Because there was no reason at all for him to be king, Richard, even more than the general run of usurpers, had to buy support and that left him peculiarly exposed to the pressure of those who had helped him to the throne. One of these was Lord Howard, who received the Duchy of Norfolk and his share of the estates and a large number of other grants. Another famous, if not infamous, beneficiary was the Warwickshire and Northamptonshire esquire William Catesby, who ensured that the private non-Duchy part of the Hastings affinity, focused primarily on these two counties, would come over to Richard. Although these were two who remained faithful unto death at Bosworth, there was no relying on the loyalty of men who had been bought. There was also a limit to how much Richard had to give and, for a king who rather prided himself on being his brother's successor in all things, including replicating his firm control of the localities, how much he wanted to give. In the longer term this proved to be the problem with the Stanleys, who had never been an intrinsic part of Richard's northern following, and were never to be a dependable part of his regime. Thomas Lord Stanley had been amongst the three others arrested with Hastings. He had somehow survived, and he and his brother Sir William were well rewarded for remaining loyal when Buckingham rebelled, with lands and office in Wales and the Welsh Marches, some of them Buckingham's. But the fact that Stanley was married to Margaret Beaufort, the mother of Henry Tudor, must always have put his reliability in doubt.

The fragility of Richard's rule is seen at its clearest in Buckingham's rebellion in October 1483. Buckingham had been showered with rewards, notably control of Wales, of the north midlands, in succession to Hastings, and of parts of southern England. He also had the promise of the half of the earldom of Hereford that had come to the crown through Henry IV, who had married one coheiress, while Thomas of Gloucester, Buckingham's great-great-grandfather, had married the other. His grants had indeed flown in the face of Richard's attempts to follow his brother's policy of not allowing great semi-independent noble power-bases to be created. Why he rebelled is obscure, other than that his appetite for reward had become insatiable. The instability and lack of judgement shown by his decision to rebel certainly vindicates Edward IV's decision not to take him seriously as politician and governor. Possibly Buckingham had some idea that a rebellion in favour of Henry Tudor might remove Richard and culminate in his own ascent to the throne, on the grounds that the Beaufort claim which Henry represented had been debarred when they were legitimised. It has even been suggested that Margaret Beaufort, anxious to obtain his participation in a rebellion in favour of her son, duped him into believing that the real aim was to place himself on the throne. He was a worthless man and probably few lamented his passing.

Buckingham's rebellion reveals one aspect of Richard's weakness; its participants demonstrate another, even more fundamental. This was in truth scarcely 'Buckingham's rebellion' at all but one in a series of revolts by the former household of Edward IV. It was observed before that it was the very unity of Edward IV's following in the midlands and the south that helped make the usurpation possible. Acting with such speed, Richard was able to seize the centre of power and with it the one directing force in the kingdom. Once the first shock was past, it was in the core of that following, the royal household itself, that he had most to fear. These were the direct servants of the crown, as opposed to the men who looked to the king indirectly through the royal estates or through other nobles. It was probably inevitable that a usurpation that could only be done over the dead body of Hastings, the linch-pin of the southern part of the royal affinity, would eventually be rejected by those in the affinity most closely connected to the king. Richard's claim to be usurping to preserve the status quo had initially received some credence with these, but as early as

July, during Richard's post-coronation progress, there was a plot involving royal servants to rescue the princes, and from July to August there were more rumblings, centred on the southern and south-midland counties that were to be the focal point of Buckingham's rebellion.

It was probably in response to this plot that the death of the princes was ordered, following the characteristic pattern seen under Henry IV and Edward IV of killing the usurped predecessor as soon as there was a rebellion on his behalf. The difficulty for Richard was that murdering children, especially if they were your nephews and the sons and heirs of a respected king, was no more acceptable in the fifteenth century than it would be now. Accordingly, while he wished it to be known that the princes were dead, to end revolts in their favour, he did not want to be known as their murderer. The compromise solution was to allow rumours of their deaths to seep out. It is more than possible that Buckingham, with his usual eye on the hereditary main chance, urged murder on the king, but the responsibility was all Richard's own.

Thus, when Buckingham's rebellion occurred, in October, the rallying cry was no longer the princes but Henry Tudor, the only viable candidate left. It was at this stage that Margaret Beaufort, who may have had some part in the July plot, first became indisputably involved in intrigues against Richard and that Tudor at last became a realistic candidate for the throne. Although Buckingham was the most eminent rebel, the fact that this was primarily a household rebellion, this time of the utmost seriousness, had far-reaching consequences. The rebels who had served Edward IV included Sir Thomas Bourchier of Surrey, a younger son of the noble family, Sir William Haute of Kent, brother of Sir Richard (councillor of Prince Edward and one of those seized at Stony Stratford), John Harcourt of Oxfordshire and Sir William Norreys of Berkshire. The rebellion lasted a month and ran through most of the southern counties of England, as far north as East Anglia. Its ramifications may have gone further, for there is evidence, for example in the north midlands, of disenchantment among those whose primary link to Edward IV had been through the Duchy of Lancaster rather than as direct servants or retainers. Buckingham's role was probably to try to draw in other nobles from the Welsh Marches, notably the Stanleys and the Talbots, and his almost complete failure to raise any significant support, which is of a piece with the rest of his political career, is what made the rebellion easier to crush than it might have been. This was in no sense a Lancastrian rising, a point that needs to be stressed, for what it revealed to Richard was that his brother's powerful network was no longer at his disposal. He would have to build a base of his own in the midlands, and in the south above all, and he did not have a great deal of time to do it, for the rebellion had also suddenly transformed Henry Tudor into a credible rival. In this new incarnation, Henry was not a Lancastrian claimant, but the Yorkist household's second-best substitute for Edward IV's dead sons. That is why, in the aftermath of the failed rebellion, Henry promised to marry Edward's daughter Elizabeth if he ever became king.

Richard found himself unable to rely on most of the leading gentry in southern England, as servants, retainers or local officers, and there must be serious doubts about the loyalty of many midland gentry. His answer was to replace them with northerners, members of his great northern affinity, and he made considerable use of lands confiscated in the rebellion to do so. To some extent he tried to exploit existing links between north and south, enhancing the position of southern families, like the Hoptons of East Anglia, that had lands or connections in the north, but clearly there was a limit to this. The more general policy was to 'plant' northerners in the midlands and south, giving them lands and then appointing them to local office. Sir Robert Brackenbury, for example, the constable of the Tower who has been implicated in the death of the princes, was given lands in Essex and Kent and appointed to county offices there. Most of these men were Richard's personal retainers as king, for the royal household too was coming to be dominated by northerners, and, like Brackenbury, few were of any great local standing in their counties of origin before the king enhanced their position in the south. They were intended to be a source of reliable local officers and a local focus around which loyalty to the new regime outside the north could be built, for it was manifestly impossible to uproot the entire gentry of the south and replace them with northerners. There were also more eminent northerners, like Sir Richard Ratcliffe, who was given land in Devon, and Viscount Lovell, one of those with southern interests, whose lands in the Thames valley, one of the key centres of the revolt, were substantially increased. In some areas it was possible to exploit existing power structures. Howard, for instance, could be used in East Anglia and we have seen that, somewhat reluctantly on Richard's part, the Stanleys were made partial replacements for Buckingham in Wales. Indeed, Richard's problems in Wales after Buckingham's death can be seen in the fact that he was also obliged to use William Herbert, formerly second earl of Pembroke, whose feebleness had led to his demotion under Edward IV.

However carefully it was done, the policy caused deep resentment and reopened those geographical prejudices that had helped stir up opposition to Margaret of Anjou as she came south after the battle of Wakefield. Most of the 'plantations' failed to work, even in the case of Lovell who was working from an existing base. The north was in many ways a world apart from the south; it was a long way from the seat of power at Westminster, it was generally poorer and it had its own agenda, most particularly the incessant border war with the Scots.[2] Much of the resentment however was focused simply on the fact that local societies were complex interwoven entities and did not take kindly to the interpolation from above of numbers of new men, wherever they came from. As has been noted several times before, kings did best when they exploited existing power structures, even if on their own terms. Radical refashioning of power in the localities could not be done, especially not at this kind of speed. The policy also dangerously overstretched Richard's own resources of manpower, for it forced him to use his closest supporters in a variety of ways in the north, in the south and within his own household. It was too narrow a base to work with or to rule from.

In the north there was no immediate problem of loyalty but here also he was overstretched, for Richard's own government of the north under Edward IV had been designed to relieve the king of the need to take personal responsibility for the region. As king himself, he would have to delegate, although he was at first reluctant to do so. He created a council of the north, nominally under his son, but actually run by himself. However, after the death of his son in January 1484, and in view of the fact that the rebellions had already revealed the insecurity of his position in the south, he accepted the need for a more than nominal leader of the council. He chose the same path as his brother, using a closely related outsider, John de la Pole earl of Lincoln, son of the duke of Suffolk and Richard's own nephew. But, unlike Richard, Lincoln had almost no lands here, and the obvious candidate for the job, who did have lands, the earl of Northumberland, was passed over. He had been well-rewarded by the king but, it has been suggested, he may have felt squeezed by Richard's policies in the north, and was another of those nobles who had no particular reason to support him in a crisis. In general, Richard remained reluctant to allow even the most trusted nobles the broad regional power that Edward IV had successfully exploited through those closest to him and this itself is symptomatic of his deep insecurity. He had the support of most of the minor northern nobility – Scrope of Bolton, Dacre, Greystoke, Fitzhugh – but, as it turned out, could not rely on the major figures.

He was also having difficulties with internal order. Again, the cause was his own feeble claim to rule, for it forced him to buy support not only with grants but also with the promise of reopening old feuds. Although it was put in more elegant terms, this is effectively what was on offer and it puts a rather different gloss on Richard's alleged concern with matters of justice. Many of these disputes had been settled in the later years of Edward IV, often after decades of conflict and violence. The consequences of this

[2] See above, pp. 55–6.

invitation can be imagined in a society where the king was the key figure in the containment of conflict. In Warwickshire numbers of disputes resurfaced under Richard, often accompanied by violence; one litigant specifically cited Richard's offer of redress as the cause of his return to the fray. In 1485 Richard's indication that he intended to reopen the affair between the Stanleys and the Harringtons which Edward and he had settled in the 1470s, and the implication that this would favour the Harringtons, who were closely attached to him, may have been the final push that took the Stanleys over to Henry Tudor. Taken more generally, the rising tide of violence can have done nothing for a king who had justified his usurpation as the best defence against the disorder of minority rule.

Things looked slightly better in early 1484, when parliament obediently confirmed Richard's title and accepted a large number of attainders, while some of the rebels asked for and secured pardons. But from the middle of July 1484 Richard faced an almost continual series of threats and insurrections, all now focused on Henry Tudor. The latter, who had been in Brittany since 1471, moved to France in September 1484, when he learned that Richard was on the verge of negotiating his forcible return. In France he was far more dangerous, for he began to receive the active support of the French king for an invasion of England. In Brittany he had been joined by numbers of Yorkist rebels, mostly former members of Edward IV's household, and these continued to arrive in France. It was indeed at this time that Henry acquired the services of some of those who were later to be his closest aides, and these, like Sir Giles Daubigny and Sir Robert Willoughby, both ennobled by Henry VII, were in many cases former servants of Edward IV. A notable addition was James Blount, scion of the family of Sir Walter that had done so well under Edward IV. He was Richard's lieutenant of Hammes Castle and, having released the earl of Oxford from captivity there, he accompanied him to France. Towards the end of the year there was a rising in Essex which spread into other counties. It was fomented by Sir William Brandon, Howard's own retainer, and it exploited lingering loyalties to the earls of Oxford who had once owned substantial lands there.

Because throughout his reign Richard remained in the position of a usurper, forced to purchase loyalty, the distribution of patronage mattered. The more he was obliged to give to his northerners to help them control the south, the less he had to give to the southerners, and so the more he needed the assistance of the northerners. In an attempt to broaden the basis of his rule, he began to make overtures to the Woodvilles towards the end of 1484 and, his wife having died in March 1485, even proposed that he marry his niece, Elizabeth of York. This proposal had the additional advantage of cutting out Henry Tudor. But it was then that his heavy dependence on the favour of his existing allies became evident, for it seems that they opposed the match because of the risk to their own gains under Richard if the Woodvilles were restored. Thus, the king who was still obliged to buy support remained at the mercy of those he had bought. Moreover, his continuing need to purchase his landed subjects' loyalty seriously drained his financial resources. Although given the customs for life in the parliament of 1484, he was unable to extract a subsidy, and probably did not dare to try. This was despite the fact that he was contemplating war with Scotland and needed to maintain his defences, in the channel and on the coasts, against first Brittany and then France. It was probably these financial needs that lay behind his efforts to extract more from the crown lands. Even so, in early 1485 he was reduced to taking forced loans, which an established king like Edward IV could ride out but a usurper could not. This was particularly embarrassing because, in the parliament of 1484, Richard had passed legislation against the use of benevolences, a clear play for the allegiance of those who had suffered from Edward's use of these, and the gap between forced loans and benevolences was more a matter of words than of reality.

It has been suggested that by spring 1485 Richard's only hope was that a confrontation with Henry Tudor would bring a victory that would at last allow him to embark on the task of reuniting the polity, rather as Edward IV was able to do after the Readeption. But this is to assume that the Yorkist affinity that so resented Richard's betrayal of his brother would not have looked for another candidate – for there were others, such as the de la Poles – and that the remainder of the midlands and south could be bought over. Arguably, it was only good and equitable kingship over many years that could have expunged the memory of the governance that Richard had destroyed. Could he have lasted long enough, even after the defeat of Tudor, to accomplish this?

On 7 August Henry landed at Milford Haven in Wales. Passing through mid-Wales, by the second half of August he was in Staffordshire. He had gathered a sizeable force, if by no means a vast one, along the way. In Staffordshire he had two secret meetings with the Stanleys; Lord Stanley was as ever reluctant to commit himself, but particularly so in this case because his son and heir, Lord Straunge, was a hostage in the king's custody. Richard mustered his men at Nottingham and then moved south to Leicester and from there towards Henry's army as it came from Lichfield. On 22 August the two sides met at Market Bosworth near Leicester. Although Richard's force was considerably the larger, neither Northumberland nor Stanley would engage the enemy and the earl of Westmorland, another northerner, was equally hesitant, if he was there at all. It is indeed less the numbers prepared to fight for Henry that impress than the reluctance to fight for Richard and the rumours of treason and disaffection that flew around his camp. At the height of the battle Richard chose to charge straight at the centre of Henry's army. It was at this point that the Stanleys intervened on Henry's side and probably saved him. Richard was killed and the battle was Henry's.

Richard had never succeeded in becoming more than a usurper and the disloyalty around him on the last day of his life reflects that fact, for in some ways Bosworth was the showdown between one usurper and another, would-be one. But it was also the Yorkist restoration, the vindication of Edward IV's rule, which had been so rudely destroyed by his brother. Both the army that Henry Tudor had and the one that Richard had not owed their existence principally to the lasting loyalty of Edward's household and of the wider body of landowners south of the Humber. If it was the north that betrayed Richard at Bosworth, it was the south that had made Henry into a real candidate for the throne and impelled the northern lords to doubt Richard's ability to win. The king who had taken the throne in the name of continuity brought down his dynasty, while propelling the dynasty's closest aides into becoming the foundation of the new ruling house of Tudor. His actions had reopened all the dynastic issues that seemed to have been settled in 1471; it would be left to his successor to try to close them.

II

HENRY VII AND THE END OF
THE WARS: 1485–1509

Study of Henry VII's reign is at a problematic but interesting turning point at the moment. For a long time it was left to the Tudor historians, for it was understood that Tudor history and the 'modern age' started in 1485. The trouble was that the reign does not really fit with the Tudor historiographical traditions. These have focused on parliamentary and administrative history and the progress of the Reformation, and, apart from some local studies, have until recently been to a large extent devoid of internal politics. Late-medieval history, on the other hand, in the McFarlane era, has put politics, especially high politics, at the centre of its concerns and it is becoming increasingly clear that the same should be true of Henry VII's reign. The neglect of politics under Henry VII has been given added impetus by the fact that the sources for the reign are still very much the same as those for late-medieval history and therefore pose similar difficulties. During the reign of Henry VIII, the class of documents known as State Papers begins, and this tells us far more about what the government was doing and why. Moreover, there is a general multiplication of informative sources, particularly of private papers, in the course of the sixteenth century. All this makes political history much easier. Thus, if any is to be done for the Tudors, their historians are going to be reluctant to tackle the reign of the first Tudor, which requires a medievalist's willingness to search around among a multiplicity of different sources, often both difficult and dirty. In some respects Henry VII's reign is in fact less well served by its sources than earlier ones in the fifteenth century. Notably, the returns for the Commons elected to most of the parliaments are missing and there is much less information on noble retaining and annuities. The medievalists, however, conscious that this reign was officially 'off-limits', have, until very recently, left it alone although they are the better equipped to study it.

This situation has had a number of unfortunate consequences. The first, as one perceptive medievalist has pointed out, is that much of the reason that the reigns of Edward IV and Henry VII look different is that they belong to different historiographical traditions, each with its own agenda. That means, secondly, that the reign of Henry VII seems not to have any politics. This is readily apparent in the standard modern account of the reign, by S. B. Chrimes, which, although written by a medievalist, has to use work by Tudor historians and, after dealing with the initial settlement of the realm, is so bereft of internal politics that it is almost impossible to use it to find out who the nobility were. In this it reflects a more generalised problem in Tudor historiography. This is that concentration on the formalised institutions of parliament and central government has given rise to a rather distorted vision of the realm. It has meant that the tendency noted by McFarlane for historians who work primarily with governmental records to become 'king's friends' and to see the realm from the top down has been particularly powerful. This is reinforced by the focus on institutions rather then people, so that politics can come to be seen as a rather dirty distraction from the real business of government by bureaucracy.

Together these perspectives produce the typical reverence of many Tudor historians for strong government, by which they mean putting the nobility in their place. Late-medievalists, on the other hand, are aware of McFarlane's profound insight that the realm must be viewed as much from below - from the perspective of nobles and gentry - as from above if historians are to make any sense of late-medieval politics. They may not always have absorbed the alternative perspective entirely but they are at least conscious of it. They can hardly fail to be, as the magnates were so manifestly important in the fourteenth and fifteenth centuries. The Tudor historiographical tradition on the other hand meets the belief that something called early-modern England did begin in 1485. This notion survives at a very deep level, despite all the acknowledged reservations, for the simple reason that 1485 still marks the normal boundary between what medievalists and Tudor historians teach and know. And the outcome of the joining of these two threads, of the king-centred approach and the idea that England changed in 1485, is the standard interpretation of Henry VII. This is that, despite the nod that it is now customary to give in the direction of Edward IV, it was Henry VII who created a modern monarchy. This monarchy is held to have rested on a sound financial basis, on putting the nobles firmly in their place and on effective order, secured by wise legislation and the disciplining of the nobility, accomplished by a new 'middle class' of professional administrators and lawyers. Although it is now generally understood that Henry's closest servants were by no means a middle-class, and although that summary does no justice to some of the more subtle work that has modified ideas in some of these areas, it is a fair representation of the account still to be found in textbooks, especially Tudor textbooks. More importantly, it indicates the range of questions that still dominates accounts of the reign.

Yet it should be obvious to anyone who has read the rest of this book that this is not what kingship was primarily about until 1485; did it really change so radically overnight? In recent years there has been some rethinking. This has come from two directions: medievalists moving forwards and Tudor historians moving backwards. Almost all the medieval work has been done at a local level, since there is little reason to end a local study in 1485. Tudor historians for their part have grown conscious that the nobles may have had some importance in the reign of Henry VIII and have become particularly interested in the politics of his court, notably in the early years, and one or two are beginning to move back into the later years of Henry VII. However, distinguished as some of this 'Tudor' work is, the view from the centre, and therefore the assumption that whatever the king did was normally justified, still dominates it. The history of late-medieval England takes for granted that no king can be evaluated without reference to his effect on his realm, yet in relation to Henry VII we have still to a large extent to acquire the knowledge that would enable us to judge him in these terms. Above all, two things need to be stressed. The first is that all interpretations of Henry VII's reign until very recently have rested on an almost complete ignorance of his dealings with the nobility, except at the most superficial level. Now, thanks mainly to the work of Steven Gunn, we are acquiring a better sense of these. The second is that the level of ignorance of what actually happened in the shires, that is of the true business of ruling, has been as bad and is only just beginning to be rectified. It is the 'medieval' perspective of placing Henry's rule in the context of political society that to a large degree informs the account of the reign that follows.

Henry VII became king under better circumstances than any other usurper in late-medieval England. Like Henry IV, he had the enormous advantage of replacing a king who had been widely disliked, although the lingering affection for Richard III in the north might prove a problem. Unlike both Henry IV and Edward IV, he started with the advantage that his predecessor was already dead. Unlike both, he had no powerful kingmaker to contend with; the noble house that gained most from

Henry's accession was that of the Stanleys, the family into which Henry's mother, Margaret Beaufort, had married, and it was improbable that the head of the family, Lord Stanley, would lead a rebellion against his own stepson. Neither did Henry have the difficulty, shared by both Henry IV and Edward IV, of bringing uncommitted nobles over to his side, for Bosworth was essentially the restoration of the regime of Edward IV and as such to be welcomed by all but the most devoted supporters of Richard III. With the restoration came the royal affinity that had been at the heart of Edward's predominance over the whole of the midlands and the south. Henry's marriage to Elizabeth of York in January 1486 set the seal on his inheritance of Edward IV's political legacy.

The remnants of Richard's supporters were disposed of in the first two years. The earl of Northumberland, who, if he had failed to fight for Richard, had at least turned up at Bosworth, was initially imprisoned, but released at the end of the year because of the need for an effective power in the region where Richard had been strongest. The earliest attempted rising, of Humphrey Stafford, a Warwickshire/Worcestershire esquire, in the west midlands, and of Lord Lovell in his two former spheres of Yorkshire and the Thames Valley, in early 1486, proved a comfortingly damp squib. Stafford tried and failed to raise the heartland of the earldom of Warwick in the name of the young earl of Warwick and Lovell's efforts to exploit Richard's own relationship with the Middleham area were equally disappointing.

Subsequent revolts proved more serious because they were actively sponsored from abroad. First there was Lambert Simnel, who masqueraded as Edward of Warwick. He had support from the earl of Kildare, described by one historian as 'in effect king of Ireland',[1] whom Henry had offended by failing to confirm him in the position of deputy-lieutenant of Ireland, and from Edward IV's sister, Margaret of York, now dowager duchess of Burgundy. She had already sheltered Lovell, who had escaped after his abortive rebellion. In early 1487 John de la Pole earl of Lincoln fled to Burgundy. As son of Edward IV's sister he was a possible Yorkist claimant, but had initially submitted to the new king. Why he changed his mind, and whether he had been in touch with Margaret long before, is obscure. In May 1487, Lovell and Lincoln arrived in Ireland, with a force provided by Margaret; Simnel, already in Ireland, was proclaimed as Edward VI. Reinforced by an Irish contingent, they landed in Lancashire in June. Some of Richard's old northern affinity joined them, and the earl of Northumberland failed to move against them. Henry was in the midlands when he heard of the landing and moved north to Nottingham,

---

[1] J. R. Lander, *Government and Community: England 1450–1509* (London, 1980), p. 339.

where he awaited the Stanleys who brought a large army. On 16 June at Stoke near Newark in Nottinghamshire Henry was victorious. Lincoln was killed, Lovell missing, presumed dead; Simnel was spared and set to work in the king's kitchens. In contrast to Simnel, whose army seems to have consisted chiefly of foreigners, Henry was well supported in this campaign, a fact which emphasises how little he had to fear from rebellion within England. What the invasion did was to give Henry the opportunity to finish off any lingering resistance in the north and this he did in August with a personal progress to Yorkshire and the north-east, the centres of Richard's northern power. This was not the last attempt at a Yorkist restoration but it did mark the end of the Gloucester tradition in the north and of the efforts to exploit it to unseat Henry in the immediate aftermath of Bosworth. From this time onwards the whole kingdom was Henry's. We must now examine how he ruled it.

Henry's nobility were an amalgam of existing peers and restored ones, mostly Lancastrian. The Stanleys were hugely rewarded. Lord Stanley was promoted earl of Derby and given large powers in the north-west - grants of both land and offices in the earldom of Chester and Duchy of Lancaster - while his brother Sir William became chamberlain of the king's house-hold and retained much, even though not all, of the power in north Wales he had acquired under Richard. The Staffordshire branch of the family, which had assisted Henry as he journeyed through Staffordshire to Bos-worth, was also well recompensed, gaining offices on the crown lands and on the Buckingham estates; these were yet again in royal custody while the heir, Duke Henry's son Edward, was a minor. Through the Buckingham lands, Derby's influence percolated from Cheshire into the north mid-lands, for his wife, the king's mother, had custody of most of them. She was indeed a great power in the kingdom on her own account. She was already the owner of large possessions as heiress to the Beauforts of Somerset and widow of Henry Stafford, second son of the duke of Buckingham killed at the battle of Northampton. In January 1487 she was given an enormous grant in addition, largely of estates in the midlands and the west country. It included most of the lands of the Duchy of Exeter that had been allowed to remain with the last duke's divorced wife, Edward IV's sister, on her marriage to Thomas St Leger, and whose ultimate descent to the heiress of this second marriage had been authorised by Edward.[2] Richard III had revoked this piece of sharp practice, chiefly because the heiress was to marry a Woodville, the son and heir of the earl of Dorset, but the whole estate had remained in the king's hands. Margaret was soon able to cut out the St Leger heiress: the latter's marriage to

---

[2] See above, p. 183.

Dorset's heir did not take place and he was married instead to one of Margaret's kinsmen. Also in the grant were some Beaufort lands that had been regained, by dubious means, from the Nevilles. This family had had them since Salisbury's marriage to the Montacute heiress, to whom they had passed, but the Neville heir, Edward of Warwick, could be easily cut out. The other major component of the grant was part of the Honor of Richmond, Henry's own inheritance, which Henry VI had given to Henry's father, Edmund Tudor.

Margaret set up a household at Collyweston in Northamptonshire, which she transformed into a palace. Her influence throughout the midlands, as far north as Yorkshire, grew during the reign. From 1499 she lived permanently at Collyweston and, in the period between 1499 and 1505 in particular, she and her council were what has been called 'an unofficial council of the midlands'.[3] Another member of the king's family to do well was his uncle, Jasper Tudor. He was created duke of Bedford but also had the earldom of Pembroke restored to him and was given leading responsibility for south Wales and the Marches until he died in 1495. He married the widow of Henry of Buckingham and thereby secured control of her dower lands. In this respect, as in some others, contrasts with Edward IV are illusory, for Henry had as much of a 'family policy' as Edward. Indeed rather more, for there was no noble of any standing outside his family whom he trusted as Edward had trusted Hastings.

The nobles who were restored included the earls of Devon – the first resuscitation of this earldom outside the Readeption since 1461 – of Oxford and of Ormond. For the last the earldom of Wiltshire was not restored because in the interim it had passed to a branch of the Stafford of Buckingham family, but the lands in Ireland and England were. It was indeed the favouring of the Butlers of Ormond under Henry that to a large extent provoked the opposition of the earl of Kildare. There were other Lancastrian stalwarts among the restorations, such as Beaumont, Hungerford and Clifford. But Thomas Grey marquess of Dorset, who was now the king's half brother-in-law, since his half sister had married Henry, was less generously treated. Although he had eventually fled to Henry in early 1484, he had subsequently tried to desert him. He was restored, but we have seen that his son did not acquire the Exter lands, as had been planned by Edward IV, and in 1492 he was put under stringent bonds, through which he could have lost his whole estate.

With the exception of the Stanleys, the existing nobility in 1485 received no special favours but, apart from Northumberland's short-lived disgrace, were not singled out for punishment; like Henry IV and Edward

---

[3] M. K. Jones and M. G. Underwood, *The King's Mother: Lady Margaret Beaufort, Countess of Richmond and Derby* (Cambridge, 1992), p. 88.

IV before him, Henry was happy to accommodate all those nobles prepared to come to an accommodation with him. Thus, for example, the earl of Shrewsbury, who had served Richard while still a minor, was given livery of his estates in 1486. The earl of Westmorland, who had given Richard more committed service, was put under bonds and had to surrender his son and heir to the king's keeping but was punished no further. The earl of Wiltshire was forgiven his rather youthful endorsement of Richard's rule. It is indeed necessary to adjust the view that Henry VII preferred to rely on the gentry rather than the nobles for his rule. It should be apparent by now that, put in these terms, such a policy would have been unworkable; the magnates still were the leaders of political society and individually they had far too much territorial power to be ignored. It is evident that they remained important both in advising the king and in the shires. The earls of Oxford and of Ormond were influential with Henry, and both were used extensively on local commissions in the areas of their estates. Oxford may have been given regional authority in East Anglia, especially in Essex, similar to that exercised elsewhere by Bedford and the Stanleys. From the 1490s Henry Bourchier earl of Essex served regularly on commissions in Hertfordshire and Essex. The earl of Shrewsbury was important in the north midlands and, after his initial disgrace, Northumberland was extensively employed in the north-east until his murder in 1489, was indeed on the king's business of enforcing the collection of a tax when he was killed. Even the restoration of the Howards, the disgraced family of the duke of Norfolk, who had been amongst Richard III's most ardent supporters and had died at Bosworth, began under Henry. Norfolk's heir, the earl of Surrey, was used in the north from 1494 to 1501.[4] By that time he had recovered enough of the family lands, by petition and purchase, to return to East Anglia, where the family was eventually to be a great power for much of the century. Nor must it be forgotten that the Stanleys and Jasper Tudor may have been family but they were also magnates.

It is equally clear that, contrary to received myth, Henry had a court, with courtiers and lavish court spectacle. The progenitor of the notion that Henry had no interest in court amusements or in expenditure on them was Sir Francis Bacon. Writing more than a century after the events, he hardly deserves his status as an authoritative source, but it has now been shown additionally that he had his own agenda. This was that he had been a victim of the court politics of James I and was all too anxious to discover, as he thought, a reign that had neither courtiers nor court politics. The history of faction at Henry's court, as opposed to those of his successors, has been little explored but there were certainly courtiers. These included leading councillors like Guildford and Risley, lesser nobles who had influence both within the household and in the localities, such as Daubigny and Lord Willoughby de Broke, and great nobles who had significant responsibilities for governance like Shrewsbury and Essex. There were also court politics, judging by the sudden falls from grace among some of Henry's courtiers, notably in the last years. Moreover, some of the more dramatic earlier downfalls associated with the great treason trials, such as those of the household officers Sir William Stanley and Lord Fitzwalter in the Warbeck plot of 1495, may have been, in part at least, the result of infighting within the court.[5] And, not surprisingly, for a world in which literacy was still limited and display was still the best propagandist tool, Henry did not eschew pageantry or entertainment, either when on state visits around his country or within his own court, and was prepared to spend large sums of money on the latter. He also spent on patronage of artists and on the building of King's College chapel, very little of which had been completed by 1485, and on his chapel in Westminster Abbey. In fact the sum of almost £20,000 given by Henry for this building was surpassed among royal contributors to the Abbey only by Henry III, the original builder, who is always seen as inordinately extravagant.

However, although the portrait of Henry as the epitome of 'middle-class' austerity requires substantial modification, there is nonetheless a real difference in style and in policy between Henry and Edward IV with respect to the nobility. Where Edward implicitly trusted the nobles until he had cause not to do so, and assumed that they were his partners in ruling, Henry VII's instincts were not to trust them and therefore to exploit their power only as far as he had to. Symptomatic of this is that the use of government spies within England, which seems to have intensified during the prolonged periods of instability in the later fifteenth century, became under Henry, as one historian has put it, 'systemic'.[6] The difference between the two kings with regard to the nobles is most evident in Henry's frequent use of bonds. This procedure was a normal peace-keeping mechanism which lay at the root of much of late-medieval peace-keeping and which bound landowners to keep the peace by putting in jeopardy their most priceless possession, their land.[7] It had already been applied by the government to both nobility and gentry, but usually only within the context of conflict and peace-keeping: for example, by Henry V in restoring order to the localities at the start of his reign and by Edward IV in dealing with Welsh Marcher lords in the 1470s.

[5] See below, pp. 241, 244.

[6] I. Arthurson, 'Espionage and Intelligence from the Wars of the Roses to the Reformation', *Nottingham Medieval Studies*, 35 (1991), pp. 143–4.   [7] See above, pp. 59–60.

What Henry VII did was to widen its use to put landowners whom he mistrusted in a position where he could take their lands if, as he thought, they were acting suspiciously. As Edmund Dudley, one of the most notorious agents of Henry's last years, said of this policy at that time: 'the pleasure and mynde of the kinges grace . . . was much sett to have many persons in his danger at his pleasure . . . wherefore divers and many persons were bound to his grace . . . in great somes of money'.[8] However, although the use of bonds is most notorious at the end of the reign, they appear early in the reign, and what is striking is the extent of mistrust of the nobility that they reveal. We have seen how both Westmorland and Dorset were put under bonds as the price of their pardons from the king, and so was Northumberland. Fines and other financial impositions were used in the same way throughout the reign, to force the victim into debt, which then obliged him to make bonds with moneylenders or the king or both. This was what happened, for example, to the young duke of Buckingham, before he was allowed to come into his estates in 1498; to the earl of Northumberland, fined £10,000 in 1505 for ravishing a royal ward; and to Lord Bergavenny, the most famous victim of the retaining legislation, who was fined over £70,000 in 1507, although he probably paid no more than £1,000 of it. All together, eleven magnates were put under bonds between 1485 and 1499. Henry also exploited attainders and confiscations to put nobles in his power. For example, although Thomas Howard was restored at the beginning of 1489, and was soon to play an important role in Henry's rule, he had to buy back most of the Mowbray lands to which he was heir. There are two telling indices of Henry's lack of trust in the nobility. One is the fact that, whereas under the Yorkists, a period which included three major political crises, two-thirds of the nobility were at some point attainted or subject to recognisance, under Henry the proportion was a little over four-fifths. The other is that extinction, mostly by natural wastage, and Henry's reluctance to create new nobles reduced the numbers of nobles from fifty-five in 1485 to forty-two by the end of the reign.

A significant aspect of Henry's negative attitude to the traditional power of the nobility is in the crucial area of their effective control of the country's military resources. This was not of course something that the king could terminate because it was built into the fundamental fabric of society, but he could try to force his own direction over it. In some respects what Henry did was very much in line with what Edward IV had done. He built further on Edward's retaining legislation and this climaxed in 1504 with legislation that removed most of the loopholes from Edward's

---

[8] C. J. Harrison, 'The Petition of Edmund Dudley', *English Historical Review*, 87 (1972), pp. 82–99.

statute of 1468. There were more prosecutions under the statutes than under Edward, and greater use of the avenue offered by the statutes of prosecution by information rather than by jury,[9] but their motivation seems to have been similarly exemplary rather than regulatory. Thus, a number of indictments in Staffordshire in 1488 and in Warwickshire the following year were apparently directly related to the serious disturbances in north Warwickshire and the north midlands at this time.[10] The huge fine of Lord Bergavenny mentioned above must be attributed to suspicion of his involvement in the Cornish rebellion of 1497[11] and his apparent inability to control his followers in Kent, the centre of his estate. However, there was more to Henry's policy towards retaining than simply disciplinary action. He seems to have been using the licensing permitted by the legislation to ensure that the only landowners allowed to retain were those he regarded as safe. Initially only a small number of people were licensed. These included Bedford and Derby, some of the gentry he trusted in the Duchy region of the north midlands and household men. As he felt more secure, the number of licensees grew. To these retinues should be added the tenants of the crown lands, who could be brought out in the king's name by their stewards. This was why these officers were so carefully chosen by the king. The importance both of control of retaining and of the officers who raised the crown tenantry can be seen in instructions on levying troops, issued in 1511, early in the reign of Henry VII's successor, to Henry Willoughby, a north midlands knight who did well under the early Tudors: 'foreseeing always that you neither prepare nor take any persons for war but such as be your own tenants or inhabitants within any office that you have of our grant'.[12] So, while he had to accept that it was others who had the military power that made rule possible, Henry was determined to control it himself as far as he could. Whether this was wise remains to be seen.

The men whom Henry really did trust were not his natural partners, the nobility, but certain officials who owed almost everything to him and who became the real powers in the land. Mostly they were of gentry origin, many of them trained in the law. Most of them had been with Henry in exile under Richard III and some, like Giles Daubigny, John Risley and Richard Guildford, had served Edward IV or were connected to men who had done so. The presence of such men at the hub of governmental affairs was hardly new; what was new was the amount of influence they wielded. Although one should avoid attributing Henry's style of government primarily to institutional change, there seems to have been a formalisation of

[9] See above, p. 196.   [10] See below, pp. 233–5.   [11] See below, p. 242.
[12] Quoted in A. Cameron, 'The Giving of Livery and Retaining in Henry VII's Reign', *Renaissance and Modern Studies*, 18 (1974), p. 21.

the work of the council under him. Conciliar power, including the power of chancery,[13] an early offshoot of the council, was used extensively to intervene in the affairs of landowners. It seems that what had been a small administrative council throughout the later middle ages, while advice on important executive decisions was given by the informal counsel of prominent landowners,[14] became a much larger body with much greater executive authority. It is accordingly appropriate in this reign to begin to talk about a *council*, in the sense of a more or less formal body which helped the king make and execute policy, and to refer to its members as *councillors*.

As a result of this formalisation, the council became to some extent departmentalised, producing various offshoots. Among these were Star Chamber, the council learned in the law, which had a primarily legal brief, and the general surveyors, which dealt with matters concerning the landed and feudal rights of the crown outside the Duchy of Lancaster. However, it is a mistake to take such compartmentalisation too literally. Star Chamber, for instance, was not a separate body and indeed it now seems that most of the business that came before it was not, as used to be supposed, royal disciplinary measures against disorderly nobles. Rather it was pleas between subjects making use of the speedy justice which the king's council had always been able to offer. Equally, 'counsel learned' was the medieval term for lawyers and it seems that the 'council learned' meant councillors with legal expertise who were dealing with legal matters concerning the king. It must be emphasised that the king's key councillors acted for him in a variety of capacities: the most prominent of them, for instance, were nearly all councillors of the Duchy of Lancaster. What gave them their power was not so much their institutional focus as the fact that they were the king's most trusted advisers and executive officers.

They were first of all known to be among the most powerful people in the realm. Reginald Bray, for instance, a former servant of Henry's mother, perhaps the most influential of them all until his death in 1503, was used frequently by landowners in such capacities as feoffee and executor of wills because he had such influence with the king. For the same reason he was granted annuities or offices by eight different members of the nobility, including Northumberland, Devon and even Henry's uncle and trusted associate the duke of Bedford. Secondly they were given land in the localities which enhanced their authority as the king's men. Often this was from the redistribution of confiscated estates. In Warwickshire, for example, many of the Catesby lands went to John Risley, a royal councillor (although it does not seem that he took a great deal of interest in affairs in that county), while Bray was able to exploit a variety of oppor-

---

[13] See above, p. 34.   [14] See above, pp. 36–7.

tunities offered by service to Henry to build up a sizeable landed estate, located primarily in the Thames Valley and south-east midlands. Thirdly, they were often employed by the king in the supervision of the localities and of the nobles and gentry whose power dominated the localities. Despite the provisos expressed above about focusing too much on institutions rather than men, the fact that the council was the fount of their power was immensely significant because it reflected Henry's intense personal control, through the body that was closest and most responsive to the king, over the governance of the realm.

Some of this control was achieved through placing trusted associates in the main local offices of sheriff and JP. For instance, James Hobart, the king's attorney-general, was the most frequent attender at those peace sessions in Suffolk which have left records, and it is probably no coincidence that a large number of indictments about royal rights came from that county. JPs might be used to keep an eye on sheriffs, and informers were encouraged to denounce sheriffs who took bribes. Between 1492 and 1495, probably in response to deteriorating local order and suspicion of a far-reaching Yorkist conspiracy,[15] Henry revived Edward IV's scheme of afforcing JPs in many counties with his own servants. But much of this supervisory work in the shires was done directly by the council. At its most direct, landowners, including nobles who were deemed to have misbehaved, could be summoned before the council, as Lord Dacre of the north was in 1488–9. Lords Dudley and Grey of Powys were imprisoned for getting involved in an affray. The duke of Suffolk was even ordered not to pursue a plea which he had begun in the common law courts. The equitable jurisdiction of chancery, which could by-pass the much slower common law, to the advantage of both plaintiff and king, was exploited and extended - for example to deal with corrupt juries - to bring large numbers of cases between landowners before the council. In fact, the entire system of bonds and recognisances owed its existence to the fact that this was the normal mechanism employed by the council and its offshoots to secure the obedience and good behaviour of those who appeared before it. Moreover, the whole conciliar apparatus, much of which was designed to discover and audit royal revenues of all sorts, could be used to put numbers of prominent subjects into the king's financial power.

Another group of men whom Henry was disposed to trust were those leading churchmen who had been trained in the Roman and canon law, a class from whom administrators of both lay and ecclesiastical government had traditionally come. Notable amongst these were John Morton, Richard Fox and Thomas Savage, all of them royal councillors. Morton,

---

[15] See below, pp. 241, 233–5.

another former servant of Edward IV, had been one of the men arrested at the famous council under Richard III when Hastings had met his end. He had survived and later fled abroad. On his return he was made chancellor and archbishop of Canterbury and remained in both posts until his death in 1500. He was responsible in large measure for the growth of chancery jurisdiction under Henry. Fox held a succession of bishoprics. He was at Durham from 1494–1501, where he brought the priorities of the king to bear on this very distant part of the kingdom, and at Winchester for an enormously long period, from 1501 to 1528, where he exercised what has been called 'a dominance of Hampshire'.[16] Savage came from a gentry family in the north-west that was allied in marriage to the Stanleys. He was bishop of Rochester and then of London and then archbishop of York from 1501. From 1497 to 1502 he was president of the king's council and in 1498 was said by the Spanish ambassador to be on a par with Margaret Beaufort, Daubigny and others in importance in the realm.

This contrast in attitude to the magnates and to his own men can be seen very clearly in Henry's governance of the north. It was unlikely that a king so mistrustful of the great nobles would delegate on a large scale here, and, after Northumberland was killed in the northern rising in 1489, Henry effectively resurrected the system used by Richard III. The difference was that he did not have the strong local roots which had enabled his immediate predecessor to sweeten the pill of intervention. Something of the sort was necessitated by Henry's drastic reduction of the salaries paid to the wardens. This made it almost impossible for any nobles, other than those who had sizeable lands on the borders, and hence large numbers of tenants, to maintain the office. Even with these advantages, Northumberland himself had been forced to spend nearly half his income on fees. After Northumberland's death, the council of the north, under the nominal leadership of Henry's second son, the future Henry VIII, was placed under Surrey, a magnate without any lands of his own in the north. From 1494 to 1501 he acted in conjunction with Richard Fox, then bishop of Durham. When the 5th earl of Northumberland came of age in 1501 Surrey gave up his position in the north, just as Fox moved south to Winchester, but Archbishop Savage, newly promoted to York, ensured that the earl would be kept under careful constraint. In the north-west heavy reliance was placed on Lord Dacre, a minor local magnate, and Percy influence, already weakened by Gloucester's governance under Edward IV, was kept at bay.

In Wales and the Welsh March there was a similar continuation of interventionist Yorkist policies, although here the Yorkists had already set a much more forceful tone. The council of the Marches was revived in

---

[16] S. Gunn, *Early Tudor Government 1485–1558* (London, 1995), p. 31.

1490 and, as under Edward IV, the Prince of Wales was its titular leader. Prominent men close to the king, such as the duke of Bedford and Sir William Stanley, were used to give it local authority, buttressed by councillors who were placed at various times in local office. In 1499, on Bedford's death, Henry experimented briefly with bringing in a complete outsider, Reginald Bray, as lieutenant of the council, but Bray had neither the land nor the time to make his direction effective. What had developed into an uneasy compromise between outside rule and the resistance of local vested interests, especially those of the increasingly anglicised and self-confident Welsh gentry, was to continue until Wales was shired and formally incorporated into the English polity in the later years of Henry VIII.

We have seen that the centrist rule of Henry's councillors was used to take the king's direction into all parts of the realm, and the lack of trust in Henry's dealings with the nobility is replicated in his handling of the shires. Although he may have recruited his closest servants from the gentry, the king was no more inclined to regard lesser landowners as a group as his allies than he was nobles. This prejudice came to a climax in the last years of the reign when large numbers of gentry, as well as nobles, were placed in bonds to the king, among them some of Henry's closer associates. But it is already evident earlier in the reign. In contrast to Edward IV's policy of rarely confiscating gentry lands, a number of gentry families suffered forfeiture for fighting against Henry at Bosworth or for subsequent rebellion. Overall, Henry passed almost as many attainders as Edward, in a reign less bedevilled by noble rebellion (138 as opposed to 140), and tended to reverse them less readily and less fully. Moreover, the confiscated lands were often handed to outsiders. Risley's gains in Warwickshire have been mentioned; the Catesby and Stafford of Grafton confiscations in the same county brought a number of estates to the king and all of them went to men from outside the shire who had an intimate association with Henry. He was also keen to use control over wardships and marriage to interpolate his own men into the county or to build up servants who had recently arrived. One example is Sir Edward Belknap, coheir to Lord Sudeley, a lord who had wielded a fair amount of power in Warwickshire. Belknap was a household esquire and in 1508 was made 'surveyor of the king's prerogative' and given wide powers to enquire into the upholding of the king's rights throughout England. He was able to purchase more land in Warwickshire and was appointed to local office there: his purchases were financed probably in the main from his crown employment, which brought him nearly £3,000 from the pursuit of outlaws alone.

At the same time the existing Warwickshire gentry received very little in the way of reward, even those who had come rapidly to Henry's side after Bosworth. Not many of them were made officers in the county, for local office here went mostly to relative newcomers like Belknap, although the established gentry were on the whole orderly and, in some cases, are known to have turned out against rebellion in 1487 and 1497. Their docility is undoubtedly connected with the fact that Henry had taken over from Richard III and Edward IV the responsibility for the Warwick earldom (still nominally on behalf of Edward of Warwick) and the part of the county that was easily dominated by the earldom – everywhere except the far north – had become disposed to follow whichever royal earl was in power. It had even accepted the rule of Richard III, up to a point. By contrast with central and southern Warwickshire, in the north midlands – Nottinghamshire, Derbyshire, Staffordshire and the north of Warwickshire – there were a number of gentry families who were close to Henry and important to him. These included the Staffordshire Stanleys, the Savages, whose Cheshire influence spilled over into Staffordshire and Derbyshire, and Henry Willoughby, a rising power who had lands in Warwickshire and Nottinghamshire. Their record in this period is not a good one. Willoughby for example was guilty of several affrays and an abduction; the Savages were heavily involved in a vicious conflict between the Pilkingtons and the Ainsworths, two local families in the Derbyshire/Cheshire/Lancashire region; one of the Stanleys, Humphrey, of the Staffordshire branch of the family, was directly implicated in the murder of a Warwickshire landowner who was also a crown servant. And yet it was these men who were favoured by the king rather than the more law-abiding gentry to the south.

It is in fact in the sphere of internal order, where he is so often held up as a paragon, usually to the disadvantage of his predecessors, that closer inspection shows Henry's record to have been particularly weak. Traditional conclusions rest on the assumption that the key to good order lay in legislation and, above all, in the king's being prepared to wield a harsh discipline over landowners, especially the nobility. There is no doubt either of the discipline, exercised especially through the council, which we have already examined, or of the legislative enthusiasm. Henry was responsible for no less than twenty-one statutes concerning the powers and responsibilities of the JPs and it is no coincidence that the first treatises on the office come from this reign. Especially notable was the extension of JPs' summary powers, that is their ability to convict on information rather than indictment and without jury. Much of this was aimed at retaining and at the corruption of justice. However, as the most sympathetic recent account of Henry's policies in this sphere has observed, 'As justice was necessary to political control, so political control was necessary to justice.'[17] Legislation then as now follows rather than creates good social order and medieval legislation on the law must be seen as propaganda or placed within its particular context and understood as responses to specific circumstances. Moreover, we have seen throughout this study that harshness was only effective when occasional and exemplary and that order was normally best secured by co-operation.

Henry's mistrust of his nobles, and of local societies as a whole, seems to have been deleterious to local order. It must be stressed that at this stage we still know very little about what really happened in the shires under Henry, so what follows must be provisional. The problem seems to have been lack of judgement over how to delegate and to whom. On the one hand Henry was relatively relaxed about giving extensive licence to those he did trust. The Stanleys in Cheshire and Lancashire and the north midlands are a case in point; so are the Savages, also in the north-west, and Henry Willoughby. These men and others like them close to the king were not only given the lands, offices, and sometimes the licences to retain, that made them powerful but they were protected against the consequences of the misuse of that power. Humphrey Stanley, for instance, was never brought to book for murder. Robert Belingham, a rather lowly member of Henry's household, was able to abduct and marry a Warwickshire heiress and not only keep her but be promoted to the Warwickshire commission of the peace, where he sat in judgement over considerably more law-abiding neighbours. On the other hand, the king would not give overall control to anyone in either the north midlands or the north-west in the way that Hastings had held sway over the north midlands in Edward IV's name.

The result, in both the north-west and the north midlands, was feuding among the king's favoured men, sometimes of an extremely violent nature, combined with contempt for the law and the legal processes. In the absence of a single ruling figure, nobody had the authority to bring all this under control. The Pilkington–Ainsworth conflict, about which we are well informed, because a long document by one of the participants survives, ultimately enmeshed the hitherto amicable Savages and Stanleys in mutual antagonism. Both sides played fast and loose with the law, and all efforts to get the affair settled from the centre failed because of the power that both Savages and Stanleys had in the king's counsels. It was still going on at the end of the century. In the north midlands in the first decade of Henry's rule there was disorder on a scale not seen since the worst period under Henry VI and there was the same sort of exploitation of Duchy of Lancaster office to local men's advantage as had occurred then. What made this situation worse was that further south, in the main body of Warwick-

---

[17] Gunn, *Early Tudor Government*, p. 72.

shire, the more law-abiding and less favoured gentry lost patience with men like Willoughby in the north, and with those in the south of the county like Belknap and Belingham who had been thrust on them, and the county became split. In 1494 the more orderly segment of the prominent Warwickshire gentry tried to prosecute the other segment, including some, like Willoughby and Belingham, well favoured by the king. At the same time, during the 1490s the king's mistrust of the bulk of the Warwickshire gentry, his grant of lands to outsiders who in some cases rarely went to the county, and the lawlessness of those he did trust meant that he was on the verge of running out of local officers with sufficient standing to put the king's law into effect.

How far these conditions were to be found elsewhere remains unknown at the moment, although even greater reluctance to delegate in a far more fragile situation seems to have caused similar problems in the north of England. In the north-east Archbishop Savage and the fifth earl of Northumberland had to be brought before the king's council to make mutual peace-keeping bonds and in the far north-west there was a continuing need to deal with breaches of the peace by the local gentry. It has been concluded in a recent study that, as long as neither Henry VII nor his son was prepared to invest substantial sums of money in turning the wardens of the northern Marches back into powerful local rulers, localism and local self-reliance would flourish on the borders. Thus, paradoxically, intervention to cut down the military strength of the border nobles produced more disorder and self-reliance rather than less. And the same point could be made more generally about Henry's rule: forceful control of the nobility's military power and political authority may in the end have been self-defeating, because it restricted their ability to assist the king in the rule of his realm and made it impossible for them to deal with lesser rogue elements, especially those close to the king. It also incidentally was later to make things difficult for a king like Henry VIII who wanted to raise troops for war. The fact was that Henry could not change the social and tenurial system, which still placed the nobles at the top of the hierarchy of power, however much they had ceased to be the dominant arbiters of provincial affairs. All he could do was render it unworkable. One of the most approving commentators on Henry's rule has written that his son's 'power as king rested in large measure on his power as bastard feudal lord'.[18] But we have seen all along that this could be only the most limited basis for royal authority and, in so far as Henry seems also to have believed that he needed to be primarily a 'bastard feudal lord', at least to some degree, it is a serious indictment of his governance.

[18] D. Starkey, 'The Age of the Household: Politics, Society and the Arts *c.* 1350–1550', *The Context of English Literature: The Later Middle Ages*, ed. S. Medcalf (London, 1981), p. 273.

What is apparent is that, in this interlinked sphere of magnate- and shire-management, Henry VII's policies look superficially like Edward IV's in his second reign but were actually very different. Both kings used their families; both used the nobles much as they wished; both intervened extensively in the localities; both relied heavily on household men to do so. But Edward started from a premise of trust in both nobles and localities, while his easy relationship with all his landed subjects meant that he, rather than Henry VII, was the one with the broad base to his government. It was not just a small clique within his household that regarded Edward as its natural lord but a far wider affinity encompassing the landed society of all England. Since we have seen that this combination of relaxed direction and firm intervention was the optimum means of achieving universal governance in late-medieval England, we should expect it to work better than Henry's more inflexible system.

This is one area where Henry VII has been taken to look 'unmedieval', and it may be that what we see is less a forward-looking monarch than one who had an imperfect understanding of his job. Another 'unmedieval' aspect of his rule which turns out to be equally problematical is the famous financial policy. We have seen already that Henry was not the miserly king of myth. Like those of all kings since 1450, his efforts to tighten up expenditure by a resumption proved unavailing: his act of 1486, which attempted to resume all the way back to October 1455, ended up with no less than 461 exemptions. However, unlike Edward IV, there can be no doubts that Henry had a financial policy. Curiously for the first two years of the reign he reverted to the use of the exchequer for all aspects of his finances, but from 1487 he had returned to the use of special receivers and chamber accounting for the crown lands. The amount of money coming into the chamber from land revenues rose from an average of £3,000 a year in 1487–9 to £40,000 in 1502–5. Even allowing for the increase occasioned accidentally, for example by the death of the Prince of Wales and the reversion of his lands in Chester, Cornwall and Wales to the crown, the growth is impressive. Most of it seems to have come from a considerable tightening of the collection of money arising from the king's feudal rights over the lands. A lot of concern for these was manifested during the reign. For example, the law was carefully examined and the thirteenth-century text, *Prerogativa Regis*, which discussed the king's rights in this regard, received its first commentaries from lawyers in this reign. One legal issue resolved in the king's favour was the extent to which tenants of the king's tenants-in-chief themselves became crown tenants, and thus subject to all the royal feudal prerogatives, when a tenant-in-chief's lands were in the hands of the crown. Since so many lordships had come to the crown by this time, the decision had far-reaching implications. In 1489 the Statute of Uses made it harder to evade the feudal obligations liable at a tenant-in-chief's death by conveying the land to feoffees, or trustees. There were commissions to investigate all the dues owed to the king, and the council learned played a large part in pursuing them. Then there were the bonds that have already featured in this chapter. Some of these were very large, for instance the £105,000 imposed on Lord Bergavenny. Between 1504 and 1507 a total of at least £200,000 and more in bonds was promised to the king. However, in the nature of things, this was potential rather than actual money, and only a little over £30,000 was paid in cash. Bonds were designed to keep the king's subjects in political thrall, not to provide the king with large sums of money.

While money was collected with increasing tenacity, it was accounted with intensifying control. More and more of the royal revenues went straight into the chamber, bypassing the exchequer. Between 1487 and 1502 the amount handled in this way grew from something over £10,000 to over £100,000. The chamber accounts were meticulously audited by trusted servants under the supervision of the king. The increasing role of chamber rather than exchequer in the royal finances and, more generally, the intensification of the king's direct control over almost all aspects of government led to a change in the use of royal seals. The king's personal seal, the signet, whose importance had already begun to grow under the Yorkists, supplanted the privy seal as authentication for large numbers of governmental instructions. A modern commentator has indeed called the chamber 'the hub of an administrative system',[19] where policies were formulated and decisions made on a wide range of governmental matters.

All this is undeniably impressive as evidence of what would now be known as productivity on the part of king and servants, but what did it all mean? It certainly did not mean that Henry ceased to exploit other levies and he was no different from his predecessors in taxing both the church and the laity. The customs were given him by parliamentary grant, although, like Richard III, he managed to obtain a life grant at the start of the reign, and, as one might expect, he was assiduous in pursuit of what was due to him. Like Edward IV in his later years, he benefited from peace in the narrow seas and from the boom in cloth exports which was partly due to this. Under Henry the annual average return from the customs rose from the £34,000 of Edward's second reign to £38,000. Like his predecessors, when it came to the very large sums of money required for war, Henry relied on parliamentary taxation, and he took lay subsidies in 1487, 1489, 1492, 1497 and 1504. Between 1487 and 1497 he was able to gather something over £200,000 by this means. Following on the two serious

---

[19] M. Condon, 'Ruling Elites in the Reign of Henry VII', *Patronage, Pedigree and Power*, ed. C. Ross (Gloucester, 1979), p. 127.

revolts of 1489 and 1497,[20] both caused by efforts to increase the yield of taxation, and a less serious one in Yorkshire against the tax of 1492, Henry grew very cautious about these demands, promising the parliament of 1504 that he would try not to call another. Since even he was unable to finance a war without taxation, the effect of this promise was to prevent him contemplating a further military campaign. This restriction on his freedom of manœuvre may well account in large part for his less impressive display in foreign policy in his last years.[21] In fact all Henry's financial policies really amounted to was applying on a grand scale the sort of 'good housekeeping' that the Commons were always demanding as the price of taxation. Not only was this inappropriate for the government but he did not even reap the political benefits, since his care for his ordinary revenues was not used to secure him the kind of flow of taxation which had been the norm during the Hundred Years War.

There is indeed no indication that Henry derived any political advantage from all the effort he put into raising revenue by non-parliamentary means and it is difficult to see what such an advantage might have been.[22] The long-running but relatively minor difficulty caused by the shortfall of ordinary revenues to finance the garrisons, especially Calais, seems to have been resolved under Edward IV. This was done apparently by the combination of the revenues from the enlarged crown lands and the increased customs returns. Even had it not been, it would not have caused more than a certain amount of friction between king and parliament over the expenditure of taxation. If the absence of short-term loans after 1490 suggests long-term solvency, we are left wondering, as with Edward IV, whether the undoubted benefits to the crown's creditors were matched by any tangible benefits to the crown. It has been calculated that all this intensive activity produced a legacy for Henry VIII of at most two years' gross permanent revenue. The most recent account of Henry's finances suggests that, although Tudor financial administration was probably at its most efficient under Henry VII, the net gain was no more than to restore crown income in real terms to what it had been in the late fourteenth and early fifteenth centuries. It could be argued that this was a substantial achievement, in that it indicates that Henry had been able to make up for the decline in the customs revenue during the century and for the sharp fall from the very high taxation of the 1370s and 1380s and Henry V's reign. On the other hand, we have seen that the customs shortfall did not amount to a serious political issue and, if the king was not fighting major wars, as

---

[20] See below, p. 241.   [21] See below, p. 250.

[22] It could on occasion provide ready money to pay off foreign countries which thought about intervening in English affairs, but we then come back to the fact that intervention was only ever possible when the king himself was weak.

Henry was not, he did not require major taxation to finance them. It is also highly dubious whether there was really any point in such close account-ancy. The exchequer was designed to do this job and, as long as the royal finances avoided the state of chaos they reached under Henry VI, did it well. Indeed, if, in the 1530s, there was a 'Tudor revolution in govern-ment' (something which is now questioned by many historians), arguably it consisted of a return to the normal medieval bureaucratic procedures which had been put aside by the personal rule of the Yorkists and, to a much greater extent, of Henry VII and Thomas Wolsey. Both Henry and his men would have been better employed in giving their attention to more urgent matters, such as the growing hostility to his government.

For what Henry's financial policies also left was another much more serious political legacy. This gathering of money, potential and actual, was mostly at the expense of the king's landed subjects. These were precisely the people he would need if his throne were threatened, and yet he was treating them in such a way that they were likely to be the chief threat to his throne. This was a strategy that had been seen before, under King John, Edward II and Richard II - John's habit of equating security with noble indebtedness to the crown is especially relevant - and every time it had led to disaster: Magna Carta and civil war and two depositions. It is note-worthy that the commission into abuses issued after Henry's death in-cluded breaches of Magna Carta in its remit. The precise point was made by a foreign observer, who noted: 'The king is very powerful in money, but if fortune allowed some lord of the blood to rise and he had to take the field, he would fare badly owing to his avarice; his people would abandon him.'[23] Henry needed not money but his landed subjects' allegiance and, by collecting money with such assiduity, he was losing what he most required. He was, after all, not even very successful at taking his subjects' money by legitimate parliamentary means: if his taxes were sometimes individually harsh, the extent of popular rebellion against taxation under Henry seems out of all proportion to the frequency of his demands and suggests a country very ill at ease with itself. Perhaps the demoralisation of the ruling classes and their lack of obvious enthusiasm for the regime restricted their ability to impose the king's will on the lower orders.

Why Henry himself thought money important, and why he felt the need to have the money and its accounting instantly accessible to him through the chamber, is a moot point. It has been suggested that large liquid reserves, readily available to kings as they travelled round the country dealing with crises, were required at a time when monarchs were insecure, and that this in many ways explains the financial policies of

---

[23] The Florentine ambassador, quoted in C. Carpenter, *Locality and Polity: A Study of Warwickshire Landed Society, 1401–1499* (Cambridge, 1992), pp. 631–2.

Edward IV and Richard III, as well as of Henry VII. A change under all three kings, albeit incomplete, from 'assigning' much royal revenue – which meant that it was simply handed over to the payee at the point of collection rather than being paid into the royal coffers – to actual collection of the money by the chamber lends some weight to this theory. However, although there is much to be said for it in principle, it neglects the fact that Edward IV ceased to be in this position after 1471, after which he led a much more settled existence, that the constant state of crisis of Richard III's reign was self-created and most unusual and that, after 1487, Henry VII should have been as invulnerable as Edward after 1471. And he did indeed travel less after his early years. It also fails to appreciate that it was Henry's amassing of his reserve that perpetuated his insecurity beyond the first few years of the reign. Henry may indeed have had some idea that, as a mercenary army had enabled him to defeat Richard III, so the ability to outbid any rivals who might want to raise such an army might guarantee his safety. What he forgot was that it was only Richard's alienation of his subjects that had made Henry's invasion with his rather paltry host possible and successful. His attitude to his finances may also have had a lot to do with the psychology of those who grow up in genteel poverty and come to equate financial security with the real thing.

Looked at as a whole, Henry's governance of England shows a comprehensive misunderstanding of the nature of medieval kingship. It is therefore no accident that the basis for his many apologists has been an anachronistic theory of a new and more 'modern' monarchy that was wholly inapposite for a king of England in late-medieval England, which is what Henry was. Henry had been an exile all his adult life. He was almost thirty when he came to the throne, perhaps too old to listen and learn to adapt. Unlike Henry IV and Edward IV he had not even been trained as a noble in England before he became king. If he preferred to surround himself with career administrators and churchmen—civil servants rather than with magnates, he would have had little chance to learn the normal modes of governance. He had spent much of his life in France, where political and governmental traditions were very different from those in England. In fact, it was at this time, notably under Louis XI, 'the universal spider', that centralisation through a royal bureaucracy, designed to break down the independent power of the great feudatories, was proceeding apace. In England, on the other hand, centralisation had been a fact of life since the later twelfth century and what has been called 'self-government at the king's command', based on the acceptance of this rule by all landowners, had been the norm for almost as long. Henry's attempts to override local powers by means of his own servants, his use of spies, his institution of a personal bodyguard on the French model – the 'yeomen of the guard' - as soon as he became king, all point to a misguided policy of emulating the French kingship, which was what he knew best. We have already seen some of the results of these misconceived policies in the disorder and alienation from the king that has been demonstrated in some parts of England and may turn out to have been more widespread. It would be surprising if local instability and Henry's deep mistrust of the nobles that bred mistrust towards the king did not raise some questions about his suitability to rule, and it is a fact that Henry was troubled by plots and rebellions for much longer than he should have been after Stoke.

In 1489 there was a rebellion in the north against the king's taxes. Although it turned out to have no dangerous political overtones, and was singularly lacking in noble or gentry support, it was in a sensitive area for the king. Moreover, it began with the murder of the earl of Northumberland, the king's own chief agent in the area, and a man who should have been more than acceptable to local opinion. It seems indeed to have been caused by the novel means by which the king was trying to increase the yield of the tax and by his unwillingness to allow the north its usual tax rebates, perhaps another indication of ill-informed rule. Northumberland, as the main tax-gatherer, became identified with royal policies. The rebellion may have been fomented by the fear, inspired by the king's intransigence, that the whole region would be punished for the murder. Then in 1491 Perkin Warbeck, a new pretender, appeared. He claimed to be Richard of York, the younger of Edward IV's sons. Like Simnel he had support from Ireland and from Margaret of Burgundy. He was briefly in France in 1492 until Charles VIII expelled him. In 1493 he acquired the backing of Maximilian, the Habsburg ruler of Burgundy. In the event, Warbeck's attempted invasion in July 1495 proved abortive but the invasion was not the most worrying thing for Henry. If there truly was a conspiracy in Warbeck's favour, and it was not the figment of Henry's over-concerned imagination, fed by his spies in the Netherlands, then it went deep into his personal entourage. The most sinister aspect for the king was the involvement of prominent members of the household: John Ratcliffe Lord Fitzwalter, his steward, and, worst of all, Sir William Stanley, his own step-uncle, chamberlain of his household and leading figure in the family that had been most comprehensively rewarded by the king.

Warbeck escaped to Ireland and thence to Scotland, but when he next threatened to invade it was under far more disturbing circumstances. The attempt at invasion from Scotland in late September 1496 was a rather half-hearted affair, but it forced the king to raise a tax in 1497 for what proved an abortive expedition to Scotland, and the levy led to a revolt in Cornwall. As in 1489, general resentment at particularly harsh taxation was specifically focused by the issue of whether a region that had to protect itself against possible foreign raids and invasion should help subsidise a national war. The Cornish believed that they paid enough for their own local defence and thought the northerners should finance the war in the north. The rebels marched on London, but this was in no sense a political rebellion. However, its repercussions went well beyond the revolt itself and until recently have been too easily dismissed. There are unmistakeable signs of disloyalty of an alarming nature amongst English landowners, especially over much of the west country: two south-western nobles, James Touchet Lord Audley and Lord Stourton, and at least twenty-five gentry from Hampshire and Dorset are known to have taken part. It has been shown recently that power over much of the south-west was concentrated in the hands of a small number of people close to Henry, chief amongst them Lord Daubigny, and that this set up resentment which, even where it did not lead to actual rebellion, left Henry exposed in 1497. For the Cornishmen to get almost as far as London, there must have been at the very least failure of reaction by the local authorities. Audley was the only peer to be executed, but Lord Bergavenny was suspected of involvement, and suspicion, as in 1495, went also into some of the innermost recesses of Henry's household. Remarkably, even Daubigny, the king's chief lieutenant in the region, and Stanley's successor as chamberlain, was among those temporarily under a cloud: his reluctance to engage the rebels allowed them to get so dangerously close to London. Although Daubigny did redeem himself at Blackheath, where the rebels were defeated, it has been suggested that he hesitated deliberately because, despite his reputation as the king's instrument in the south-west, he had connections with so many of the noble and gentry rebels. There is no question of a Yorkist conspiracy, although, had Warbeck and the Scots managed to invade then, it would have been a serious matter. All the same, the rebels' demands that men like Morton, Bray and Fox be removed from about the king's person may well have struck a chord with many English landowners. It was fortunate for Henry that he was organising the Scottish expedition at the time, for it provided him, crucially, with an army near the capital.

A treaty with Scotland ended the threat of invasion and it was preceded by Warbeck's departure from that country. He moved to Ireland; invading from there later in the year, he was captured. In 1499 both Warbeck and Edward of Warwick, Clarence's son, the last heir of York through the male line, were executed. This was a logical response to rebellion: in particular, had the rebels of 1497 been able to reach London and release Edward from the Tower, there might have been a very different outcome. But there were still de la Poles; in 1501 there was a plot in their favour and two of the de la Pole brothers fled to Maximilian's court. If in the event none of these plots came to anything, we cannot ignore their presence for much of the reign. It has usually been assumed by historians that the extent of resistance to a monarch who is taken to be the epitome of kingship merely emphasises the hopelessness of the 'dinosaur-like' nobility who could not accept Henry's modern ways. Historians are now realising that, since neither nobles nor gentry normally rebelled unless heavily provoked, resistance to Henry VII may indicate less noble or gentry moral turpitude and more monarchical incompetence. If we take the abortive invasion by the earl of Oxford to be the last equivalent act under Edward IV, then Edward, ascending the throne in an almost impossibly difficult situation that was unresolved for ten years, was secure within twelve years, while Henry, with a much better hand from the start, was still coping with conspiracies after sixteen years. After 1473 foreign rulers knew support for challengers to Edward's throne was a waste of time and money; that unequivocal message never reached them from Henry.

It is a moot point whether these plots really ramified as far as was alleged, although close investigation of the rising of 1497 does make it look alarming for the king. It is not impossible that at least some of the alleged conspirators of 1495, including Stanley, were placed on a hit-list by the king to resolve the acute problems of disorder in the north midlands and north-west. It was a dreadful warning to those others close to the king who had misbehaved in local politics but whom he considered too important to his security to be brought to book. But Henry's intensification of the use of bonds suggests that he, at least, believed in all these plots, and that was a large part of the problem, for his suspicion made him treat his landed subjects ever more harshly, which bred more resentment and more suspicion. What is striking is the extent to which the king's own household, the very sphere where he was personally most vulnerable but should have been most secure, was implicated in the conspiracies and rebellions of 1493 to 1497. Before Henry, it was almost unheard of for a king to find disloyalty here: the problem was more often a perception by outsiders that those within the household were too close to the king. The creation of the privy chamber in 1495 was in large measure a response to the supposed plots of the previous two years. It was effectively a household within the household and designed to restrict access to the king to all but a favoured few. Even so, as we shall see, this by no means ended Henry's problems here. Another index of his unease is that virtually the entire Stanley family was put under bonds towards the end of the reign. This seems to be partly an overdue reaction to misuse of the power the king had given them and partly an indication of the fear of even the noble families that were closest to him. Increasingly from the later 1490s, the only noble he really trusted was his mother, and her vow of chastity in 1499, which led her to reside permanently at Collyweston,[24] may well have been part of the process by which both mother and son distanced themselves from the Stanleys. Henry's unease increased after the rebellion of 1497, leading him to intensify his use of spies, and grew particularly acute after the death of the Prince of Wales in 1502. That left a single male heir aged ten. Henry now faced the very real risk of a repetition of the events of 1483, and that was on the assumption that his son even survived to inherit.

Although there was once some disagreement about whether the king's rule did become harsher in these last years, there is now general agreement that it did and that the main cause was insecurity born of fears for the succession. It was in this period, from 1502 to the end of the reign, that the search for security through bonds, imposed in some cases on the king's own key officers, and exploitation of financial resources, grew really intense. It was also then that the two notorious agents of Henry's last years, Empson and Dudley, came into their own. There is little doubt that the polity was put under extreme pressure in these years, nor that Henry was highly fortunate; he survived long enough for his son to be of age and to repudiate his father's policy by cancelling bonds, by initiating an investigatory commission and by killing the two hated royal servants. Most of this apparent enthusiasm on the part of the young Henry VIII to rectify the misdeeds of the last years of his father's reign was, as has been pointed out, highly spurious, but that was not the point. The fact was that it was his father's own kingship that Henry VIII was disowning. Although we now know that there were great continuities of personnel and policies from Henry VII to Henry VIII, it was of crucial importance for the survival of the Tudor dynasty that the first Tudor king to inherit the throne was an adult able to endorse an outward return to a more conventional style of kingship.

There was a sense of tension around the king in these years. It was a period notable for the fall of courtiers, especially in the last three years: for example, Dorset and Lord Courtenay were both imprisoned at Calais and even the king's close councillor James Hobart was dismissed as attorney-general in 1507. The king was making military preparations in his last two years, perhaps fearing foreign invasion on behalf of a rival on his death. Anyone who doubts the real dangers to the dynasty in Henry VII's last years should read Flamank's Information, an account of an alleged conversation at Calais at this time involving Sir Hugh Conway, one of Henry's oldest and most loyal servants. It does not have to be true to reveal the uncertainty about the succession and the poisonous atmosphere of mutual mistrust around the throne at this time. It is worth noting that in this

[24] See above, p. 224.

alleged conversation doubts were voiced about the long-term commitment to the dynasty of Lord Daubigny, the king's chamberlain and commander at Calais since 1486, who had acted so equivocally in 1497, in the same breath in which his enormous power about the king was affirmed. It seems therefore that Henry had still not been able to deal with the problem of loyalty about his very person. Much the same impression of lack of settled stability at the very heart of power comes over from the 'petition of Edmund Dudley', a confession he made between condemnation and execution, apparently in a genuine effort to save the late king's soul and the lives of some of the king's servants. Henry's death itself was kept secret for nearly thirty-six hours and the arrest of Empson and Dudley followed rapidly upon it. These events suggest that there was a real fear of resistance to the succession, and recognition that measures against the previous king's closest servants would be necessary to prevent it. On the interpretation advanced here, which rests on a medieval perspective, Henry VII's reign shows that what we think of as medieval kingship was the means of effective governance and that Henry's supposed modernity is merely symptomatic of inadequate rule.

However, before leaving this subject, we should look at the most recent contributions to the re-evaluation of Henry VII, both of which in different ways imply the revival of the concept of a 'new monarchy', although on very different terms. Both are at one with the present work in emphasising the novelty of the centralisation occurring in the governance of England in the later fifteenth and early sixteenth centuries but in some other respects they differ from each other and from the evaluation of Henry offered here. The most extended treatment, by Steven Gunn, to which this chapter is greatly indebted, places Henry's reign in the middle of a long period of governmental development and centralisation from Edward IV to the accession of Elizabeth. While recognising that Henry's rule had deleterious effects, the author is generally positive about its benefits to the monarchy and to most of the king's subjects; it is an interpretation which leans to the view that 'you can't make an omelet without breaking eggs'. The present author parts company with Gunn in two respects: first, in rejecting the idea that Edward IV and Henry VII had similar intentions as rulers and that resemblances between their governmental methods are anything more than the result of their both having to deal with similar political, financial and administrative crises in similar circumstances.[25] Secondly, it does not seem that there was any need to make an omelet, much less to break any eggs, and too many eggs were broken for the king's security or for the political nation's comfort. The constitution of late-

---

[25] For more on their circumstances, see below, pp. 259–66.

medieval England, as inherited by Henry VII, was more than adequate to the needs of any reasonably able king, once he had dealt with the immediate crisis of Richard III's legacy, something which had really been done after the victory at Stoke. For example, Gunn defends Henry's policies on internal order, by arguing that there was something of a crisis of order which his draconian policies largely resolved. However, it is noteworthy that the small amount of existing work which makes possible a comparison of the governance of Edward and Henry on the ground is a strong endorsement of Edward's methods, and that any crisis of order under Henry has been shown to have been created largely by the king himself.

Both Gunn and the present writer accept the conventional view that intense personal involvement is the hallmark of Henry's rule, but a new interpretation by John Watts suggests the opposite. Like Carpenter and, to some degree, Gunn, Watts stresses Henry's unfamiliarity with England but this leads him to raise the possibility that his reign represents a takeover by bureaucrats, who acquired their own momentum and took much of the personal element out of the heart of monarchy. One might gloss this argument further by adding that the king's ignorance of England was compounded by constant crisis, which deprived him of the time to learn about his new domain, and might have made him complacent about leaving the details of governance in the hands of men he felt he could trust. It is an attractive theory, which is in a sense implicit in the generally accepted view that Henry's council was enormously important to him, for it could be argued that real personal monarchy, in which the king has absolute freedom to consult whom he wishes and do as he likes, cannot coexist with a powerful council. This is one of the grounds for not believing that there was a formal advisory council of this sort earlier in the period.[26] Moreover, it is an idea that is supported by a surprising amount of existing work. For example, it was observed many years ago that the main reason for the enormous power of Empson and Dudley in Henry's last years was that the king was almost continuously ill from 1507 to 1509. From this perspective, their arrest after the king's death could be seen as the revenge of the other servants of the king, who survived to serve his son and may have been itching for a chance to dispose of these two. Gunn implies that most of the real upheavals and experiments in governance and major mistakes were made before 1500 and that thereafter government became more settled and predictable. As part of this argument, he shows how 'mini-empires' were created within the administration, especially after 1500, by royal servants like John Heron, under whom the chamber became a self-propelling institution. In the same vein, at the height of their

[26] See above, pp. 36–7.

power, Empson and Dudley are alleged to have held sessions of conciliar courts in their own houses.

This tendency for bureaucracies to grow of their own accord if the controlling hand is absent or weak is not only common to all governments but had already been crucially important in the development of English government under the absentee kings of the late twelfth century, Henry II and Richard I. If Henry was enmeshed in dealing with rebellion and, to ward off rebellion, in diplomacy and espionage, he may have had neither the time nor the inclination to direct the other aspects of his government, as long as they provided what he wanted: money and security. Unfortunately the only historian who has done recent close research on Henry's chamber accounts, and who implies that her work reinforces the usual view of Henry's close personal involvement, has not published the promised extended discussion, so we are not in a position to know whether there is a fundamental objection of this sort to Watts' hypothesis.[27] If Watts is right, then Henry's reign fits still more firmly within the period of development postulated by Gunn: it would mean that the institutionalisation of many of the personal aspects of monarchy, which Elton placed in the 1530s, but which it seems everyone would now accept had occurred to some degree by the accession of Elizabeth, began under Henry VII, that allegedly most personal of monarchs.

Both Watts and the present author would agree that Henry's rule grew less out of the deliberate intent which is implicit in Gunn's interpretation than out of crisis, error and misunderstanding. Watts would presumably attribute both Gunn's experimental period before 1500 and what came after to the activities of bureaucrats. As Watts points out, the bureaucratisation of the very centre of power which he is arguing for is remarkably like Sir John Fortescue's blue-print for reform of the government of England and it is not impossible that Henry's servants, many of them lawyers, were familiar with the writings of this royal judge. Fortescue's ideas do in many ways constitute a bureaucrat's paradise, in which the whim of a mere king is subsumed to the more sensible policies of the administrator. If Watts is correct, then in a curious way we are back with the rule of the bureaucrats under the mythical Henry VII of Francis Bacon and later historians, except in this case it would be without the king's knowledge rather than by his own bureaucratic genius.[28] It could thus be argued that Watts adds force to the negative judgement on Henry that is the theme of this chapter, since it is clear that Fortescue had a very limited notion of how the fifteenth-century English polity worked.[29] It is also beyond argument, in the light of recent work, that bureaucratisation of Henry's governance, far from

---

[27] Condon, 'Ruling Elites', p. 127 and n.92 on p. 141.   [28] See above, p. 225.
[29] See above, p. 22.

denoting the disinterested impersonal service that the word implies for us, would mean the rampant and unrestrained pursuit of their own interests, and what were perceived to be the king's, by men like Bray, Risley, Daubigny, Empson and Dudley, with large egos and larger personal ambitions: a collection of small-scale and rather grubby Henry VIIs. The almost complete lack of policy with which some of the king's revenues and victims were hunted down in fact offers strong support to Watts' theories. A further commentator, trying to reconcile the views of Watts and Carpenter, has suggested that the reign be seen as 'one long usurpation crisis', which, because Henry did survive and thus did not make way for a better ruler, in the end amounted to a major turning-point in English history.[30] One's view of the nature of the crisis - whether caused by the king himself or by the debasement of monarchy in the period since 1450, culminating in the events of 1483–5 - would of course affect one's evaluation of the king. Whether the effects of Richard's usurpation, and indeed of what had gone before, were lastingly deleterious is something to which we must return in the conclusion,[31] but it should be noted that, if they were, then Gunn's case for Henry VII becomes a lot stronger.

For the present, with the proviso that Watts may be right about the limited extent of Henry's personal role in all this, the present writer remains an unrepentant critic of the king. However, although it can be shown that the chances of the Tudor dynasty disappearing on the death of Henry, or even before, had he lived much longer, were quite high and that the effects of his rule on the country were to a large extent malign, he did die in his bed after close to twenty-four years on the throne. We should not leave him without asking why this was so, against all the odds. First there was Henry's tenacity, his most outstanding quality, acquired no doubt in those long years of hopeless exile. Secondly, he seems to have been a capable soldier and commander, not perhaps the capacity that we associate most readily with him. But he won all his battles - Bosworth, Stoke, Blackheath - any one of which could have proved decisive had it gone against him. Most important was his ability to manage foreign policy. Since Henry was unable to make himself secure enough to discourage foreign intervention, this was undoubtedly of the first importance. It was the one sphere for which his earlier history would have given him an excellent training. From it he would have acquired broad experience of the courts and rulers of England's neighbours, along with the diplomatic virtues of patience and a feel for minutiae.

In the dangerous early years Henry was able to keep on reasonable terms with Scotland, and the assassination of James III in 1488, leaving a young

---

[30] B. Thompson in the same volume as Watts and Carpenter (see bibliographical note to this chapter), on p. 9.   [31] See below, pp. 257–8.

heir, turned the Scots' attention away from England for a while. In 1489–92 he made the mistake of getting himself dragged in to support Brittany against its absorption by Charles VIII of France and, after the rapid French victory, needed a quick accommodation, while indicating token displeasure, to avoid any lasting hostility with France. Luckily Charles himself was keen to go off to Italy to fight, and in the Treaty of Etaples in 1492, which produced a truce for the lifetime of both kings, he agreed not to support Henry's opponents. It was the preliminaries to this treaty which resulted in Warbeck's departure from France in 1492. Unfortunately almost the whole of the coast of north-west Europe was now in French hands, which, even apart from the Warbeck issue, made an agreement with Maximilian, as ruler of Burgundy, and therefore of the rest of the channel coast, especially urgent. There was also the importance of trade with the Netherlands for the customs revenues. A link with Burgundy was eventually to come through a mutual Spanish connection forged by marriage. In 1489 the Treaty of Medina del Campo with Ferdinand of Aragon had arranged for the future marriage of Prince Arthur and Catherine of Aragon, Ferdinand's daughter, and in 1496–7 there was a double marriage between Maximilian's and Ferdinand's families. But, immediately, the most important aspect of Medina del Campo for Henry was that, like his later treaty with France, it included a mutual promise not to aid rebels, which, in view of the proliferation of Yorkist plots, was greatly to Henry's benefit.

More important than marriages, in preventing the rulers of the countries facing England across the narrow seas being ranged against Henry, were Charles VIII's adventures in Italy from 1494. These united Ferdinand, Maximilian - who, as Holy Roman Emperor from 1493, was especially concerned about that country - and others against France and made them favourably disposed to England. This was as well since Margaret of Burgundy had taken up Perkin Warbeck's cause, Maximilian was persuaded to recognise him as king of England in 1493, and there were efforts to harness the support of Isabella. When Warbeck made his failed attempt to land in England in 1495, it was with Burgundian backing. Despite this continuing uncertainty regarding Henry's security, Spain was prepared to renew its treaty in 1496 and 1497, and in 1501 the marriage between Arthur and Catherine finally took place. The executions of Warbeck and Edward of Warwick may have been a precondition for it, removing the obvious threats to Henry's heir. Although the death of Arthur soon after seemed to have nullified all the good work, agreement to marry Catherine to the new heir, the future Henry VIII, preserved the Spanish alliance. Meanwhile Maximilian, although he received the de la Poles in 1501, remained too preoccupied with Italy to support any Yorkist plots after 1495.

In the mean time relations with Scotland had deteriorated dangerously.

James IV, now old enough to rule, had agreed to a truce from 1492–4 but had received Warbeck in 1495 and in 1495–6 offered him the assistance that made possible the invasion of England in 1496. It was vital to Henry not to look vulnerable at this time for fear of losing the Spanish match. Having missed his opportunity to profit from the Cornish rising in 1497, James was persuaded to expel Warbeck and to agree to a series of truces. These began later that year and culminated in the Treaty of Perpetual Peace in 1502 - the first peace treaty between the two countries since 1328 - and the marriage of James to Henry's daughter Margaret in 1503. Throughout the 1490s, despite consistent provocation by the Scots, Henry had upheld the system of Marcher law[32] which made a relatively normal life either side of the Scottish border sustainable, and the treaty was a reward for his patience over the whole issue of Scotland. Ireland, which had seemed so threatening at the time of Simnel's conspiracy and had continued to offer some help to Warbeck, had been tamed, chiefly by the efforts of Sir Edward Poynings between 1494 and 1495, and the earl of Kildare, now reconciled to Henry. In 1495 Warbeck left Ireland, foreseeing no further help there. In 1498 Kildare was given official charge of the province.

The death of his queen in 1503, and of various other players in these dynastic politics about the same time, led Henry into a number of grandiose marriage and alliance schemes in his last years, all of which proved abortive. Reluctance to tax a country which seemed all too ready to rebel when he did so may well have contributed to the relative failure of his foreign policy in these years.[33] By 1509 England had become rather isolated in European politics, something which might have proved dangerous had Henry VIII's accession been challenged. But there was no internal crisis in 1509 and Henry VII's foreign policy had done its job of keeping foreign intervention largely at bay at the time when it could have exploited unrest and rebellion within England. France's ambitions in Italy had helped greatly from 1494, in distracting other European countries from the relatively minor matter of England and in making Henry a desirable ally, however reluctant to commit himself, against this destabilising force. However, Henry had been an effective diplomat and done much to facilitate his own survival.

If the qualities that enabled Henry to remain king despite his serious weaknesses are important to the story, much more so are the changes that appear to have been taking place within England in the later part of the fifteenth century. This is something on which all the recent commentators on Henry are in agreement and which they see as intrinsic to what was happening to the English monarchy in the century or so after Edward IV's accession. It is not a question of 'modernity', it was not brought about by

---

[32] See above, p. 56.   [33] See above, p. 238.

Henry and had indeed begun under Edward IV, but it does mark the beginnings of a new political dispensation. Albeit under very different conditions, and with a much more widely based political society, the English monarchy began to resemble again the strongly centralised model of the late twelfth and thirteenth centuries. This is the type of rule that had been Richard II's ambition and his attempt to bring it about had brought about his downfall. Henry VII, although an abler king than Richard, abused his authority in ways that it seems inconceivable that a king of the fourteenth or earlier fifteenth century could have surmounted. What had happened to bring about what looks like a change in the structure of English politics and make possible a reign like Henry VII's? In the next chapter we shall survey the course of politics from the 1440s and see whether there were indeed any long-term changes.

12

CONCLUSIONS

——— . ———

This account has been a deliberate attempt to restore the public dimension
to historians' increasingly 'privatised' account of kingship and politics in
the fifteenth century, while giving the private element its proper place
within the body politic. It has aimed to place politics within a context of
structures of private power and public government and to examine how
they affected the whole of the political society that participated in those
structures, nobles and gentry as much as monarchs. What has emerged
very clearly is the degree to which fifteenth-century governments, like all
others, were bounded by recognised limitations, and the importance of
discovering what those limitations were. Thus, for example, there is little
point in berating a ruler for failing to punish infractions of the peace by
landowners systematically, once it is apparent that he was not expected to
do this, did not expect to do it himself and had not the means to do it. It is
equally inapposite to lament non-interventionist rule if that was the norm
and if it worked. These long-term structures should not normally be
labelled 'long-term weaknesses': no governmental system is perfect, all
systems will have areas where they function less well than the participants,
whether rulers or consumers of rule, would like. The test is whether the
polity can absorb and find ways round such shortcomings. It has been
argued in this work that under normal circumstances the constitution of
late-medieval England was perfectly workable. The trouble was that from
the later 1430s circumstances were far from normal. Dependence on the
capacity of the monarch can hardly be called a fundamental weakness,
since some monarchsw ere exceedingly able and the polity could cope
quite adequately with even a king who was no more than moderately
competent. However, the arrival at nominal adulthood of a king for

whom the word 'incompetence' is a pale reflection of the grisly reality turned out to be more than the polity eventually could bear.

As there were no long-term weaknesses, so it must be emphasised that the causes of the lengthy political and constitutional crisis which began then were not long-term but were rooted in the king's personal incapacity and everything which followed from that. The monarchy had not been weakened by developments under Edward III, but, if anything, strengthened, and it had become still more indispensable to the lives of a yet larger number of subjects: hence the momentous reverberations of a wholly inadequate king. The temporary diminution of the majesty of kingship occasioned by the Lancastrian usurpation had been more than remedied by the time of Henry VI's accession. Neither did the crisis arise from local feuds or a social system that allegedly bred them. Landowning society was structured as much to contain as to create conflict, and intrinsic to the way it worked was that a properly functioning monarchy could contain feuding, even among the king's most powerful subjects. It was the failure of central governance that led to local conflict and ultimately made conflict among the nobles nationally divisive, not that conflict created governmental failure and irreconcilable division. Seeing the 'Wars of the Roses' in terms of 'an escalation of private feuds' is the ultimate act of 'Namierisation': reducing all political motivation to the immediate interests of each of the participants.[1] By the same token, it is crucially important to differentiate 'battles' which grew out of private feuds, like those at Heworth and Nibley Green,[2] from real battles at which the king was present and on whose outcome depended the control or identity of the king. The 'escalation' interpretation, on the contrary, takes a battle where the king took part to be merely the highest form that a private conflict can rise to. What is wrong with this approach is that it fails to identify the king's public persona as something apart from the private world of the subject, and to realise that it was the failure of kingship, much more than private conflict, which caused both the feuding and the battles. Neither were there long-term economic causes: the Wars occurred neither because the nobility were too poor to sustain themselves – they were not – nor because they were too rich to be controlled by the king. In any case they did not need to be controlled, they were not normally interested in attacking the king. Despite the decline of the customs revenues, there was no insurmountable monarchical financial frailty: from the mid-fourteenth century, kings who fought wars were able to tap the country's resources as no ruler of England had been able to do before; those who did not fight wars did not need this scale of subsidy.

---

[1] See above, pp. 21–2.   [2] See above, pp. 128, 175.

Moving to more immediate causes, the French war itself did not bring about the Wars of the Roses. We have seen that York's focus on Somerset's loss of Normandy as a *casus belli* was highly spurious. If some former commanders in France, like Andrew Ogard and John Fastolf, had served York there and remained in his service after their return, they were mostly too old to participate, or dead, by the time full hostilities erupted. Ogard in any case had moved towards the household before his death in 1454. Since the numbers of men of any status willing to fight in France had dwindled since the later 1430s, the numbers of former soldiers active enough to take part in the battles cannot have been large. William Oldhall, in his consistent enthusiasm for York's cause, at some risk to himself, is exceptional. Of those who still had any sort of stake in France, the Calais garrison, brought over by Warwick to support the Yorkists in 1459, made it clear at Ludford Bridge that its first allegiance was to the king. Indeed, one of the reasons for the apparent amateurishness of some of the fighting in the Wars was not that the participants were amateur, for almost all landowners were routinely trained in the rudiments of war, but that so many of them had not got the experience in battle that is crucial to the effectiveness of all armies. Where the war may have had importance is less as a stimulus to division *after* 1450 than as an incitement to unity *before* then. If the new analysis of the period from 1437 to 1450 is correct, then the war was the principal reason for the nobility to unite behind the semblance of the king erected by Suffolk in these years. As late as 1453, when it looked as if something could be salvaged from Gascony, the whole political nation came together behind the king, as represented by Somerset, making York's opposition temporarily untenable. Once France was irretrievably lost, there was less incentive for the nobility to pull together if other things were pulling them apart.

Similarly, foreign relations and diplomacy loomed large over much of the period because of internal problems; they neither caused nor resolved them. The parameters of the north-west European balance of power were undoubtedly among the long-term circumstances of the English polity, as far back as the later years of Edward I's reign. It was in the interests of France and Scotland to keep England weak and of England to keep these two both weak and apart. In the fifteenth century Burgundy became a major player in this game, wooed by both England and France as an important trade partner of England, as the engrosser of almost all that part of the channel coast which did not belong to France and as a potential underminer of the French monarchy. On a smaller scale and more intermittently, Brittany played the same kind of part. But it was France, not England, that was accustomed to invasion and attempts at dismemberment. So unused were the English that they tended to become hysterical over a French coastal raid, a Scottish invasion or the prospect of a French one. What made things different from 1450 onwards was the divisions within England, of a sort seen more often in France. This made England vulnerable to outside intervention and gave a peculiar significance to her foreign relations, but the cause was internal, not external.

What there was from about 1437 was quite simply a crisis of kingship which threatened eventually to become a crisis of the crown. It is the elucidation of the nature and effects of this crisis that is the key to understanding the politics of the period, and, for this, a grasp of political and governmental structures, as set out in chapters 2 and 3, is essential. The question at its most basic is why did it matter that Henry VI was unable to rule? The conventional answers, focusing on patronage and on personal antagonism, take us only a very small part of the way. Patronage was relatively unimportant to the normal process of ruling. Certainly, its abuse under Henry VI caused some bad feeling, and the absence of effective monarchical power in Henry's adulthood made nobles' relations with the royal court more significant than they should normally have been, but this was by no means the normal process of ruling. The clash of powerful personalities, like York's feud with Somerset from 1450 to 1455, although it could have serious consequences, was the result, not the cause, of the breakdown. The real answer is that it was the king's pivotal position, at the meeting-point of the public and private spheres whose interaction was the basis of successful governance, that made him indispensable. We must now summarise the effects, both short-term and long-term, of Henry's inability to fill this position.

Immediately, there were certainly those who were prepared to exploit a state of affairs that gave great opportunities to the greedy and the power-hungry. What is most striking, however, is that all the main protagonists were caught in a situation created by cracks in the basic structures of rule which resulted from the incapacity of Henry VI. No-one would claim greatness for Suffolk, York or the duke of Somerset who died at St Albans, but all three were operating in an impossible situation. There simply was no solution to an inept king other than deposition, because the medieval polity, with the emphasis on unity under the single figure at the apex, did not allow for legitimate opposition. The king could choose his advisers, the king had to be left free to act impartially, therefore no-one could dictate to a king, however inappropriate his choices and decisions. Previous experience had shown that deposition was indeed a possible answer to this conundrum, and it might succeed. But, while deposition required the active involvement of only one or two great nobles, an essential prerequi-

site was that virtually all the rest of the political nation should first have
removed its allegiance. Since this was a massive step to take, only the most
extreme behaviour on the part of the king could provoke it and both the
previous depositions – Edward II and Richard II – had therefore been
accomplished in conditions of near unanimity. What made Henry VI's
rule so peculiarly damaging was his nothingness, which engendered the
near-impossibility of achieving a deposition.

At first there was what turned out to be a misconceived substitution for
his rule. This occurred initially because his youth and extreme pliability
merged with ideas on the king's obligation to listen to counsel to disguise
his true nature. By the time the true extent of his inertness had become
apparent amongst a limited body of people with close access to the throne,
it must have seemed best to continue as they were. The system in place had
after all worked well during the minority and this was in many ways a
continued minority. The need to maintain unity in the face of the French
threat was a vital incentive to stay with this form of government, in fact if
not in name. Only gradually did it become apparent that neither collective
responsibility nor unity could be preserved when there was no minority
council any more, and the king was nominally an adult and free to sign
whatever was given him. Nor was it obvious until 1450 that those who
accepted the task of substitute rule must take responsibility for its shortcomings when their surrogacy and its consequences reached the public
consciousness.

No sooner was the nature of the problem recognised in 1450 than its
solution was rendered impossible by both York and Somerset putting
themselves up for the job of standing in for the king. Since neither would
give way, only a king could have adjudicated a confrontation of this order,
a solution that by definition was out of the question. Most of the other
nobles continued to seek the mirage of unity throughout the decade but
against a consistent background of internal conflict which was the inevitable outcome of lack of a single unitary authority. This succession of
disputes kept on pushing each of the nobility to one side or the other. Even
so, with a few wholly committed exceptions, they never ceased to try to
regroup in the middle, especially after a victory for one of the sides raised
the possibility of restoring a single authority. But this could not be done
until one of them was comprehensively defeated, and the efforts to restore
unity only inhibited the destruction of either side. In all these years the
unity that would have been required for so great a step as deposition was
lacking because what was wrong with Henry VI was not positive bad rule
which could have provoked removal but negative lack of rule from which
disunity grew. Corporate unwillingness to support the king – as in 1327
and 1399 – would have been enough if there was anyone bold enough to

overthrow him, but the nature of Henry's misrule ensured that it was not there. The only reason that any solution was achieved was that the decades of misrule gradually wore away the king's natural support among landowners; that the politics of the 1450s, especially the queen's intervention, inexorably pulled the nobles away from the centre where most wanted to be; and that the Yorkists' decision to claim the throne forced a final confrontation. And that was only a partial solution until 1471, when Edward could bring about the complete defeat of his opponents and the rival pole of authority could be eliminated.

Had that been the end of the story, the consequences might well have been less far-reaching, but it is possible all the same to argue that the effects of the events up to 1471 were still reverberating in 1483. Certainly the period from 1471 to Edward's death was one of successful rebuilding and can by no stretch of the imagination be called a crisis. Nevertheless, the results of almost forty years of non-kingship under Henry VI, especially of the twenty-four years when there was an inactive adult king, followed by ten years in which the throne remained in doubt and the change of ruler was twice reversed, should not be underestimated in the events of 1483. From its own or its parents' experience, the generation in power in 1483 was still familiar with the devastating impact of the last king to ascend the throne as a child. The Woodvilles may have seemed possible look-alikes for Suffolk and for the duke of Somerset who died at St Albans. If all this amounted to a misreading of what had gone before, it was an understandable one and it gave Richard a platform for his attack on the Woodvilles and then for his claim to represent the best means of continuing his brother's extremely successful rule. Moreover, this generation or its fathers had seen a king dethroned three times and may well therefore have regarded the act as less unthinkable than its forebears had done. Most important of all, in 1461 a precedent had been set when for the first time both a reigning king and his son and heir had been removed. And finally, the removal meant that the dynasty whose representative died in 1483 was vulnerable because it had yet to establish its permanent right to the throne by passing it to the next direct heir.

If the crisis that had been resolved in 1471 left a legacy which played some part in 1483, the crisis of 1483 was to have far-reaching consequences for monarchs and the monarchy. It was not just that it led to another round of depositions, rebellions and usurpations, leading to another dynasty without a secure title, but that another precedent was created. Richard's threadbare justification opened up the possibility of anyone with a title to the throne, however dubious and distant, and however successful the reigning monarch, making an attempt on it. The accession of Henry Tudor is itself exemplification of the point about dubious claims. It is at this juncture that we can perhaps speak, at least for a while, of a dynastic insecurity which is often, erroneously, held to have been introduced by the Lancastrians. Throughout the middle ages, because of marriages into English noble houses of royal children who were not matched abroad, there were always several nobles who were cousins of some sort of the king. Mostly this had had no political significance but suddenly anyone who could claim some sort of proximate relationship could be, or be seen to be, a danger to the throne. The Tudor dynasty remained for long as insecure as it seemed to its founder, especially once the survival of a male heir to Henry VIII was in doubt. In the 1530s the Wars of the Roses were still going on in the mind of the king, as the last descendants of rival claimants were murdered by his orders. It is thus in the second phase of the Wars, from 1483, that we may have to begin to talk about a crisis of the crown. Even if, as was argued earlier, Henry VII did his level best to make the dynasty more insecure, it is possible that this period did bring about some cheapening of the crown and that the early Tudor obsession with security may have had some justification. It undoubtedly led to some distortion of the monarchy, since the constitution was designed around a king, not a usurper. It will be argued that there were other more cogent causes for changes in the style of politics from the later fifteenth century,[3] but the accession of two successive usurpers, neither of whom was able to attain an unquestioned right to rule, could only accentuate unease and suspicion around the ruler and the importance of the reward and punishment that the king could offer.

Given the monarchy's pivotal place in the English polity, such an extended monarchical emergency was likely to have significant effects on the king's subjects. Until recently, one of the results of the 'McFarlane revolution' was to minimise them. Devastation was down-graded from the near-universal mayhem depicted by Stubbs, Plummer and their successors to localised destruction which had limited impact on the economy and society of the country at large. Focus on the quality of the individual kings, accompanied by a lack of interest in the structures of rule, has meant that the repercussions for the polity of breakdown at the centre have been largely unexplored: bad times followed from the rule of Henry VI and Richard III, better times were restored by Edward IV (eventually) and Henry VII. What 'bad' meant and whether what was restored was the same as before have been neglected questions. As a relatively recent historian of the Wars has put it, 'there have been some signs of the growth of a counter-legend . . . a legend which writes the Wars of the Roses off as a brief and harmless episode'.[4]

[3] These are considered below, pp. 261–6.   [4] Gillingham, *Wars of the Roses*, p. 14.

It is still difficult to assess the direct effects of the Wars, not least because we are so uncertain of the size of the armies. By and large we are probably right not to make too much of them. Campaigns were mostly short. Some battles were not only probably small in scale, perhaps because of the incompetence of some of the commanders, but, like the first battle of St Albans, closer to skirmishes than to genuine military encounters. Ludford Bridge, where the Yorkist forces made off overnight, was barely a skirmish. The forces at Towton seem to have been exceptionally large, although here also we have no certain figures. One of the reasons for the brevity of the campaigns and the small size of many of the armies was that, without the financial and logistical support that a king could command, opponents of the crown found it hard to keep armies in the field, and the same was true of kings for much of the time. Henry VI's government retreated to the midlands in the later 1450s, and between 1469 and 1471 Edward IV's hold on the apparatus of government was either unsure or non-existent. Thus, in most cases, the full army would assemble only shortly before the battle and, once the battle was over, it would disperse rapidly, leaving concentrated devastation only in the places where the whole army spent the night and where the battle itself had been fought. In 1461, after the battle of Wakefield, when Margaret's army did stay together and fed itself as it came south by plunder, the only means it had, the fact was noticed. Equally, because England was such a unified country, there were few sieges, and it was these which could bring prolonged devastation to an area through the besieging army's need to feed itself. The exceptions, where there were sieges and more sustained campaigns, were the Scottish border, and, to a lesser extent, Wales. However, these, especially the northern border, were areas where violence and plunder were considered more normal. The Wars certainly had some deleterious economic effects, and not just in these regions. For example, the lords' uncertain hold on their Welsh Marcher revenues was not improved by the near-collapse of English rule in Wales and the March during the middle of the century. The strained economy of the north-east during the period of the Wars cannot have been helped by the siege warfare and rebellions of the 1460s and may, of course have been one of the causes of the revolts. Coventry's economy, probably increasingly less buoyant from the 1450s, was not improved by the large fine levied after the Readeption for its support of Warwick and Clarence in 1470. But, even in instances such as these, it does not seem that the Wars did more than accentuate existing tendencies.

Where the extended series of crises is likely to have had far wider and more profound effects is in its consequences for the inhabitants of England in general, not just those who were caught up in armies or who suffered destruction at their hands. The commons of England were of course the group most exposed to this direct destruction but more significant for them in the longer term are further signs of the political awareness which can first be seen in 1381. Those townsmen and tenants who were recruited into armies in the Wars, the surviving veterans of the French wars, the coastal inhabitants subjected to raids from the 1440s, first by the French and then by Yorkists and Lancastrians, could hardly be unaware of what was going on. The manifesto of the Cade rebellion shows a far more mature understanding of the mechanisms of local government than the vague statements of 1381, which is not surprising when we consider that several of its participants were local officers. How far the commons were manipulated in the rebellions of the north and in Lincolnshire under Edward IV is a moot point, but they were clearly defending their own interests in 1489 and in 1497 – on the last occasion in an organised and, to authority, deeply threatening manner. As ever, Kent was frequently in the forefront of revolt but the geographical spread of rebellion in the second half of the century is striking and went well beyond the traditionally 'difficult' regions, East Anglia and the south-east. Self-evidently, the progress of lower-class revolt owes more to the critical economic and social changes of the century than to political events, but we should not dismiss folk-memory of earlier rebellion, common to much of England by 1500, as a stimulant to the great popular demonstrations of the sixteenth century.

The church on the other hand seems to be the part of society most untouched by the crisis. Like other landowners it might suffer from the destruction caused by local and national conflict, but church land was essentially secure against counter-claimants, where lay land was not. Even though some of the higher clergy seem to have meddled dangerously in politics, remarkably few suffered for it. A few had to put up with temporary imprisonment or disgrace, mostly of a brief nature. Ayscough and Moleyns were murdered in the events of 1450. George Neville lost the chancellorship and was later disgraced at the Readeption because of over-identification with his family's politics. Stillington, bishop of Bath and Wells, was pardoned his advocacy of Richard's claim to the throne but then took part in the Simnel conspiracy and was imprisoned until just before his death, in 1491. Neither Neville nor Stillington, however, lost his bishopric. Rather surprisingly, none of the bishops in England promoted from Henry VI's household, some of them distinctly partisan, suffered seriously when Edward became king. Lawrence Booth of Durham is a case in point. As bishop and lord of the palatinate, he had immense power in a region that was very vulnerable in the early years of Edward IV, and, even if he had at first been more conciliatory to the Nevilles than might have been expected, he had rather grievously offended them in the last years of Henry VI. But after two years of suspension he was reinstated, was impeccably loyal thereafter and was finally promoted to York by Edward on George Neville's death in 1476. The exceptions to this rule of Edwardian leniency were in Wales, which was probably seen as too vulnerable for Edward to leave Lancastrian bishops in post in the early 1460s.

The group that was most profoundly touched by the events of this period was of course the landowners of England. Of these, it was the nobles who could least well escape the consequences of a crisis of kingship. The myth that they took no interest in national events should now be buried for good. If they failed to come to parliament it was because these gatherings were usually of no great interest or importance for them. If they stayed away from key parliaments and great councils in the 1450s, it was because attendance implied commitment to the side that called them. In a few cases, they had already given their allegiance to the other side but, in most cases, they were trying to stay neutral. What we must not do is mistake neutrality, a political stance which grew logically out of their own position in the polity, for lack of interest. It is indeed inconceivable, once their key role in the constitution has been understood, that the nobles could have remained on the sidelines. They were involved whether they liked it or not and, as the crown demanded in the later 1450s that they commit themselves, they could no longer hide.

Whether in the longer term their experiences of the 1450s and 1460s encouraged withdrawal or even brought about demoralisation, as has been suggested by some historians, is a debatable point. The old belief that the nobility were wiped out by the wars, leaving the way open for 'Tudor absolutism', was long ago laid to rest by McFarlane. While recent work suggests that we should take fuller cognisance of the death rate among them, that is not to deny that very few lines were ended entirely by the Wars.[5] However, the death rate could be seen as a critical factor in assessing the psychology of the survivors. If, as has been noted, 'No less than four Courtenays in the direct male line perished in the years 1461–71',[6] that must have had some effect on the surviving Courtenays. Such deaths in the family would surely have made nobles still more reluctant to commit themselves to either side. When the victory of either side seemed to have no pressing urgency for the polity, reluctance must have become stronger and, as this was usually under conditions in which the reigning monarch was in no position to command their military participation, non-participation was highly attractive. Such a state of affairs existed in 1469–71, when

[5] McFarlane, 'Extinction and Recruitment', *Nobility*, pp. 146–9 (a point he restated in 'Wars of the Roses', pp. 247–9). *Cf.* Gillingham, *Wars of the Roses*, p. 14.

[6] Gillingham, *Wars of the Roses*, p. 14.

the opposition to Edward IV had little to be said for it, while Edward himself, although he had begun to look like a viable and worthwhile king from 1465, was in too precarious a situation to demand allegiance, at least until after Barnet. It also existed under Richard III and is seen most obviously in the equivocal behaviour of some of his supposed supporters at Bosworth, who could not entirely disregard the call to arms against Henry Tudor but could at least wriggle out of actually fighting. The eventual sustained resistance of Edward IV's old following to his usurping brother, although it was mostly of gentry rather than nobles, shows that passive cynicism was still not universal when there was a cause worth fighting for. However, it cannot be denied that some of the passivity of the nobility in the face of Henry VII's aggression, even when offered alternative claimants, may have come from the battering they had received in the politics of the previous half-century. As with the effect on the monarchy, it is the unexpected renewal in 1483 of a mode of politics that had apparently been buried in 1471 that is likely to have been especially debilitating.

If the gentry could mostly escape into neutrality more easily than the nobles, we have seen that the reason they wished to do so was that in many ways they were more likely to suffer from the failure of monarchy than their lords. To understand why this period was indeed peculiarly destructive to all landowners, but especially to the gentry, we must remove our focus from the direct consequences of the Wars of the Roses themselves – whether death, disgrace or local destruction – to the wider repercussions for a landed ruling class of the threatened breakdown of the polity. At almost every phase of national crisis, the scale of local conflict and attack on landed property rose alarmingly. Throughout the period, uncertain or inadequate kingship was accompanied by increasing local discord. Perhaps worst of all was the ultimate dislocation of political society under Henry VI. Because they had no direction from the king, the nobility were unable to perform their function of acting pivotally between crown and provinces. Because the nobility were therefore unable to give them direction, the gentry could not do their job of supplying the bedrock of private noble power in the shires which made possible the king's public rule. Nor could they easily act in their other role, as the local executive officers of that rule. Moreover, because the source of power under him was at first obscure and then contested, it was Henry VI's unique failure that he made all the normal processes of landowning life inoperable, from high politics to mundane marriage and property settlements. For reasons that were explained in the account of the 1450s,[7] all this was still more damaging to the gentry than to the nobility because the lives of even the greater gentry

---

[7] See above, pp. 149–52.

were essentially lived on a small local scale compared with those of all but the most meagre nobles. The nobles, who had widespread lands and a political life lived in both national and local politics, might choose, or be forced, to sacrifice local equilibrium in the wider political forum. For all but the small number of gentry who were wholly committed to a particular lord, this would be madness.

In their contrast, Henry's reign and his successor's, particularly after 1471, show very clearly what landowners at all levels needed from the king; co-operation laced with firmness, the ability to listen and, perhaps above all, predictability. The two keys to governance as they were understood in the fifteenth century, counsel and will, were present in equal proportions under Edward; under Henry there was plenty of listening to counsel but a complete absence of will. Landowners had to cope with a prolonged crisis of kingship which really began with Henry VI's nominal adulthood in about 1437, intensified from 1450 and lasted to 1471, in which there was first wholly insufficient rule and then rival claimants for control of the king, followed by rival claimants to the throne itself. In 1483, although politics never again reached the depths of the 1450s and much of the 1460s, the throne came into question again and remained an uncertain inheritance until at least 1509, and arguably well into the Tudor period. What is remarkable is that the polity held together at all, as it did for most of the period. Until 1450 this was principally the achievement of the nobles, who managed both war and diplomacy abroad and government at home. From 1450, as the nobility got drawn into an increasingly more uncontrollable political maelstrom, it was the gentry who gave politics some stability. It is landowners' responses, in trying to maintain some kind of normality in this lengthy period of distorted politics, especially in the worst years, from 1450 to 1471, that may hold the key to the emergence of the new monarchical style towards the end of the century.

In examining the events of the later 1450s it was suggested that the gentry may have begun to withdraw their support not just from the monarch but also from the nobles whose involvement in national politics was beginning to make them behave in ways that the gentry could not approve and demand behaviour from the gentry that they could not offer. Indeed, the lack of inclination of the lesser landowners to follow their lords into rebellion or battle, which has sometimes been seen as indicative of the instability of 'bastard feudalism' is, on the contrary, potent evidence of the depths of allegiance to the crown. Moreover, there is some evidence that in the 1450s the gentry were starting to establish or strengthen cross-factional groupings, and for the first time looking less to the nobles for local leadership. Such groupings existed in spite of, rather than because of, the magnates. We must remember that together the gentry were always territorially more powerful than the nobility, but the individual might of the magnates meant that they would always be the natural local leaders as long as the gentry automatically looked to them for leadership. These habits were self-reinforcing, for an effective network built around noble leadership was not something to be disturbed. But it is possible that the mid-century crisis forced the gentry into new habits; once they had become conscious of their ability to manage without noble leadership, radically different political structures could develop. Under the direction of the nobles, the gentry found in the 1450s that their destiny was not in their own hands, so they took hold of it for themselves.

The late-medieval polity was constructed around a hierarchy of power and deference that allowed royal authority to filter down through nobility to gentry and from all landowners to their tenants, and response to move in the opposite direction. Thus, if the gentry began to operate without automatic reference to the magnates, the nature of governance and response had to alter. Once the magnates no longer had the undisputed leadership of the shires, it was possible for the king to bypass them and make direct contact with the gentry. The gentry in their turn, realising that it was now the king who held the key to the rule of the localities, would go to him direct, either to the royal court or to his local representative. The magnates, deprived of their unique position as gate-keepers in the shires and spokesmen for their inhabitants, would become vulnerable, as the gentry allegiance that lay at the root of their local power was no longer theirs to command. Their lands could be taken under dubious pretexts, they could be executed on doubtful charges, they could be firmly disciplined.

In the later fifteenth century we can see the emergence of what is recognisably the Tudor polity. This is a court-centred realm, in which nobles remain a vital adjunct to royal power but are a much more exposed group. The gentry rule the shires at the command of the monarch and, since political life focuses on the court, politics and the building of political connections centre on the giving and receiving of royal favours, in a way which is not true of the late-medieval polity. Under Henry VII, we can even see the start of that percolation of the king's direct authority still further down the social scale which was to become increasingly common during the sixteenth century. Although lesser gentry and yeomen would still normally use the local noble as their conduit to the crown, they were beginning to exercise the option of bypassing him if he was unwilling or unable to do what they wanted. Moreover, the continued expansion of royal authority into geographical and social spheres hitherto relatively untouched made that authority so essential to the polity that any uncertainty about individual kings was bound to be accompanied by even greater elevation of the status of the crown. There is little doubt that Tudor England does look different from late-medieval England, nor that the change begins to occur in this period. It happened at different times and different rates in different parts of the kingdom and in 1500 there was still a long way to go – another century really – before the whole realm was integrated into a unitary political structure around the monarchy. Nevertheless, the way Edward IV and Henry VII ruled was possible because of these changes, and without them Henry could probably not have kept his throne. Thus, even if it seems that the crown may have been damaged by the upheavals of the second half of the century, those very events seem to have been operating ultimately to adjust the balance of power within England in the interests of the king. So, if Henry VII had some justification in feeling ill-at-ease after the occurrences of 1483–5, the fact remains that he failed to realise that the structure of the polity he ruled was now positively helpful to his survival.

What remains obscure is how and why these changes in the style of monarchy happened, and we shall need several more studies of the interplay of local and national politics in both the fourteenth and fifteenth centuries before we reach any real understanding. There was certainly a measure of institutional change: the expansion of the household as a political force; the rapid development of the council and its offshoots, especially under Henry VII; the development of summary justice, less touched by local interests. But we have seen that all this stemmed from centralisation, it did not cause it. It has been suggested that the growth of the crown lands, and therefore of the crown affinity connected to the lands, may have played a significant role in extending royal power, and there must be some truth in this. But the lands themselves could only grow if there was a gap opening between noble and gentry which allowed the king to confiscate magnate lands permanently, without stirring up the local resentment at the disturbance of networks and allegiances that would have resulted earlier on. In any case this would not apply to regions where there were no crown lands, nor does it allow for the granting away of many of these estates under Henry VIII. For the moment the hypothesis of gentry/noble divorce in the middle of the century seems the most likely explanation, but it remains a hypothesis.

The consequences were by no means uniformly beneficial, as Henry VII's reign, especially its later years, immediately shows. There was no certainty that firm royal direction of the shires from outside would inevitably be any more just than the older system of self-rule with minimal royal intervention. At least self-rule would provide a locally endorsed distribution of power and favour and there was always the possibility of appealing to the king. By trying to look at politics both ways – from the king's and his landed subjects' perspectives – this study has shown that consensus between monarch and landed subjects was normally the most acceptable form of government, as long as the king was able to enforce such a consensus when it broke down in the shires. From the fourteenth century until the later fifteenth that was also far and away the most efficacious method for the king, so that at its best it was an extraordinarily successful method of achieving a balance between the desires of the ruler and the ruled. From the last decades of the fifteenth century, it was possible for the monarch to override the wishes of the localities with diminishing resistance. There could still be an Edward IV but there could also be Henry VIIs. The Tudors present a depressing picture to the late-medievalist. Once the monarch was the single focus of power, and once the nobles could no longer represent the realm to the king, the wish for access to the king became so general that the ruler had to be shut away in the privy chamber; the days of open-access kingship were over. The monarch's image had to be glorified in keeping with his or her universal and unshared authority. That was indeed partly why he or she could be less open to the public gaze. The court, now the single centre of politics, became a focus of back-biting and intrigue as it was before only under inept kings like Richard II. The open shouting match that was reported as occurring in 1297 between the earl of Norfolk and Edward I, perhaps the most majestic and authoritative king ever to rule in England, would have been as inconceivable at the Tudor court as Norfolk's subsequent impunity. Amidst the intrigues, nobles could be destroyed for little more than a whiff of treason about them, dragging lesser men and women down with them. The deaths of Sir William Stanley and Lord Fitzwalter under Henry VII, and even of Clarence under Edward IV, are a foretaste of what was to come.

Naturally this is only one part of the story, as one-sided an account of the sixteenth century as those of the fifteenth that stress disorder and weak kingship. What it should do is invite reconsideration of both late-medieval and Tudor kingship from the perspective of the landed subject, as well as the king's. It should also encourage exploration of this kingship, in all its manifestations, across the barrier that still remains fixed between the later Plantaganets and the Tudors. There are both more similarities and more differences than is often supposed and the similarities and differences are not always the obvious ones. Historians are just on the verge of a proper exploration of the century from 1450 to 1550 as a period in its own right, and study of these hundred years and of the fifty years that preceded them is changing very fast at present, so that everything that has been said in this book must be regarded as an interim report. Within the period 1450 to 1550 we must begin to evaluate the significance for what came after of the more acute years of crisis: 1450 to 1471, and 1483 to 1485 or 1487. The peaks and troughs of kingship in the fifteenth century are an admirable laboratory in which to investigate the governance of England in the later middle ages and the legacy that was left to the Tudors.

This study closes with four admonitions. The first is to avoid making connections that look neat on paper but do not bear close scrutiny. Almost all the bad history of the period has been written in this way, especially in the search for deep-laid causes, whether in the rise or decline of great nobles, in the Lancastrian usurpation or, above all, in the reign of Edward III. Secondly, no account of the past will ever be remotely free from anachronism unless the historian can put himself imaginatively into the mind-set of the main participants. This is not the derided 'empathy' of the GCSE examination but an understanding of the preconceptions which would have shaped their responses, as individual actors and as social groups. They could not see into the future but they would have their sense of what the present amounted to and strong views about what had just happened. When looking over their shoulders, they would have seen not the working-out of long-term causes but their own recent past, or their fathers', not necessarily correctly interpreted. We have seen how the participants in the events of the last two decades of the century could not fail to have been influenced by the perceptions and, in some cases, memories of the mid-century crisis. It is a common-place that much of the harping on respect for the crown and on the urgency of political stability in the next century came from collective memories about the Wars of the Roses, but one that takes new force from consideration of what this prolonged crisis had really meant to landed society and the crown. If we can put ourselves imaginatively into the position of the nobles and gentry, as they contemplated what was going on around them at that time, we shall have a much better understanding of why they responded as they did, sometimes with deep and lasting results.

This brings us to the third point, which is that, while we should be looking not at long-term causes but at long-term structures, the way the participants in this succession of crises responded could inadvertently change the structures, and this has been one of the major themes of this book. Because people cannot see into the future, the results of political events are nearly always unforeseen. By making neat patterns, as with the supposed connections between Edward III and the Wars of the Roses, historians can be badly led astray. However, if they focus carefully on what people seem to have thought they were doing, and follow the consequences through without preconceptions, the assessment of long-term results can be rooted in the normal messiness of human relations rather than in schemata dreamt up by historians. Fourthly, the largely unpromising evidence for discovering what was going on in the minds of land-owners need not be an insuperable bar if we are prepared to think in terms of their expectations. Careful study of their routine business, linked to exploration of the body politic of which they were an indispensable part, will get us a long way in uncovering these. These four precepts can be summed up as respecting the people we study; not deriding them for having beliefs we do not share nor dismissing them as aliens who share nothing with us at all. If the apparently incoherent politics of the last sixty years of the fifteenth century are studied as a period in which human beings with certain kinds of expectations were suddenly confronted with the wholly unexpected and struggled to understand and to cope with it, as human beings will, they begin to make a surprising amount of sense.

BIBLIOGRAPHICAL NOTES

This is by no means a comprehensive bibliography but it is designed to take the interested reader further into the literature. All the works listed below contain further references for those who wish to study any subject in depth. Note that in most cases works are listed once only, although they may well be relevant to other chapters. This is almost invariably the case with studies of a particular reign, which will normally be cited for the first chapter on that reign and not for subsequent chapters. Works listed more than once are fully referenced on their first citation only.

I SOURCES AND HISTORIOGRAPHY

There are a number of general works or collections of essays on the period, some of which contain discussions of the sources and historiography, and several of the works listed for other chapters also have historiographical discussions. The most useful of the general works are A. J. Pollard, *The Wars of the Roses* (London, 1988) and *The Wars of the Roses*, ed. A. J. Pollard (London, 1995). F. R. H. Du Boulay, *An Age of Ambition: English Society in the Late Middle Ages* (London, 1970) is quite a nice introduction to the period. R. L. Storey, *The End of the House of Lancaster* (London, 1966) has an introduction which spends some time on the history and applicability of the term 'Wars of the Roses'. See also J. R. Lander, *Crown and Nobility 1450–1509* (London, 1976), 'Introduction: Aspects of Fifteenth-Century Studies', pp. 1–56. Two works are primarily on the military history of the Wars: J. Gillingham, *The Wars of the Roses* (London, 1981) (but see also under chapter 8, below) and A. Goodman, *The Wars of the Roses* (London, 1981). They cover similar ground but in different ways. Text-books covering all or part of the period include G. A. Holmes, *The Later Middle Ages 1272–1485* (2nd edn, London, 1967) (still the best short account of late-medieval England), M. H. Keen, *England in the Later Middle Ages* (London, 1973), A. Tuck, *Crown and Nobility 1272–1461* (London, 1985), J. A. F. Thomson, *The Transformation of Medieval England 1370–1529* (London, 1983) (which has an extremely useful compendium of information), J. R. Lander, *Government and Community: England 1450–1509* (London, 1980), C. S. L. Davies, *Peace, Print and Protestantism 1450–1558* (London, 1977), D. M. Loades, *Politics and the Nation 1450–1660* (London, 1973). The historiography and wider historiographical background are specifically addressed in C. Carpenter, 'Political and Constitutional History: before and after McFarlane', *The McFarlane Legacy*, ed. R. H. Britnell and A. J. Pollard (Stroud, 1995), pp. 175–206, which leans heavily in part on J. W. Burrow, *A Liberal Descent* (London, 1981) and P. B. M. Blaas, *Continuity and Anachronism: Parliamentary and Constitutional Development in Whig Historiography and in the Anti-Whig Reaction betwen 1890 and 1930* (The Hague, Boston, London, 1978) and includes references for the work of Stubbs, Tout and other nineteenth- and early twentieth-century historians. The classic account of 'Whig' history is H. Butterfield, *The Whig Interpretation of History* (London, 1931). Both Fortescue's ideas and Plummer's work on 'bastard feudalism' can be followed up in Sir John Fortescue, *The Governance of England*, ed. C. Plummer (Oxford, 1885). For other pre-McFarlane developments, see C. L. Kingsford, *Prejudice and Promise in XVth Century England* (Oxford, 1925) and S. B. Chrimes, *English Constitutional Ideas in the Fifteenth Century* (Cambridge, 1936). McFarlane's work is best approached through two collections: *England in the Fifteenth Century*, ed. G. L. Harriss (which includes his classic essays, 'Bastard Feudalism' and 'The Wars of the Roses') (London, 1981) and *The Nobility of Later Medieval England* (Oxford, 1973). The McFarlane legacy is summarised and discussed in Harriss' introduction to *England in the Fifteenth Century*, C. Carpenter, *Locality and Polity: A Study of Warwickshire Landed Society 1401–1499* (Cambridge, 1992), chapter 1, the Carpenter article, above, and E. Powell, 'After "After McFarlane": The Poverty of Patronage and the Case for Constitutional History', *Trade, Devotion and Governance: Papers in Later Medieval History*, ed. D. J. Clayton, R. G. Davies and P. McNiven (Stroud, 1994), pp. 1–16. A representative post-McFarlane account is C. Ross, *The Wars of the Roses* (London, 1976). The Wars of the Roses as 'an escalation of private feuds' is proposed in Storey (as above). An excellent critique of lingering 'Whiggery' is J. W. McKenna, 'The Myth of Parliamentary Sovereignty in Late-Medieval England', *English Historical Review*, 114 (1979), pp. 481–506.

The three gentry correspondences can be most conveniently found in the following editions: *The Paston Letters*, ed. J. Gairdner (6 vols., 1904, rpt. in 1 vol., Gloucester, 1983); *The Plumpton Letters and Papers*, ed. J. Kirby, Camden, 5th ser. 8, (1996); *Kingsford's Stonor Letters and Papers 1290–1483*, ed. C. Carpenter (Cambridge, for the Royal Historical Soc., 1996). A useful collection of sources on the Wars themselves is integrated into the narrative of J. R. Lander, *The Wars of the Roses* (London, 1965) and a substantial collection of sources for late-medieval England in general is *English Historical Documents*, iv, *1327–1485*, ed. A. R. Myers (London, 1969).

2 THE GOVERNANCE OF ENGLAND IN THE FIFTEENTH CENTURY I

The best general guide to the mechanisms of government is A. L. Brown, *The Governance of Medieval England 1272–1461* (London, 1989). The view that war weakened the late-medieval state is stated most fully in R. W. Kaeuper, *War, Justice and Public Order: England and France in the Later Middle Ages* (Oxford, 1988) and there is a trenchant criticism of this view and an excellent summary of state growth in this period in G. L. Harriss, 'Political Society and the Growth of Government in Late Medieval England', *Past and Present*, 138 (1993), pp. 28–57. See also his interesting synthesis of the post-McFarlane work on English politics, 'The Dimensions of Politics', *The McFarlane Legacy*, pp. 1–20. For discussion of ideas of kingship and references to further reading, including contemporary texts, see J. L. Watts, *Henry VI and the Politics of Kingship* (Cambridge, 1996). This also deals with the council/counsel issue and has full references to works on the council. The development of parliamentary taxation is summed up in the classic work, G. L. Harriss, *King, Parliament, and Public Finance in Medieval England to 1369* (Oxford, 1975). See also G. Bernard, *War, Taxation and Rebellion in Early Tudor England: Henry VIII, Wolsey and the Amicable Grant of 1525* (Hassocks, 1986). Brown, as above, has a summary of the king's financial position. The development of the law is summarised in E. Powell, *Kingship, Law, and Society: Criminal Justice in the Reign of Henry V* (Oxford, 1989), chapter 2 (especially good on the fourteenth century) and there is a more basic account in A. Harding, *The Law Courts of Medieval England* (London, 1973) (less good on the fourteenth century but useful on the thirteenth). On the economic position of the nobility, see McFarlane, *Nobility of Later Medieval England*, and of the gentry, see Carpenter, *Locality and Polity*, chapter 5, and, for a more general survey of the English economy in relation to the wars, R. H. Britnell, 'The Economic Context', *The Wars of the Roses*, ed. Pollard, pp. 41–64. The argument for 'welfare dependency' is put forward in C. Given-Wilson, *The English Nobility in the*

Late Middle Ages (London, 1987), chapter 6. For the main social groups in late-medieval England, see McFarlane, *Nobility* (nobles), Carpenter, *Locality and Polity*, chapter 3 (gentry), T. B. Pugh, 'The Magnates, Knights and Gentry', *Fifteenth-Century England 1399–1509: Studies in Politics and Society*, ed. S. B. Chrimes, C. D. Ross and R. A. Griffiths (Manchester, 1972), pp. 86–128 (nobles and gentry) and I. M. W. Harvey, 'Was There Popular Politics in Fifteenth-Century England?', *The McFarlane Legacy*, pp. 155–74 (commons). On the Commons' role in parliament there is a large literature, of which the classic item is K. B. McFarlane, 'Parliament and "Bastard Feudalism"', *England in the Fifteenth Century*, pp. 1–21, and the most recent L. Clark, 'Magnates and their Affinities in the Parliaments of 1386–1421', *The McFarlane Legacy*, pp. 127–53. For this chapter and the next, see also a useful recent summary, W. M. Ormrod, *Political Life in Medieval England 1300–1450* (London, 1995), which, although wide-ranging in its review of the literature, especially recent 'revisionist' work, ends rather unconvincingly in an attempt to shift the 'declining late-medieval monarchy' thesis into Henry V's reign.

3 THE GOVERNANCE OF ENGLAND IN THE FIFTEENTH CENTURY II

There is now a large amount of work on 'bastard feudalism' and the localities. A survey of the former is M. A. Hicks, *Bastard Feudalism* (London, 1995) and a summary and critique of the latter is in C. Carpenter, 'Gentry and Community', *Journal of British Studies*, 33 (1994), pp. 340–80. The local studies include R. Virgoe, 'The Crown, Magnates and Local Government in Fifteenth-Century East Anglia', *The Crown and Local Communities in England and France in the Fifteenth Century*, ed. J. R. L. Highfield and R. Jeffs (Gloucester, 1981), pp. 72–87, S. Wright, *The Derbyshire Gentry in the Fifteenth Century* (Derbyshire Record Soc., 8, Chesterfield, 1983), M. J. Bennett, *Community, Class and Careerism: Cheshire and Lancashire Society in the Age of Sir Gawain and the Green Knight* (Cambridge, 1983), C. Arnold, 'The Commission of the Peace for the West Riding of Yorkshire, 1437–1509', *Patronage, the Crown and the Provinces in Later Medieval England*, ed. R. A. Griffiths (Gloucester, 1981), pp. 116–38, A. J. Pollard, *North-Eastern England during the Wars of the Roses: Lay Society, War, and Politics, 1450–1500* (Oxford, 1990), S. J. Payling, *Political Society in Lancastrian England: The Greater Gentry of Nottinghamshire* (Oxford, 1991), C. Moreton, *The Townshends and their World: Gentry, Law and Land in Norfolk, c. 1450–1551* (Oxford, 1992) and Carpenter, *Locality and Polity* (which tries to construct a view of the polity as seen from the provinces). Some of these make important contributions to the history of

England as a whole within this period and a discussion of 'bastard feudalism' within a local context is to be found in nearly all of them. Specific works on 'bastard feudalism' include McFarlane's article and Harriss' comments (see under chapter 1), Pugh, 'Magnates, Knights and Gentry', M. Cherry, 'The Courtenay Earls of Devon: The Formation and Disintegration of a Late Medieval Aristocratic Affinity', *Southern History*, 1 (1979), pp. 71–97, C. Carpenter, 'The Beauchamp Affinity: A Study of Bastard Feudalism at Work', *English Historical Review*, 95 (1980), pp. 514–32, J. M. W. Bean, *From Lord to Patron: Lordship in Late Medieval England* (Manchester, 1989) (a very 'institutional' discussion), S. Walker, *The Lancastrian Affinity 1361–1399* (Oxford, 1990). There is a not very satisfactory debate on the origins of 'bastard feudalism' which suffers from an outdated over-emphasis on retaining as an institution but it is almost the sole occasion for a serious discussion of origins: P. Coss, 'Bastard Feudalism Revised', *Past and Present*, 125 (1989), pp. 30–9, followed by D. Crouch, D. A. Carpenter, 'Debate: Bastard Feudalism Revised', ibid., 131 (1991), pp. 165–89. An extremely useful survey of the development of indentures, which goes well beyond this limited brief, along with an excellent series of illustrations, is *Private Indentures for Life Service in Peace and War*, ed. M. Jones and S. Walker (Camden Miscellany, 32, Camden Soc., 5th ser., 3 (1994)). The new approach to 'feudalism' is introduced in B. Golding, *Conquest and Colonisation: The Normans in Britain 1066–1100* (London, 1994), chapters. 4 and 6. Law in local society is considered most fully in Powell, *Kingship, Law, and Society*. Powell has also made the major contributions on arbitration: 'Arbitration and the Law in England in the Late Middle Ages', *Transactions of the Royal Historical Society*, 5th ser., 33 (1983), pp. 49–67 and 'Settlement of Disputes by Arbitration in Fifteenth-Century England', *Law and History Review*, 2 (1984), pp. 21–43. See also C. Carpenter, 'Law, Justice and Landowners in Late-Medieval England', *Law and History Review*, 1 (1983), pp. 205–37 and P. C. Maddern, *Violence and Social Order: East Anglia 1422–1441* (Oxford, 1992). Carpenter, *Locality and Polity*, chapter 9(i) includes a fairly comprehensive bibliography up to 1988 on the public/private interrelationship in its notes. On all this see also Ormrod, as listed in chapter 2. A very useful introduction to legal process, helpfully illustrated with documents, although most of it focuses on the earlier middle ages, is R. C. Palmer, *The Whilton Dispute 1264–1380: A Social-Legal Study of Dispute Settlement in Medieval England* (Princeton, 1984). For the contrast with Scotland in governmental terms, see A. Grant, 'Crown and Nobility in Late Medieval Britain', *Scotland and England 1286–1815*, ed. R. A. Mason (Edinburgh, 1987), pp. 34–59. Stimulating recent work on the borders includes S. G. Ellis, *Tudor Frontiers and Noble Power: The Making of the British State* (Oxford, 1995), Ellis, 'Crown,

Community and Government in the English Territories 1450–1575', *History*, 71 (1986), pp. 187–204, A. Goodman, 'The Anglo-Scottish Marches in the Fifteenth Century: A Frontier Society?', *Scotland and England 1286–1815*, pp. 18–34, C. J. Neville, 'Keeping the Peace on the Northern Marches in the Later Middle Ages', *English Historical Review*, 109 (1994), pp. 1–25, R. Frame, *The Political Development of the British Isles 1100–1400* (Oxford, 1990). Useful older work is R. L. Storey, 'The North of England', *Fifteenth-Century England*, pp. 129–44 and R. A. Griffiths, 'Wales and the Marches', ibid., pp. 145–72. The Norman frontier can be explored in C. Allmand, *Lancastrian Normandy, 1415–1450: The History of a Medieval Occupation* (Oxford, 1983).

4 THE LANCASTRIAN KINGS TO C. 1437

There is no satisfactory full-scale study of Henry IV, but see the notable short accounts, A. L. Brown, 'Henry IV', *Fifteenth-Century England*, pp. 1–28, and K. B. McFarlane, *Lancastrian Kings and Lollard Knights* (Oxford, 1972), chapters 4–6. Helen Castor's work on the Duchy of Lancaster in the Lancastrian polity is at present available as a whole in thesis form only but two important articles drawn from it are listed for later chapters and the work as a whole will be published before long. Henry V's reign is very well covered in *Henry V: The Practice of Kingship*, ed. G. L. Harriss (Oxford, 1985). The subject of Powell's important chapter in this is more fully explored in *Kingship, Law, and Society*. The main accounts of Henry VI's reign are B. P. Wolffe, *Henry VI* (London, 1981) (good on the minority) and R. A. Griffiths, *The Reign of King Henry VI* (London, 1981). See also Wolffe, 'The Personal Rule of Henry VI', *Fifteenth-Century England*, pp. 29–48. Far and away the most important and innovatory study of the reign is Watts, *Henry VI and the Politics of Kingship*. G. L. Harriss, *Cardinal Beaufort: A study of Lancastrian Ascendancy and Decline* (Oxford, 1988) has an excellent account of politics in the minority from a Beaufort perspective, and its discussion for the whole period from 1399 to Beaufort's death in 1447 of the interplay of the royal finances and war in France is most illuminating and helpful. For the Hundred Years War itself, see C. Allmand, *The Hundred Years War: England and France at War c. 1300–c. 1450* (Cambridge, 1988) and A. Curry, *The Hundred Years War* (London, 1993).

5 HENRY VI'S ADULT RULE: THE FIRST PHASE C. 1437–1450

The vexed question of the king's character and abilities is discussed in the studies of the reign listed for chapter 4 and in most of the general works.

See also J. Watts, 'When did Henry VI's Minority End?', *Trade, Devotion and Governance*, pp. 116–39, R. Lovatt, 'John Blacman: Biographer of Henry VI', *The Writing of History in the Middle Ages*, ed. R. H. C. Davis and J. M. Wallace-Hadrill (Oxford, 1981), pp. 415–44, and Lovatt, '"A Collector of Apocryphal Anecdotes": John Blacman revisited', *Property and Politics: Essays in Later Medieval English History*, ed. A. J. Pollard (Gloucester, 1984), pp. 172–97. There are also interesting contemporary comments in Storey, *End of the House of Lancaster*. Important contributions for this period additional to those listed for chapter 4 are R. A. Griffiths, 'The Sense of Dynasty under Henry VI', *Patronage, Pedigree and Power in later Medieval England* (Gloucester and Totowa, N. J., 1979), pp. 13–36, A. Crawford, 'The King's Burden?: The Consequences of Royal Marriage in Fifteenth-Century England', *Patronage, the Crown and the Provinces*, pp. 33–56, M. Jones, 'John Beaufort, Duke of Somerset and the French Expedition of 1443', *ibid.*, pp. 79–102. Significant studies of local conflict and disorder in this period are M. Cherry, 'The Struggle for Power in Mid-Fifteenth-Century Devonshire', *Patronage, the Crown and the Provinces*, pp. 123–44, A. Smith, 'Litigation and Politics: Sir John Fastolf's Defence of his English Property', *Property and Politics*, pp. 59–75, Maddern, *Violence and Social Order*, chapter 6, and see also the local studies listed for chapter 3. Helen Castor's work on East Anglia in the 1440s is not yet in print but a taster is her entirely novel perspective on the period before, in 'The Duchy of Lancaster and the Rule of East Anglia 1399–1440: A Prologue to the Paston Letters', *Crown, Government and People in the Fifteenth Century*, ed. R. Archer (Stroud, 1995), pp. 53–78. On the duke of York, see P. Johnson, *Duke Richard of York 1411–1460* (Oxford, 1988) and T. B. Pugh, 'Richard Plantaganet (1411–60), Duke of York, as the King's Lieutenant in France and Ireland', *Aspects of Late Medieval Government and Society*, ed. J. G. Rowe (Toronto, 1986), pp. 107–41. The financial situation in the later 1440s is considered in an important article by G. L. Harriss, 'Marmaduke Lumley and the Exchequer Crisis of 1446–9', *ibid.*, pp. 143–78. For the war, see items listed earlier (notably Harriss on Beaufort), R. Massey, 'The Land Settlement in Lancastrian Normandy', *Property and Politics*, pp. 76–96 and M. Keen, 'The End of the Hundred Years War: Lancastrian France and Lancastrian England', *England and Her Neighbours, 1066–1453* (London, 1989), pp. 297–311. These last two are also relevant for chapter 4.

6 THE ROAD TO WAR: 1450–1455

An important collection of documents for the 1450s, with a very significant commentary by J. L. Watts, is in *The Politics of Fifteenth Century*

England: John Vale's Book, ed. M. L. Kekewich *et al.*, (Stroud, 1995). Watts' ideas on the ideology of the 1450s can be pursued in his book and in 'Ideas, Principles and Politics', *Wars of the Roses*, ed. Pollard, pp. 110–33. On York, see works in chapter 5 and M. K. Jones, 'Somerset, York and the Wars of the Roses', *English Historical Review*, 104 (1989), pp. 285–307. The most up to date and fullest account of the Cade rebellion (although a little naive in its handling of the evidence) is I. M. W. Harvey, *Jack Cade's Rebellion of 1450* (Oxford, 1991). For local conflict, see local studies, Cherry (as for chapter 5), Storey, *End of the House of Lancaster*, chapters 5, 7–8, 10–11, R. A. Griffiths, 'Local Rivalries and National Politics: The Percies, the Nevilles and the Duke of Exeter, 1452–1455', *Speculum*, 43 (1968), pp. 589–632, S. J. Payling, 'The Ampthill Dispute: A Study in Aristocratic Lawlessness and the Breakdown of Lancastrian Government', *English Historical Review*, 104 (1989), pp. 881–907 and H. Castor, '"Walter Blount was Gone to Serve Traytours": The Sack of Elvaston and the Politics of the North Midlands in 1454', *Midland History*, 19 (1994), pp. 21–39. Griffiths, *Reign of Henry VI*, incorporates his work on Wales in the 1450s.

7 THE END OF LANCASTRIAN RULE: 1455–1461

Most of the relevant work is listed under chapter 6. See also Storey, *End of the House of Lancaster*, chapter 13. The key article for noble participation is C. Richmond, 'The Nobility and the Wars of the Roses', *Nottingham Mediaeval Studies*, 21 (1977), pp. 71–85. For the debate on London in the 1450s, with particular reference to the events of 1460–1, see C. M. Barron, 'London and the Crown 1451–61', *Crown and Local Communities*, pp. 88–109, and J. L. Bolton, 'The City and the Crown, 1456–61', *London Journal*, 12 (1986), pp. 11–24.

8 EDWARD IV'S FIRST REIGN: 1461–1471

Many of the works listed for the first three chapters remain relevant. The standard study of Edward IV is C. Ross, *Edward IV* (London, 1974): it is essential, solid and rather lacking in penetration and is perceptively reviewed by B. P. Wolffe in *English Historical Review*, 91 (1976), pp. 369–74. It incorporates some important work by J. R. Lander on the king's dealings with the nobility, especially the Woodvilles. See also Ross' summary, 'The Reign of Edward IV', *Fifteenth Century England*, pp. 49–66. Gillingham, *The Wars of the Roses* has some helpful insights into Edward's rule, especially his first reign. The key work on the Yorkist finances, with which several later writers, including Ross, have disagreed is by B. P. Wolffe. It is published in its shortest and most accessible form in

Wolffe, *The Crown Lands 1461–1536* (London, 1970). For the costs of Edward's queen, see Crawford (as for chapter 5). Outside one or two of the local studies the only work to deal with Edward's peace-keeping with any depth is a rather specialised one, P. M. Barnes, 'The Chancery *Corpus cum Causa* File, 10–11 Edward IV, *Medieval Legal Records Edited in Memory of C. A. F. Meekings*, ed. R. F. Hunnisett and J. B. Post (London, 1978), pp. 430–76. There is an excellent close analysis of the politics of the crisis of 1469–71 in M. A. Hicks, *False, Fleeting Perjur'd Clarence: George Duke of Clarence 1449–78* (Gloucester, 1980), chapter 2. Significant additions to the literature on the 1460s since Ross include also Hicks, 'The Case of Sir Thomas Cook, 1468', *English Historical Review*, 93 (1978), pp. 82–96, P. Holland, 'Cook's Case in History and Myth', *Historical Research*, 61 (1988), pp. 21–35 and Hicks, 'The 1468 Statute of Livery', *Historical Research*, 64 (1991), pp. 15–28. There are useful documents, especially from 1469–71, in *John Vale's Book*, although the commentary on this section is somewhat bizarre.

9 THE TRIUMPH OF YORK: 1471–1483

Most of the literature is listed under chapter 8. There are two important post-Ross articles on the Woodvilles: M. A. Hicks, 'The Changing Role of the Wydevilles in Yorkist Politics to 1483', *Patronage, Pedigree and Power*, pp. 60–86 (this also deals with the 1460s) and D. E. Lowe, 'Patronage and Politics: Edward IV, the Wydevills, and the Council of the Prince of Wales', *Bulletin of the Board of Celtic Studies*, 29 (1982), pp. 545–73 (the latter much less harsh in its judgement than the former). Clarence's fall is discussed in J. R. Lander, 'The Treason and Death of the Duke of Clarence', *Crown and Nobility*, pp. 242–66, Hicks, *Clarence*, chapters 2 and 3 and C. Carpenter, 'The Duke of Clarence and the Midlands: A Study in the Interplay of Local and National Politics', *Midland History*, 11 (1986), pp. 23–48 (this is given in summarised form but placed more fully in the context of Edward's second reign in Carpenter, *Locality and Polity*, chapter 14). See *Locality and Polity*, chapter 14 also for the most recent discussion of Hastings' retinue (with references for further reading). The key work on Richard of Gloucester in the north is R. Horrox, *Richard III: A Study of Service* (Cambridge, 1989), chapter 1, and Edward's southern affinity gets some coverage here in the author's account of its later rebellions against Richard III. See also M. A. Hicks, *Richard III as Duke of Gloucester: A Study in Character* (University of York, Borthwick Papers, 70 (1986) (informative but tries to go into realms where the evidence cannot take us). The key article on Edward's affinity (which begins its discussion in the 1460s), against which both Carpenter (*Locality and Polity*, chapter 14) and Horrox (see immediately above) argue is D. A. L. Morgan, 'The King's Affinity in the Polity of Yorkist England', *Transactions of the Royal Historical Society*, 5th ser., 23 (1973), pp. 1–25. The 'Croyland Continuation', an important source for both Edward's second reign and Richard III, exists in a modern edition, which also discusses authorship and reliability: *The Crowland Chronicle Continuations: 1459–1486*, ed. N. Pronay and J. Cox (Richard III and Yorkist History Trust, 1986).

10 RICHARD III AND THE END OF YORKIST RULE: 1483–1485

The key work is Horrox, *Richard III*. There is also C. Ross, *Richard III* (London, 1981). There has been a lot of discussion of the reliability of the sources for the period 1483–5, especially the period leading up to the usurpation. A quite useful survey is A. Hanham, *Richard III and his Early Historians 1483–1535* (Oxford, 1975). The 'Croyland Continuation' is mentioned above, under chapter 9 and another important source is D. Mancini, *The Usurpation of Richard III*, ed. and trans. C. A. J. Armstrong (Oxford, 1969, rpt. in paperback, Gloucester, 1984). Horrox has rather downgraded Mancini as a reliable source (see the comments in the text to this chapter). There is a rather absurd debate about the date of Hastings' execution arising out of Hanham's work which is briefly summed up in *Kingsford's Stonor Letters*, Intro. by Carpenter, p. 15 n. 60, where references to the contributions to it are given. Carpenter, *Locality and Polity*, chapter 14, deals with Richard's rule in a local context at some length. M. Bennett, *The Battle of Bosworth* (Gloucester, 1985) has a lot of useful background to the battle and a serious attempt to grapple with the difficult problem of who actually fought there.

11 HENRY VII AND THE END OF THE WARS: 1485–1509

A clear sense of the traditional interpetation, which can be a great help in seeing where it still lingers, can be found in many accounts of the Tudors, classically in G. R. Elton, *England under the Tudors* (London, 1955) (although Elton later produced a second edition, his account of Henry VII barely changed). The reader could also use A. Grant, *Henry VII: The Importance of his Reign in English History* (London, 1985) and T. B. Pugh, 'Henry VII and the English Nobility', *The Tudor Nobility*, ed. G. Bernard (Manchester and New York, 1992), pp. 49–105, for the same purposes. The standard modern account of the reign is S. B. Chrimes, *Henry VII* (London, 1972) and a summary of Chrimes' views is 'The Reign of Henry VII', *Fifteenth-Century England*, pp. 67–85. R. L. Storey, *The Reign of Henry VII* (London, 1968) has more room for messy things like politics and the nobles. J. R. Lander's important work on Henry, the nobility and bonds is incorporated into and referenced in Chrimes, as is the debate between Elton and J. P. Cooper on Henry's last years. Wolffe, *Crown Lands* remains important. Two key sources, alluded to in the text, are 'Flamank's Information', which can be read in *Letters and Papers Illustrative of the Reigns of Richard III and Henry VII*, ed. J. G. Gairdner (Rolls Series, 2 vols., London, 1861–3), i, pp. 231–40, and 'The Petition of Edmund Dudley', ed. C. J. Harrison, *English Historical Review*, 87 (1972), pp. 82–99. Work which has begun to take discussion of the reign beyond the purely institutional includes R. Virgoe, 'The Recovery of the Howards in East Anglia, 1485–1529', *Wealth and Power in Tudor England*, ed. E. W. Ives, R. J. Knecht and J. J. Scarisbrick (London, 1978), pp. 1–20, M. M. Condon, 'Ruling Elites in the Reign of Henry VII', *Patronage, Pedigree and Power*, pp. 109–42, Condon, 'From Caitiff and Villain to Pater Patriae: Reynold Bray and the Profits of Office', *Profit, Piety and the Professions*, ed. M. A. Hicks (Gloucester, 1990), pp. 137–68, S. J. Gunn, 'The Accession of Henry VIII', *Historical Research*, 64 (1991), pp. 278–88, Gunn, 'Henry Bourchier, Earl of Essex (1472–1540)', *Tudor Nobility*, pp. 134–79, Gunn, 'The Courtiers of Henry VII', *English Historical Review*, 108 (1993), pp. 23–49, M. K. Jones and M. G. Underwood, *The King's Mother: Lady Margaret Beaufort, Countess of Richmond and Derby* (Cambridge, 1992), chapter 3, D. Luckett, 'Crown, Patronage and Political Morality in Early Tudor England: The Case of Giles, Lord Daubeny', *English Historical Review*, 110 (1995), pp. 578–95, Luckett, 'Crown Office and Licensed Retinues in the Reign of Henry VII', *Rulers and Ruled in Late Medieval England: Essays in Honour of G. L. Harriss*, ed. R. E. Archer and S. Walker (London, 1995), pp. 223–38. The role of the privy chamber is discussed in D. Starkey, 'Intimacy and Innovation: The Rise of the Privy Chamber', *The English Court from the Wars of the Roses to the Civil War*, ed. D. Starkey (London, 1987), pp. 71–118. On risings of the commons under Henry VII, see I. Arthurson, 'The Rising of 1497: A Revolt of the Peasantry?', *People, Politics and Community in the Later Middle Ages*, ed. J. Rosenthal and C. Richmond (Gloucester, 1987), pp. 1–18, M. A. Hicks, 'The Yorkshire Rising of 1489 Reconsidered', *Northern History*, 22 (1986), pp. 39–62, M. J. Bennett, 'Henry VII and the Northern Rising of 1489', *English Historical Review*, 105 (1990), pp. 34–57 and M. Bush, 'Tax Reform and Rebellion in Early Tudor England', *Historical Research*, 76 (1991), pp. 379–400 (which has interesting material on earlier periods as well). Current debate on Henry VII, which has developed in very recent times, can be followed in the magisterial S. Gunn, *Early Tudor Government, 1485–1558* (London, 1995) (apart from anything else, this is an excellent survey of work on late-medieval political structures and masterful on early-Tudor governance), Carpenter's deliberately revisionist chapter 15 in *Locality and Polity* and the following articles in *The Reign of Henry VII*, ed. B. Thompson (Stamford, 1995): Thompson, 'Introduction: The Place of Henry VII in English History', pp. 1–10, Carpenter, 'Henry VII and the English Polity', pp. 11–30, and J. L. Watts, '"A New Ffundacione of is Crowne": Monarchy in the Age of Henry VII', pp. 31–53. See also in the same volume D. Luckett, 'Henry VII and the South-Western Escheators', pp. 54–64.

12 CONCLUSIONS

Most of the relevant literature is listed above. On the church, see R. G. Davies, 'The Church and the Wars of the Roses', *Wars of the Roses*, ed. Pollard, pp. 134–61. Further reading on the subject of change between c. 1450 and c. 1550, additional to that given for chapter 11, includes Carpenter, *Locality and Polity*, chapters 16 and 17, which elaborates and sums up the thesis of changes in political structures advanced here and, at greater length, in *Locality and Polity*, G. R. Elton, 'Tudor Government: The Points of Contact, ii, The Council', *Transactions of the Royal Historical Society*, 5th ser., 25 (1975), pp. 195–211, D. Starkey, 'Which Age of Reform?', *Revolution Reassessed*, ed. C. Coleman and D. Starkey (Oxford, 1986), pp. 13–27, the whole of *The English Court*, S. Gunn, 'The Structures of Politics in Early Tudor England', *Transactions of the Royal Historical Soc.*, 6th ser., 3 (1995), pp. 59–90, R. H. Britnell, *The Closing of the Middle Ages? England 1471–1529* (Oxford, 1997), and *The End of the Middle Ages? England in the Fifteenth and Sixteenth Centuries*, ed. J. L. Watts (Stroud, 1998), especially Watts' introduction. The 'Tudor revolution' issue can be followed directly in G. R. Elton, *The Tudor Revolution in Government* (Cambridge, 1953) and the debate in *Past and Present*, 25 (1963), pp. 3–58, under the heading 'A Revolution in Tudor History?': P. Williams, 'Dr Elton's Interpretation of the Age' and 'The Tudor State', pp. 3–8, 39–58 and G. L. Harriss, 'Medieval Government and Statecraft', pp. 8–39, and it is also addressed in most of the works which examine the early Tudor state, notably Gunn, *Early Tudor Government*.

INDEX

Cambridge Medieval Textbooks

Already published

Other titles are in preparation